The
U.S. Navy
in the **Korean War**

The
U.S. Navy
in the Korean War

EDWARD J. MAROLDA, EDITOR

Published in cooperation with the
Naval Historical Center and the Naval Historical Foundation

NAVAL INSTITUTE PRESS
Annapolis, Maryland

Naval Institute Press
291 Wood Road
Annapolis, MD 21402

© 2007 by the United States Naval Institute
Annapolis, Maryland

Library of Congress Cataloging-in-Publication Data

The U. S. Navy in the Korean War / Edward J. Marolda, editor.
    p. cm.
Includes bibliographical references and index.
ISBN-13: 978-1-59114-487-8 (alk. paper)
ISBN-10: 1-59114-487-6 (alk. paper)
1. Korean War, 1950–1953—Naval operations, American. 2. United States.
Navy—History—Korean War, 1950–1953. I. Marolda, Edward J.
DS920.A2U85 2007
951.904′2450973—dc22

                                                                    2006033336

Printed in the United States of America on acid-free paper ∞
14 13 12 11 10 09 08 07   9 8 7 6 5 4 3 2
First printing

Contents

Foreword

THE KOREAN WAR was a historic milestone for the U.S. Navy during the long, sometimes hot, Cold War. In the epic struggle from 1950 to 1953, naval forces operated in the Yellow Sea and the Sea of Japan, ashore on the Korean peninsula, and in skies overhead to defeat invading Communist armies. Our Sailors and Marines had to battle not only a determined, skillful, and ruthless foe but also the extreme weather common to northeast Asia. Cold, biting wind and snow characterized the Korean winter and blistering heat, the summer. That our fighting men overcame those challenges and fought successfully to preserve the independence of South Korea and the freedom of the Korean people is a testament to the American spirit. Sailors and Marines, many of whom had served with distinction in World War II, responded once again to the call to arms. Members of the Naval Reserve formed the core of many units deployed to Korea.

The war tested new aircraft, including jet-powered fighter-bombers and medical evacuation helicopters, but also validated the continued worth of warships, amphibious vessels, and planes that had served the nation so well in World War II. In that regard, *Iowa*-class battleships and 8-inch-gun cruisers provided critical gunfire support to troops ashore; LVTs, LCVPs, and LSTs did yeoman service in the amphibious role; and the gull-winged, piston-powered F4U Corsairs saved many American lives with their precise and devastating close air support.

We are gratified that the U.S. Naval Institute has agreed to this compilation presenting the first-rate research and writing of distinguished authors initially engaged to produce booklets commemorating the Korean War. The work of these scholars analyzes air, amphibious, gunfire support, and logistic operations; decision making by naval leaders; and the contributions of Sailors—young and old, black and white, officer and enlisted—who gave their all in the fight for freedom during the early days of the Cold War.

My special thanks go to Dr. Edward J. Marolda, senior historian/chief of the Naval Historical Center's Histories and Archives Division and a distinguished scholar of the Navy's modern history. He oversaw preparation of the Korean War commemorative series under the director of naval history, Rear Adm. Paul E. Tobin, USN (Ret.), and his predecessor, Dr. William S. Dudley. Equally deserving is Sandra J. Doyle, the center's senior editor, who managed the entire editorial and publication process with exceptional professional skill.

James L. Holloway III
Admiral, U.S. Navy (Ret.)

Preface

FROM 1950 TO 1953, the world witnessed a bloody, drawn out, and inconclusive struggle between Communist and United Nations soldiers for control of Korea. Images abounded of fierce fighting in Korea's cold, rugged mountains and in the fortified trench lines along the 38th parallel. Critics of the allied war effort bemoaned President Harry S. Truman's decision to deploy American troops ashore in Asia within reach of the sizable armies of the People's Republic of China, the Democratic People's Republic of Korea, and potentially of the Soviet Union. In short, the Korean War was and is commonly seen as a ground war that cost the lives of thirty-seven thousand Americans and hundreds of thousands of Koreans, Chinese, and other belligerents.

A prime purpose of this book is to highlight the considerable maritime dimension of the Korean War. The United States and its allies were able to deploy combat troops on the Asian continent and logistically sustain that presence for more than three years because UN naval forces enjoyed the numerous advantages that came with control of the sea around Korea—a peninsula. The U.S. Pacific Fleet's rapid deployment from the Philippines, Japan, and the United States of surface warships, aircraft carriers, troop-laden transports, and supply vessels at the war's outset saved the UN command from defeat at the hands of the fast-advancing North Korean army. Thereafter, the allied navies exploited their mobility to deploy U.S. and South Korean ground forces far behind enemy lines at Inchon and dramatically turn the tide of battle.

When enormous Chinese Communist armies entered the fray and forced U.S. Marine and other UN units from the mountains of North Korea, the fleet expeditiously reembarked the troops and their equipment and redeployed them to South Korea to fight again. Throughout the Korean War, allied naval forces ranged along the coasts of the peninsula to bombard enemy troop units and other targets ashore; launch carrier air strikes against North Korean supply depots, bridges, railways, dams, and ports; and land naval commandos in the enemy's rear.

Allied control of the sea denied the Communists those benefits. Fear of another Inchon-like operation behind their lines compelled Mao Tse-tung and other Communist leaders to keep badly needed troops in reserve and out of the fight on the 38th parallel. Moreover, UN control of the waters lapping Korea's shores prevented the enemy from threatening allied flanks, cutting the UN sea lines of communication, or reinforcing and resupplying their own combat units except by land. The U.S. Navy's powerful presence in the Western Pacific and ability to attack coastal targets in China and the Soviet Union also discouraged the enemy from spreading the conflict beyond the Korean theater. Maritime power was critical to keeping the first "limited war" of the Cold War era confined to Korea.

Another objective in the preparation of this volume is to highlight the contributions of the 1,601,000 naval personnel who fought the Korean War and to honor the service of those 659 Sailors and 4,509 Marines who made the ultimate sacrifice for their country. In 1999, the Naval Historical Center and the Naval Historical Foundation enlisted the services of a number of highly regarded authors in the preparation of monographs on key naval aspects of the war. This joint endeavor resulted in the publication between 2001 and 2005 of well-researched, engagingly written, and colorfully illustrated booklets by Col. Joseph H. Alexander, USMC (Ret.), the late, distinguished historian Thomas B. Buell, Capt. Richard C. Knott, USN (Ret.), Bernard C. Nalty, and Malcolm Muir Jr. In this volume we present their work in addition to a previously published monograph by Curtis Utz and an original manuscript by Lt. Cdr. Thomas J. Cutler, USN (Ret.). Several of the works concentrate on fleet operations during the first critical year of the war and later years when UN forces fought a "static war." Others focus on the leadership of Adms. Forrest P. Sherman, C. Turner Joy, James H. Doyle, and Arleigh A. Burke; carrier-based and ground-based naval air operations; and the contribution of African American Sailors to the successful effort to preserve the independence of the Republic of Korea.

At the end of the Korean War, many observers concluded that this "limited war" in northeast Asia had been an aberration that was unlikely to be replicated in the age of long-range bombers, ballistic missiles, and nuclear weapons. In fact, the Korean War was the first in a long line of twentieth-century and early twenty-first-century conflicts that involved U.S. naval forces confronting Communist and nontraditional adversaries in distant regions of the globe and projecting conventional power ashore in such places as Vietnam, Lebanon, Panama, Kosovo, Afghanistan, and Iraq. Hence, understanding the U.S. Navy's Korean War experience promises critical insights about the role of sea power in the modern age.

Edward J. Marolda
Editor

Acknowledgments

THE EDITOR AND AUTHORS of these chapters gratefully recognize, appreciate, and thank the staffs of several historical organizations for their help in preparing this volume, aiding in research, and supplying photographs. This group comprises professional staff members of the Histories and Archives Division, the Naval Warfare Division, the Photographic Section, and the Navy Department Library of the Naval Historical Center, Washington, D.C.; the Naval Historical Foundation; the History, Reference, and Preservation Branch of the U.S. Naval Institute, Annapolis, Maryland; the U.S. Marine Corps Historical Division, now at Quantico, Virginia; the Prints and Photographs Division and the Map and Geography Division of the Library of Congress; the Still Pictures Branch of the National Archives and Records Administration, College Park, Maryland; and the Association of Naval Aviation, Alexandria, Virginia.

The editor and authors also appreciate the encouragement of colleagues, especially Director of Naval History Rear Adm. Paul E. Tobin, USN (Ret.), and former directors Dr. Dean C. Allard and Dr. William S. Dudley, who supported this book and publication of the original booklets to commemorate the fiftieth anniversary of the Korean War.

List of Acronyms

AGC	amphibious force command ship
AKA	attack cargo ship
AM	minesweeper
AMS	minesweeper, high speed or auxiliary motor minesweeper
APA	attack transport
APD	high-speed transport
ASW	antisubmarine warfare
ATF	fleet ocean tug
CCRAK	Covert Clandestine and Related Activities, Korea
CINCFE	Commander in Chief, Far East
CINCPACFLT	Commander in Chief, Pacific Fleet
CINCUNC	Commander in Chief, United Nations Command
COMNAVFE	Commander Naval Forces, Far East
CNO	Chief of Naval Operations
CPO	chief petty officer
DCNO	Deputy Chief of Naval Operations
DMS	destroyer minesweeper
DPRK	Democratic People's Republic of Korea
DUKW	amphibious truck
ECM	electronic countermeasures
FEAF	Far East Air Force
FECOM	Far East Command
GCA	ground control approach
CGI	Ground Controlled Intercept
HVAR	high-velocity aircraft rocket
JCS	Joint Chiefs of Staff
JOC	Joint Operations Center

JSPOG	Joint Strategic Plans and Operations Group
KATUSA	Korean Augmentation to the U.S. Army
KMAG	Korean Military Advisory Group
KMC	Korean Marine Corps
LCM	landing craft, mechanized
LCVP	landing craft, vehicle, and personnel
LSD	landing ship, dock
LSM	landing ship, medium
LSMR	landing ship, medium, rocket
LST	landing ship, tank
LSU	landing ship, utility
LVT	landing vehicle, tracked
LVT(A)	landing vehicle, tracked (armored)
MCM	mine countermeasures
MSO	minesweeper, ocean
MSR	major supply route
MSTS	Military Sea Transportation Service
MTB	motor torpedo boat
NAACP	National Association for the Advancement of Colored People
NGFS	naval gunfire support
NKAF	North Korean Air Force
NKPA	North Korean People's Army
NROTC	Naval Reserve Officer Training Corps
OPNAV	Office of the Chief of Naval Operations
POW	prisoner of war
RCT	regimental combat team
ROK	Republic of Korea
ROKN	Republic of Korea Navy
SCAJAP	Shipping Control Administration, Japan
SCOROR	Secretary's Committee on Research and Reorganization
TACC	Tactical Air Control Center
TACP	Tactical Air Control Parties

UDT	underwater demolition team
UNICOM	Committee on Unification
UNREP	underway replenishment
VCNO	Vice Chief of Naval Operations
VT	variable time
WAVES	Women Accepted for Volunteer Emergency Service
WESTPAC	Western Pacific
WP	white phosphorus

CHAPTER 1

Sea Power and Defense of the Pusan Pocket, June–September 1950

THOMAS J. CUTLER

As we look back on the war in Korea after the passage of fifty years, there are several conclusions to be made. In the account that follows, the importance of sea power—then and now—should be obvious. It should also be evident that the current emphasis on the concept we call "jointness" is appropriate and warranted as we develop the nation's future strategy. And it should also be quite apparent that, for all the doubts we often have about ourselves—"too soft," "spoiled," "self-centered"— Americans can be a tough lot once committed, no matter how reluctantly, to the battlefield.

As will be made clear in the pages that follow, the Korean War could not have been fought as it was without American control of the sea. The United States Navy, despite an enormous drawdown at the end of World War II, was still more powerful in 1950 than any other naval force on earth. It was this dominance that made the difference when UN forces fought to hold the line in the early days of the war. Even when the tide of war had shifted after the landing at Inchon in September 1950, American sea power was needed to protect the vital logistical tail that stretched across the vast Pacific.

In the years just prior to the Korean War, the world witnessed the dawn of a global conflict between the United States and the Soviet Union and their respective allies. Coupled with this development were technological advances that unleashed the power and destructive capability of the atom. These and other factors fostered a reorganization of the American defense establishment and a reassessment of the traditional roles of the armed forces. Interservice rivalry was never more acute—and certainly never more bitter—than it was during this period when the services were going through major postwar reorganization.While some of that rivalry was put aside to fight the common enemy at the outbreak of the Korean War, interservice friction continued to complicate military operations.

In James Michener's classic novel *The Bridges at Toko-ri*, the protagonist, Harry Brubaker, comes to Korea as a reluctant warrior, a reservist who wants nothing more than to get back to the good life he has left behind in Colorado. Nevertheless, he flies against the bridges at Toko-ri with courage and determination that would make any Spartan warrior proud. Although the Brubaker character is fictional, what he represents is not. History shows that Americans do not eagerly embrace war. It also shows that their reluctance frequently causes them to arrive on the battlefield dangerously unprepared. But the record also reveals that once committed to a fight, these hesitant warriors become tenacious combatants who are the equal of their fiercest enemies. Americans have proven time and again that they can leave the comforts of home and meet head-on a rigorously trained and ideologically driven enemy.

Korea was no exception. The "Brubakers" of America rose to the occasion, despite the ambiguities of a so-called police action and even though many of them had already cheated death in the world's greatest war just a few short years before. This is testimony to the mettle of America's men and women in uniform.

The story of the U.S. Navy's role in helping to defend the Pusan Perimeter is a proud one. It was a moment in our long history in which American Sailors, fighting side by side with Marines, soldiers, airmen, and allied forces, preserved a small toehold of freedom on the Korean peninsula. It is a story worth telling and retelling for as long as there is a United States of America and a Navy operating in distant waters.

INTRODUCTION

IN HIS 1976 BOOK *The Sea Power of the State*, Soviet Admiral of the Fleet Sergei Gorshkov discussed the role of the United States Navy in the Korean

War—a struggle in which his nation played no small role and had great interest. Gorshkov accurately assessed the importance of sea power in war when he observed, "without wide, active use of the fleet, the interventionists [Communist jargon for the UN side] could hardly have escaped military defeat in Korea. The fleet was the force which materially influenced the course of the war as a whole."

Because the conflict in Korea occurred only a few years after World War II, in which great fleets had slugged it out in dramatic battles, there is the temptation to underestimate the significance of the less-spectacular naval aspects of the war. Naval surface operations in the Korean War included amphibious landings and evacuations, thousands of naval gunfire missions, and the deployment of commando teams behind enemy lines. Submarines inserted some of these commandos and exploited the boats' capacity for stealth to reconnoiter enemy positions. Navy and Marine Corps planes flew tens of thousands of reconnaissance, interdiction, patrol, and close air support missions throughout the war. The Seventh Fleet served as a deterrent to Chinese Communist and Soviet naval activity elsewhere in the Pacific, especially in the waters separating Communist and Nationalist China. The most vital and successful mission of the fleet during the war was to keep the sea-lanes open so that troops and supplies could be brought in at will. UN forces would have lost the Korean War had the United States Navy not seized and maintained control of the sea.

Naval operations in Korea have not commanded as much attention as ground operations because more than thirty-two thousand soldiers and Marines were killed in action, compared to 458 Sailors. The desperate and dramatic struggle of UN air forces in the skies over Korea to maintain air control also drew the interest of the world. But control of the sea was never in doubt. United Nations naval forces, led by the United States Navy, took control of the sea shortly after the war began and never lost it.

While the U.S. Navy contributed the vast majority of naval vessels to the conflict, other nations—most notably those of the British Commonwealth—deployed warships to the Korean theater. By war's end, combatants from Great Britain, Australia, Canada, New Zealand, France, Colombia, the Netherlands, and Thailand had taken part. The Royal Navy's HMS *Maine* was the first hospital ship to arrive, and the Danish later sent *Jutlandia* to handle casualties. On hand at the outset of the Korean War was the small but fearless Republic of Korea Navy (ROKN).

The U.S. Navy worked side by side not only with America's allies in the Korean War but also with U.S. armed forces. Interservice relations in Korea were a mixed bag. The establishment of the Department of Defense in 1947 and the massive cutbacks in military spending in the years before the war had resulted in bitter and public differences among the leaders of the armed forces. The advent of atomic weapons and globe-spanning heavy bombers persuaded some U.S. Air Force and U.S. Army leaders that huge fleets of naval vessels and a Marine Corps focused on amphibious operations were no longer needed.

Once the shooting started, most military men were professional enough to put past differences behind them in favor of accomplishing their mission, but the failure to cooperate in previous years affected operations. The air war, in particular, suffered because the services followed different philosophies with regard to command and control of air forces and their tactical employment. The Air Force advocated centralized control of all American and allied air resources while the Navy and Marine Corps believed in a more decentralized, flexible approach.

If nothing else, the Korean War reaffirmed the vital importance of the Navy's aircraft carrier and bombardment units and Marine amphibious forces to the success of American arms in the post–World War II era. Had these naval forces not been on hand in the combat theater during the first three months of the war, the attacking Communists would have destroyed the South Korean army, forced the evacuation of American and allied troops forces from the peninsula, and called into question the credibility of U.S. and UN power. American and South Korean ground troops fought hard and paid the highest price in blood to hold the Pusan Perimeter, but their sacrifice would have been in vain if UN naval forces had not been on hand in the summer of 1950. The naval services interdicted enemy supply lines from the air and the sea, gave ground troops close air support, rushed army and marine units to the peninsula, and ensured the unhindered flow of tanks, trucks, fuel, and ammunition to the fighting forces ashore.

These naval contributions have never caught the public eye in the same manner as the great sea battles of World War II. They have not been the subject of great classical works, nor secured the attention of many who study naval strategy and policy. But the lessons of this time must not be ignored nor forgotten. Once the decision was made to hold Korea against the Communist invasion, establishing sea control made all else possible. Power projection from the sea was a significant factor in holding the Pusan

Perimeter, and set the stage for the decisive amphibious assault at Inchon in September. Today, as in the desperate, chaotic days of June, July, and August 1950, sea power is a vital component of America's war-fighting establishment.

OPENING SALVOS

THE FAMILY HAD MOVED from the screened porch into the study where the open windows admitted enough air to make the room comfortable that evening late in June 1950. It had been a hot and humid day in Independence, Missouri, and the relative cool of the evening was welcome. It was too early in the year for the crickets and no automobiles traveled the streets outside, so the ringing of the telephone in the hall at 9:20 PM was particularly piercing. There were few telephones in this quiet midwestern town, and it was rather unusual to hear one ring so late in the evening. But, there was little doubt who was being summoned, so the man of the house rose from his chair and walked out of the study.

In the hall, he picked up the receiver and, placing it to his ear, heard a familiar voice from far away. "Mr. President," Secretary of State Dean Acheson said, "I have some very serious news."

When he returned to the study, Harry Truman's daughter, Margaret, saw that her father was deeply concerned. She later wrote that in the moments that followed, the president "made it clear . . . that he feared this was the opening of World War III."

Truman was informed that in the early morning hours (local time) of 25 June, the Communist North Korean People's Army (NKPA) began a full-scale invasion of the Republic of Korea. At 0400 artillery batteries opened fire across the 38th parallel that had served as the dividing line between the two Koreas. After forty-five minutes of heavy bombardment, more than a hundred thousand troops surged across the boundary.

By the time Secretary Acheson had informed the president of the event, a mere seven hours had passed, but the situation was already critical. With no tanks of its own and untested troops in its ranks, the Republic of Korea army proved no match for the NKPA. The North Korean army boasted Soviet-made T-34 tanks and battle-hardened veterans who had fought for the Communist side in the civil war in China. Even retreating proved difficult for the South Korean army because of the thousands of refugees who clogged the dusty roads as they too fled south to escape the onslaught. It was soon evident to all but the most optimistic or the most uninformed that, without outside help, South Korea was doomed.

Truman's concern that the outbreak of fighting heralded the beginning of World War III would prove unwarranted, but at the time it seemed to be a real possibility. The two Koreas were virtual surrogates of the Soviet Union and the United States, two powerful nations contending for world dominance. The sequence of events leading up to this calamitous moment in world history had ensured that South Korea would be unable to withstand an invasion from North Korea (with support from the Soviet Union and the People's Republic of China). Thus, the United States and its Western allies had to decide whether or not to come to the armed assistance of South Korea, understanding that such a move risked global war with the Soviet Union and its Communist allies.

GENESIS

FOR MUCH OF ITS HISTORY, Korea had been known by the sobriquets "land of the morning calm" and "Hermit Kingdom." Ironically, there had been little calm in Korea during the twentieth century, and by 1950, the would-be "hermits" found themselves at the center of the world stage.

When the Japanese set out to build an empire and dominate the Pacific early in the twentieth century, the Korean peninsula had been one of their first acquisitions. Korea became a protectorate of Japan as a result of the latter nation's victory over Russia in the Russo–Japanese War of 1904–5. Between then and the end of World War II, the Japanese government ruled Korea with an iron hand, dominating every aspect of Korean life and culture.

At the conferences in Cairo and Yalta during World War II, the United States and the Soviet Union agreed to a UN trusteeship over Korea to prepare the country for eventual independence. Russia's entry into the war and Japan's surrender to the Allies in August 1945 prompted quick decisions about the occupation of Korea. In early September 1945, as Soviet forces moved into northern Korea from their Far Eastern territories, the U.S. Seventh Fleet landed two divisions (about forty-five thousand men) in the south. Moscow and Washington agreed to divide their respective occupation zones at the 38th parallel, splitting the peninsula roughly in half. Though intended as a temporary measure, this demarcation had

EARLY KOREAN
HISTORY

WHEN WAR BROKE OUT in Korea, many Americans had to consult a world atlas to locate the country. Despite its obscurity, Korea is one of the world's oldest nations, tracing its beginning to 2333 BC. Anthropologists have linked the Korean people to the same Mongol tribes believed to have crossed from the Eurasian landmass into North America to become what are known today as the Native American tribes.

From about 100 BC to the middle of the seventh century AD, the Korean peninsula was divided into three autonomous kingdoms: *Koguryo* in the north; *Paekche* in the center, along the Han River basin; and *Silla* in the southeast. But in 660, *Silla*—the kingdom that included the area that would be known as the Pusan Pocket in the summer of 1950—conquered *Paekche* and eight years later unified the entire peninsula by conquering *Koguryo*. Korea remained unified for nearly two millennia until the division into North and South in 1945.

In 935, a member of the Koryo Dynasty overthrew the ruler of *Silla*, giving Korea its name. The Koryos continued to rule for several centuries but were eventually absorbed into the Mongolian Yuan Dynasty after the Mongol Kublai Khan conquered both China and Korea, the latter falling in 1259.

When the Ming Dynasty in China overthrew the Mongols, a native Korean general, Yi Song-gye, led a revolt against the pro-Mongol Koryo ruler in 1392. The succeeding Yi Dynasty ruled Korea until the early twentieth century, while maintaining close ties to China and fighting off Japanese attempts at subjugation. One of these attempts occurred in

1592, when much of a Japanese fleet was destroyed by a number of iron-clad vessels known as "turtle ships," led by Korean Admiral Yi Sun-sin.

Through much its history, Korea has been the battleground for outsiders. Korea was a pawn in the struggles between the Chinese and Mongolians in the thirteenth century. In the sixteenth century, the Japanese and Chinese fought a series of major battles on Korean soil, devastating large portions of the countryside. Again, in 1894, when the Koreans asked the Chinese for help in quelling an internal uprising, the Japanese sent a detachment of soldiers to Seoul to protect Japanese interests, which provoked a war between China and Japan. In 1903, Russia suggested to the Japanese that they divide Korea between them (at the 39th parallel of latitude). The Japanese did not accept this offer and the disagreement contributed to the outbreak of the Russo–Japanese War in 1904. The treaty ending this war, brokered in part by Theodore Roosevelt, forced Russia to recognize Japanese interests in Korea and led to Japanese annexation of Korea as a colony in 1910.

The Japanese occupation of Korea, lasting from 1910 until the Japanese defeat at the end of World War II in 1945, was not something Koreans remember with fondness. The brutal oppression of the Korean people caused them to revolt in 1919. The Japanese occupiers crushed the rebellion, killing nearly seven thousand people, wounding another sixteen thousand, and jailing nearly twenty thousand more in the process. Many Korean nationalists fled the country after this rebellion, and the Korean Provisional Government was established in exile in Shanghai, China, headed by Syngman Rhee. He was the man destined to lead the Republic of Korea during the Korean War of 1950–53. This latter war began primarily as a civil war between the North and South Korean governments that had been created by Japan's conquerors in 1945. But, as had happened many times before in Korea's history, outsiders became involved in the civil conflict and Korea became a battleground for a struggle of ideologies with more than twenty nations eventually participating.

become by 1948 a Cold War boundary, separating the Soviet-sponsored Democratic People's Republic of Korea (DPRK) from the American-supported Republic of Korea (ROK).

Despite the roughly equal geographic division provided by the 38th parallel, the two newly created nations were *not* equal in many important ways. For example, most of the Korean people lived in the south; the division separated agricultural lands in the south from fertilizer resources in the north; and most of the country's hydroelectric power sources and coal reserves were found in the north.

Syngman Rhee—the belligerent and unpredictable ROK leader—made it clear that he intended to unify the Korean peninsula under his regime. So too did Kim Il Sung, his equally bellicose Communist opponent. In the years before the Korean War, the supporters of these two leaders fought a bloody civil confrontation. The Soviets withdrew their troops from North Korea in late 1948 but not before they had ensured that their clients were well prepared for war. The Soviets set up an NKPA military academy, trained and equipped ten infantry divisions and an armored brigade, and provided Kim with scores of modern aircraft.

In the south, it was a much different story. Officials in Washington worried that Rhee—if adequately armed—would invade the Communist north and risk starting a third world war. As a result, the United States did not supply Rhee with offensive weapons. The Americans did not provide the ROK with tanks, medium or heavy artillery, or military aircraft.

If this were not encouragement enough to Kim Il Sung, subsequent American actions and statements inadvertently signaled the Communists that the United States would not defend South Korea from attack. In June of 1949 the United States withdrew all of its combat forces from South Korea. Only a contingent of five hundred advisors remained. Perhaps the most significant signal coming from the United States occurred in a speech delivered at the National Press Club in Washington by Secretary of State Dean Acheson in January 1950. He described a U.S. defense perimeter in the Pacific that encompassed the Aleutian Islands off Alaska, Japan, the Ryukyu Islands, and the Philippines. One did not need a detailed map of the Western Pacific to see that this imaginary line excluded Korea and Taiwan. Most observers concluded that the United States would not commit armed forces to defend the ROK if the Communists invaded from the north.

It was not just the North Koreans who were misled by Acheson's pronouncement. Soviet Premier Josef Stalin for some time had discouraged

Kim from attacking the south for fear of provoking an American response. After the Acheson speech, Stalin gave Kim the green light for an offensive. Chairman Mao Tse-tung, leader of the People's Republic of China, was likewise encouraged by the American strategic demarcation that seemed to exclude Taiwan from American protection. Mao planned to seize the island, one of the last refuges of Chiang Kai-shek's Chinese Nationalist government.

Seemingly faced by only the weak ROK armed forces, Kim Il Sung ordered the invasion of South Korea following a Soviet-designed attack plan. With good reason, Kim expected a quick victory. And for a time, it seemed he was right.

THE POLITICAL RESPONSE

NIGHT AIR TRAVEL WAS still considered risky in 1950, so President Truman remained at his Missouri home on 25 June. Not wanting to alarm the nation, he spent Sunday morning, 26 June, visiting relatives and inspecting a new milking machine before boarding his plane, *Independence*, for Washington. While the nation—indeed the world—wondered what the U.S. response to the North Korean invasion might be, the president's daughter, Margaret, apparently had no doubt. That evening, as her father met with key advisors to determine an appropriate course of action, she confided to her diary, "Northern or Communist Korea is marching in on Southern Korea and we are going to fight."

Margaret Truman was right. Her father's willingness to take such a stand had been long coming. Shortly after the end of World War II, Truman had written to then–Secretary of State James F. Byrnes, "Unless Russia [USSR] is faced with an iron fist and strong language another war is in the making. Only one language do they understand—'How many divisions have you?' " In the same letter, he listed some of the places of strategic concern. He included Korea. Truman ended the letter with the observation, "I'm tired of babying the Soviets."

This resolve to stand up to the Communists resulted, in large part, from Truman's nature, but it was also born of his interpretation of history. On the flight from Missouri to Washington, he recalled the days preceding the outbreak of World War II, remembering, "how each time that the democracies failed to act it encouraged the aggressors to keep going ahead." Truman concluded: "If the Communists were permitted to force their way into the Republic of Korea without opposition from the free world, no small nation would have the courage to resist threats and aggression by stronger Communist neighbors. If this was allowed to go unchallenged, it would mean a third world war, just as similar incidents had brought on the second world war."

Other Americans shared this view. From Tokyo, where he was negotiating the World War II peace treaty with Japan, John Foster Dulles, a prominent Republican and future secretary of state, sent a cable to the State Department. He counseled "to sit by while Korea is overrun by unprovoked armed attack would start [a] disastrous chain of events leading most probably to world war."

In meetings over the next several days, Truman and his advisors made a series of decisions that committed the United States armed forces to the emerging conflict. At the first meeting, it was decided that the Army would provide more equipment to the beleaguered ROK forces, the Navy would evacuate American civilians from South Korea, and the Air Force would cover the exodus. Truman then ordered the Navy and the Air Force to conduct air operations against the invading enemy and the Army to dispatch reinforcements to South Korea from Japan. American aircraft were authorized initially to strike targets only in the South but soon throughout Korea. And, to ensure that the aggression in Korea did not spread throughout the Far East, the president ordered the Seventh Fleet to sortie from its base at Subic Bay in the Philippines and steam along the coast of China. Truman made it clear the United States would prevent a Communist invasion of Taiwan.

On 27 June, the U.S. House of Representatives voted by a margin of 315 to 4 to extend the Selective Service Act and the Senate passed the act unanimously. That same afternoon, the United Nations Security Council endorsed Truman's actions and voted to assist the Republic of Korea in repelling the invasion. The Soviet Union, a member of the Security Council, would have vetoed the measure, but its representative had absented himself from the chamber over an earlier dispute.

The die was cast. Less than five years after the final shots were fired in World War II, the international community was once again engaged in a major military conflict.

NAVAL ORDER OF BATTLE

AT THE END OF WORLD WAR II, the Truman administration ordered a major reduction of the U.S. Navy and concentration of most remaining

THE FIRST
AMERICAN WAR
WITH KOREA

IN 1866, BARELY A YEAR AFTER the end of the American Civil War, a U.S. merchant vessel, the *General Sherman*, anchored in the Taedong River downstream from Pyongyang. The ship had come to open trade with this mysterious land, known as the Hermit Kingdom because of its resistance to foreign influence. Nearly two decades earlier, the U.S. Congress had passed a resolution calling for the opening of trade with Korea, but the Civil War and other factors prevented any action on the resolution for nearly two decades.

Those who wanted to open the way to trade with Korea were encouraged in 1866 when the Koreans saved the crew of the American merchantman *Surprise* after she had been wrecked off the Korean coast. Shipwrecks and traders were apparently two different things to the Koreans, however. As *General Sherman* made her way up the river, the crew saw signs posted along the banks warning them to leave. Ignoring these warnings, the American ship continued up the river, taking advantage of the favorably high tide. But the high tide did not last, and the ebb left the ship stranded in the mud of the river. The Koreans sent burning rafts across the shallow water, deliberately aimed at the American vessel. When she caught fire, and the crew tried to swim ashore, they were slaughtered by the waiting Koreans.

Some intervening attempts at diplomacy were unsuccessful, so on 30 May 1871, an American naval expeditionary force, under the command of Rear Adm. John Rodgers, dropped anchor near Chemulpo (later renamed Inchon). The squadron consisted of the frigate *Colorado*

U.S. Sailors battle Korean troops during Commodore John Rodgers's attack on the forts near Inchon in 1871. (Naval Historical Center)

(serving as flagship), gunboats *Monocacy* and *Alaska*, sloop *Benicia*, and tug *Palos*. Embarked was Frederick Low, U.S. minister to China, hoping to smooth over hard feelings and negotiate a commerce treaty. Before any negotiations could be arranged, one of the five forts along the river opened fire on *Palos*. A subsequent exchange of fire wounded two Americans, and Admiral Rodgers demanded an apology.

When no apology was offered, Rodgers sent a landing force of 109 Marines and 575 Sailors ashore on 10 June. Supported by gunfire from *Monocacy* and *Palos*, the Americans advanced on the forts. On the first day, the defenders of the first two forts withdrew without much of a fight, but on the second day, the American bluejackets and Marines assaulted the main fort—known as The Citadel—and its two supporting fortifications. A Navy lieutenant leading the assault was run through by a spear as he came over the wall, and a fierce battle ensued. At the end of the struggle, 243 of the Korean defenders lay dead alongside 3 Americans. Only 20 Koreans, some of them wounded, surrendered. The victorious Americans suffered 7 wounded, while capturing 481 cannon and hundreds of matchlock muskets. Six Marines and nine Sailors were later awarded the Medal of Honor for their valor. Despite this victory, the Korean king rejected all further attempts by Low to negotiate. Rodgers rightly decided that his force could do no more and, on 3 July, the expedition left a still-closed Korea.

Reaction to the incident in the United States was less than enthusiastic. The heroes of the battle were acknowledged, but the American press criticized the government for sending a force "altogether too large for the delivery of the message of peace and too small for the prosecution of war."

No further attempts at opening trade with the Hermit Kingdom were attempted by the United States until after Japan had negotiated a treaty in 1876 that at last prompted Korea to open its doors to the world. The United States would eventually become the first Western power to negotiate a treaty with Korea when the two nations finally signed an accord in 1882.

forces in Europe. Still, though anemic by World War II standards, Vice Adm. Arthur D. Struble's Seventh Fleet remained the most potent naval force in the Western Pacific. Its strongest formation was the Striking Force (Task Force 77), which consisted of attack carrier *Valley Forge* (CV-45), cruiser *Rochester* (CA-124), and eight destroyers. Embarked in "Happy Valley" (as *Valley Forge* was known to her crew) was Carrier Air Group 5, numbering eighty-six aircraft—two jet fighter squadrons of F9F-2 Panthers, two squadrons of F4U-4B Corsair propeller-driven fighters, and one propeller-driven squadron of AD-4 Skyraider attack planes.

After steaming along the China coast at the outset of the war, the Seventh Fleet deployed to Buckner Bay in Okinawa ready either to return to Chinese waters or support operations in Korea. While it was initially unclear what role they might play in the ensuing conflict, Seventh Fleet submarines *Segundo* (SS-398) and *Catfish* (SS-339) took on full loads of torpedo warheads in the Philippines on 26 June and proceeded north for Japanese waters the next day.

U.S. Navy ships in Japanese waters when war broke out were under the operational control of Commander Naval Forces, Far East (COMNAVFE), Vice Adm. C. Turner Joy. He also wore a second hat as Commander Task Force 96, which included the light cruiser *Juneau* (CLAA-119), four *Allen M. Sumner*-class destroyers, one diesel submarine, and an assortment of minesweepers. Before the war, Task Force 96 had shown the flag in Japanese ports, conducted antismuggling patrols, and cleared mines remaining in surrounding seas from the last war.

Also in Japanese waters and subordinate to COMNAVFE was the Amphibious Task Force (Task Force 90). Commanded by Rear Adm. James H. Doyle, it consisted of the amphibious command ship *Mount McKinley* (AGC-7), attack transport *Cavalier* (APA-37), attack cargo ship *Union* (AKA-106), fleet tug *Arikara* (AT-98), and one tank landing ship (LST). These ships had recently arrived in Japan to conduct amphibious training exercises with units of the U.S. Eighth Army.

The United Kingdom deployed aircraft carrier *Triumph*, light cruisers *Belfast* and *Jamaica*, destroyers *Cossack* and *Consort*, and frigates *Alacrity*, *Hart*, and *Black Swan* to the theater. Soon Australia, Canada, and New Zealand proffered ships as well. Joy welcomed these British ships, which were placed under his operational control. He assigned several ships to Task Force 96 in Korean waters and sent *Triumph*, *Belfast*, *Cossack*, and *Consort* to Okinawa to join Task Force 77.

The Republic of Korea Navy was not only newly formed but small in size. At Inchon, port city for the capital at Seoul, the ROKN operated four motor minesweepers (YMS), two steel-hulled minecraft (JML) inherited from the Japanese, and its only LST. Two more YMS and an assortment of small craft were based at Mokpo on the southwestern tip of the peninsula. Another nine YMS operated in the Pusan–Chinhae area along with an American-supplied patrol craft (PC) and some smaller craft. Three more

PCs were in Hawaii en route from the United States when the North Koreans began their invasion.

The U.S. Navy's Patrol Squadron 47, with PBM Mariner antisubmarine warfare seaplanes—homeward bound when war broke out—was recalled. The unit returned to the Western Pacific and joined Patrol Squadron 46 flying surveillance of the waters around Japan and Korea.

The Communist navies potentially arrayed against this agglomeration of allied naval forces were not formidable. The North Korean navy numbered fewer than fifty small craft, including several sixty-foot aluminum-hulled torpedo boats supplied by the Soviets. The Chinese Communist navy consisted of a "junk assault force," so insignificant that it had not even been included in *Jane's Fighting Ships,* a British publication then recognized as the most authoritative assessment of the world's naval forces. And the USSR's Pacific fleet (except for a significant force of submarines) was the weakest component of a relatively small, coastal-focused Soviet navy. In contrast to the U.S. Navy, which operated bases throughout the Pacific, the Soviet navy in the Far East had only one ice-free port—Vladivostok.

Bound for Korea, leathernecks of the 5th Marine Regiment board the attack transport *Pickaway* (APA-222) in San Diego, California, on 12 July 1950. (National Archives 80-G-416566)

Such was the naval situation in the Pacific at the outbreak of war. It is indeed fortunate that no enemy or potential enemy—even the Soviet Union—had sufficient forces to challenge the U.S. Navy at this crucial time, or the Korean War might well have had a far different outcome. With the minimal forces at hand, the U.S. Navy began carrying out the missions that would maintain control of the sea for the forces of the United Nations.

NAVAL FORCES
INTO THE BREACH

THE SITUATION IN KOREA only worsened. The South Korean capital of Seoul fell just three days after the war began, forcing the government to flee southward to Taejon. To make a bad situation worse, retreating UN forces prematurely destroyed the Han River Bridge at Seoul, trapping many South Korean soldiers and civilians north of the river. Despite the decisions of the United States and the United Nations to come to South Korea's aid, there was serious concern that the North Koreans might occupy the entire peninsula before significant military assistance could reach the battlefield. With less than 250 miles between the 38th parallel and the southern tip of the narrow peninsula, the South Koreans would soon run out of retreating room. And, with close to five thousand miles of water lying between Korea and the west coast of the United States—source of most of the supplies and reinforcements that could ultimately turn the tide—it was not an encouraging race. For a while at least, the UN would have to make do with resources already in the Western Pacific.

Because there were no other allied naval forces in Korean waters at the outset of the war, the first action, which would probably be the most important surface engagement of the war, fell to the ROKN. In the dark hours of the first night of the invasion, ROKN forces put to sea in search of enemy vessels. Soon after Commander Nam Choi Yong got his PC-701 under way from Chinhae and headed northeast, he encountered an armed, 1,000-ton North Korean steamer. The ship, with six hundred Communist troops embarked, was heading for the nearly defenseless port of Pusan. In a running gun battle, the South Korean patrol craft sank the enemy ship, whose passengers and crew drowned. Since Pusan became the toehold bastion of allied ground forces on the Korean peninsula and the primary port of entry for vital reinforcements and supplies, this victory was critical.

At the same time, Admiral Joy, headquartered in Japan, dispatched the destroyers *De Haven* (DD-727) and *Mansfield* (DD-728) to Inchon and

Pusan to evacuate American nationals. *De Haven* and the cruiser *Juneau* were then called upon to escort the ammunition ship USNS *Sgt. George D. Keathley* (T-APC-117) from Tokyo to Pusan. *Mansfield* and another destroyer, *Collett* (DD-730), escorted ammunition ship *Cardinal O'Connell* on a similar mission. On 27 June, Admiral Joy designated *Juneau*, *De Haven*, *Mansfield*, *Collett*, and another destroyer, *Lyman K. Swenson* (DD-729), as the South Korea Support Group (Task Group 96.5) and ordered them to patrol Korean waters south of the 38th parallel. The group's mission was to oppose any landings by hostile forces, provide fire support to friendly troops, engage any enemy vessels encountered, and escort friendly shipping involved in evacuation or resupply operations.

During the night of 28–29 June, *Juneau*, operating north of latitude 37° N, picked up two groups of surface contacts on radar. Believing reports that all ROKN units were far from the scene, *Juneau* opened fire on the unidentified contacts, sinking one vessel. Unfortunately, the *Juneau* had encountered ROKN units involved in evacuation operations. *Juneau* had sunk a South Korean minecraft.

The next night *Juneau*, armed with sixteen 5-inch guns, conducted the first shore bombardment of the war, shelling Mukho about thirty miles south of the 38th parallel on the east coast. Three days later, *Juneau*, joined by the Royal Navy's cruiser *Jamaica* and frigate *Black Swan*, encountered four North Korean torpedo boats and two motor gunboats. In the ensuing battle, the Anglo-American force destroyed three of the enemy torpedo boats and both motor gunboats.

The following day, *Juneau* attacked several enemy ammunition trawlers. But the enemy was not toothless. Two North Korean aircraft, believed to be Russian-made Stormoviks, strafed *Black Swan*, inflicting minor damage on the destroyer before escaping.

On 1 July, the day after President Truman approved the commitment of American ground forces to the war, Admiral Joy's headquarters began coordinating the transport of available troops from Japan to Korea. Part of the U.S. Army's 24th Infantry Division was airlifted to the war zone, but the rest of the troops were embarked at Sasebo in Task Group 96.3 LSTs belonging to the Shipping Control Administration, Japan—known more commonly as SCAJAP. These ships were manned by Japanese crews and, prior to the outbreak of hostilities, had provided logistic support to American occupation forces and repatriated Japanese prisoners of war from the Asian mainland. Chartered Japanese merchant vessels and the ships of Admiral Doyle's amphibious Task Force 90, augmented by ships of the

Military Sea Transportation Service (MSTS), deployed the Army's 24th and 25th Infantry Divisions to Pusan.

By 1 July some—though not all—of the initial concern over possible widening of the war had subsided. Neither the Chinese Communists nor the Chinese Nationalists seemed to be seriously contemplating an immediate crossing of the Taiwan Strait, and earlier anxiety over positioning the Seventh Fleet within tactical range of Soviet air bases also had diminished. Consequently, the Seventh Fleet was ordered out of Buckner Bay and sent north to the Yellow Sea for raids against North Korean targets. On 3 July, aircraft from "Happy Valley" and HMS *Triumph* suddenly pounced on the airfields of the North Korean Air Force (NKAF), destroying many planes on the ground.

Thus, only days after the North Korean invasion, allied naval forces in the Western Pacific were in the thick of the action, as they would be for the next three years of the war.

STRIKING THE ENEMY'S FLANKS

THE SUPERIOR NKPA DIVISIONS continued to roll back their southern counterparts. Even the introduction of U.S. ground forces from Japan failed to stem the tide. The North Koreans had considerable momentum and the American ground troops—coming from rather static occupation duties in Japan—were not honed to full combat capability. During July, the NKPA pushed the United Nations forces into a precariously small perimeter on the southeast corner of the peninsula centered on Pusan.

The geography of Korea gave UN forces some advantages. The invading NKPA divisions could never get very far from the sea, no matter which side of the peninsula they came down, because of the mountain ranges that ran down the center. Their flanks and their supply lines were vulnerable to attack from the Sea of Japan on the east side of the peninsula and the Yellow Sea on the west. Enemy-held roads and rail lines on the coast were subject to attack by surface ships, amphibious forces, and commando units.

On the fourth of July, *Juneau* celebrated Independence Day by bombarding bridges and roads along the east coast between Samchok and Chumunjin, just south of the 38th parallel in what was now enemy-dominated territory. The Royal Navy's *Black Swan* joined her in the bombardment but presumably not the Independence Day celebration. The next day, HMS *Jamaica* and HMS *Hart* joined up, and *Juneau* departed for Sasebo to replenish fuel and ammunition. For the next few days, the British ships bombarded targets ashore as they worked their way up and down the coast.

By 8 July, *Juneau* had returned from Sasebo and with destroyers *Mansfield, Swenson, Collett*, and *De Haven* continued bombardment operations. On 13 July, a U.S. Army artillery major embarked in *De Haven* established good radio communication with elements of the 25th Division. He coordinated effective naval gunfire against North Korean troops in Ulchin and Mukho. *De Haven* and *Juneau* also shot up a railroad yard and an oil storage facility.

On 15 July, with spotting assistance from an Army plane, *Juneau* and *De Haven* fired 645 rounds of 5-inch ammunition at troops, shore batteries, and various other targets along the coastal road. The two ships continued firing missions into the night, with the aid of star-shell illumination. The next day, *Mansfield* joined the pair and all three combatants engaged targets along the highway.

Even heavier naval firepower came to the defense of the Pusan Perimeter at the end of July. Heavy cruisers *Helena* (CA-75) and *Toledo* (CA-133), each armed with nine 8-inch and twelve 5-inch guns, had made a hurried departure from Long Beach, California, several weeks earlier. While *Helena* steamed in Chinese waters to deter Communist aggressive behavior, *Toledo* pounded away at enemy revetments, supply points, and troop concentrations near the front lines of the advancing army. On 7 August, *Toledo* struck targets near Samchok identified by aerial reconnaissance. Then *Helena* joined up, bombarding the town of Tanchon, north of the 40th parallel.

James Alexander, in *Inchon to Wonsan*, his account of destroyer operations during the Korean War, described a firing mission during the evening of 19 August: "The destroyer *Swenson* (DD-729) put 102 rounds into iron works, harbor installations, railroad yards, and radio stations at Chongjin with devastating effect. By the time she concluded her evening's work of destruction, flames from the burning facilities were visible for eighteen miles seaward."

The Royal Navy handled bombardment on the west coast and the U.S. Navy attacked the east coast. By early August, British cruisers *Jamaica, Kenya*, and *Belfast*, and destroyers *Cossack, Cockade*, and *Charity* had formed the West Coast Support Element. Australian destroyer *Bataan*, Dutch destroyer *Evertsen*, and Canadian destroyers *Athabascan, Cayuga*, and *Sioux* reinforced the Royal Navy contingent. On 1 August, *Belfast* and *Bataan* entered the approaches to Haeju Man, an enemy supply hub where rail and port facilities converged just north of the 38th parallel, and fired on shore batteries. The British destroyers *Cossack* and *Cockade*, based on intelligence reports of a large contingent of enemy shipping at Mokpo near the southwestern tip of the peninsula, headed for that port. The two ships wound their way thirty miles up a narrow channel, fighting ten-knot tidal currents much of the way, only to find one steamer at the site. With spotting assistance from a Patrol Squadron 6 Neptune plane based in Japan, the destroyers sank the steamer and bombarded surrounding docks and railroad sidings before threading their way back down the tortuous channel.

Throughout this period, American and British cruisers, destroyers, and frigates hampered NKPA supply and combat movements by firing on trains, bridges, oil tanks, troop concentrations, shore batteries, roads, and rail lines. These operations, while not decisive, complicated and slowed the enemy's logistical support effort. Combined with air interdiction operations, these naval bombardments forced the North Koreans to abandon daytime movements of supplies and reinforcements, thus cutting their logistical workday in half. James Alexander, an enlisted destroyer Sailor off Korea, observed:

> With the sea cut off as a route of supply and with rail lines being made inoperable by aircraft strikes during daylight, the North Koreans turned to their only other alternative to resupply themselves. They moved at night. Aerial photographs revealed camouflaged bypass railroad tracks around ruined bridges, crude log caissons placed in streambeds, and tunnels that showed smoke from trains that were hiding in them, waiting for nightfall. Infrared photography revealed trucks running at night.

In a report dated 3 August, the commanding officer of *Juneau* strongly recommended, "this force continue concentrated bombardment of enemy troops along the coast and prevent landings and resupply of troops. It is believed that naval gunfire during this period was effective in slowing enemy movements which were confined along the coast to hours of darkness."

Even more welcome to the UN troops ashore was the naval gunfire support provided during North Korean ground attacks. At Yongdok on 18 July for example, *Juneau* and a number of destroyers broke up a full-scale enemy assault. On 27 July, the cruiser *Toledo* and destroyers *Mansfield* and *Collett* provided direct support to besieged troops ashore. Again at Yongdok, on 4 and 5 August, Navy ships combined with U.S. Air Force fighters firing rockets to disperse concentrations of NKPA troops. In the early morning hours of 16 August the heavy cruiser *Helena* and destroyers *Theodore E. Chandler* (DD-717) and *Wiltsie* (DD-716) delivered concentrated fire against advancing North Korean troops at Chongha near Pohang on the southeastern coast, holding back the tank-led troops while amphibious vessels evacuated a ROK force.

BLOCKADE

DENYING THE ENEMY USE OF THE SEA for reinforcement and resupply was an especially important mission for UN naval forces in Korean waters. On 30 June—just five days after the start of hostilities—Chief of Naval Operations Adm. Forrest P. Sherman recommended a blockade of Korea as a component of U.S. strategy. The next day President Truman concurred. Operation Order 8-50, detailing plans for escorting shipping in the area and establishing a blockade, followed on 3 July. The coasts south of latitude 37° N were assigned to the South Korean naval forces, designated Task Group 96.7. North of 37° on the east coast, blockading responsibilities were assigned to the East Coast Support Group (Task Group 96.5), which was a mix of U.S. and other ships. The west coast, north of 37°, was the responsibility of the British ships operating in the Yellow Sea; this was the West Coast Support Group (Task Group 96.8). To preclude an unwanted confrontation with Chinese or Soviet military forces, these blockading units were prohibited from operating north of 41° on the east coast and 39°30' on the west.

Beginning on 5 August, when the front line was far to the south, British ships in the Yellow Sea established three barrier stations between 38°08' and 36°45'. On 13 August, blockading stations were established from 39°50' to 40°50' in the east.

The ROKN was a hard-hitting component of the blockading effort. Early in July, ROKN minesweeper *YMS-513* destroyed a trio of North Korean supply vessels on the southwestern coast at Chulpo and later in the month sank another three enemy boats loaded with supplies nearby. Submarine chasers PC-702 and PC-703, only recently transferred to the ROKN from the U.S. Navy, destroyed twelve North Korean ammunition vessels off Inchon. During August these and other South Korean naval forces sank or captured sixty enemy boats. As the Communists tried desperately to reinforce their assault divisions advancing on Pusan, the ROKN sank numerous troop-laden vessels on both coasts.

The ROKN subchaser *Chiri San* (PC-704) sorties from San Francisco on her way to South Korea in June 1950. Her sister ship, *Bak Du San* (PC-701), engaged and sank a Communist steamer loaded with troops and headed for the critical port of Pusan on the first night of the war. (Naval Historical Center)

The limited number of UN ships—already tasked with numerous other missions—precluded an effective blockade during the early weeks of the war. In his report to Commander in Chief, Pacific Fleet on 3 August, the commanding officer of *Juneau* recommended "that additional ships be assigned to carry out effectively the proclaimed blockade. International law requires that a blockade to be legal must be effective. It is not felt that an effective blockade of the N. Korean Coast has been established from Lat 38° N to northern established limit." Ultimately, the goal of the blockade was achieved with the strong presence of UN naval forces in Korean waters, and the early frustration of the enemy's seaborne resupply effort.

This strategy was in keeping with Alfred Thayer Mahan's contention sixty years earlier when he wrote, "it is not the taking of individual ships or convoys" that defines sea power, but the "overbearing power on the sea which drives the enemy's flag from it, or allows it to appear only as a fugitive." The overwhelming strength of the U.S. Navy, relative to its real and potential adversaries, was sufficient to meet this Mahanian criterion. Professor George Baer, chairman of the Naval War College's Department of Strategy and Policy, later assessed the blockade as successful, noting that it had "cut the enemy's seaborne maneuvers and closed its seaborne supply lines" as well as having "secured the flanks of the battle line" by the interdiction of the vital coastal arteries.

FROM THE SEA

THE NAVY'S INHERENT ABILITY to project power ashore was especially relevant in the context of the struggle for the Korean peninsula. Commando raids and sabotage operations were a significant feature of the naval war in Korea.

Just as the first watch began on the evening of 11 July, the executive officer of *Juneau*, Cdr. William B. Porter, and his team of four Marines and four Navy gunner's mates transferred to the destroyer *Mansfield*, which then headed for a target area well north of the 40th parallel near the village of Tanchon. In complete darkness, *Mansfield* closed to within a thousand yards of the beach and lowered her whaleboat. Once ashore, the men—armed with small arms and lugging high explosives—made their way over rough terrain to their target, a tunnel through which passed a vital enemy rail line. After setting two 60-pound demolition charges to detonate when the next train passed through, the commandos made their way back to the waiting destroyer, arriving just before the midwatch. Intercepted North Korean radio transmissions later indicated that the mission had been a success. Moreover, Commander Porter's Navy-Marine team had the distinction of being the first formation of the U.S. armed forces to invade North Korea.

On the night of 4 August, an American underwater demolition team (UDT) from the high-speed transport *Diachenko* (APD-123) went ashore just north of the railroad town of Yosu near the Pusan Perimeter. Their mission was to destroy several bridges. They were foiled, however, when a North Korean patrol traveling by railroad handcar happened upon them. In the ensuing firefight, the enemy drove the team away from the target, but all the men returned safely to the ship.

On 6 August the high-speed transport *Horace A. Bass* (APD-124), which had been converted to carry four landing craft, vehicle, and personnel (LCVP) and 162 troops, received a Special Operations Group consisting of a Marine reconnaissance contingent and a team of underwater demolition personnel. Between 13 and 16 August, *Bass* conducted daylight firing missions against rail targets between latitudes 38°35′ N and

41°28' N, but at night she moved in close to shore to insert her raiders. Over the three nights, the UDT Sailors and recon Marines of the Special Operations Group went ashore and successfully destroyed three tunnels and two bridges.

AMPHIBIOUS OPERATIONS

THE EARLY SUCCESS OF NKPA forces quickly made reinforcing the ROK Army an imperative. The U.S. Air Force had flown seven hundred men from the U.S. 24th Infantry Division from Japan to Korea in the first days of July. Airlift resources were much too limited to fly troop units to Korea. But it was clear that more soldiers would be needed—and fast.

Naval leaders searched for landing sites from the outset of the war. Their first thought had been to deploy units into Inchon, port city for the capital at Seoul, but that option faded when Seoul fell just three days later. The next site considered was Kunsan, at the mouth of the River Kum on the west coast. The troops would then advance on the Communist right flank. Naval leaders shelved that idea when it was clear that the enemy would be across the Kum River before such an operation could be executed. Soon, naval leaders just wanted to get reinforcements ashore before the Communists overran the entire peninsula.

By 10 July, the seriously outnumbered American and Korean troops had fallen back to take up defensive positions outside of Taejon in the middle of the peninsula. Four NKPA divisions, supported by tanks and artillery, closed on Taejon from several directions. General of the Army Douglas MacArthur wanted to deploy the 1st Cavalry Division from Japan to the battlefront via Pusan, but the port was already clogged with supply ships and transports. Further complicating the situation, the roads between Pusan and Taejon were saturated with military vehicles and refugees fleeing the fighting. Admiral Doyle's TF 90 staff began planning an amphibious landing at Pohang, sixty-five miles north of Pusan on the east coast.

Because little was known about the potential landing site, a team of Navy and Army personnel flew into Pohang on 11 July. The men returned to Japan on 13 July with as much information as they had been able to gather in two days. Pohang had been chosen because it had a half-mile strip of sandy beach conducive to an amphibious landing, a functioning airfield, and decent anchorages. Most significant was Pohang's proximity

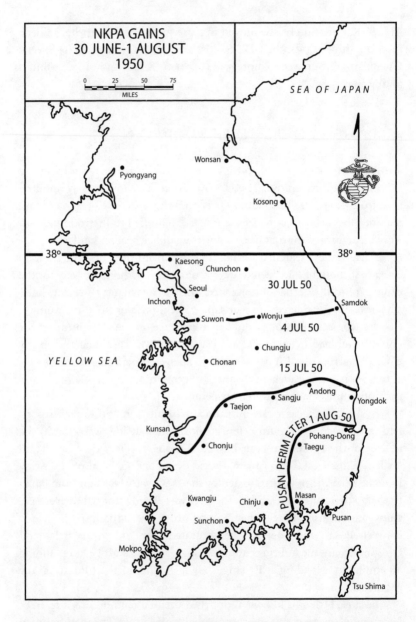

Even though UN forces quickly established sea and air control in the Korean theater, by July 1950 Communist ground forces had pushed ROK and U.S. troops into the southeast corner of the peninsula, leaving Pusan as the only major port under allied control. The map illustrates how quickly the enemy had advanced. (Steve Karp)

to rail lines, which connected it to Pusan to the south and, more importantly, to Taegu in the west. The freshly landed troops could be rapidly moved to Taegu, then northward to Taejon where they could be brought to bear on the central front of the NKPA.

Planners feared that the enemy would seize Pohang before the fleet could land the Army troops there. Delaying actions by ground, air, and naval forces kept the Communists from reaching Pohang, but no one knew for how long. The staff drew up plans for both an opposed and an unopposed landing.

Task Force 90's original complement of ships—one command ship, an attack transport, an attack cargo ship, and an LST—were not nearly enough for the task, so the Navy collected ships from throughout northeast Asia. The Navy's MSTS provided two attack cargo ships, *Oglethorpe* (T-AKA-100) and *Titania* (T-AKA-13), SCAJAP dispatched fifteen LSTs, and occupation authorities reactivated and pressed into service six landing ships, utility (LSUs) that originally belonged to the Imperial Japanese Navy. As a result of the cutbacks after World War II, the number of crewmembers in the MSTS ships had been radically reduced and much amphibious equipment stripped from the vessels. So, Fleet Activities Yokosuka worked around the clock installing debarking nets, boat and vehicle slings, prefabricated boat skids, towing bridles, and other necessities, and collecting landing craft. The Navy reinforced the crews with Sailors flown in from the amphibious base at Coronado, California. Ironically, the SCAJAP LSTs were crewed by Japanese Sailors who, just five years earlier, had been the enemy.

Amphibious landings normally take weeks or even months to plan, but Admiral Doyle's staff began putting together Operation Order 9-50, code named "Bluehearts," on 10 July. Only four days later, the task force got under way with the Army's 1st Cavalry Division embarked. As the ships departed Yokosuka, an Army band sent them off to the strains of "Anchor's Aweigh." Amazingly, at 0558 on 18 July, just eight days after the decision had been made to land at Pohang, Admiral Doyle signaled the traditional "Land the Landing Force." In short order, Task Force 90 deployed the soldiers ashore. The landing was unopposed, and only the press was disappointed that this was not a guns-blazing near thing like the great amphibious assaults of just a few years before.

By 22 July, the 1st Cavalry Division was on the front lines near Taejon, bringing sorely needed relief to the beleaguered 24th Division. Admiral Joy later asserted, "I do not believe the [Pusan] perimeter could have been held

Senior allied naval leaders meet on board heavy cruiser *Rochester* for operational planning in early summer 1950. Left to right, Captain A. D. Torlesse, RN, the commanding officer of British carrier *Triumph*; Rear Adm. John. M. Hoskins, Commander Task Force 77; Vice Admiral Arthur D. Struble, Commander Seventh Fleet; and Rear Admiral Sir William G. Andrewes, RN, commander of British Commonwealth naval forces. (National Archives 80-G-416423)

without the timely reinforcement of our forces by the First Cavalry Division." The landing at Pohang lacked the drama of the later landing at Inchon, but without it the UN command might not have been able to stem the Communist tide in Korea.

With the assistance of naval gunfire, Army artillery, and F-51 Air Force fighters based at Pohang airfield, the ROK 3rd Division successfully held on to Pohang against stiff enemy opposition. By early August, however, it was clear that South Korean forces would not be able to do so much longer. The enemy cut the ROK unit's line of communication to the south. As NKPA forces converged on Pohang and nearby Chongha, three LSTs arrived on 8 August to remove Air Force ground personnel and heavy equipment from the site. UN leaders decided to evacuate the ROK troops and their American advisors in the Korean Military Advisory Group (KMAG) before they were overwhelmed. Meanwhile, fleet units pounded away at the enemy forces, brought in medical supplies by helicopter, and transported gasoline ashore by motor whaleboat. Then carrier planes struck enemy positions around the precarious perimeter at Chongha.

Four LSTs—one manned by Korean and the others by Japanese mariners—arrived on 16 August to evacuate the beleaguered ROK troops. Escorted by the destroyer *Wiltsie*, these landing ships headed for the beach. They were guided to the evacuation site by the headlights of appropriately positioned jeeps. Throughout the night, the heavy cruiser *Helena* and her escorting destroyers kept up a steady bombardment of enemy positions while the South Korean troops and KMAG Americans embarked in the beached LSTs. Finally, at 0415 the LSTs took a strain on their stern anchors and backed off the beach. They were loaded with nearly six thousand military personnel, about one hundred vehicles, and more than twelve hundred civilian refugees. There were no friendly casualties in the entire operation. As James A. Field Jr. concluded in his official history of naval operations in the Korean War, "this first amphibious operation in reverse of the Korean War was thus a signal success." And the authors of the classic work *The Sea War in Korea*, Malcolm Cagle and Frank Manson,

Heavy cruiser *Helena* fires her powerful 8-inch guns against targets in North Korea in August 1950. The 8-inch guns could fire shells farther into enemy territory and do more damage than could the smaller 5- and 6-inch guns on other U.S. and allied ships. (Naval Historical Center)

observed, "to these troops [rescued at Chongha], 'control of the sea' assumed a fresh, new meaning."

Less than two years earlier, General of the Army Omar N. Bradley, then chairman of the Joint Chiefs of Staff, observed before the House Armed Services Committee: "I predict that large-scale amphibious operations will never occur again." Pohang and Chongha might not have qualified as "large-scale," but they were certainly amphibious operations. Pohang would not be the last amphibious landing of the Korean War, nor would Chongha be the last "amphibious operation in reverse."

NAVAL AIR OPERATIONS

MILITARY LEADERS AND STRATEGISTS agreed that air power had played a significant role in the Allies' World War II victory, but long after the conflict they continued to debate whether or not it was *the* decisive factor. Leaders of the Air Force (the Army Air Forces became the U.S. Air Force in 1947) and others argued that long-range, shore-based strategic bombers armed with atomic weapons should be considered America's primary war-winning force. Some air proponents even suggested that naval aviation in general and aircraft carriers in particular had outlived their usefulness. In 1949, these advocates persuaded Secretary of Defense Louis A. Johnson to cancel completion of USS *United States*, which was to be the Navy's newest carrier and capable of handling jet aircraft. Navy and Marine Corps leaders contended that there would continue to be conflicts in which atomic bombs, for political and military reasons, could not be used. For such wars, carriers and shore-based aircraft armed with conventional weapons would continue to be indispensable. The often-heated interservice dispute was far from settled when North Korean forces stormed across the 38th parallel in June 1950.

In Korea, as in World War II, there were three major aspects of the employment of air power: (1) air superiority; (2) interdiction; and (3) close air support. There was clear consensus between Air Force and naval leaders that air superiority had to be gained before other operations could succeed afloat and ashore. The Air Force put more emphasis than the naval services on destroying the enemy's munitions plants and other war-making facilities over interdicting supply lines to the front. But, North Korea had a miniscule military-industrial complex with few worthy targets, so the allied air forces by necessity had to concentrate on knocking out rail lines and rail and highway bridges.

"REVOLT OF THE ADMIRALS"

A LITTLE MORE THAN a year before war broke out in Korea, another battle was being waged on the other side of the world, along the shores of the Potomac River. In this struggle the opponents were the U.S. Navy and the newly created U.S. Air Force.

The origins of this conflict were complex, but a somewhat simplistic account begins with the resignation of James Forrestal as secretary of defense. Forrestal, the former secretary of the navy, was succeeded by Louis Johnson, who, as assistant secretary of war in the late 1930s, had played a role in strengthening the Army Air Corps. No friend of the Navy—he had once declared that the Air Force could do anything the Navy could do—Johnson confirmed the anxiety of many senior naval officers when, less than a month after taking office, he halted construction of the Navy's newest aircraft carrier, USS *United States*. To make matters worse, he did so when Secretary of the Navy John L. Sullivan was out of town. When Sullivan resigned in protest, the secretary of defense hand-picked as Sullivan's successor Francis P. Matthews, a man he believed would make loyalty to Johnson his highest priority.

In an attempt to discredit the B-36 bomber program, the special assistant to the undersecretary of the Navy delivered an anonymous document to several members of Congress alleging that the secretary of defense and the secretary of the Air Force, Stuart Symington, had personally benefited from the procurement of the new bomber being built for the Air Force. These allegations were subsequently proven untrue but prompted a series of hearings in Congress that brought a sizable number of dissenting admirals forward and into the limelight. Their testimony before

The Joint Chiefs of Staff meet in 1948 after discussions on service roles and missions with Secretary of Defense James V. Forrestal. Left to right, Gen. Hoyt S. Vandenberg, Chief of Staff, U.S. Air Force; Adm. Louis E. Denfeld, Chief of Naval Operations; and Gen. Omar N. Bradley, Chief of Staff, U.S. Army. (National Archives USAF K-4823)

Congress—decrying cancellation of *United States* and accusing the secretary of defense of unfairly hurting naval aviation—prompted the press to coin the term "revolt of the admirals." The toadying secretary of the Navy subsequently relieved Adm. Louis E. Denfeld, then-chief of naval operations, for supporting the testimony of the Navy witnesses. Several other senior naval officers were punished for their complicity, including Capt. Arleigh A. Burke, a hero of World War II and popular officer.

This unhappy sequence seemed to gain little if anything—budgetary cuts into naval aviation allocations continued after the hearings—the revolt was seen at the time as a defeat for the Navy. However, the testimony of these senior naval officers actually had the desired effect of convincing key members of Congress of the importance of naval aviation, thereby setting the stage for the revitalization that would subsequently occur.

Another more immediate factor in naval aviation's survival was the outbreak of the Korean War. When aircraft carriers were able to "show the flag" in the Taiwan Strait, interdict the enemy's supply lines in Korea, provide crucial close air support to troops on the front lines, and help wrest control of the air from the North Korean Air Force, the future of naval aviation was made secure.

The rivalry of the Navy and Air Force was diminished by the appearance of a new and common enemy, but the antagonism that had manifested itself in the hearing rooms of Congress was not completely eradicated. Many of the differences between the two forces were the legitimate result of dissimilar philosophies born of different origins and priorities. Others resulted from budgetary squabbling and other less-noble impulses. Some Navy–Air Force differences continued to trouble the relation of these services and indeed outlasted the Korean War, but cooperation was the more common factor in the hard fight against the Communist foes.

The strongest disagreements occurred over the importance and conduct of close air support. With its focus on long-range strategic bombing, the Air Force devoted few resources or command attention to close air support, and saw that mission as bombing support to ground troops a few miles behind the front. Control of such operations was to be handled at the division, corps, or even army level. The naval services, based on their experiences in the bloody island assault battles of the Pacific in World War II, considered close air support a complement to artillery support. Navy and Marine Corps leaders expected air units to drop their bombs as close to the front-line troops as was safe and as directed by aerial and ground spotters. They wanted the immediate and flexible employment of air support.

These philosophical differences, while complicating air operations in Korea, certainly did not seriously impede the overall effort. U.S. and allied air forces, shore-based and carrier-based, brought devastating firepower down on the enemy.

AIR SUPERIORITY   The North Korean Air Force, although larger than its practically nonexistent South Korean counterpart, had fewer than two hundred combat aircraft at war's beginning. All of these were propeller-driven, World War II–vintage, Russian-made hand-me-down planes, and their pilots were not up to American qualitative standards. It was clear from the outset that the North Koreans would not be able to maintain control of the skies over Korea against U.S. air forces.

Two factors potentially offset the air superiority enjoyed by the allies. The first was hypothetical—at least at war's beginning. Intervention in the war by the Soviet Union—either directly or by sending the NKAF more modern aircraft—could have a significant impact on UN command of the air. The other factor was not hypothetical but very real. As the North Korean army advanced south from the 38th parallel, forcing allied forces into the Pusan Pocket, they seized the few air bases in South Korea that hosted U.S. Air Force planes. Aircraft based in Japan consumed so much

A Grumman F9F-3 Panther of Fighter Squadron 52 taxies forward for a catapult launch from *Valley Forge*. The only U.S. carrier in the Western Pacific at the outbreak of the Korean War, *Valley Forge* began launching attacks against North Korean targets on 3 July. (National Archives 80-G-428152)

fuel flying to and from the targets in Korea that they had little on-station time. The allies' qualitative edge was meaningless when they could not operate effectively over Korea.

The obvious answer was to bring aircraft carriers into the theater. Since the U.S. Navy held control of the sea, these floating airfields were immune to the enemy's advance and could be positioned—and repositioned—at will, close offshore where they could directly influence the battle.

Valley Forge, the only American carrier in the Far East when the war began, was soon joined by HMS *Triumph*. Because *Triumph* carried a different mix of aircraft and her maximum speed of twenty-three knots was ten less than *Valley Forge*'s, the Americans adjusted their operations to accommodate the British; but the added punch of a second carrier clearly was worth the effort.

On the evening of 1 July, Task Force 77 sortied from Buckner Bay in Okinawa and headed northwest for the Yellow Sea. The two carriers, accompanied by two cruisers and ten destroyers, arrived on station early on 3 July. For the first time since the end of World War II, aircraft carriers prepared to launch combat strikes against a hostile shore. Airfields in and around the North Korean capital city of Pyongyang were chosen as targets for these first strikes. The designated launch point, 130 miles from the target area, was only one hundred miles from Chinese Communist airfields on the Shantung Peninsula and less than two hundred miles from the Soviet air garrison at Port Arthur. At 0500, *Valley Forge* launched combat air patrols in a protective screen over the task force, just in case any Chinese or Soviet planes showed up to contest the allied presence. As an added precaution, the carrier also launched a number of antisubmarine patrols. Forty-five minutes later, British Fireflies and Seafires took off from *Triumph* and headed for the enemy coast. American Corsairs and Skyraiders then launched from "Happy Valley" to join their British counterparts.

When these propeller-driven aircraft were airborne and well on their way, a group of Panther jets took off from *Valley Forge*. (The sortie of these eight Panthers marked the first time in aviation history that naval jets flew in combat.) The speed of these jets would place them over the target area before the propeller-driven planes arrived. As the Panthers arrived over the enemy airstrips, numerous North Korean, Soviet-made Yak fighters frantically tried to get airborne. Several of these aircraft almost collided on the ground, prompting one Panther pilot to describe the scene as "too hairy to watch." The Panthers swooped in on the Yaks, destroying at least nine on

HMS *Triumph*, a light fleet aircraft carrier commissioned after World War II, was the Royal Navy's carrier in the Far East when war broke out on the Korean peninsula. (Naval Historical Center)

the ground and shooting two out of the air. The Corsairs and Skyraiders reached the scene soon afterward and, pushing over at seven thousand feet, dove on their targets. Firing rockets and dropping bombs, they demolished three hangars, cratered the runways, and scored a direct hit on the field's fuel storage facility.

Meanwhile, the British aircraft struck at Haeju airfield sixty miles south of Pyongyang. It was perhaps fortuitous that the British and American aircraft had gone to separate targets on this first strike of the war. Later, the American pilots found that the British planes were not only unfamiliar to them, but the Seafire fighters resembled the Communist Yaks. More than once in the war, their allies would fire on the British Seafires and actually shoot one down (the pilot survived). On this first strike, however, all British aircraft returned safely to their carrier.

This initial raid was followed by another that afternoon, with more the following day. The British and American pilots concentrated on railroad facilities around Pyongyang, destroying fifteen locomotives and assorted rolling stock, as well as dropping one of the spans of a key railroad bridge across the Taedong River.

All American aircraft returned to *Valley Forge* after the two days of strikes. On the second day, however, heavy antiaircraft fire took its toll, hitting one of the Skyraiders with a 37-mm cannon shell and damaging its hydraulic system enough to necessitate a landing without flaps. When this wounded bird landed on the straight-deck carrier, it bounced over the crash barriers and careened into other aircraft spotted forward. (This result would be avoided with the advent of angled-deck carriers after the war.) The crash wrecked and damaged six other aircraft.

The message of these first strikes of the war was clear. Allied aircraft could strike at the enemy capital with virtual impunity. No site on the Korean peninsula was beyond the reach of this aerial weapon. This operation affirmed the wisdom of an earlier Soviet decision not to intervene in the air war.

Because strategic planners were still concerned about the possibility of a flare-up in the Taiwan Strait, Task Force 77 headed back to Buckner Bay after these Pyongyang strikes. While the task force was there, aircraft carrier *Philippine Sea* (CV-47) left San Diego and headed for the Western Pacific. After a workup period in Hawaiian waters, she joined Task Force 77 at the beginning of August.

At the same time, the attack carrier *Boxer* (CV-21) prepared to depart for the war zone, but for an unconventional mission. Instead of a normal air wing load-out in San Diego, she took aboard 145 Air Force F-51 Mustangs. These propeller-driven fighters had served the Army Air Forces in World War II and after the war were relegated to reserve and Air National Guard units in the United States before their retirement. But the jet-powered F-80 Shooting Star fighter-bombers the Air Force had been using in Korea were gas-guzzlers, ill suited for operating over Korea. When the F-80s got to Korea from Japanese air bases, they could be on-station for only a short time before having to return to Japan. As a result, the Air Force decided to deploy the more fuel-efficient, propeller-driven F-51 Mustang to Korea. The fastest way to get them to the combat theater was to have them transported by the Navy. The carrier *Boxer* loaded the planes in San Diego and delivered them to Yokosuka, Japan, in a record-setting eight days and sixteen hours.

Although the changeover had some distinct advantages, it also caused some problems. The Mustangs conserved fuel and carried a heftier bomb load than the F-80s, but their slower airspeed kept pilots in the cockpit much too long. The flights from Japan to Korea exhausted the airmen. The

The oil refinery at Wonsan in North Korea under attack by *Valley Forge* Corsairs and Skyraiders in July 1950. The carrier planes destroyed much of the plant and twelve thousand tons of refined petroleum products. American Sailors on ships far out to sea could see the plumes of smoke that resulted from the strike. (National Archives 80-G-707876)

older Mustangs also needed more maintenance than the jets. Worst of all, the lightly armored Mustang was more vulnerable to antiaircraft and small-arms fire. In one report, an Air Force historian related what some airmen felt about the Mustang: "A lot of pilots had seen vivid demonstrations of why the F-51 was not a ground-support fighter in the last war and weren't exactly intrigued by the thought of playing guinea pig to prove the same thing over again."

Still working with only *Valley Forge* and *Triumph* (*Philippine Sea* would not join the fray until 1 August and *Boxer* would not be available until the Inchon landing in mid-September), Task Force 77 sortied from Okinawa on 16 July and headed for the eastern side of Korea to support the amphibious landing at Pohang. Because enemy opposition to the landing did not materialize, strike coordinators sought other targets. Seven Panthers launched from *Valley Forge*, flew along the eastern coast of North Korean, and verified that the Wonsan Oil Refining Factory, which produced five hundred tons of refined petroleum product each day, was a prime candidate. Soon, ten Corsairs and eleven Skyraiders were in the air and headed north, armed with an assortment of rockets, bombs, and gun ammunition. These predators swooped in and destroyed the facility. A tower of smoke rose, visible for sixty miles, rose into the summer sky. The refinery burned for four days. Some months later, when the allies seized Wonsan, witnesses to the earlier strike reported that the main power plant, coke furnaces, water tanks, air compressors, and storage buildings had all been hit, and that oil had run in the streets as deep as two feet. The carrier strike ended production at the refinery.

The Pyongyang strikes decimated the NKAF and in so doing further discouraged Soviet involvement in the air war. The Navy's destruction of the Wonsan oil refinery also dealt a serious blow to the North Korean war machine.

INTERDICTION From the earliest days of the Korean War, American and British carrier aircraft, in conjunction with U.S. Navy and Royal Navy surface ships, devoted considerable attention to North Korean troops and supply convoys advancing south toward Pusan. In contrast to the naval vessels, however, the aircraft could attack the enemy's rear far inland. Enemy tanks, towed artillery pieces, and trucks transporting critical food, fuel, and ammunition became excellent targets for the allied aviators.

As the North Korean army moved farther south, its lines of communication grew longer and more vulnerable to attack from the sky. Allied fighter-bombers pounced on one convoy after the other, littering the landscape with burned out and destroyed vehicles. Eventually, the North Korean logistical units traveled only at night, reducing their operating time by half. The NKPA devoted an increasing amount of time trying to conceal and protect their supply vehicles. The constant air attacks also lowered the morale of enemy soldiers. By late August, attacks by Communist infantry and armor units against the Pusan Perimeter occurred less frequently and on narrower fronts. As allied ground units and supplies poured into Pusan, the enemy offensive, starved of fuel and ammunition, lost steam. Thanks to the hard fighting of American and South Korean troops, and the air interdiction operations of U.S. and British naval aircraft and surface ships, the North Korean army was in a precarious position—too weak either to press on or disengage.

CLOSE AIR SUPPORT In *The Bridges at Toko-ri*, Michener brings up a touchy subject when two of his characters discuss the Korean War:

> With his cup he [Admiral Tarrant] indicated on the chart where the permanent snow line, heavy with blizzards and sleet, hung a few miles to the east, while to the west the mountains of Korea hemmed in the ships. "Imagine the United States Navy tied down to a few square miles of ocean. The marines are worse. Dug into permanent trenches. And the poor air force is the most misused of all. Bombers flying close air support. Militarily this war is a tragedy."

The Navy and the Air Force considered close air support a legitimate use of air power and had doctrine covering its use. However, each service viewed the function through a different philosophical lens. While the Navy and Marine Corps consistently referred to these operations as *"close* air support," the Air Force often used the term *"tactical* air support"—a telling distinction.

Faced with operations on a wide, ever-changing front in Europe during World War II, the Army Air Forces (predecessor of the U.S. Air Force) had developed a centralized, highly structured system for controlling air power. Thus, in Korea the Air Force continued to employ a Joint Operations Center (JOC) staffed by ground and aviation personnel who coordinated air operations for the combat theater. The JOC and its affiliated Tactical Air Control Center (TACC), received, prioritized, and reacted to requests for support from ground-based air control parties or airborne forward air controllers. Often, however, requests for air support from a front-line combat unit went through corps and division headquarters. The process was time-consuming and could not accommodate fleeting targets of opportunity.

In Central Pacific operations, control of air power was much more decentralized. Navy and Marine Corps aircraft reported to ground commanders and for the most part flew directly above the battle line ready to strike. This immediate fire support was necessary because artillery was not deployed ashore in the first waves of amphibious landings.

Admiral Burke, who served as chief of staff to Commander Naval Forces Far East, Admiral Joy, described the different service approaches to air power and the result:

> They had a lot of trouble with coordination at that time [during the defense of the Pusan Perimeter] and during the whole Korean war between the ground forces and front-line troops, because the two systems that were being used by the Air Force and Navy were completely different. The Navy had a system developed by the Marines and the Navy, in which the front-line troops, the men who needed it, controlled the aircraft. That is, they had direct communication with the aircraft and directed the aircraft, and when they said "close air support" they meant close air support, within a couple of hundred yards, quite frequently. The Air Force and the Army did not have that system. They had theirs controlled by the air, they had small planes in the air that controlled . . . the airplanes, and their close air support was sometimes miles away from the troops.

The theater commander, General MacArthur, directed that all services operate through the Air Force system, with the JOC as the central coordinating headquarters. Hence, when naval aircraft arrived over the battlefront, they could not drop their bombs until an Air Force ground or air controller authorized a mission, which required approval by higher authority and took too long. Often, to the frustration of the naval aviators, they had to ditch their ordnance in the sea and return to their carrier.

Incompatible communications equipment caused other problems. For example, *Valley Forge* pilots reported that when they arrived over the battle line along the Pusan Perimeter on 25 July, they could not make radio contact with the air controllers on station, or with the JOC. They watched helplessly while Air Force F-80s from Japan with smaller ordnance loads attacked the primary target. Finally, in exasperation, the *Valley Forge* pilots flew off to search for targets of opportunity. After bombing a few trucks, and jettisoning remaining ordnance, the naval aviators returned to the ship. Soon afterward, Commander Seventh Fleet, Admiral Struble, informed Forrest Sherman, the Chief of Naval Operations, that "the results [of close air support] were disappointing" and that naval aviators would need "training [in the Air Force system] before minimum Navy standards can be attained."

Adm. John S. Thach, who devised the famous "Thach weave" fighter tactic in World War II and commanded the escort carrier *Sicily* in the early days of the Korean War, also described the air control problem:

> Of course the U.S. Air Force wasn't too interested in close air support. The people in high command in the Air Force were primarily hepped on the big bomber idea, that you really didn't even need troops to win a war; just fly over and bomb them, and then wait for a telegram saying that they surrender. So they were utterly unprepared to do close air support the way it had to be done if you were going to help the troops at the front lines. And it wasn't a matter of just a communication problem. It was a matter of education over a long period and experience and doctrine built up.
>
> I was amazed that it could be so bad. . . . The pilots would come back and say, "We couldn't help. We wanted to. We were there and we couldn't get in communication with people." Those that did would get in touch with the Joint Communications Center [sic] and they wouldn't have any target, or by the time they got it, it was old information.
>
> The Air Force went on the principle that any aircraft committed had to go through a pretty high echelon of command before it did anything. They wanted to keep tight control in high places. The idea was never would they let anybody in the trenches control one of their airplanes.

The official history of the U.S. Air Force in the Korean War takes a different view, observing, "during the Korean war the favorable results achieved with it justified the wisdom and practicality of the USAF-Army system for managing air-ground operations." The report does, however, concede that "early in the war . . . demonstrations of the Marine system of close support . . . caused some Army officers to assert requirements for their own organic air support."

Captain John S. Thach, a highly decorated World War II veteran, originator of the "Thach weave" fighter tactic and commanding officer of the escort carrier *Sicily* (CVE-118), discusses a mission with 1st Lt. Roland B. Heilman (left) and Maj. Robert P. Keller of VMF-214. Marine fighter squadrons operating from *Sicily* and *Badoeng Strait* (CVE-116) flew hundreds of ground support sorties during August 1950. (National Archives USN 417110)

The Air Force, however, did seek to accommodate the Navy and Marine Corps approach. Joint talks and a number of procedural modifications did satisfy naval close air support requirements. The Air Force integrated the naval services' Air and Naval Gunfire Liaison Companies into the system, accepted naval officers on the staff of the JOC, and allowed Marine attack squadrons to operate exclusively with the 1st Marine Division. Most important, the services improved their radio communications.

When the North Koreans launched an all-out effort in early August to break through to Pusan, General MacArthur ordered all air resources in the theater—including those of the Seventh Fleet—to concentrate on

Marines atop a ridgeline along the Naktong River watch for signs of an enemy attack. The Naktong formed part of the boundary on the Pusan Perimeter defended by the allies in the summer of 1950. (Naval Historical Center)

interdicting Communist supply lines near the battle front and to provide the hard-pressed ground troops with close air support. Admiral Struble put *Valley Forge* and *Philippine Sea* on a rotation that assured at least one of them was on station off Korea. The admiral also moved his logistic support ships from Okinawa to Sasebo to put them closer to the operational area. As a result, the carriers left station only briefly to replenish their ammunition, fuel, and food.

While the Navy launched a "maximum all-effort," the Air Force system could not handle multiple naval aircraft over the battlefield. Rear Adm. Homer Hoskins, Commander Carrier Division 3, believed that positioning only four aircraft overhead would have sufficed. Rear Adm. Edward C. Ewen, Commander Task Force 77, concluded that only 30 percent of the fleet's air assets were being used in close air support operations, and that the effort was "wasteful and ineffective."

As a result, at the end of August Admiral Joy asked General MacArthur to release the carriers from close air support duties so they could deploy off North Korea, which held many more lucrative targets. A final, all-out enemy offensive on the Naktong River line in early September, however, cut short these plans. Despite continued frustration with the inefficiency of the close air support organization, *Valley Forge* and *Philippine Sea* mounted 263 sorties that helped stem the tide of the last Communist offensive.

Even more critical to defense of the Pusan Perimeter during August and September were the Marine aviators flying from escort carriers *Sicily* and *Badoeng Strait* (CVE-116). Admiral Burke credited the "Marine pilots in those two jeep carriers" and Marines on the ground without whom, the allies "would have been driven into the sea."

At war's beginning, *Sicily* and *Badoeng Strait*, home ported in San Diego, immediately headed for the war zone. Captain Thach, *Sicily*'s commanding officer, later described the tenor of the times:

> Admiral Radford sent a message directing that we . . . go to Yokosuka and pick up a Marine Squadron, VMF-214, which was the famous Black Sheep Squadron that Pappy Boyington had during World War II. . . . I was directed on the 31st [of July] to go to Kobe [Japan], where the *Badoeng Strait* was, and the supply vessels that were carrying Marine Corsair spare parts and their squadron personnel. . . . We got into Kobe and went alongside a pier. I'd just got the brow over when a call came up, "Captain, Tokyo wants you on the telephone," . . . and it was the duty officer at ComNavFE . . . saying, "How soon can you get underway?"
>
> "Well," I said, "there's a lot of spares and stuff here to be put aboard. I think I could get underway first thing in the morning."

A crane lifts a Marine Corsair of Marine Aircraft Group 33 on board *Badoeng Strait* for a July 1950 departure from the United States for the Korean War zone. (Naval Historical Center)

He said, "You don't understand. I mean how soon can you get underway right now." And he said this over the phone in plain English. "Because if you don't, there won't be any use in getting underway. It'll be too late."

Well, all right, things were really popping, so I said, "In thirty minutes." Then I figured, what can I do in thirty minutes. I knew I could cast off my lines easily, so I got on the public address system and addressed everybody, the people on the pier, everybody, everybody who could hear me, "I don't care what you are, unless you are on watch, go over to those two vessels, pick up something that's good for a Corsair and bring it back over to *Sicily*. Make one trip. I'm leaving right after that."

And it was amazing how much they got. Everybody, the ones in the other ships and all my crew—I didn't realize I had so many of them—streaming over there and they'd bring a carburetor and another one would bring something. Other people would bring rockets in their arms and walk right aboard, put them down. I got everybody that wasn't supposed to be on the *Sicily* off, cleared the lines, and away we went.

On 3 August, Corsairs from VMF-214 joined *Sicily* off the coast of Korea. They were immediately refueled, armed with incendiary bombs and rockets, and launched to provide close air support to the besieged Eighth Army. Within minutes of their launch these aircraft were hitting Communist positions at Chinju and Sinban-ni on the western side of the perimeter. These were the first Marines to enter combat in support of the Eighth Army, but they were soon joined by the troops of the 1st Provisional Marine Brigade who had just arrived at Pusan. Actually little more than a reinforced regiment, these Marines, too, were rushed to the front, and soon, with close air support from the *Sicily* and *Badoeng Strait*, not only prevented the collapse of the precarious perimeter in that sector but *advanced*—one of the few successful attacks by U.S. troops since the war began.

In the first half of August, the two carriers flew nearly 1,400 sorties in direct support of the 1st Provisional Marine Brigade. Marine Commandant Gen. Clifton B. Cates told his men, "I am very proud of the performance of your air-ground team. Keep on hitting them, front, flanks, rear, and topside! Well done!"

While the differing service approaches to close air support, indeed air operations in general, outlasted the Korean War, the imperfect system still enabled U.S. and allied air forces to lend vital assistance to the ground troops ashore on the Korean peninsula.

CONCLUSION

THE ALLIES CONTINUED TO HOLD the Pusan Pocket. U.S. and South Korean troops, backed up by Navy, Marine, Air Force, and British

THE GROUND
WAR

ON 25 JUNE 1950, a huge artillery and mortar barrage across the 38th parallel signaled the beginning of the invasion. The NKPA surged across the boundary between the two Koreas in a full-scale assault led by Soviet-built tanks and supported by heavy artillery, neither of which the South Korean Army possessed. The NKPA drove southward along natural corridors, several of which converged on the capital city of Seoul. The South Korean units were quickly routed and individual soldiers fled south.

Three days after the invasion began, the NKPA rolled into Seoul. In the terrible chaos, South Korean engineers destroyed the bridges over the Han River before much of their fleeing army could cross. The North Koreans continued south, slowed only by their need to resupply.

On 1 July, the first American ground combat troops arrived in South Korea—coming straight from relatively soft occupation duty in Japan. The 1st Battalion of the 21st Infantry Regiment, 24th Infantry Division—dubbed Task Force Smith after its commander, Lt. Col. Charles B. Smith—joined the battle four days later, fighting a disastrous delaying action at Osan. More of the division deployed to Korea, and in the days that followed, these American infantrymen slowed the advance of the NKPA in a series of engagements at Chonan, Chochiwon, the Kum River, and Taejon. American performance on the battlefield reflected the troops' poor state of training and readiness, and casualties were high, but they succeeded in buying desperately needed time for the retreating remnants to regroup and for the buildup at Pusan to continue.

The 25th Infantry Division was the second U.S. Army division to land in Korea, transported by U.S. Navy shipping to Pusan, 10–18 July. This

Tanned and sweating gunners of the Army's 64th Field Artillery Battalion operate a 105-mm howitzer in defense of the Pusan Perimeter. Fighting with determination and skill, Lt. Gen. Walton H. Walker's Eighth Army units defeated one NKPA attack after another during the brutally hot summer of 1950. (National Archives 111-SC-347107)

division entered the fray almost immediately, also helping to slow the advance of the NKPA. On 20 July, the 25th launched the first successful counterattack of the war at the town of Yechon, an important rail hub about fifty miles north-northeast of Taegu.

The Navy put the 1st Cavalry Division ashore in an unopposed amphibious landing at Pohang, 18–22 July, sixty-five miles north of Pusan on the east coast. The fresh troops were rapidly moved by rail to Taegu, then northward to Taejon where they were committed to battle against the central front of the NKPA.

The first major Marine contingent to arrive in Korea was the 5th Marine Regiment, which would serve as the nucleus of the 1st Provisional

Marine Brigade. After its arrival in mid-July, it was augmented by an influx of Marine personnel from called-up reserve units and from other parts of the active force in other theaters. Soon sent to the front, they also played a vital role in stopping the North Korean onslaught.

Gradually, as the NKPA's lines became extended and allied strength increased, the retreat ended and the Americans and their allies were able to solidify their lines in the Pusan Perimeter. The allies now stood nearly shoulder to shoulder along this front with the advantage of interior lines in their favor and a continuing logistic build-up in their rear. Despite the tenacious—sometimes reckless—attacks by NKPA forces, this line held until a counterstroke—the daring and brilliant landing at Inchon—at last turned the tide of battle.

air forces, slowed and then stopped the North Korean assault on Pusan. During the desperate days of July, August, and early September of 1950, the U.S. Navy hit the enemy from the air and from the sea, rushed reinforcements and supplies to the theater, and set the stage for the decisive counterstroke at Inchon.

Holding Pusan, however, a very near thing had not been guaranteed. The post–World War II dissolution of the U.S. armed forces and fixation on long-range atomic warfare almost doomed the UN effort to preserve the independence of the Republic of Korea. Admiral Burke, revered by many as one of the finest naval officers this nation has ever produced, made the point well when he said:

> There's [a] simple point here that is so obvious that people have forgotten it. We had absolute control of the sea around there. It was never contested in Korea. If our control of the sea had been contested just a little bit, it would have interfered with a lot of those operations, and Korea would have been lost very fast.

THOMAS J. CUTLER *is a retired lieutenant commander and former gunner's mate second class who served in patrol craft, cruisers, destroyers, and aircraft carriers. His varied assignments included an in-country Vietnam tour, small craft command, and nine years at the U.S. Naval Academy where he served as executive assistant to the chairman of the Seamanship and Navigation Department and associate chairman of the History Department. While at the Academy, he was awarded the William P. Clements Award for Excellence in Education (military teacher of the year). Founder and former director of the Walbrook Maritime Academy in Baltimore, he now serves as Fleet Professor of Strategy and Policy with the Naval War College and senior acquisitions editor for Naval Institute Press. Winner of the Alfred Thayer Mahan Award for Naval Literature, he is the author of* Brown Water, Black Berets: Coastal and Riverine Warfare in Vietnam *(Naval Institute Press, 1988),* The Battle of Leyte Gulf *(HarperCollins, 1994), and* A Sailor's History of the U.S. Navy *(Naval Institute Press/Naval Historical Center, 2005) and has revised* Dutton's Nautical Navigation *(15th ed.) and* The Bluejacket's Manual *(22nd and 23rd eds.). His books have been published in various forms, including paperback and audio, and have appeared as main and alternate selections of the History Book Club, Military Book Club, and Book of the Month Club. He and his family live in Annapolis, Maryland.*

CHAPTER 2

Assault from the Sea
The Amphibious Landing at Inchon

CURTIS A. UTZ

INTRODUCTION

ON 25 JUNE 1950, the army of the Democratic People's Republic of (North) Korea stormed across the 38th parallel and invaded the Republic of (South) Korea. North Korea's Communist leader, Kim Il Sung, intended to destroy the rival government and abolish the division of Korea that had resulted from international tensions after World War II. Kim launched the attack because he, and the Communist leaders in Moscow and Beijing, believed that the United States would not protect South Korea. This was a critical mistake, however, because President Harry S. Truman roundly condemned this blatant act of aggression and persuaded the United Nations to resist the invasion. Truman also ordered U.S. ground, air, and naval forces into combat in Korea. Thus began the Cold War's first major armed conflict.

Weakened by the drastic cutbacks in defense spending after World War II, the U.S. armed forces were hard-pressed to delay—much less stop—the onrushing North Korean People's Army (NKPA). Only a small number of Navy carrier and Air Force planes were on hand to strike enemy front-line units and supply convoys. A hastily gathered and deployed Army unit made a brave but futile stand in central South Korea. By early August, the hard-charging NKPA armored and infantry forces had pushed the U.S.

Eighth Army and Republic of Korea (ROK) troops into an ever-tightening pocket around the port of Pusan on the southeastern tip of South Korea. Barring a dramatic turn of events, it looked as though the U.S. and the ROK troops would be forced to evacuate the Pusan Perimeter under fire, much as the British and French had done at Dunkirk in World War II.

The effort to rescue South Korea, however, was under way. General of the Army MacArthur, the U.S. Commander in Chief, Far East, and Commander in Chief, United Nations Command (CINCUNC), persuaded his superiors in Washington to approve an amphibious assault at Inchon, a major port 110 miles behind enemy lines on South Korea's west coast. Because of the port's treacherous waterways, he reasoned that the North Koreans would not expect an attack there, so it would be relatively poorly defended. The UN force could advance rapidly from Inchon and capture the nearby key air base at Kimpo and then mount an attack on Seoul, the capital of the Republic of Korea. Seoul was also the key link in the NKPA's line of communications and once taken would then serve as an anvil on which an Eighth Army offensive from Pusan would hammer the enemy army. The hoped-for result of this coordinated action was the complete destruction of the NKPA and the recovery of all of South Korea.

Inchon was a classic demonstration of how naval forces can be decisive in regional wars and littoral operations. During July, August, and early September 1950, fleet units in the Far East established superiority in the Yellow Sea and in the air over it. The presence there of surface ships, submarines, carrier aircraft, and shore-based patrol planes served to deter or, if necessary, warn the CINCUNC of Chinese or Soviet intervention in the war. Control of the sea and the air also blinded the North Koreans to UN military movements. This enabled the 230 ships of Vice Admiral Struble's Joint Task Force 7, which steamed toward the west coast of Korea in mid-September, to achieve a clear advantage over their foe through strategic surprise.

On 13 September 1950, Struble's forces began their assault from the sea against Inchon. Carrier-based aircraft squadrons, as well as cruisers and destroyers, devastated enemy fortifications, coastal artillery batteries, and supply points for two days. Then, on 15 September, landing ships and transports began disembarking the 1st Marine Division, which quickly seized Inchon. By 19 September, the Marines captured Kimpo air base, into which flowed Marine close air support aircraft and Air Force supply transports. U.S. Army troops also pushed out from the beachhead and on 27 September linked up with their comrades advancing north from the

Pusan Perimeter. UN casualties were light, especially when compared to the thousands of dead, wounded, and captured North Korean soldiers.

Provisioned by the Navy's transport and cargo ships, Marine, Army, and South Korean troops captured Seoul on 28 September. Only a battered remnant of the NKPA was able to flee South Korea and the closing UN trap. Because of Chinese intervention in October 1950, the struggle in Korea would drag on for almost three more bloody and inconclusive years. Inchon, however, was a strategic masterstroke that clearly turned the tide of battle in the opening phase of the war.

KOREA: THE "COCKPIT OF ASIA"

KOREA HAS LONG BEEN an Asian battleground. The mighty Genghis Khan and his Mongol horde swept into Korea in the thirteenth century. For the next six hundred years, the Mongols and their successors to the throne of China dominated the diminutive Kingdom of Korea. Every year, the Korean king pledged his fealty to the emperor in Beijing, but aside from this connection with the outside world, the Koreans jealously guarded their isolation. In fact, the Korean monarchs banned overseas trade and discouraged contact between their subjects and foreigners. The ruggedness of the coastline and the perilous seas around the Korean peninsula helped enforce their royal edicts. Outsiders appropriately referred to Korea as the Hermit Kingdom.

In the latter half of the nineteenth century, Americans learned just how serious the Koreans were about their desire to be left alone. In 1866, the Koreans massacred the crew of American merchant schooner *General Sherman*, which had run aground in the Taedong River near Pyongyang. The Navy dispatched Cdr. Robert W. Shufeldt, commanding officer of the screw sloop-of-war *Wachusett*, to discuss the incident with the King of Korea. The monarch refused to deal with him.

Despite this rebuff, U.S. naval leaders in the Far East convinced Washington that Korea could be "opened" for trade and diplomatic relations. The visits of Commo. Matthew C. Perry and his "black ships" to Japan in the 1850s, which stimulated the Japanese to cultivate contacts with the Western world, clearly influenced these officers. In 1871, Rear Admiral Rodgers led five U.S. Navy warships up the Salee River until they were under the guns of the Korean forts above Inchon. The Koreans, as they had done in the past, greeted the foreigners with gunfire. Rodgers's ships returned fire and put ashore a landing party of Sailors and Marines, who seized the forts. The admiral, however, did not have enough men to march on the Korean capital and impose a treaty on the king, so the Americans and their ships withdrew.

The Navy now enlisted the support of the Chinese, who encouraged the royal head of the subordinate kingdom to work with the Americans. Finally, on 22 May 1882, in sight of the U.S. screw sloop *Swatara*, Commodore Shufeldt and Korean officials signed a treaty that provided for peace, friendship, and an exchange of diplomats. The agreement also granted the United States most-favored-nation treatment, with special trading rights on the peninsula. The Koreans hoped this unique relationship with the United States would help fend off their more demanding neighbors, particularly the Japanese.

This proved an illusion, however, because the American interest in Korea faded even as the focus of the Chinese, Japanese, and Russians sharpened. The Imperial Japanese Navy's sound thrashing of the Chinese fleet in the naval Battle of the Yalu in 1894, during the Sino-Japanese War, ended Beijing's domination of Korea. Russian designs on the kingdom met the same fate as a result of the Russo-Japanese War of 1904–5. That conflict, fought partly on the Korean peninsula, was capped by the Japanese destruction of a Russian fleet in the Strait of Tsushima and the declaration of a "protectorate" over the country. President Theodore Roosevelt, in the interest of balancing Japanese and Russian power in Northeast Asia, endorsed Tokyo's direction of Korean affairs. Finally, in 1910, Japan formally annexed the kingdom, establishing a brutal regime that lasted until Japan's defeat by the Allied powers in 1945.

Before the end of that global conflict, Allied leaders agreed to set up a United Nations "trusteeship" over Korea, with the United States and the Soviet Union occupying Korea on either side of the 38th parallel, which was intended to be only a temporary dividing line. After disarming Japanese forces, the occupying powers planned to withdraw and restore Korea's independence. To carry out this mandate, in August and September 1945, Soviet and U.S. troops moved into their respective occupation zones in North and South Korea.

Ideological conflict and balance-of-power politics after World War II soon disrupted the process of Korean unification and independence. The world witnessed the dawning of the Cold War. The United States and the

An American-educated Nationalist, Syngman Rhee, president of the Republic of Korea, was a vehement anti-Communist. (Library of Congress photograph)

other Western allies were increasingly at odds with the USSR and its ruthless dictator, Joseph Stalin. The Soviets suppressed basic freedoms and undermined governments in Poland, Czechoslovakia, and the other Eastern European nations that had been occupied by the Red Army. Moscow fueled an insurgency in Greece and made territorial demands on Turkey and Iran. In 1946, Mao Tse-tung Chinese Communists launched an all-out campaign against Chiang Kai-shek's Nationalist government that would culminate several years later in the conquest of the entire mainland of China. The Soviet menace loomed especially large in August 1949 when the USSR detonated an atomic bomb, ending the U.S. monopoly of these weapons of mass destruction.

Meanwhile, in Korea, the Soviets supported the ascendancy if Kim Il Sung, a Communist leader whose forces had fought the Japanese in North China and Manchuria during the war. U.S. officials favored Dr. Syngman Rhee, an American-educated Nationalist, and his ardent anti-Communist supporters. In both sections of the country, the Korean antagonists suppressed their opponents, often ruthlessly. Voters south of the 38th parallel

Kim Il Sung, leader of the People's Democratic Republic of Korea, gives a speech in 1948 with a depiction of a united Korean peninsula behind him. (Department of Defense)

eventually elected Rhee as the first president of the Republic of Korea, formally established on 15 August 1948. The following month Kim Il Sung announced his leadership of a second political creation, the Democratic People's Republic of Korea.

During the next year and a half, the two Korean governments engaged in low-level hostilities. They sent agents, saboteurs, and raiding forces across the 38th parallel and fought artillery duels along the dividing line. In the last six months of 1949 alone, there were more than four hundred "border incidents."

With the establishment of friendly regimes in their respective occupation zones, the USSR and the United States withdrew their occupation forces. The Soviet armed forces left behind a military advisory group and large amounts of WWII–vintage munitions and equipment, including tanks, artillery, and combat aircraft. The North Korean armed forces continued to grow in number and capability under Soviet tutelage.

Except for the 500-man Korean Military Advisory Group (KMAG), the United States withdrew all of its forces from Korea by June 1949. They left behind large quantities of small arms and ammunition but, unlike the

Soviets, no tanks, medium or heavy artillery or combat aircraft. The administration of Harry Truman opposed giving Rhee such "offensive" weapons, fearing that he would try to unify Korea by force. The Americans thought Rhee's new government needed only U.S. training of its armed forces, modest arms supplies, and economic and political support.

The simultaneous drawdown of U.S. conventional forces and reliance on military advisors and assistance reflected the Truman administration's global approach to the threat posed by the Soviet Union and its allies after World War II. In 1947, President Truman proclaimed a new strategy for dealing with the Communist's militant and expansive policies—containment. The United States and her allies would prevent the spread of Communist ideology and Soviet influence by strengthening the economies, political systems, and military organizations of friendly countries. The containment strategy anticipated using U.S. ground troops, tactical aircraft units, combat fleets, and other conventional forces to defend only vital national interests.

REDUCED FORCES

AT THE END OF WORLD WAR II, the U.S. armed forces comprised 12 million men and women who had answered the greatest call to the colors in American history. This massive establishment fielded ninety-five infantry, armor, airborne, and Marine divisions; 92,000 aircraft; 1,307 warships; and 82,000 landing craft. But, with the war now over, the American public clamored to "bring the boys home." Operation Magic Carpet and similar movements transported millions of American soldiers, Sailors, airmen, and Marines home to the United States and then discharged them from the military.

Another motivation for the reduction of the military establishment was Truman's desire to improve America's financial health. Being the "Arsenal of Democracy" in World War II had been a great drain on the public treasury of the United States and had disrupted the production of consumer goods. Truman believed that it was more important to balance the budget and encourage the private sector than to buy new weapons or station large forces overseas.

Key leaders in Washington also suggested that the United States could reduce defense spending significantly because America had the atomic bomb. Proponents concluded that the American atomic arsenal (which was not that powerful or ready for war during the 1945–50 period) either would deter or defeat Soviet invasions of vital areas such as Western Europe. The U.S. Air Force, separated from the Army in 1947, believed that the delivery of atomic weapons should be the mission of only its bombers. The Air Force argued that this made conventional forces, especially Navy carrier forces, much less valuable and that they should be reduced in number and capability. The Navy countered that a balanced military establishment, in which no weapon system or service predominated, best served the global interests of the United States.

All the services were involved in sometimes-acrimonious disputes over dwindling budgets, their respective roles and missions in the new postwar world, and unification of the defense establishment. James V. Forrestal, the first secretary of defense (the National Military Establishment, later to become the Department of Defense, was established in 1947), literally worked himself to death trying to accommodate the differing views of each service. His successor, Louis A. Johnson, an incompetent political appointee with little experience in defense matters, reinforced Truman's inclination to drastically cut the defense budget. Johnson also accepted the proposition that only the Air Force should be allowed to conduct long-range atomic bombing. Without consulting the Navy's civilian or military leaders, he canceled construction of *United States* (CVA-58), the first aircraft carrier designed to carry atomic-capable aircraft. In the uproar over this and other issues, collectively called the "revolt of the admirals," Secretary of the Navy John L. Sullivan resigned in protest and his successor forced Admiral Denfeld, the Chief of Naval Operations (CNO), to retire.

From 1945 to 1950, all the services suffered from the loss of critical resources. The last budget approved by Congress before the outbreak of the Korean War provided for only 238 naval combatants, including six fleet aircraft carriers, one reduced-status battleship, and nine carrier air groups; six battalions and twelve aircraft squadrons for the Marines; and fourteen reduced-strength Army divisions. Even the favored Air Force was expected to operate with forty-eight air groups instead of the seventy-one it considered essential.

THE ROAD TO WAR

IN EARLY 1950, INTERNATIONAL miscalculation over Korea resulted in war. For several years, Kim Il Sung had urged his Communist patrons to support a North Korean invasion of South Korea but they refused him each time. The leaders of the Soviet Union and the People's Republic of China did not want a major war to break out in northeast Asia. Stalin was more concerned about the growing strength of the North Atlantic Treaty Organization alliance in Europe. Mao Tse-tung was concentrating his forces for the invasion of Taiwan and climactic last battle with Chiang Kaishek's Nationalists.

The United States did not want a war in Asia either. The Truman administration focused its attention and the combat power of the U.S. military on Europe. Truman and his secretary of state, Dean Acheson, were determined to limit U.S. Far Eastern commitments, a desire unfortunately made public. On 12 January 1950, Acheson told the Washington press corps that the United States would fight to defend Japan, Okinawa, and the Philippines but, by failing to mention them, neither Taiwan nor Korea. So, when Kim once again asked Moscow and Beijing to approve his plans to conquer South Korea, they agreed, although Mao Tse-tung was somewhat reluctant. However, Mao promised to send the substantial number of ethnic Koreans in the Chinese Communist forces back to Kim.

By the late spring of 1950, the North Koreans had amassed formidable military forces. The NKPA then consisted of one hundred thirty-five thousand men. The principal ground elements of this force were ten infantry divisions, an armored brigade, two independent regiments, and border constabulary troops. Two of these divisions recently had returned from China; many of the other soldiers were veterans of Mao's forces. The NKPA fielded 150 Soviet-made T-34 tanks, hundreds of light and medium artillery pieces, and numerous heavy mortars. The North Korean Air Force included seventy Yakolev Yak-3 and Yak-7 fighters and sixty Ilyshin Il-10 "Shturmovik" attack planes, all propeller-driven. The Navy operated a few small patrol boats.

The Republic of Korea military was inferior to the NKPA in quantity and quality. The ROK Army, composed of eight infantry divisions, various support units, and headquarters elements, numbered only one hundred thousand men. They lacked good field artillery and had no tanks. The air force flew only twenty unarmed training planes. The ROKN manned seventeen old U.S. and Japanese minesweepers, a few picket boats, one tank landing ship, and one subchaser, renamed *Baek Du San* (PC-701), which the U.S. Navy sold to the Koreans in 1949.

The U.S. naval forces in the Western Pacific in June 1950 were a pale reflection of the mighty armada that surrounded the battleship *Missouri*

(BB-63) at Tokyo Bay in September 1945. Admiral Struble, a veteran of WWII amphibious operations in the Philippines, commanded the Seventh Fleet, based at Subic Bay in the Philippines. In this fleet steamed fleet air-craft carrier *Valley Forge* (CV-45), heavy cruiser *Rochester* (CA-124), eight destroyers, four submarines, and five logistics support ships. Fleet Air Wing 1, with two patrol squadrons, provided the fleet with long-range search and reconnaissance aircraft. Vice Admiral Joy, Commander Naval Forces, Japan, led a force that consisted of light cruiser *Juneau* (CLAA-119), the four ships of Destroyer Division 91, and the seven minesweepers of Mine Squadron 3. Also under Joy were the five ships of Rear Admiral Doyle's Amphibious Group 1. Joy was also Commander Naval Forces, Far East, and in the event of an emergency, Seventh Fleet would come under his direction, as well.

The closest American ground forces to the Korean peninsula were the four infantry divisions of Lt. Gen. Walton H. Walker's Eighth Army, which served as the occupation force for Japan's Home Islands. Walker's units—the 7th, 24th, and 25th Infantry Divisions and the 1st Cavalry Division (also infantry)—were in poor shape. Because of postwar defense cutbacks, these units were severely undermanned and badly equipped. Much of their mate-rial had been salvaged from WWII battlefields and restored in Japanese shops. Lacking adequate training and resources, and softened by occupa-tion duty, the American troops in Japan were ill prepared for war.

Manpower and material shortages also hobbled the U.S. Far East Air Force (FEAF), commanded by Lt. Gen. George E. Stratemeyer. FEAF was made up of three air forces—the 20th, 13th, and 5th, which operated from Okinawa and the Mariana Islands, the Philippines, and Japan. FEAF oper-ated mostly jet-powered Lockheed F-80 Shooting Stars in both the fighter and fighter-bomber roles, even though they were not well suited to the lat-ter mission. The only planes in FEAF designed solely for the attack role were the propeller-driven Douglas B-26 Invaders of the 3rd Bombardment Wing (Light). Also flying with FEAF were North American F-82 Twin Mus-tang all-weather fighters, Boeing B-29 Superfortress bombers, and Dou-glas C-54 Skymaster transports.

While the United States could not assume its WWII allies would sup-port it in any new crisis, Australian and British forces operated in the region during early 1950. Australian occupation forces stationed in the Japanese Islands were an infantry battalion, a fighter squadron equipped with North American F-51 Mustangs, and the frigate HMAS *Shoalhaven* (K-535). The UN was fortunate that in June 1950 light aircraft carrier HMS

Triumph, two light cruisers, two destroyers, and three frigates of the Royal Navy's Far East Station were steaming toward Japan to escape the summer heat at their Southeast Asian home ports.

As U.S., Australian, and British forces in the Far East carried out business as usual in the late spring of 1950, there were ominous developments on the Korean peninsula. After months of probing south across the border, the NKPA suddenly halted such activity in May. Intelligence sources in Taiwan and South Korea warned that the Communists would soon take stronger armed action. These warnings, however, fell on deaf ears. American political and military leaders believed that none of the countries interested in the Korean situation would benefit from a war on the Korean peninsula. KMAG officers told visiting American officials that all was quiet on the Korean front. On 19 June, the Central Intelligence Agency forecast that the North Koreans would continue their low-level hostilities near the 38th parallel but not launch a major attack across it that summer.

NORTH KOREAN INVASION AND UN REACTION

EARLY ON THE MORNING OF 25 June 1950, the hills around the 38th parallel reverberated with artillery fire. This caused little alarm among the American advisors, however, because of the numerous border incidents that had occurred there during the past year. This complacency soon changed to shock as they discovered North Korean combat forces in their midst. When U.S. Army Capt. Joseph R. Darrigo neared the railroad station at Kaesong, five miles south of the parallel, he discovered several NKPA battalions detraining. Overnight, the Communists had connected their rail lines to those in the south and rushed troops forward. He now knew that this was no border incident—this was an invasion.

By early afternoon, NKPA infantry and armored formations, heavily supported by aircraft and artillery, were attacking all along the border. As T-34 tanks spearheaded the main assault on Seoul, landing forces stormed ashore at several places on the east coast and outflanked ROK positions.

Some of the South Korean units fought well, but many did not. None was equipped or trained to hold off a mechanized assault. Surprised as they were, most of the ROK units disintegrated or retreated in the face of the powerful offensive. At least one South Korean unit, however, scored a victory over the attackers. After putting to sea with the few other combatants of the ROKN, the newly arrived submarine chaser *Baek Du San* discovered a 1,000-ton armed North Korean steamer off the east coast. In a vicious surface battle, the South Koreans sank the steamer, whose six hundred embarked soldiers were meant to land and seize Pusan. This proved to be one of the most important fights of the campaign for it prevented the short-term loss of this key port, soon to be vital to the survival of UN forces in Korea.

Meanwhile, chaos reigned in Seoul. With South Korean defenses around the capital crumbling, U.S. ambassador John J. Muccio ordered the evacuation of American dependents. Protected by the destroyers *Mansfield* (DD-728) and *De Haven* (DD-727), the Norwegian freighter SS *Rheinholdt* took on the evacuees at Seoul's port, Inchon, and headed for Japan. In the next several days, Air Force transports flew other Americans and UN personnel out of nearby Kimpo and Suwon airfields. During these evacuation operations, escorting U.S. fighters shot down seven North Korean fighter and attack planes.

Even though surprised by the North Korean invasion, President Truman and his advisors in Washington took immediate action to oppose it. Truman called for an emergency meeting of the UN Security Council to consider the North Korean aggression. The council met only twenty-three hours after the start of the invasion and it discussed a resolution advocated by the United States that condemned the North Korean aggression, demanded an end to hostilities, and called for the restoration of the 38th parallel dividing line. With the USSR's delegate absent because of an earlier dispute over the UN's failure to seat the People's Republic of China on the Security Council, there was no Soviet veto and the council passed the resolution. Then, on 27 June, the Security Council approved a second resolution, encouraging UN members to come to the armed assistance of the Republic of Korea.

Meanwhile, despite earlier uncertainty over the importance of South Korea to America's interests, Truman decided that U.S. forces should defend the country. Truman and the Joint Chiefs of Staff (JCS) were concerned that the attack on Korea was only a diversion for a major Communist offensive in Europe. Still, they ordered the combat deployment of air and naval forces in the Far East, including the Seventh Fleet, to the Korean theater.

The Seventh Fleet was important not only for the help it could provide to UN forces fighting in Korea but for its impact on North Korea's potential military allies, the People's Republic of China and the USSR. Fearing that the Communists might mount a regional offensive, Truman ordered the Seventh Fleet to "neutralize" the Taiwan Strait and then made that directive public. Truman wanted to prevent a Chinese Communist invasion of Taiwan as well as an attack on the mainland by Chiang's Nationalist forces.

After steaming from Subic Bay on 27 June, the Seventh Fleet sent carrier planes flying up the Taiwan Strait as it passed close to the island on 29 June. Throughout the Korean War, Seventh Fleet forces operated along the coast of China, from the Yellow Sea in the north to Hainan in the south, discouraging the Chinese use of the sea and the air over it. Beijing later revealed that it respected the power of the fleet's air, surface, and subsurface forces.

The fleet also maintained naval forces in the waters around the Soviet Far East. Shore-based patrol planes kept a close watch over Soviet air and naval bases. U.S. submarines also prowled the waters off Vladivostok and the straits from the Sea of Japan.

Meanwhile, as units of the Seventh Fleet headed for the Yellow Sea at the end of June, Admiral Joy's Naval Forces, Japan, dispatched units to Korea. Early on 29 June, cruiser *Juneau* and destroyer *De Haven* deployed off Korea's east coast to stop Communist seaborne movement and to bombard enemy ground forces advancing down the coastal road. In the confusion during the withdrawal of South Korean forces to the south, *Juneau* in a tragic accident sank the ROKN minelayer *JML-305*, which the cruiser mistook for an enemy ship.

Early in July, Joy sent part of Struble's Seventh Fleet dashing into North Korean waters to hit the enemy's central nerve center, the capital at Pyongyang. Struble's Striking Force (Task Force 77), reinforced by several of Rear Adm. William G. Andrewes's Royal Navy warships, mustered twenty-four ships. On 3 and 4 July, only eight days after the North Korean invasion, planes from *Valley Forge* and HMS *Triumph* pounded the air base, rail yards, and bridges near Pyongyang.

In addition to launching Navy carrier and Air Force bombing attacks against the advancing North Korean forces, General MacArthur ordered Air Force transports to deploy a hastily assembled Army infantry–artillery team, Task Force Smith, to Korea. NKPA armor and infantry units overran and destroyed this brave force of 24th Infantry Division soldiers in a bloody action near Osan on 5 July.

MacArthur pleaded with the JCS for reinforcements to stop and then counterattack the invading NKPA. Since General Bradley and the service representatives of the JCS suspected that Korea was only a Communist diversionary move, they were reluctant to dispatch a sizable portion of the understrength U.S. armed forces to the Far East. The gravity of the UN situation in Korea and MacArthur's insistent pleas, however, soon persuaded them to grant most of the general's requests.

Naval forces answered the call for help with alacrity. During July and August, Pacific Fleet units streamed into the Korean theater. These included heavy cruisers *Helena* (CA-75) and *Toledo* (CA-133) and *Essex*-class carriers *Philippine Sea* (CV-47) and *Boxer* (CV-21). The latter ship brought with her from the U.S. west coast 171 aircraft, including 146 F-51 Mustang fighters desperately needed by the Air Force. *Boxer* set a transpacific speed record, reaching Yokosuka, Japan, in only eight days. Also dispatched to Korea were the Pacific Fleet's two escort carriers, *Sicily* (CVE-118) and *Badoeng Strait* (CVE-116). *Sicily* embarked antisubmarine aircraft and thirty other fighter, attack, and transport planes. *Badoeng Strait* embarked not only Marine Fighter Squadron (VMF) 214, assigned to the ship, but also the aircraft of three squadrons of Marine Aircraft Group (MAG) 33. The UN naval contingent expanded with the arrival in Korean waters of the Royal Navy's light cruiser HMS *Kenya* and British, Canadian, New Zealand, Dutch, and French destroyers and frigates.

Those reinforcements soon entered the fray. On 27 July, *Toledo* shelled positions on the east coast of Korea, and on 5 August, planes from *Philippine Sea* attacked targets at Iri, Mokpo, and Kunsan. Early in August, VMF-214, the "Black Sheep" squadron of WWII fame, and VMF-323, based respectively on *Sicily* and *Badoeng Strait*, began to strike enemy forces ashore.

UN air forces responded in similar fashion. In early July, General Stratemeyer ordered several of his Philippine-based squadrons to Japan. He also ordered that some fighter–bomber squadrons be reequipped with F-51 Mustangs stockpiled in Japan because his F-80s experienced difficulty in the close-air-support role, and they could not operate from the rough Korean airfields. In addition, the Air Force deployed several B-29 bomber groups to the Western Pacific. The Australian F-51 squadron in Japan also joined the FEAF.

As important as naval and air forces were to the allied defensive effort in Korea, ground forces were absolutely essential. On General MacArthur's orders, Admiral Doyle's Amphibious Group 1, Military Sea Transportation Service (MSTS) cargo ships, and Japanese time-chartered ships transported three infantry divisions (24th, 25th, and lst Cavalry) from Japan to

Korea, where General Walker quickly plugged them into the front line. Only the understrength 7th Infantry Division remained in Japan. MacArthur also requested and received the infantry and artillery battalions needed to bring his Eighth Army divisions up to battle strength. The JCS also ordered the U.S.-based 2nd Infantry Division, a regimental combat team (RCT) from the 11th Airborne Division, and various armor, artillery, and engineer units to the Far East.

Marine combat units and Navy amphibious forces were especially critical to MacArthur's anticipated operations on the Korean peninsula. Supported by General Cates, Commandant of the Marine Corps, MacArthur persuaded the JCS to fully man and equip the 1st Marine Division and deploy the unit to Korea by mid-September. General Cates partially filled the understrength division with Marines pulled from bases throughout the United States, but this was not enough. President Truman then approved Cates's request for mobilization of the entire ground element of the Marine Corps Organized Reserve and attached Navy medical units. The first contingent of the division to arrive in Korea was the 5th Marine RCT.

The amphibious ships that transported the Marine units from the United States also bolstered Admiral Doyle's amphibious force. The newcomers included three dock landing ships (LSDs), two attack transports (APAs), one tank landing ship (LST), and one medium landing ship. To complement this force, Doyle got control of LSTs operated by the Army in Japan and enlisted the assistance of the SCAJAP, a civilian occupation agency that controlled Japanese merchant shipping. In the SCAJAP inventory were thirty-four former U.S. Navy LSTs, manned by Japanese, and Doyle quickly integrated seventeen of them into his force.

Despite the growing strength of UN ground, naval, and air forces, the North Korean offensive rolled on. Coordinated NKPA tank assaults and infantry flank attacks often broke the thin U.S. and ROK defensive lines, which led to a series of demoralizing retreats. With his command in dire straits, General Walker ordered UN forces to withdraw behind the Naktong River, the last natural barrier to Pusan, on 1 August. This defensive bastion soon became known as the Pusan Perimeter.

To stiffen the ground defenses, MacArthur reinforced the Eighth Army with the 2nd Infantry Division and the Marine Brigade, comprising the 5th Marine RCT and MAG-33. During the first two weeks of August, the NKPA launched four major attacks. The Marine Brigade repelled two of them, including a serious penetration in the vital "Naktong Bulge" sector. Navy cruisers and destroyers provided gunfire support that helped repel assaults near the coast as well. In early September, the Marine Brigade countered one last NKPA breakthrough at the Naktong Bulge.

Throughout this period, U.S. Air Force, Navy, and Marine, as well as British and Australian, planes struck targets throughout Korea. Navy UDT and Marine reconnaissance detachments executed raids ashore from the high-speed transport *Horace A. Bass* (APD-124). By 4 September, Communist forces were spent. There would be no more major attacks on the perimeter, but MacArthur expected the NKPA to be just as tough on the defense as it had been on the offense. The general had no intention of launching the Eighth Army on a frontal assault against the dogged North Koreans.

COUNTERSTROKE

MACARTHUR, THE VETERAN COMMANDER of numerous littoral operations in the Southwest Pacific during World War II, was quick to see the strategic possibilities offered by the Korean peninsula. Less than one week after Kim Il Sung's Communist legions poured across the 38th parallel into the Republic of Korea, CINCUNC began to consider how he could defeat his land-bound adversary. MacArthur's visit to the Korean battlefield on 29 June convinced him that the NKPA would push the underequipped, battered, and demoralized ROK Army, even if bolstered by U.S. reinforcements, far to the south of Seoul. MacArthur felt that his forces could turn the tables on the enemy by exploiting one key advantage over them—strategic mobility. He decided that a decisive stroke, an amphibious assault somewhere behind NKPA lines, could liberate South Korea.

MacArthur concluded that his enemy was most vulnerable to a landing on Korea's west coast at Inchon. Capture of this sizable port and the nearby air base at Kimpo would enable the UN to mount a major attack on Seoul, not only the capital of South Korea but also the key road and rail link in the NKPA's line of communication. A northwestward UN offensive from the Pusan Perimeter would then push across the peninsula, trapping most of the enemy army in the south. The U.S. divisions from the perimeter would also link up with the units at Inchon. The isolated NKPA formations would be forced to surrender or be crushed between the UN forces. Success at Inchon could lead to a glorious, one-stroke UN victory in the war, a prospect the gifted but vain MacArthur could only relish.

MACARTHUR SELLS INCHON

MACARTHUR SELECTED THE SMALL Joint Strategic Plans and Operations Group (JSPOG) of his Far East Command (FECOM) staff to bring his concept to fruition. The general's advocacy of an amphibious operation sometime before October and selection of Inchon as the site were, according to Admiral Struble, the general's "earliest and most important" decisions.

Planners were free to concentrate on overcoming the Inchon site's difficulties, and they were serious, indeed. In the words of Lt. Cdr. Arlie G. Capps, Admiral Doyle's gunnery officer, "We drew up a list of every natural and geographic handicap—and Inchon had 'em all." The approaches from the Yellow Sea were two restricted passages, Flying Fish and Eastern channels, and they joined at Palmi-do. The island stood at the end of the narrow Salee River, ten miles downstream from Inchon. Both channels and the Salee could be easily blocked by mines. In addition, the normal harbor current at Inchon was a dangerously quick two to three knots and sometimes even eight knots. The anchorage was small, there were few docks and piers and no landing beaches—in the usual meaning of that term—there were only seawalls, piers, salt pans, and, according to one intelligence report, "rocks with patches of sand." Just offshore, a triangular-shaped island, Wolmi-do, and an islet, Sowolmi-do, separated the city from the Salee River.

Several heights dominated the landing area. The 315-foot-high Radio Hill on Wolmi-do completely commanded the harbor. Presenting a sheer cliff to the harbor side and rising to 102 feet, Cemetery Hill guarded the eight-hundred-yard-long causeway that led to Wolmi-do. Observatory Hill, 238 feet high, and the smaller British Consulate Hill overlooked the city itself.

Perhaps the most critical factor was Inchon's extreme tidal range of thirty-two feet, which limited a daylight landing to three or four days each month. Tidal waters had to be high enough to cover the wide mudflats that fronted the city. Since the highest tides in September occurred in mid-month, the JSPOG selected 15 September as D-day. FECOM had less than two months to plan an assault that normally took three to five months of work. Nonetheless, MacArthur's headquarters issued Operation Plan 100-B, code named "Chromite," with Inchon as the objective.

Doyle and many of the officers on the staff were concerned that Inchon might be too risky, so they investigated alternative sites. Doyle

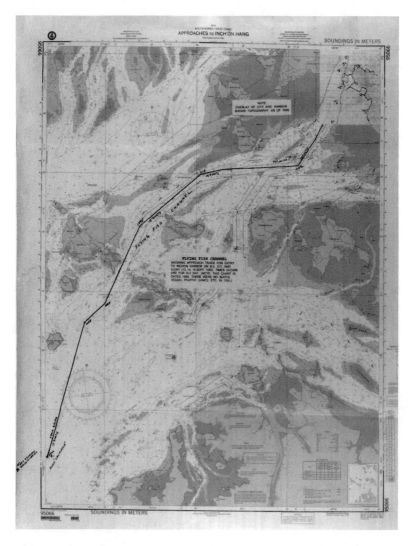

This 1950 map of the Inchon area details the narrow passages and numerous mud and tidal flats in the approaches to the harbor. (Library of Congress Geography and Map Division)

dispatched *Horace A. Bass* and her UDT/Marine team to scout Kunsan, which they found to be better suited to an amphibious assault. The JSPOG prepared a plan for a Kunsan operation, just in case MacArthur changed his mind on the attack site.

General MacArthur takes Admiral Sherman, Chief of Naval Operations, and Gen. J. Lawton Collins, Army Chief of Staff, in tow for his forthcoming Inchon "performance." The JCS concurred in the attack on Inchon, in large measure because Sherman told his colleagues it could be done. (National Archives 80-G-442492)

Although commanders in the Far East understood the difficulties of the proposed assault, the JCS was "somewhat in the dark." On 20 August, Admiral Sherman, the CNO; General Collins, the Army Chief of Staff; and other high-ranking officers flew from Washington to MacArthur's Tokyo headquarters for a briefing on the planned amphibious operation in Korea.

Admiral Doyle's staff summarized the details of the assault: weather, hydrography, landing craft, beaches, naval gunfire, and air support. Intelligence on the enemy forces at Inchon suggested that only a few weak units operated there and that the harbor's defenses were not completed. Doyle, a veteran of Guadalcanal and other WWII landings, ended the briefing with the statement that "the best I can say is that Inchon is not impossible." This reinforced the misgivings already felt by some of the assembled officers, so they asked probing questions about alternative landing sites such as Kunsan.

MacArthur, at that time revered by many Americans as a military genius and legendary hero, slowly rose to address the assembled officers. In his well-known theatrical style and sonorous voice, the general spent the next forty-five minutes delivering an oration that awed his audience. MacArthur never swayed from his choice of Inchon as the landing site. He observed that because the conditions at Inchon were so difficult, the enemy would not expect a landing there. Success at Inchon could end the war, while a seizure of Kunsan or an alternative site would be indecisive and lead to a brutal winter campaign. Looking at Admiral Sherman, the general spoke with conviction: "The Navy has never let me down in the past and it will not let me down this time." Concluding this masterful performance, MacArthur quietly but forcefully stated that "we shall land at Inchon and I shall crush them!"

PREPARING FOR OPERATION CHROMITE

WHEN SHERMAN AND COLLINS returned to Washington, the JCS formally approved MacArthur's intention to assault Inchon on 15 September, and this spurred FECOM's preparation effort. MacArthur's greatest concern was the availability and readiness of ground troops for Operation Chromite. Many of the forces that he hoped to hold in reserve for the amphibious assault at Inchon had been thrown into battle on the Naktong or would arrive in the theater late. The 5th Marine RCT of his primary assault force, the 1st Marine Division, spent much of August and early September fending off NKPA thrusts into the Pusan Perimeter. The unit had only eight days to rest from combat, prepare for the amphibious operation, and embark for the passage to Inchon. The division's third regiment would not arrive in the Far East until two days after the landing. When MacArthur ordered the 2nd Infantry Division, his first choice for the Army component, to the front in Korea, he had to replace it with Maj. Gen. David G. Barr's half-strength 7th Infantry Division based in Japan. The Army channeled to Barr's division all arriving replacement personnel, including experienced noncommissioned officers from the schools at Fort Benning, Georgia, and Fort Sill, Oklahoma. This was still not enough, so MacArthur authorized the division to incorporate more than eight thousand Korean troops, called KATUSAs (Korean Augmentation to the U.S. Army). Finally, for lack of alternatives, the American planners were compelled to use the understrength, ill-equipped —but enthusiastic—1st Korean Marine Corps (KMC) Regiment as the reserve contingent and Inchon mop-up unit.

Doyle's staff focused their efforts on the operational aspects of Chromite. They decided that amphibious ships and craft would approach Inchon by way of Flying Fish Channel, which was a rougher seaway than Eastern Channel but less subject to enemy artillery fire. Two days prior to the landing, cruisers and destroyers would steam into the harbor to shell Wolmi-do and check the waters for mines.

Even though the Japanese and American tide tables did not agree, planners estimated that high tides would occur shortly after sunrise and then just after sunset on 15 September. Since most of the amphibious ships would need daylight to navigate the narrow, swift waters of Flying Fish Channel and the Salee River, the planners decided that the smaller initial landing would take place on the morning tide. A reinforced Marine battalion would storm ashore at Green Beach on Wolmi-do and seize this island that dominated the harbor. With close air and naval gunfire support, the unit was expected to hold off any North Korean counterattacks during the day. The main assault would occur as the tide rose in the evening. Two Marine battalions would land at Red Beach, just north of the causeway from Wolmi-do, and seize the three hills in town. An entire Marine regiment would land at Blue Beach, three miles to the south of Red Beach.

Both "beaches" were in actuality built-up industrial areas largely bounded by seawalls. Vehicle and personnel landing craft (LCVP) and mechanized landing craft (LCM) were responsible for deploying the leathernecks to shore at Red Beach. Tracked landing vehicles (LVT), also known as amtracs, would transport the Marines in the first waves at Blue Beach, because the approach crossed two miles of mudflats covered by shallow water. LCVPs would bring in the rest of the regiment in later waves. Navy and Marine planners concluded that both beachheads were defensible, even though separated by the built-up section of Inchon.

The planners paid special attention to logistics support, which would be vital to the success of not only the initial assault on Inchon but also the breakout to Seoul. They knew that the existing port facilities were rudimentary and even those would probably be destroyed in combat. Initially,

THE
"BLACKBEARD OF
YONGHUNG-DO"

ACCURATE INTELLIGENCE ABOUT INCHON and its water approaches was absolutely vital to the success of Operation Chromite, and no one did more to provide that information than Lt. Eugene F. Clark, a daring and resourceful naval officer.

The staffs planning Chromite needed detailed information about the Inchon harbor, the local tides, the waterways leading to the port, and enemy defenses. While UN forces fought to hold the Pusan Perimeter, South Korean naval forces raided the peninsula's west coast and occupied Yonghung, an island only fourteen miles from Inchon.

FECOM decided to dispatch a reconnaissance team to the island under Lieutenant Clark. This sixteen-year veteran had joined the Navy as an enlisted man, earned a commission, and commanded an LST and a transport after World War II. Because Lieutenant Clark knew that Inchon was the actual site of the forthcoming UN invasion, he decided he would kill himself rather than divulge that information if captured by the enemy. During the operation, the lieutenant carried a grenade with him everywhere because he believed it to be "more certain than . . . a pistol."

His small team included two South Korean interpreters, both of whom had served as officers in the Japanese military during World War II, and an individual identified in one account as a U.S. Army major but who may have been a member of a U.S. intelligence agency.

Clark's team landed on Yonghung-do on 1 September and quickly organized a force of local men and boys to keep watch on the nearby enemy-held island of Taebu-do. As a gesture of good will, Clark

The resourceful Lieutenant Clark, far right, stands with his band of daring fighters, interpreters, and possibly a South Korean navy officer on Yonghung-do, just fourteen miles from Inchon. These men gathered crucial intelligence on the Inchon approaches and landing areas for the planning of Operation Chromite. (OPAR Manson & Cagle Papers)

dispensed rice and dried fish to the islanders. Clark, who later said he felt like Blackbeard the pirate, equipped Yonghung-do's one motorized sampan with a .50-caliber machine gun and armed his men with carbines and submachine guns. To acquire information about the enemy, the team seized local fishing sampans—interrogating crewmen who generally professed loyalty to South Korea—and explored Inchon harbor. Clark's young Korean comrades also infiltrated Inchon, Kimpo air base, and even Seoul, and returned with valuable intelligence.

Clark informed Tokyo that the Japanese-prepared tide tables were accurate, that the mudflats fronting Inchon would support no weight, and that the harbor's seawalls were higher that estimated. Clark also reported that Wolmi-do was heavily fortified and studded with

Soviet-made artillery pieces. Grateful naval planners incorporated these facts into the landing plan.

The North Koreans were aware of Clark's presence on Yonghung-do, but they sent only small parties to the island to investigate. On 7 September, however, two days after several British ships bombarded Inchon, the enemy sent one motorized and three sailing sampans loaded with troops to Clark's hideaway. South Korean lookouts spotted the approaching boats, so Clark and his men got their "flagship" under way. As the antagonists closed on one another, a 37-millimeter antitank gun mounted in the bow of the Communist motorized craft opened up. A shell splashed well in front of Clark's sampan. Undeterred by this poor shooting, and in "Nelsonian style," Clark directed his flagship to close to within one hundred yards of the enemy squadron. His .50-caliber machine gun raked two of the North Korean vessels, sinking one and demolishing the other. Witnessing this slaughter, the remaining boats fled the scene.

After Clark reported this engagement to headquarters, the destroyer *Hanson* (DD-832) showed up to take off the team. Clark, who had not asked to be extracted, instead requested *Hanson*'s skipper to pound Taebu-do. *Hanson* blasted the island with 212 5-inch rounds, and Marine Corsairs covering the destroyer also bombed and strafed the North Korean lair.

The team stayed on the island and continued their mission. Clark scouted Palmi-do, an island centrally located in the approaches to Inchon, and reported that Canadian raiders had only damaged the lighthouse beacon. Tokyo ordered Clark to relight the lamp at midnight on 15 September. On 14 September, Clark's team left Yonghung-do for Palmi-do and repaired the light.

Meanwhile, the North Korean commander at Inchon sent a contingent to wipe out the bothersome force on Yonghung-do. At dusk on 14 September, the enemy troops crossed the mudflats from Taebu-do to Yonghung-do. The Communists overwhelmed the island defenders and executed more than fifty men, women, and children.

Clark avenged their sacrifice for the UN cause when he activated the beacon atop the lighthouse at midnight on 15 September. With this light to guide them, the ships of the Advance Attack Group safely threaded their way through the treacherous approach to Inchon.

In recognition of his heroic work off Inchon, the Navy awarded Clark the Silver Star and the Army presented him with the Legion of Merit.

all material would have to be moved across the beach. In addition, the narrow approaches from the sea would allow only a few ships at a time to operate off Inchon.

The Navy's LSTs, which were designed to operate in shallow water and unload cargo directly onto the beach, were key to success at Inchon. Doyle assembled seventeen U.S. Navy LSTs and thirty Japanese-manned SCAJAP vessels. The admiral, understanding the importance of keeping the Marines supplied with ammunition and equipment in the early, critical stage of the landing, planned to leave some of his LSTs aground as the evening tide receded. They would be replaced by other ships with the following morning's tide. Hence, the LSTs, which in World War II were often referred to by their crews as "large, slow targets," would in this instance be "large, stationary targets."

The planners knew that accurate intelligence was critical to the success of an operation as complex as an amphibious assault. Consequently, in late August, the FECOM acted to gather more information about the waterways leading to Inchon. On 19 August, the Canadian destroyer HMCS *Athabaskan* (DDE-219) escorted a ROKN vessel to Yonghung-do, an island only fourteen miles from Inchon. Lt. Cdr. Ham Myong Su led a small team ashore where they found the inhabitants sympathetic to the South Korean cause. Armed with this information, on 1 September FECOM dispatched to the island Navy Lieutenant Clark, a former LST skipper. Under the noses of nearby NKPA island garrisons, Clark's team gathered information on surrounding waterways. The lieutenant informed Tokyo that the Japanese tide tables were accurate, the area's mudflats would support no weight, seawalls were higher than estimated, and Wolmi-do was heavily fortified and bristled with numerous artillery pieces. Clark reported that even though the Canadians had disabled Palmi-do lighthouse, it was easily repairable. Tokyo told the intrepid officer to relight the beacon just after midnight on 15 September.

A TIME OF DECEPTION
AND UNCERTAINTY

AS IMPORTANT AS IT was to provide friendly forces with current intelligence, it was absolutely vital to deny the enemy information on the UN landing site. Without the element of surprise, the Marines, Sailors, and soldiers might find a heavily armed and dug-in enemy waiting for them at Inchon.

To prevent such a catastrophe, MacArthur's command staged an elaborate deception operation. The purpose was to encourage the North Koreans to believe the landing would occur at Kunsan, 105 miles south of Inchon. FEAF bombers began isolating Kunsan on 5 September by bombing roadways and bridges leading to the port. On 6 September, Admiral Andrewes's cruisers and destroyers bombarded Kunsan, a day after shelling Inchon. During early September, planes from HMS *Triumph* and *Badoeng Strait* hit railroads and bridges from Kunsan north to Pyong-yang. Meanwhile, ROKN small boats raided enemy positions along the west coast.

Disinformation was also part of the deception effort. On a Pusan dock, Marine officers briefed their men about the landing beaches at Kunsan despite the numerous Koreans within earshot.

As the actual landing date came closer, activity near Kunsan increased. In addition to the regular FEAF attacks, on 11 September B-29 bombers struck Kunsan's military installations. During the night of 12–13 September, the British frigate HMS *Whitesand Bay* (F-633) landed U.S. Army special operations troops and Royal Marine commandos on the docks, who made sure the enemy knew of their short presence ashore.

FECOM worked even harder to keep the true destination of Admiral Struble's task force secret. With men, supplies, and ships concentrating in the ports of Japan and at Pusan, there was no way to hide the fact that an amphibious operation was about to take place. So widespread was the speculation that the press in Japan referred to the impending landing as Operation Common Knowledge. Confirming MacArthur's worst fears, in early September, counterintelligence agents uncovered a North Korean–Japanese spy ring. When the leader of the ring was arrested, he had a copy of the Chromite operation plan. No one knew if he had been able to transmit the plan to Pyongyang.

Not only were UN commanders uncertain about how the North Koreans would react to an amphibious assault, but also how the Chinese and Soviets would respond. Communist ships and aircraft operated from bases that were only one hundred miles from UN fleet units in the Yellow Sea. The eighty submarines of the Soviet Pacific Ocean Fleet at Vladivostok also posed a potential threat. U.S. submarines, surface ships, and patrol aircraft, based on shore and afloat, maintained a constant watch in the Yellow Sea and the Sea of Japan to detect any hostile activities.

Anxiety rose on 4 September when the radar picket destroyer *Herbert J. Thomas* (DDR-833) picked up an unidentified aircraft contact heading from Port Arthur in Manchuria toward the UN task force in the Yellow Sea. Air controllers vectored a flight of four Fighter Squadron 53 Vought F4U Corsairs from the combat air patrol toward the intruder. Thirty miles north of Task Force 77, the Corsair pilots saw one twin-engine plane dive and head for Korea. The flight leader, Lt. (jg) Richard E. Downs, closed on the suspicious aircraft. It was an American-made Douglas A-20 Havoc light bomber, many of which were provided to the USSR in the WWII lend–lease program. The A-20, emblazoned with the red star of the Soviet air force, suddenly fired at Downs. After receiving permission from *Valley Forge*, Downs opened up on the hostile. Downs overshot the target, but his wingman riddled the bomber and sent it slamming into the ocean. When crewmen from *Herbert J. Thomas* recovered the pilot's body, they confirmed that he was a Russian. Leaders in Washington and Tokyo wondered if this event presaged Soviet and possibly Chinese intervention in the war.

INTO THE GALE

SOON AFTER THE SHIPS of Admiral Doyle's amphibious armada put to sea from the ports of Kobe and Yokohama, Japan, they faced age-old enemies: howling winds and raging waters. Warnings from Navy weather planes and aerologists days earlier that Typhoon Kezia was headed his way caused Doyle to speed up the fleet's loading and departure process. Hard work on the docks and on board the ships allowed the task force to sortie by 11 September, one day ahead of schedule. Doyle's flagship, *Mount McKinley* (AGC-7), already being pounded by the rising swell, was the last vessel to leave Kobe. Still, on 12 September, Kezia battered the fleet with ninety-knot winds and massive waves. Doyle later described it as the worst storm he ever experienced.

The tempest sorely tested the ships and Sailors of the flotilla. After losing her port engine, *LST-1048* had to fight to maintain steerageway.

The salvage ship *Conserver* (ARS-39) came alongside the struggling landing ship and floated down a hawser. Working on a wet, pitching deck, the LST's sea and anchor detail chocked the line into place and soon had secured a towing cable passed by *Conserver.* While only making six knots, the two ships proceeded together and reached Inchon on time for the fight.

On 12 September, Capt. Norman W. Sears's Advance Attack Group and three attack transports stood out of Pusan with the 5th Marines embarked. After a second Naktong Bulge battle, the regiment barely had time to refit and integrate reinforcements from the United States. Before leaving Pusan, Marine leaders selected Lt. Col. Robert D. Taplett's 3rd Battalion, 5th Marines to make the initial assault on Wolmi-do.

Meanwhile, Doyle's *Mount McKinley* steered for Sasebo, Japan. There, MacArthur came on board with his entourage, which included ten of the general's favorite journalists, all of whom Doyle later quipped "wanted to travel in the light of the sun." They joined Maj. Gen. Edward M. Almond, Commander X Corps; Lt. Gen. Lemuel C. Shepherd, Commander Fleet Marine Force, Pacific; and Maj. Gen. Oliver P. Smith, Commander 1st Marine Division, and their respective staffs, all of them cramped in one relatively small ship.

By 14 September, the entire invasion force was headed for the Yellow Sea and Inchon. Admiral Struble's Joint Task Force 7 comprised forces from nine nations, including 230 warships, amphibious ships, and auxiliaries; the 1st Marine Division and the 7th Infantry Division; twenty-one aircraft squadrons; and special amphibious, engineer, logistic, and UDT units. His subordinate, Admiral Doyle, was responsible for executing the actual assault and getting the Marine and Army troops ashore.

As laid out in Joint Task Force 7 Operations Plan 9-50, Struble divided his command into six components. The aircraft of the Fast Carrier Force (Task Force 77) flew fighter cover, interdiction, and ground-attack missions. Admiral Andrewes's Blockade and Covering Force (Task Force 91) carried out prelanding deception operations with naval gunfire and air strikes, protected the amphibious force from surface and air threats, and patrolled the waters off the west coast of Korea. The patrol squadrons and seaplane tenders of Rear Adm. George R. Henderson's Patrol and Reconnaissance Force (Task Force 99) stood ready to provide aerial escort for the transports and search the surrounding waters. Logistic support was the responsibility of Capt. Bernard L. Austin's Service Squadron 3 (Task Force 79).

As detailed in Amphibious Group 1 Operation Order 14-50, Doyle led the major invasion element, the Attack Force (Task Force 90). This formation included all the amphibious and transport ships, a gunfire support group, and the escort carriers embarking Marine air squadrons. Additional Navy transports, MSTS ships, and chartered merchantmen would start bringing in the 7th Division on 18 September. Once a beachhead was established, Almond would take charge of forces ashore and direct their push toward Seoul and the UN forces advancing north from Pusan.

"TEN ENEMY VESSELS APPROACHING"

ON THE MORNING OF 13 September, Rear Adm. John M. Higgins's gunfire support ships steamed up the narrow channel toward Inchon. At 1010, during the day's first flood tide, destroyers *Mansfield, De Haven, Lyman K. Swenson* (DD-729), *Collett* (DD-730), *Gurke* (DD-783), and *Henderson* (DD-785), followed by cruisers *Rochester, Toledo,* HMS *Jamaica,* and HMS *Kenya,* entered the outer harbor. Aware that one disabled ship could block the vital channel, destroyer officers had their boatswain's mates rig-towing gear to quickly pull a damaged or grounded ship out of the way. Repair parties, armed with Browning automatic rifles, carbines, and submachine guns, stood by to repel enemy boarders who might attack from nearby sampans or the mudflats. Overhead, a combat air patrol of Task Force 77 Grumman F9F Panther jets provided cover.

At 1145, a lookout on *Mansfield* cried out, "Mines!" Cdr. Oscar B. Lundgren, *De Haven*'s commanding officer and a mine warfare expert, spied the menacing black shapes of seventeen contact mines. The three leading destroyers fired on the mines with their 20-mm and 40-mm guns, plus small arms. A thunderous explosion tore through the air and a plume of muddy water leapt skyward as one mine exploded. Capt. Halle C. Allan Jr., Commander Destroyer Squadron 9, ordered *Henderson* to stay behind and eliminate the remaining mines. Soon afterward, the destroyer Sailors discovered, from the piles of Soviet-made mines they spied ashore, that the enemy was in the process of completely mining the water approaches to Inchon.

As the ships moved to their firing positions, propeller-driven Douglas AD Skyraiders from *Philippine Sea* blasted Wolmi-do with bombs, rockets, and gunfire. The cruisers remained in the outer harbor while the destroyers dropped anchor above and below the island. The destroyers swung on their anchors on the incoming tide, bows downstream, prepared to exit quickly, if necessary. The gunners loaded their 5-inch guns, trained them to port and located their assigned targets.

"Ten enemy vessels approaching Inchon," the North Korean commander radioed in the clear to NKPA headquarters in Pyongyang. He added, "Many aircraft are bombing Wolmi Do. There is every indication that the enemy will perform a landing." The Communist officer assured his superiors that his defense force was prepared for action and would throw the enemy back into the sea.

In *De Haven*'s gun director, Lt. Arthur T. White, saw North Korean soldiers run out and load a gun just north of Red Beach. White requested permission to open fire and Lundgren gave it. *De Haven*'s fire, which quickly eliminated the enemy weapon, proved to be the opening salvo of the prelanding bombardment.

The object of this effort was to stimulate the enemy guns in Inchon and emplaced on Wolmi-do to return fire so that UN ships could target and destroy them. For a long eight minutes, the North Koreans failed to rise to the bait. But then the defenders, men of the 918th Coastal Artillery Regiment, wheeled out their weapons—mainly Soviet-made 76-mm anti-tank guns—and opened fire, hitting *Collett* seven times and *Gurke* three. The response was devastating. The gunfire support ships poured 998 5-inch rounds into the island and defenses in front of the city. At 1347, with many enemy guns silenced, Allan signaled the retirement order to his destroyers, which headed for the open sea. The cruisers provided covering fire for this movement and then brought up the rear of the column.

Before the ships could clear the harbor, however, one of the few remaining Communist guns exacted revenge on *Lyman K. Swenson*. Two North Korean shells exploded just off the destroyer's port side, killing Lt. (jg) David J. Swenson (no relation to the Sailor for whom the ship was named). Enemy fire wounded another eight men in the bombardment force that day.

That night Higgins and Allan conferred with Struble in *Rochester*. Although pleased with the day's action, Struble ordered the ships and aircraft to give Wolmi-do "a real working-over" the following day. The mine threat remained because gunfire had eliminated only three of the devices and the task force minesweepers were several hundred miles away from Inchon. Because of the lack of small combatants, the minesweepers had been assigned to troop transport escort duty. Struble now ordered the ships to make best speed to the operational area, even though they would not arrive until 15 September. Soon after midnight the admiral dismissed his officers so they could grab a few hours of sleep and prepare for the next day's combat.

The following morning, the ships of the bombardment group hove to, with colors at half-mast and crews at quarters. A boatswain's mate in *Toledo* piped "All hands to bury the dead." After a simple service, a Marine rifle salute, and the playing of "Taps," bluejackets committed Lieutenant Swenson's remains to the deep. Somber but determined after this ceremony, the men of the cruiser-destroyer group again prepared for action.

The ships once again moved up Flying Fish Channel. As the force closed Inchon, *Toledo* fired on one mine, exploding it. The damaged *Collett* dropped off and destroyed another five of the deadly "weapons that wait."

At 1116, when they came in range of targets ashore, the cruisers loosed a salvo. NKPA gunners then opened up on HMS *Kenya*, the closest cruiser to shore. Capt. Patrick W. Brock, RN, *Kenya*'s skipper, felt that "the enemy gunners were either very brave or very stupid," because even before the cruiser could return fire, attack aircraft obliterated the offending guns. In the next seventy-five minutes, the destroyers hurled more than seventeen hundred 5-inch shells into Wolmi-do. The cruisers reentered the fray and as Marine and British Fleet Air Arm pilots spotted targets, they blasted positions near Inchon and on Wolmi-do. One *Valley Forge* pilot observed that "the whole island," referring to the once-wooded Wolmi-do, "looked like it had been shaved."

The Advance Attack Group, then in the Yellow Sea, stood in toward Flying Fish Channel. Near dusk and sixty-five miles from the objective, Cdr. Clarence T. Doss Jr., in charge of three rocket bombardment ships (LSMRs), spied a huge pillar of smoke on the horizon to the east. Doss knew this meant that UN ships and planes were plastering the enemy defenders. He passed that welcome news to all hands.

"LAND THE LANDING FORCE"

JUST AFTER MIDNIGHT ON D-DAY, 15 September, the Advance Attack Group and the bombardment group formed into an eighteen-ship column and entered Flying Fish Channel. Two hours later, lookouts in the lead ships noticed a rhythmically flashing light in the darkness ahead of them. The rotating beacon atop the Palmi-do lighthouse guided each ship safely

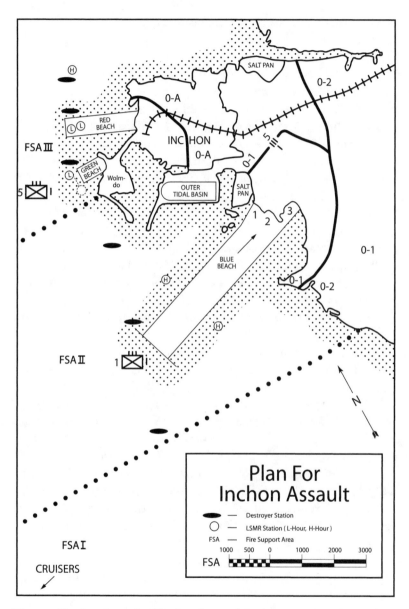

The assault plan shows landing beaches and fire support areas from which cruisers, destroyers, and LSMRs would operate at Inchon. (Steve Karp)

through the narrow passage. Lieutenant Clark, who had activated the light, shivered in his lofty perch not only from the chilly night air but also from the thrill of seeing the fleet steaming into Inchon.

At 0508, *Mount McKinley* dropped anchor in the channel and the gun-fire support ships and amphibious vessels moved to their assigned positions. At 0520, Doyle hoisted the traditional signal that had preceded many amphibious assaults in naval history: "Land the landing force."

Marines in *Horace A. Bass*, *Diachenko* (APD-123), and *Wantuck* (APD-125) climbed into the LCVPs that would carry them to shore. *Fort Marion* (LSD-22) prepared to disgorge three utility landing ships carrying tanks and equipment. At 0540, the cruisers and destroyers inaugurated the third day of shelling Wolmi-do and other targets in and around Inchon. Soon after first light, Marine Corsairs launched from *Badoeng Strait* and *Sicily* and once again churned up Wolmi-do with bombs, rockets, and machine-gun fire. Task Force 77 fighters formed combat air patrols to seaward and scoured the roads behind Inchon for enemy reinforcements and supplies.

Fifteen minutes before L-hour, set for 0630, two of the ungainly LSMRs began an ear-splitting, two-thousand-rocket barrage of the reverse slope of Radio Hill on Wolmi-do. Their object was to destroy any remaining mortar positions and prevent reserves from reaching the defenders of the island. Commander Doss's third ship, *LSMR-403*, moved in front of the LCVPs on their way to the shore and raked Green Beach with rockets and 40-mm fire. That done, signalmen on the control vessel lowered flags signaling the assault. The coxswains in the first wave put their controls at full throttle and the landing craft roared across the line of departure.

To cover the final run into the beach, Corsairs from VMF-214 and VMF-323 screamed over the LCVPs and strafed the shoreline. Two destroyers using proximity-fuzed ammunition scoured the forward slope of Observatory Hill and the waterfront with deadly airbursts of shrapnel.

At 0633, G and H Companies of Colonel Taplett's 3rd Battalion, 5th Marines stormed ashore. When three men stepped off one LCVP, they sank in water well over their heads. Not wanting a repeat of the tragic experience at Tarawa in World War II when many Marines drowned because they had to move long distances through neck-high water, the boat crews moved their vessels closer to the shore. Succeeding waves brought in the rest of Colonel Taplett's Marines and ten M-26 Pershing tanks, including one equipped with a flame-thrower and two more with bulldozer blades.

The Marines advanced rapidly across the island. Company H seized and fortified the Wolmi-do end of the causeway to Inchon, while engineers sprinted onto the roadway to lay an antitank minefield. Company G assaulted Radio Hill and by 0655 the stars and stripes flew over that position.

Meanwhile, Taplett landed with his I Company, which moved into areas supposedly secured by the assault units. North Korean troops, hidden in caves on the east side of the island, fired on several I Company squads. When, despite the pleas of a Marine interpreter, the NKPA soldiers refused to surrender, a tankdozer entombed them in their positions.

By 0800, Taplett reported Wolmi-do secured. His leathernecks dug in to fend off any counterattacks and herded the few prisoners of war (POWs) into a dry swimming pool. Some of the NKPA soldiers fought to the last; others, especially local Koreans recently "recruited" by the Communists, readily surrendered. Fanatical enemy troops, however, soon opened up from the nearby islet of Sowolmi-do with light antiaircraft weapons. A reinforced rifle quad and several tanks rapidly moved against them. Supported by Marine Corsairs, the ground force quickly silenced the enemy guns.

With the outer harbor secured, at the cost of only seventeen wounded, the first phase was now over. General MacArthur asked Doyle to send the following message to Task Force 90: "The Navy and Marines have never shone more brightly than this morning." With a large smile, the old soldier then looked at the Army, Navy, and Marine officers gathered on Doyle's flagship and said, "That's it. Let's get a cup of coffee." As he drank his cup of thick Navy java, MacArthur penned a message to General Bradley and the other Joint Chiefs: "First phase landing successful with losses slight. All goes well and on schedule."

A SHORT INTERLUDE

NOW BEGAN THE LONG, eight-hour wait as the tide receded and rose and the sun began to set in the direction of the Yellow Sea. Not until then could the other Marine units storm Red and Blue beaches. The Navy–Marine task force did not stand idly by during this period. The troops on Wolmi-do improved their fighting positions and naval combatants and aircraft continued to pound the enemy on the mainland.

During this temporary lull in the battle, Admiral Struble's barge came alongside *Mount McKinley* and he asked if anyone would like to tag along with him for a closer look at Wolmi-do and the other beaches. "Certainly," replied MacArthur. Soon, Generals Almond and Shepherd, and three other flag-rank officers joined Struble in his barge. After inspecting Green Beach, they moved toward Red Beach. Shepherd reminded MacArthur that because the boat was less than a thousand yards from shore, an enemy soldier might "take a pot shot" at the commander of all UN forces in the Korean theater. Struble promptly ordered his coxswain to return to the flagship.

Meanwhile, in response to the seizure of Wolmi-do, the enemy headquarters in Seoul frantically ordered the 70th Regiment near Suwon and 18th Division, then approaching the Pusan Perimeter, to head toward Inchon. But this action was tardy, because despite two days of bombardment and the garrison commander's warning on 13 September, North Korean authorities did not believe Inchon to be the site of the main amphibious assault. No doubt thanks to the UN deception operations, Communist commanders were fixated on Kunsan until too late. The enemy reinforcements would not be able to reach the battle area by the evening of 15 September, when the Navy–Marine assault forces would hit Red and Blue beaches.

The NKPA garrison at Inchon, composed of the 226th Marine and 918th Coastal Artillery Regiments, was a motley force that included some South Koreans forced into service. The 226th had been further weakened when headquarters earlier sent a large detachment toward Yonghung-do to knock out Clark's guerrillas. In addition, after the loss of Wolmi-do, the best-prepared position in the harbor, the 918th was in bad shape.

The North Korean defensive effort was further hampered by attacks every hour and a half by eight Marine Corsairs, which dropped fragmentation bombs and napalm. The latter ordnance was especially effective against enemy troops, whether dug in or exposed. In addition, to keep pressure on the enemy, twelve Navy carrier aircraft rotated between Yellow Sea combat air patrol and strike operations inland.

One of the latter missions proved to be extremely advantageous. While flying along the road to Suwon, Ens. Eldon W. Brown Jr. of VF-53 stitched a long row of neatly stacked wooden crates with machine-gun fire. When the rounds impacted, there was a massive explosion, the force of which violently jolted Brown's plane. He climbed quickly, but an enveloping cloud of dust and debris passed him at four thousand feet. In Inchon harbor, miles away, ships rocked at their anchors. *Mount McKinley* radioed the strike leader, Lt. Cdr. Joseph N. Murphy, and asked him, "What the hell happened?" Murphy replied dryly, "We just exploded some ammunition."

On that critical day, 15 September, aircraft carrier *Boxer* arrived on station and ready for battle, culminating two months of Herculean effort by her crew. During that time the ship crossed the vast expanse of the Pacific three times, fighting Typhoon Kezia on the last passage, to transport badly needed aircraft to UN forces in the Korean theater. But this effort took its toll on a ship that was scheduled for an overhaul before the outbreak of war. Early on 15 September, a reduction gear in the engineering plant suffered a major casualty. With no time to lose, the chief engineer and his engine room crew, or "snipes," used their skills and experience to coax twenty-six knots out of the damaged propulsion system. Through their efforts, *Boxer* was able to join Task Force 77 and launch her first air strike on time in support of the Inchon landing.

As the day wore on, elements of Naval Beach Group 1's Amphibious Construction Battalion—the Seabees—came in with the tide. Off Wolmi-do, they began building a pontoon dock and causeway, but the vicious tides carried away two sections. Despite this setback, the Seabees completed the pontoon causeway in time for the twilight assault. Meanwhile, other Seabees crossed Wolmi-do. They would advance with Taplett's men an hour after the Red Beach landing to determine the extent of damage to the harbor facilities and seawalls.

At 1445, for the second time that day, Doyle ordered his signalmen to communicate the order to the amphibious force, "Land the landing force." To prepare the beaches for the 1730 H-hour, Higgins's destroyers and cruisers increased the tempo of their fire. *Toledo* and *Rochester* slammed salvos of 8-inch rounds into the roads east of Inchon, creating a gauntlet of steel for enemy reinforcements trying to reach the city. The British cruisers blasted the area around Blue Beach while *De Haven* and *Lyman K. Swenson* shelled the buildings near Red Beach. The structures near the waterfront belched fire and smoke. Navy Skyraiders and Marine Corsairs, whose missions were coordinated by a team from Tactical Air Control Squadron 1 in *Mount McKinley*, added their firepower to the maelstrom.

Meanwhile, off Red Beach, the 1st and 2nd Battalions of the 5th Marine Regiment climbed down rope nets draped on the sides of *Henrico* (APA-45) and *Cavalier* (APA-37) and joined their comrades crowding into the LCVPs and LCMs bobbing alongside. In front of Green Beach, the men of the 11th Marines prepared to go ashore. Farther south, the

1st Marines squeezed into LVTs for the long ride over the mudflats to Blue Beach.

For many of these Marine veterans of WWII amphibious assaults, the Inchon operation was different. In the bottom of each landing craft were two long planks that the men could use to reach shore if their vessels got stuck in the mud. Other landing craft carried wooden or aluminum ladders with hooks at the top for scaling seawalls. In other boats, Marines stood by with sledgehammers to pound grappling hooks attached to cargo nets into the seawalls.

During the twenty minutes before H-hour, the shore bombardment force fired as many rounds as it had in the previous nine hours. *Rochester* and *Toledo* plastered the hills of Inchon while the destroyers scoured the landing areas with airbursts. Like her two sisters off Blue Beach, *LSMR-403* sent two thousand 5-inch rockets, at the rate of one hundred per minute, screaming over the heads of the Marines and Sailors heading for Red Beach.

Despite all this firepower, the enemy dropped rounds into the wave of approaching boats. Before the fire of a destroyer off Blue Beach knocked out an NKPA gun, rounds from this weapon destroyed one LVT with a direct hit. *Gurke* and close air support planes quickly silenced a high-velocity gun on Observatory Hill that tried to duel with the Americans. Flying a massive ensign, the small, unarmored *LSMR-401* engaged another enemy weapon with her single 5-inch gun. Even though the gun crew had to manually ram shells into the breach because of a mechanical problem, they kept up a high rate of fire that scorched paint off the barrel.

STORMING ASHORE AT RED BEACH

IN THIS CRESCENDO OF exploding bombs, rockets, and shells, *Horace A. Bass*, the control ship for Red Beach, gave the signal for assault. Coxswains in the eight LCVPs of the first wave gunned their engines and conned their boats across the line of departure. Corsairs strafing the beach rained 20-mm shell casings on the Sailors and Marines in the landing craft.

The assault forces welcomed all of this extra firepower. The causeway on the right flank of Red Beach reminded Capt. Francis I. "Ike" Fenton

Navy LCVPs, loaded with Marines of the 5th Regiment, proceed in formation for the line of departure on the approach to Red Beach. Earlier reconnaissance revealed that the seawalls were higher than expected so the LCVPs carried crudely built wooden ladders to scale the walls. (National Archives W&C #1418)

Jr., commander of Company B, 1st Battalion, 5th Marines, of the bloody WWII battle of Tarawa. Fenton considered the worst—if the enemy occupied the causeway "we were going to have a tough time making that last 200 yards to the beach."

At 1731, the first LCVP hit the seawall just ahead of the others in the boat wave. Coxswains skillfully used their engines to hold their boats in place as Marines tossed grenades over the wall. Amidst the explosions, ladders clattered against the rocks and riflemen scrambled over the top. NKPA machine gunners in the few bunkers still unscathed sprayed the top of this rampart, cutting down some leathernecks and pinning others near the seawall. The Marines had landed, but just barely.

Nearby, a Navy coxswain rammed his LCVP into a breach in the seawall. The Marines stormed ashore right under a machine gun, fortunately silent, which protruded from a pillbox. This platoon from Company A quickly grenaded the position, and six wounded Koreans stumbled out to surrender. They rapidly cleared nearby trenches, advanced into town, and secured the massive Asahi Brewery on the flank of Cemetery Hill. At the base of the Wolmi-do causeway, Company E occupied the Nippon Flour Company compound.

Not everything at Red Beach went so well. Most of Company A was pinned down and the second wave troops crashed in amongst them. 1st Lt. Baldomero Lopez silenced one pillbox and moved to attack a second when an enemy burst hit him. Lopez fell on the grenade he was about to throw, sacrificing his life to save his men. The NKPA gunners continued to fire, killing two more Marines. Company A finally destroyed the pillbox, but above them loomed Cemetery Hill. Then, the platoon at the brewery attacked the back side of the hill and captured several dozen dazed enemy infantrymen. These victories had a cost; eight Marines lay dead on the little flat in front of the graveyard knoll and Navy corpsmen tended another twenty-eight wounded leathernecks.

Although the 5th Marines held Cemetery Hill, the NKPA still threatened Red Beach. Observatory and British Consulate hills remained in enemy hands and until they fell, Communist troops could fire directly into the landing area. It was especially critical that the Marines on Red Beach take the high ground because the assault waves would be followed by the LSTs loaded with ammunition, vehicles, and supplies. Without this resupply, it was unlikely that the Marines could hold their positions overnight.

The consolidation of Red Beach continued, but in ragged fashion. One passenger in the fifth wave, New York *Herald-Tribune* reporter Marguerite "Maggie" Higgins, remarked on the scene. She described a "strange sunset combined with the haze of flaming docks," which created a panorama "that a movie audience would have considered overdone." Poor visibility contributed to a breakdown in coordination. The LCVPs of the fourth and fifth waves became intermingled and many touched land in the wrong areas. These boats carried the two infantry companies that were to seize the most important position in Inchon, Observatory Hill. Hindered by battle smoke and a late-afternoon drizzle, it took the two companies several minutes to reorganize ashore. One platoon and a mortar section, however, almost immediately struck out for their objective.

Meanwhile, the eight LSTs destined for Red Beach maneuvered offshore. Each ship had embarked only five hundred tons of supplies to lighten their loads and thus prevent grounding in the mudflats. All of the LSTs carried the same proportion of food, water, ammunition, fuel, and vehicles, ensuring that the loss of any one ship would not be catastrophic. Doyle's staff calculated that the Marines needed a minimum of three

BALDOMERO LOPEZ, A UNITED STATES MARINE

1ST LT. BALDOMERO LOPEZ represented the best of the Korean War era Marine Corps. Lopez displayed dedication to the Marine Corps, concern for his men, dynamic combat leadership, personal bravery, and a willingness to sacrifice his life for his fellow leathernecks.

The son of an orphaned Spanish immigrant, Lopez enlisted in the U.S. Navy during World War II. He served with distinction until the service discovered that he was underage, which mandated his discharge. Undeterred, Lopez applied for and was admitted to the U.S. Naval Academy. Graduating in Class 1948-A on 6 June 1947, Second Lieutenant Lopez entered the Marine Corps. Because he had boxed at the Academy, he earned the nickname "Punchy." He served with the Marines in North China and then joined the 1st Marine Division at Camp Pendleton, California.

Lopez was scheduled for schooling at Quantico, Virginia, when the Commandant of the Marine Corps ordered the Marine brigade at Pendleton to ship out for Korea. In the words of a fellow Marine officer, Lopez "couldn't stand it. Before the brigade sailed, Punchy swore he would move heaven and earth and get out to us." Sure enough, Lopez was among the replacements from the States when the brigade returned to Pusan after the Naktong battles to refit for Inchon. The eager officer, now a first lieutenant, took command of the 3rd Platoon, Company A, 5th Marines.

Company A made one of the initial assaults at Red Beach. Since Lopez was the only platoon leader without combat experience, the company commander placed the other two rifle platoons in the first wave and his in the second. Despite this precaution, two of the three platoons, including

As the second assault wave lands on 15 September 1950, Marine 1st Lt. Baldomero Lopez leads his platoon over the seawall on the northern side of Red Beach. Within minutes after this photograph was taken, Lopez was killed shielding his own men from a grenade. His sacrifice earned him a Medal of Honor. (National Archives 127 GK-2341-A 3190)

Lopez's, were soon pinned down just over the seawall. Automatic weapons fire from two pillboxes crisscrossed the area. With other waves coming in, Lopez knew that the situation called for decisive action.

In the face of enemy fire, Lopez led a fire team in an attack on the two positions. The intrepid officer silenced one bunker with a grenade. Just as he pulled the pin of another grenade, a burst of machine-gun fire hit him in the chest and right arm. Badly wounded, he dropped the grenade and its arming handle flew off. The entire fire team was now at risk. Shouting "Grenade!" the lieutenant swept the live ordnance against his side. Lopez smothered the explosion with his own body, sacrificing his life for the lives of his men.

In recognition of this selfless act, the Navy Department awarded 1st Lt. Baldomero Lopez the Medal of Honor. Fellow Marines remember his courage and self-sacrifice when they serve with USNS *Baldomero Lopez*, a maritime prepositioning ship named in his honor in 1985 by the Secretary of the Navy.

thousand tons of material to hold during the night. The planners also figured that because of the hostile environment of Inchon harbor and expected enemy opposition, two of the eight ships would be lost.

At 1630, in the wake of the assault waves, *LST-859* crossed the line of departure. She was followed at five-minute intervals by her seven sisters. The LST skippers knew this would be a difficult approach, even in a non-battle situation, and what they saw ahead of them heightened their anxiety. Gun flashes from the battle at Cemetery Hill dominated the north end of Red Beach. Large groups of Marines hugged the waterfront in the center of the beach, apparently unable to advance inland.

By the time the second ship, *LST-975*, crossed the line, *LST-859* was already taking fire. Communist gunners on Observatory Hill sprayed the landing ship with heavy machine-gun rounds, and rifle bullets clanged on their superstructures. NKPA mortars firing from within the city quickly struck several ships. A fire began to blaze among the ammunition trucks on board *LST-914*, but alert Sailors and Marines put it out with CO_2 canisters and fog dispensers. A burst of automatic weapon fire holed eighth drums of gasoline on *LST-857*, and the deck ran with the volatile fuel. In response, the LSTs wildly swept the beachhead with their 3-inch, 40-mm, and 20-mm guns in an attempt to stop the enemy fusillade.

Ashore, the 2nd Battalion's Weapons and Headquarters companies came under intense "friendly" fire from the LSTs. These units, which had not yet suffered casualties, soon counted one killed and another twenty-three wounded. The platoon on Cemetery Hill abandoned the crest

THE
VITAL LST

THE TANK LANDING SHIP (LST), which proved so crucial to UN success at Inchon, was developed during World War II to deploy tanks, vehicles, and critical supplies directly onto assault beaches soon after infantry troops stormed ashore. The ships used a ballast system that allowed them to operate effectively on the open ocean, in shallow coastal waters, and on the beach. The LST had a 328-foot length and 50-foot beam and could carry a 2,100-ton load. These ships were the stars of many WWII amphibious operations, and their crews proudly served in them; but because the LSTs could only muster ten knots, Sailors sometimes referred to them as "large, slow targets."

Because of defense cutbacks, by January 1950, only 135 of the 1,051 LSTs America produced during the war remained in commission world-wide. SCAJAP, an occupation agency responsible for inter-island trade and the return of Japanese POWs from other parts of Asia, operated another thirty-nine LSTs. A few others served the U.S. Army in Japanese waters.

Soon after the sudden outbreak of war in Korea, the Navy feverishly concentrated LSTs in Far Eastern waters. These vessels would be essential to the transportation of vehicles and supplies from Japan and to MacArthur's amphibious operations in Korea. Vice Admiral Joy, Commander U.S. Naval Forces, Far East, quickly pressed into service the SCAJAP and Army LSTs. Several of these ships were returned to Navy control in the summer of 1950 and were manned largely by reservists recalled to duty. Many of these ships were in a serious state of disrepair.

LST-799, a former SCAJAP tank landing ship, was recommissioned and assigned for the Inchon landing. (National Archives USN 1045713)

Lt. Erwin E. J. Hauber, executive officer of *LST-799*, described his former SCAJAP ship as overrun with "rats bigger than footballs" and stinking with the "penetrating odor of fish heads and urine." The American Sailors rearmed their LSTs with guns removed from frigates, which the Navy had provided to the Soviet navy in the WWII lend–lease program and the USSR then returned to U.S. control. Test firing these weapons was an adventure; some of the 20-mm antiaircraft guns failed to stop firing or "ran away." One gunnery officer feared that a decrepit 3-inch gun would explode, so he tied a 45-foot lanyard to the firing key.

The crews of the seventeen American-manned LSTs and thirty Japanese-manned SCAJAP LSTs of Rear Admiral Doyle's Task Force 90 performed small miracles to prepare their ships for Operation Chromite. For instance, when Lt. (jg) Leslie H. Joslin, MSC, was ordered to set up an operating room on board *LST-898*, the officer and his men turned to. Joslin's resourceful team scrubbed the small, filthy space assigned to them, brought onboard a mountain of supplies, "scrounged" medicines from the Army, and installed an operating table that they had removed from mothballed U.S. ships tied up at Kobe since World War II. Thanks to the ingenuity and plain hard work of American and Japanese Sailors, when *LST-898* and her sister ships departed for Inchon, they were ready for action.

and harbor face for the Inchon side, preferring to confront the NKPA heavy machine guns on Observatory Hill rather than the LSTs' weapons. Some Navy LST gunners, however, were on target, destroying a North Korean automatic weapon firing at the men on Cemetery Hill.

Despite some disorganization and both enemy and friendly fire, the 5th Marines continued to move forward. Company E took British Consulate Hill at 1845 as the lone rifle platoon and mortar section seized a portion of Observatory Hill. By 2000, and after a sharp firefight, Captain Fenton's Company B secured half of the hill. Company D occupied the rest of the position, even though a Communist machine gun killed one Marine and wounded four others, including the unit's medical corpsman. This Sailor refused evacuation until he had treated the wounds of his comrades and ensured their safety.

TAKING THE INITIATIVE AT BLUE BEACH

MEANWHILE, THE ASSAULT ON Blue Beach had gone better. First, several U.S. destroyers and the LSMRs raked Won-do and Tok Am, small bits of land flanking the approach route taken by the landing craft, and the British cruisers shelled high ground just behind the beach. Then, more than 170 LVTs, including eighteen gun-equipped armored amtracs (LVT[A]s) of the Army's 56th Amphibian Tractor Battalion, moved toward Blue Beach in twenty-five waves. The first wave, consisting of all the

LVT(A)s, crossed the line of departure at 1645. With the help of four guide boats manned by Navy UDTs, the first three waves made landfall where they were supposed to, although some of the LVT(A)s remained just offshore firing on the beach.

Confusion, however, soon set in among the remaining waves. Established procedures called for thirty-two guide boats to direct a landing of this size, instead of the four available. Rain squalls and smoke from the fighting at Inchon spread across the approach waters off Blue Beach, so succeeding waves could not guide on the first three. Visibility degenerated so quickly that the primary control ship could not even see the landing area. In addition, unanticipated crosscurrents threw many of the LVT(A)s off course.

A number of the more experienced amphibious warfare officers realized that a disaster could occur if they did not take bold action. One such Marine, Maj. Edwin H. Simmons, a veteran of WWII Pacific landings, grew concerned when the LVT in which he was embarked cut across several boat lanes. Simmons pulled out his map, sought out the LVT driver, and asked him if he had a compass. "Search me," replied the Marine, a recently recalled reservist, "six weeks ago I was driving a truck in San Francisco." Many of the other LVT(A)s were manned by inexperienced crews, and because the craft had been hastily pulled out of storage some lacked radios and other essential equipment.

Despite these handicaps, company-grade Navy and Marine officers took the initiative to restore order and put the troops ashore at the best locations. Even though the LVT(A)s landed most of the 1st Battalion, 1st Marines two miles to the left of their designated beach, others disgorged their passengers close to intended landing areas near the seawall. Thirty minutes after H-hour, the units at Blue Beach started moving inland.

For a second time that day, the senior UN commanders decided they needed a closer look at Inchon. In the fading daylight and with mortar rounds exploding in the water nearby, Admiral Struble's barge brought Generals MacArthur, Shepherd, and Almond alongside the seawall at Blue Beach. A Marine noncommissioned officer bellowed, with characteristic directness, "Lay off, you stupid bastards! We're going to blast a hole in the wall!" With equal vigor the coxswain retorted, "*This* is Admiral Struble's barge!" The leatherneck responded, "I don't give a shit whose barge it is, get it clear before I blow the seawall!" An amused Struble directed the coxswain to back off immediately. Thirty seconds later, a large section of seawall was blown sky high.

The first and second assault waves approach Blue Beach on D-day. *De Haven,* one of six destroyers that subdued North Korean artillery batteries at Wolmi-do before the Inchon invasion, appears at the lower right. (Naval Historical Center)

Meanwhile, the Marines at Blue Beach pressed on toward their objectives. On the right flank, an LVT silenced a machine gun nest in a tower five hundred yards inland and the 3rd Battalion, 1st Marines seized several commanding hills and forced an NKPA company to flee their well-prepared positions on Tok Am. On the left flank, the regiment's 2nd Battalion killed fifty NKPA soldiers, captured another fifteen, and secured the large hill east of Inchon, at a cost of one Marine killed and nineteen wounded.

A NIGHT IN INCHON

MARINE REINFORCEMENTS ALSO HEADED for Green Beach in the twilight. Inchon's severe currents swept off course some of the underpowered amphibious trucks, or DUKWs, which carried the 105-mm guns of the 11th Marines' two howitzer battalions. By 2150, however, all of the "ducks" had waddled ashore and the artillerymen had registered the guns to fire in support of the infantry. After these units came two Marine armored companies, equipped with Pershing tanks, which rumbled across the causeway and prepared to push toward Kimpo and Seoul.

During the night, *Lyman K. Swenson* and other destroyers and cruisers of the bombardment force fired star shells over the Red Beach perimeter so that the Marines could detect enemy movement. Not all sightings, however, resulted in combat. In the light of one illumination round, Captain Fenton, who was relieving himself at the time, reacted with surprise when a heavily armed enemy soldier emerged from a hole at his feet. Instead of attacking the startled American officer, the North Korean bowed deeply and surrendered his weapon.

Throughout the night, Navy surgeons and corpsmen of the 1st Marine Division and medical personnel in the LSTs at Red Beach tended the wounded, whose numbers were far below the three hundred projected by Doyle's staff. The joint task force suffered 174 wounded in action and fourteen nonbattle injuries. The improvised operating room set up by the surgical team in *LST-898* treated only forty-two military and thirty-two civilian cases. One man was missing and another twenty-one had been killed in action.

As 15 September ended, it was clear to all that the landing had succeeded. The joint task force had sustained relatively few casualties and lost only two planes (whose pilots were recovered). General Shepherd, a veteran of many landing operations, credited much of his success to the Task Force 90 commander: "Doyle is a great commander and is the best amphibious naval officer I have ever met."

OBJECTIVE: SEOUL

UN FORCES WERE NOW firmly ashore, but the seizure of Inchon was only the opening phase of the campaign to cut off the North Korean army and liberate South Korea. The next step was to capture Seoul, whose military, political, and psychological importance was paramount. Critical to this effort was the fleet's ability to keep pumping reinforcements, transportation resources, ammunition, fuel, and supplies into the ever-expanding beachhead.

By the time the LSTs backed off Red Beach with the rising tide on 16 September, the men of Naval Beach Group 1 and the Marine Shore Party Battalions had unloaded four thousand tons of supplies and equipment. Another nine fully loaded LSTs soon replaced the first group on the beach, and the resupply process continued unabated. Other logistics ships and craft disembarked material onto the pontoon dock installed by the Seabees.

Early on the morning of 16 September, a column of six North Korean T-34 tanks rumbled down the road toward Inchon. Two flights of VMF-214 Corsairs operating from *Sicily* pounced on the Soviet-built armored vehicles about a mile short of Marine lines. Even though enemy antiaircraft fire turned one plane into a fireball, the other F4Us destroyed or heavily damaged half of the enemy force. Still, the intrepid Communist tankers kept on coming toward the ridgeline fighting positions of the 5th Marines. Suddenly, Marine Pershing tanks crested the rise, chose their targets, and destroyed the rest of the T-34s with accurate fire.

The way now clear of the enemy, the infantrymen of the 1st Marines and the 5th Marines advanced and around 0730 linked up east of Inchon. South of town, the leathernecks occupied an abandoned coastal artillery position and captured a 120-mm mortar battery. At the same time, General Smith ordered the 3rd Battalion, 1st KMC Regiment, into Inchon to mop up enemy troops and sympathizers, whose hiding places local civilians gladly revealed. Incensed by civilian reports of Communist atrocities, for the remainder of the day the South Korean marines ruthlessly sought out the North Koreans and other "subversives."

As UN forces secured Inchon and strengthened the beachhead on 16 September, the UN command took other steps to engage the North Korean army. General Walker's Eighth Army attacked out of the Pusan Perimeter, working to prevent the early withdrawal of NKPA units from the southern front. Then, the U.S. Army and ROKN mounted an operation to cut the north-south road at Changsa-Dong on the peninsula's east coast. A Korean LST attempted to land a guerrilla force, but the ship grounded and broached just offshore. The irregulars finally made it to the beach, only to be attacked by a nearby North Korean

OVER-THE-BEACH
LOGISTICS

THE SUCCESS OR FAILURE of an amphibious operation often depends on how soon the assault forces get resupplied with ammunition, weapons, vehicles, food, and fuel. It is equally important for naval logistics forces to keep supplies and troop reinforcements flowing into the beachhead. If they do not, the enemy might push friendly forces into the sea or prevent a breakout from the coast. At Inchon, the lack of adequate port facilities or sea room in which to stage logistics ships made it essential that the naval logistics forces rapidly move supplies "over the beach."

The Navy, the Marine Corps, and the Army had developed sophisticated methods and organizations for over-the-beach logistics support based on their experiences in the Pacific in World War II. Naval Beach Group 1, commanded by Capt. Watson T. Singer, included beachmasters and small boat units that, along with the 1st Marine Division's Shore Party Battalion led by Lt. Col. Henry P. Crowe, directed the movement of supplies to the beach and then inland. Watson's group also included UDTs that cleared obstacles and Seabees responsible for reconstructing the harbor installations and initially operating the port. The Army's 2nd Special Engineer Brigade, which had supported MacArthur's campaigns in the southwest Pacific during World War II, took over port operations from the naval units.

On the afternoon of 15 September, the Seabees built a large pontoon dock and causeway at Green Beach on Wolmi-do. After the evening landing, some of Singer's Sailors and Crowe's Marines had to unload, organize, and distribute the supplies from the eight LSTs temporarily immobilized

Four "high-and-dry" LSTs disgorge supplies onto Red Beach on or about 16 September. (National Archives USN 420027)

on Red Beach on the evening's high tide. Bringing order out of the dark and chaotic night challenged Crowe, who had come up through the ranks and was decorated for heroism at Guadalcanal and Tarawa.

Enemy snipers in Inchon shot at Crowe's leathernecks and Singer's Sailors, outlined as they were in the glare of the floodlights installed by the Seabees. Nonetheless, the men continued to toil throughout the long night to accomplish their vital mission. All of the LST captains withdrew their emptied ships on the morning's high tide.

By 19 September, one day after the 2nd Special Engineer Brigade took over port operations, the Navy, Marine, and Army shore parties had unloaded every ship of the first echelon. Army engineers and the Seabees also had trains operating almost eight miles inland. Once the airstrip at

Kimpo was opened for business, Air Force transports flew in critical aviation gas and ordnance for the Marine aircraft operating there.

By 22 September, the multiservice logistics forces had pushed ashore a staggering amount of material: 25,512 tons of cargo, 6,629 vehicles, and 53,882 troops. As a result, MacArthur's assault forces were able to seize their lodgment ashore, defend it from counterattack, and speedily break out of the coastal enclave.

garrison. The operation a failure, the battleship *Missouri* and cruiser *Helena* and Air Force F-51 Mustangs hit the enemy with their fire so another LST could extract the guerrillas.

On 17 September, the North Koreans counterattacked the UN beachhead at Inchon, so Communist reinforcements might have time to reach Seoul. Early that morning, the NKAF made its one and only assault on the amphibious force off Inchon. A pair of Yak fighters dove on the warships anchored south of Wolmi-do. Except for a lone Sailor on sentry duty at the stern of the cruiser *Rochester*, who fired his rifle at the planes, the crew of the cruiser was caught off guard. The enemy planes dropped several bombs on the Americans but the only weapons that hit a ship failed to explode. The Yaks then strafed HMS *Jamaica*, mortally wounding one seaman and hitting two others. The Royal Navy took its revenge, splashing one of the attackers with fire from 4-inch guns and automatic weapons. The cruiser's skipper, Capt. Jocelyn C. S. Salter, RN, later felt that it was "foolhardy" of the North Koreans "to go for two cruisers when they had a choice of transports and freighters galore."

As that futile attack ended, an NKPA rifle battalion supported by a platoon of T-34s advanced against the lines of the 5th Marines. The North Korean units, which made no reconnaissance of UN positions, moved into a trap. The 5th Marines quickly destroyed the tank column. To the south, Col. Lewis B. Puller's leathernecks had a tougher fight. Elements of the 1st Marine Regiment, with the help of five Corsairs, fought their way through a heavily fortified defile on the road to Seoul.

Much to the distress of General Smith, MacArthur went ashore that morning and insisted on traveling just behind the front line, at one point

After a hard-fought battle in downtown Seoul in which M-26 Pershing tanks proved invaluable, UN troops round up North Korean prisoners of war. (Naval Historical Center)

directing his jeep driver to a ridge crest to observe a firefight. Smith was greatly relieved when CINCUNC returned safely to *Mount McKinley*, particularly when he learned that his Marines had flushed seven heavily armed NKPA soldiers from the culvert on which MacArthur's jeep idled as he viewed some burning T-34s.

With the NKPA attack spent, the 5th Marines seized the south end of Kimpo air base and a KMC battalion advanced to cover their left flank. North Korean counterattacks that night failed to dislodge the Americans from Kimpo. Artillery fire from the 11th Marines and small arms fire decimated the ranks of the enemy infantry forces moving against the air base perimeter.

On 18 September, the 3rd Battalion, 1st Marines, stormed Hill 123. Assistance in this attack came from HMS *Kenya*, which poured three hundred 6-inch rounds on the enemy. Still unbeaten, NKPA gunners inflicted thirty casualties on the Americans when they shelled the slopes of the hill. Throughout the hour-long barrage, the senior naval medical officer present, Lt. Robert J. Fleischaker, MC, moved about the hill to treat the wounded, without regard for his safety. The Navy awarded Fleischaker the Bronze Star for his bravery under fire.

In support of the 5th Marines, the cruisers *Rochester* and *Toledo* and U.S. Navy Skyraiders bombarded Communist forces on both sides of the Han River northwest of Kimpo. Despite these heavy attacks, the naval aviators reported that the enemy units were "still active."

That same day, the Joint Task Force 7 transports began disembarking several Army units. The 7th Infantry Division's 32nd Infantry Regiment landed and advanced to cover the 1st Marine Division's right flank. The 96th Field Artillery Battalion and the 2nd Engineer Special Brigade also came ashore, with the engineers relieving the KMC battalion in Seoul.

On 19 September, the 1st Marine Division continued to advance on Seoul. The 5th Marines, still within supporting distance of the task force cruisers, prepared to cross the Han north of the capital. To the south, the 1st Marines began a three-day battle for the industrial suburb of Yongdungpo.

Critical close air support for this fight would come from VMF-212 and night-fighting squadron VMF(N)-542, which flew into Kimpo from Japan that day. Marine Brig. Gen. Thomas J. Cushman, the X Corps tactical air commander, directed these units. FEAF's Combat Cargo Command, with C-54 and Fairchild C-119 Flying Boxcars, also began flying ammunition and aviation gas into Kimpo on 19 September. The experienced Air Force cargo handlers of the 1st Combat Support Unit (Provisional) quickly unloaded and pushed forward the vital material.

The UN advance toward Seoul continued on 20 and 21 September. After an initial setback, Marine LVTs carrying the 3rd Battalion, 5th Marines, crossed the Han River and, with the assistance of *Sicily*'s VMF-214 fighters, established a lodgment on the far bank. The ground force received a welcome reinforcement when the Army's 31st Infantry Regiment, the ROK 17th Infantry Regiment, and the 7th Marines came ashore at Inchon. The Sixth Fleet's attack transport *Bexar* (AP-237) and attack cargo ship *Montague* (AKA-98) had completed the long journey from the Mediterranean to deliver one of the 7th Marines' battalions.

As these reinforcements moved up to the front, the Communists struck back. On 21 September, NKPA troops crossed the Han and assaulted South Korean marine positions northwest of Kimpo airfield. Carrier aircraft and the naval gunfire of *Toledo* obliterated the Communist attacking force. In addition, Navy Skyraiders reduced enemy resistance in Suwon before the 7th Division's Reconnaissance Company occupied the city.

As these actions took place, as planned, Admiral Struble's force dissolved Joint Task Force 7 and turned over operational control of

Operation Chromite to Almond, who desperately wanted to take Seoul by 25 September—exactly three months after the North Korean invasion. He believed that the Communists must be on the brink of collapse. General Smith was not as optimistic.

The leathernecks assaulted Seoul's western defenses on 22 September and found enemy resistance especially strong. The Seoul garrison now included several heavily armed and well-led NKPA units that had been rushed to the city from all directions. The Marines had to battle their way through Seoul, house-to-house, street-to-street. The fighting battered the South Korean capital. Marine casualties, light up to that point, steadily mounted. Navy surgeons and corpsmen, especially the latter who often exposed themselves to enemy fire when helping wounded Marines, paid a heavy price for their bravery. By midday on 24 September, every corpsman with F Company, 5th Marines, had either been killed or seriously wounded. NKPA soldiers cut down Hospital Corpsman Third Class James J. Ergesitz as he pulled a wounded Marine from a fire-swept slope. Communist mortar rounds hit the 1st Battalion, 5th Marines' aid station and wounded a surgeon, Navy Lt. Francis T. H'Doublei, MC. He continued to treat casualties until incapacitated by another wound. Chief Hospital Corpsman Wayne D. Austin, already hit in the face and ankle, took over and tended forty more men before being relieved. Only when a replacement arrived did Chief Austin, wounded once more, consent to evacuation. For his actions, Austin received the Navy Cross.

General Almond, dissatisfied with the Marine progress through the city, moved the 32nd Infantry and the 17th ROK Infantry across the Han to flanking positions. The enemy continued to fight with determination and skill, but Almond was persuaded that their resistance would be short-lived. Just before midnight on 25 September, he declared Seoul liberated.

To the leathernecks and soldiers in the city this was a cruel joke, because the NKPA still held 60 percent of the city and that night launched three counterattacks. Despite taking heavy casualties, the North Koreans stubbornly hung on until 28 September. Even the next day, when General MacArthur and President Rhee presided over a ceremony returning the capital of the Republic of Korea to its people, attendees could hear the sound of artillery and small arms fire coming from the northern suburbs.

Meanwhile, General Walker's 8th Army had broken out of the Pusan Perimeter, raced to the northwest, and joined forces with Almond's X

Corps. When the 1st Cavalry Division's legendary 7th Cavalry Regiment met elements of the 7th Infantry Division near Osan, on the morning of 27 September, the campaign for South Korea was almost over. Of the seventy thousand North Korean soldiers engaged at Pusan, much less than half escaped death or capture. Only thirty thousand men, with virtually no heavy weapons, recrossed the 38th parallel into North Korea. A better-coordinated attack by the Eighth Army that concentrated on isolating forces, rather than racing to Inchon, might have netted the entire NKPA. Nonetheless, the bloody campaign in South Korea and the hasty retreat from Pusan had exhausted and demoralized the survivors of the once mighty NKPA invasion force. Of paramount importance, the UN forces that stormed ashore at Inchon had achieved their primary purpose—liberation of the Republic of Korea.

CONCLUSION

THE AMPHIBIOUS ASSAULT at Inchon showed how the skillful use of naval force enables theater commanders to bring decisive power to bear on enemy nations touched by the sea. The cruisers, destroyers, frigates, and carriers, along with UN air forces, first secured control of the Yellow Sea, the Sea of Japan, and the air spaces over these waters. This unexpected display of strength led North Korea's international Communist supports to reconsider their policies regarding the Korean peninsula.

After eliminating the North Korean air force, UN ship- and land-based air power battered military facilities in North Korea and logistical lines to the Communist troops in South Korea. At the same time, U.S. and Royal Navy warships bombarded NKPA front-line troops and supply routes near the coasts, providing vital support to the U.S. and ROK ground units. Because of post-WWII defense cutbacks, however, the lack of ships, air-craft, and material ready for combat almost doomed the UN cause in Korea in July and August 1950.

Control of the sea and the ability to assemble and organize enough merchantmen, transports, and cargo ships allowed the UN command to move reinforcements to the Far East from all parts of the world. General MacArthur, the theater commander and an experienced practitioner of amphibious warfare, knew that he now possessed a clear advantage over his enemy. He was able to choose the best time and place to strike the rear of the North Korean army. If success crowned his efforts, he would liberate South Korea.

The naval forces in the Far East, under the command of Admirals Joy, Struble, and Doyle, worked to execute MacArthur's concept. Despite the difficulties in gathering relevant intelligence and assembling the variety of units needed, these veteran commanders and their expert staffs quickly planned the assault of a site that presented many physical problems. They then coordinated the necessary naval, air, and ground forces for the complex operation.

Almost every type of naval unit contributed to the victory at Inchon. Carrier-based Navy and Marine planes and surface combatants prepared the battlefield and, in conjunction with the Air Force, helped to deceive the enemy about the actual invasion area. Continued attacks by naval air and surface forces throughout the landing, consolidation, and breakout phases of Operation Chromite added considerably to the woes of the North Korean defenders. Other naval units cleared Inchon's approach waters of mines. Most important, the Sailors manning the assault ships and craft and the Marines storming the enemy's positions exhibited the skill and bravery necessary to the success of any opposed landing. Once ashore, the 1st Marine Division soundly defeated their foes and secured the objectives with typical courage and professional skill.

The Navy, particularly its often forgotten support services, remained critical to the success of the operation. Corpsmen, surgeons, and chaplains were on hand to treat the wounded and comfort the dying. The ungainly LSTs provided essential materials and services for the beachhead. The Naval Beach Group's Seabees, UDTs, beachmasters, and boat units, and the Marine Shore Party kept vehicles, equipment, and supplies flowing across the beach. Transports and cargo ships brought in additional U.S. and ROK soldiers and Marines. Oilers, tenders, and stores ships supplied combatants on station, enabling the fleet to remain off Inchon and to provide the ground forces with continued naval air and gunfire support.

Often in war, good intelligence, careful planning, and bold execution favor one side with relatively light casualties, and this was the case at Inchon. During the first seven days of Chromite, the joint task force counted approximately 70 killed, 470 wounded, and 5 missing. Because of the bloody fighting for Seoul, the toll rose to 600 killed, 2,750 wounded, and 65 missing. At the same time, UN forces killed 14,000 North Korean soldiers and captured another 7,000.

Of greater importance, Admiral Struble's joint task force carried out the theater commander's directive to strike the NKPA a lethal blow and drive the aggressors from the Republic of Korea. To General MacArthur, "the Navy and Marines . . . never shone more brightly" than at Inchon.

CURTIS A. UTZ *is a historian and the head of the Naval Historical Center's Naval Aviation History Branch. He graduated from the University of Maryland with a bachelor of arts degree in history in 1984 and a master of arts degree in history in 1989. He worked for the National Park Service and as an intern at the Smithsonian's National Air and Space Museum. He served as a historian with the Contemporary History Branch from 1992 to 1994 and was a historian with the Defense Intelligence Agency from 1994 to 2003. Utz authored* Cordon of Steel: The U.S. Navy and the Cuban Missile Crisis, *published by the Naval Historical Center.*

CHAPTER 3

Naval Leadership in Korea
The First Six Months

THOMAS B. BUELL

INTRODUCTION

IT WAS THE STRANGEST of all naval wars, if it could even be called a naval war, for a naval war has opposing navies. The United States Navy in Korea was unopposed by a conventional enemy navy. Five years before the shooting started in Korea, the United States was the world's greatest sea power, having defeated the Axis powers, a victory culminating in the surrender ceremony on board USS *Missouri* in Tokyo Bay. The Navy then had some sixty-eight thousand vessels of all types on hand and over four million people—Sailors, Marines, and Coastguardsmen—in uniform. The postwar demobilization left the naval service with but a remnant of its wartime strength, and the Truman administration intended to emasculate it yet further.

By limiting appropriations in peacetime, American politicians had managed to devastate the naval service as had no enemy in war. They acted neither for vengeance nor for want of gratitude for the victory in World War II, but because they could perceive no need for a navy in the circumstances of the late 1940s. The Soviet Union was a looming threat to the security of the free world, but the U.S. Air Force had argued convincingly that its long-range bombers and atomic bombs were the primary deterrents to Soviet aggression. As the Soviet Union was then a land power with a negligible navy, conventional wisdom reasoned that the U.S. Navy would have no great role in the event of war on the continent.

The naval establishment had blundered by not making its case and by allowing the Air Force to define the terms of the acrimonious roles-and-missions debates in Congress, the Pentagon, and the press. Ostensibly, armed forces unification was the overriding interservice quarrel—the Navy was against it, the Air Force and Army were for it. The root of the dispute, however, was whose aircraft would do what. Flag officers like Vice Adm. Arthur W. Radford, Vice Chief of Naval Operations (VCNO), argued that the aircraft carrier had been proven in war as the core of sea power. Thus when the Air Force argued that the B-36 intercontinental bomber made the aircraft carrier redundant, and that in any event an atomic bomb would sink a fleet in an instant, the Navy was stung and came out swinging. The Navy–Air Force brawl became predicated upon a single issue: Which system—carrier or bomber—was best suited to drop atomic bombs on Russia?

By advocating that the carrier's (ergo the Navy's) primary mission should be strategic bombing, and that it could do it better than the B-36, the Navy adopted a narrow, all-or-nothing argument. If it lost that argument, it would lose everything, for no other plausible justification for the Navy's existence was forthcoming. And lose that argument it surely would, owing to the Navy's long-standing ineptness in public relations and its inability to justify itself.

Other arguments rarely materialized. Control of the sea, the once traditional role of the Navy, now seemed irrelevant in the absence of any other sea power. When in his ignorance General Bradley, chairman of the JCS, shrilly dismissed the Marine Corps and amphibious warfare as wholly unnecessary in any future war, the Navy did not respond.

To be convincing in political and public forums required officers to present articulate, well-thought-out arguments, but the Navy Department in the late 1940s suffered from an intellectual vacuum. Flag officers then leading the Navy had made their number during World War II and had learned by doing. Hence, there evolved among many of them an institutional disdain for war college training and the associated disciplines of sound reasoning, abstract thought, and verbal clarity. Things learned in the school of the ship were of little value in Washington, and as a consequence, the Navy floundered when confronting Air Force propaganda.

In countering the Army–Air Force public relations campaign for unification of the services, the Navy first relied upon a group of Office of the Chief of Naval Operations (OPNAV) officers known as the Secretary's

Committee on Research and Reorganization (SCOROR), established in late 1945 and initially headed by Admiral Radford, then Deputy Chief of Naval Operations (DCNO) for Air. As the Navy's principal proponent for naval air power and for preserving the independence of the naval service, Radford fiercely opposed nearly every unification scheme proposed by the Army and its allies. Although a shrewd, persuasive bureaucrat skilled in the give and take of Washington politics, Radford achieved only limited successes on behalf of the Navy Department. He became so strongly identified as a foe of unification and Air Force aspirations that his opponents wished him out of Washington.

He left for a time to command the Second Fleet but returned in January 1948 to serve as Vice Chief of Naval Operations, a tour that lasted eighteen months. Louis E. Denfeld, a submariner, had just been appointed CNO, and he told the Chief of Naval Personnel that he wanted "an aviator who had the complete confidence of Naval aviators, both young and old, one who had a good war record and one who would be completely loyal in working out the unification legislation as it affects the Navy." After returning to Washington, Radford resumed his struggles against the Air Force and President Harry S. Truman's relentless whittling of the strength of the armed services.

Meanwhile the Secretary of the Navy's Committee on Unification (UNICOM) had replaced SCOROR, functioning since June 1948 as the coordinating agency for "unification problems relative to Navy basic concepts, doctrines and policies." Still the Navy continued to sustain losses to the smooth-talking Air Force spokesmen. Recognizing the sterility of UNICOM, Secretary of the Navy John L. Sullivan dissolved it seven months after it had been established.

Sullivan, Denfeld, and Marine Commandant General Cates discussed what, or who, would replace UNICOM. Two imperatives occupied their attention. First, unification strategy had to be coherent and coordinated to ensure the Navy's independence, if not its survival. Second, naval policies had to be developed that would be universally supported within the service. As the so-called revolt of the admirals concerned solely aviation, surface and submarine officers felt that their interests were being disregarded. Moreover, bungling leadership exacerbated the unbroken unification disasters that demoralized and humiliated the naval officer corps as an institution. Sullivan, Denfeld, and Cates were on the spot, and as one observer described it, "They were determined that something had to be done to get the Navy back into believing in itself."

Despite all the flag officers at its disposal, the high command chose a captain, Arleigh A. Burke, to act as the Navy's brainpower. Burke was a famous surface warrior who had served as chief of staff to one of the Navy's greatest aviators, Adm. Marc A. Mitscher, former commander of the Fast Carrier Task Force in the Western Pacific. Hence, Burke was persona grata to both the surface and aviation communities, the "black shoes" and the "brown shoes." Furthermore, Burke had served on the General Board after the war and demonstrated an extraordinary intellectual capacity to think, analyze, reason, and write on great and complex issues. Summoned to Washington from his cruiser command on Christmas Day 1948, Burke learned he was about to undertake a potentially career-ending assignment on the unification battlefield. There was the likelihood that the Truman administration, the Office of the Secretary of Defense, and the Air Force would consider him an enemy, that the press would portray him as acting with intrigue and duplicity, and that special interests in the Navy might deem him disloyal if he proposed unpopular policies.

Taking such hazards in stride and pressing on, Burke took charge of OP-23, titled the Organizational Research and Policy Division in the Office of the Chief of Naval Operations. But developments beyond Burke's control continued to rock a Navy in distress. Louis A. Johnson replaced the ailing James V. Forrestal as Secretary of Defense on 28 March 1949. Less than a month later Johnson cancelled construction of the new carrier USS *United States*. The Air Force rejoiced. Secretary Sullivan resigned in protest.

For political reasons Johnson wanted a prominent Roman Catholic layman as Sullivan's replacement. Francis P. Matthews was that and little more. His religion being sufficient unto itself, and unburdened with either relevant skills or experience, Matthews was sworn in as the new Navy secretary on 25 May 1949. Naval officers soon loathed him because of his subservience to Johnson and his hostility to their interests. Internal turmoil intensified, and the Navy's decline accelerated. A hostile leak infuriated Matthews, and he suspected that Burke's shop, with intent to embarrass him, was the source. Matthews ordered the Inspector General to impound OP-23's files, but nothing incriminating was discovered. Nonetheless, a vengeful Matthews attempted, unsuccessfully, to stymie Burke's selection to rear admiral.

Meanwhile congressional hearings went on, and the naval aviators led by Radford (by then a full admiral in command of the Pacific Command

THE INSPECTOR
GENERAL'S RAID

CDR. SNOWDEN ARTHUR, A member of the OP-23 staff, periodically cruised by the CNO's office to hear the latest rumors from a friendly lieutenant. It was late afternoon, 29 September 1949. The lieutenant had startling news. "They're going to raid you," he warned. "The IG's headed toward you." Alarmed, Arthur scurried to Burke's office. Burke said he did not know why he was being targeted, but in any event there were files he did not want discovered. Opening file drawers, he and Arthur immediately began to stash papers into a briefcase.

Shortly, Rear Adm. Allan R. McCann, the Inspector General, entered Burke's office. Marine staff officer Col. Samuel R. Shaw saw the expression on McCann's face. "You looked at that man," he recalled, "and you knew something was afoot." Arthur stood frozen with briefcase in hand as McCann ignored him and confronted Burke. "Arleigh, it's a raid," he said coldly. "I want to talk with you in the hall." Burke and McCann went out and closed the entryway door. "I took off like a catapult," Arthur recalled, one step ahead of McCann's Marine sentries who closed every exit. In a nearby office, he found a friend who agreed to put the briefcase in his safe, and then went home.

While Burke and McCann were outside, Shaw told staff officer Cdr. Joseph L. Howard the probable reasons for the IG raid. The Navy's top flag officers were preparing to testify before the House Armed Services Committee, which had held hearings that allowed the Air Force to promote successfully the B-36 program, hearings which coincidentally had greatly embarrassed the Navy. Despite Air Force protests, the Navy

The Air Force's B-36 intercontinental bomber was at the crux of the bitter argument between the Navy and the Air Force over the mission of dropping bombs on targets in the Soviet Union. (Naval Historical Center)

(but not Matthews) wanted to testify in rebuttal, ostensibly to advocate the need for aircraft carriers. Just before the hearing was to begin, Matthews had ordered the admirals not to bring up the B-36. Recoiling, they protested that the Air Force had made claims that had to be challenged. The next morning an article in the *Washington Post* charged that Matthews had muzzled the witnesses. While in reality VCNO Vice Adm. John Dale Price had leaked the story, an enraged Matthews suspected Burke and had sent the IG to investigate. Rear Admiral Howard recalled the incident: "Sam Shaw seemed to sense, right away, what it was all about. I didn't, but Sam Shaw did. And he and I—just the two of us— began frantically to adjust our files and make damn sure that if they were going to go through the files that there would be some things they wouldn't be able to find."

Rear Admiral Burke, future Chief of Naval Operations, joined the Naval Forces Far East staff just before Inchon. Admiral Sherman wanted Burke to report on developments by a separate and privileged communications system, but Burke insisted that Vice Admiral Joy see everything that he sent or received from Washington. (U.S. Naval Institute)

As additional IG people surrounded the OP-23 offices, McCann told Burke to order his staff to remain in their offices and to recall those who had left. Burke could scarcely restrain his fury, but at his direction the entire staff was assembled and confined to their offices into the night. One by one they were taken to the IG offices for interrogation. Burke was the first to be summoned.

The IG interrogators were severe and intimidating but did not reveal the purpose of the investigation. Shaw remembered it was like being questioned in a police station. Their questions largely centered on office routine and contacts with the press, leading some of the staff to suspect that the morning's *Washington Post* article was the cause. As no one in Burke's office had leaked the article, it was foreordained that McCann would find no evidence, but the process reduced nearly all of the staffers to nervous exhaustion. McCann concluded his investigation in the early hours of the morning, dismissing Burke's staff with a warning to say nothing of what had happened.

Burke had dodged the bullet.

Adapted from Jeffrey G. Barlow's **Revolt of the Admirals.**

and the Pacific Fleet) decried the B-36. To Matthews's dismay, Denfeld testified that the aviators were right and that, by implication, Matthews was wrong—since Matthews's own testimony had portrayed the aviators as a cabal without support by the Navy's rank and file. Matthews and Johnson subsequently fired Denfeld for testifying to what he believed. The Navy cheered Denfeld for his act of self-immolation.

Whoever relieved Denfeld as CNO would have to resolve the ethical conflict between obedience to hostile civilian authority and loyalty to a naval service dissatisfied with that authority. Presumably Johnson and Matthews wanted someone who would enforce Johnson's intentions, namely not to build a new carrier, to reduce the size of the Navy, and to avoid further opposition to the B-36 program. Any such officer would, of course, be considered a betrayer by his colleagues.

Vice Adm. Forrest P. Sherman, thought by many to be overly ambitious, was willing and available. He commanded the Sixth Fleet in the

Mediterranean and, although a naval aviator, figuratively and literally, had stood clear of the mud-slinging B-36 hearings. Thus, in Matthews's mind, he was not one of them. Sherman was universally recognized as an intellectual and a planner, and as a staff officer he had been close to Chief of Naval Operations Fleet Adm. Chester W. Nimitz. When Nimitz became CNO, Sherman followed him to Washington as his DCNO for Operations. There he undertook the difficult job of representing the Navy in negotiations culminating in an agreement on unification, which in turn became the basis for the National Security Act of 1947. The act created an independent Air Force and a Secretary of Defense who presided over a unified National Military Establishment. Predictably Sherman's role was resented within the Navy, but with Nimitz as his mentor and the White House giving its approval, Sherman's career path remained unimpeded.

Matthews summoned Sherman from the Mediterranean for consultations without telling Denfeld. Under normal circumstances Sherman would have made a courtesy call on Denfeld; moreover, by protocol, only the CNO directed flag officers to come to Washington. But in this instance Sherman avoided Denfeld altogether. The embittered CNO confided to aides, "I guess Forrest Sherman is down there telling them everything they want to hear."

Viewed as an opportunist by a good portion of the naval establishment, Sherman was announced as the new CNO on 1 November 1949, at fifty-three the youngest officer ever to hold the post. Sherman quickly abolished OP-23.

Months earlier Radford had gotten his fourth star and gone to Pearl Harbor to command the remnants of the once-mighty Pacific Fleet. He had returned to Washington temporarily to testify in the October 1949 B-36 hearings, but he had been the last strong spokesman for naval air. The aviators despaired when Vice Admiral Struble, DCNO for Operations, became by default the principal naval representative in the development of military policy with the JCS. As a black shoe, he was not one of the club, and he avoided disputes. Those still fighting the problem desired him out of Washington, and they wanted Denfeld to assign him to command of the Seventh Fleet in the far-off Western Pacific in the summer of 1949. "He can't do us any harm there," remarked one critic.

By August Denfeld had not acted, so Struble remained in Washington, in the eyes of the aviators, hurting their cause. In an exchange of letters with another senior aviator, Radford wrote:

> Struble has done more harm to the Navy in the time he has been there than anyone else could have possibly done. I discussed this with Louis [Denfeld] before I left in April, and at that time Louis assured me that he would appoint a separate JCS assistant. . . . If Struble were relieved of his contacts with the JCS he could not do much damage—although I would favor getting him completely out of the operations picture.

In all likelihood Denfeld retained Struble for reasons of continuity, and certainly he was the kind of staff officer that Sherman wanted when he became CNO in November 1949. In mid-1950 Sherman did indeed send Struble to command the Seventh Fleet, but as a normal rotation and not as an exile. He would report to Radford, who distrusted him.

In many ways, the confrontation between the Air Force and the Navy that involved Sherman, Radford, and Struble, and the disagreements among these naval flag officers, prepared them for the exacting task of leading U.S. naval forces during the chaotic first six months of the Korean War.

NORTH KOREA ATTACKS

REAR ADMIRAL DOYLE WAS a master practitioner of amphibious warfare. He had seen it all during World War II. He had been Adm. Richmond Kelly Turner's operations officer during the Guadalcanal and Solomons campaigns, when the Navy was first learning amphibious warfare by trial and error. In the latter part of the war, when amphibious ships had numbered in the thousands, Doyle was a principal amphibious planner on Fleet Adm. Ernest J. King's staff in Washington. After a postwar hiatus he returned to the "alligator navy" in 1948. For two years he commanded the Amphibious Training Command in Coronado, California, keeping alive a form of warfare derided as obsolete by many in the Air Force and Army. Absorbed in the disagreements with the Air Force over aviation matters, even the Navy had given low priority to its amphibious capability. Because the Marines were fighting to survive against an antagonistic president, it was questionable whether the Navy would even have a landing force.

Doyle finally got to fly his flag at sea when he took command of Amphibious Group (PHIBGRP) 1 in January 1950. A vestige of a once mighty naval force, PHIBGRP 1 comprised but five ships, one of each type: a flagship (AGC), an attack transport (APA), an attack cargo ship (AKA), a tank landing ship (LST), and a fleet tug (ATF). No one ventured to say exactly what it was expected to do as the Navy retrenched in the aftermath of the unification fight. Perhaps this was Doyle's twilight cruise. Since he was in the Navy's backwater force, a promotion to vice admiral seemed unlikely. It might be time for him to think of retirement and a new career, for he was also a lawyer.

In the spring an unexpected summons came from General MacArthur, Commander in Chief, Far East (CINCFE). The general had let it be known that he wanted amphibious training for his army occupation forces in Japan. Ecstatic that a senior Army officer of MacArthur's prestige still thought that the Navy's amphibious forces were useful, the Navy sent Doyle and his ships to Japan. It was a logical and fortuitous decision: Doyle was accustomed to conducting amphibious training and had already embarked Marines from the Troop Training Unit, Coronado. They would train MacArthur's army. No other ships were available in the entire Pacific Fleet, so pitiably few were the numbers of amphibious vessels in commission.

When he arrived in Japan in late June 1950, Doyle called on Vice Admiral Joy, COMNAVFE, whose office was down the street from MacArthur's Tokyo headquarters. A decorated warrior, Joy had commanded a cruiser and later a cruiser division during several of the greatest battles of the Pacific war. When the war ended, he was commanding an amphibious group preparing for the invasion of Japan. Before and after the war he had operated in Far Eastern waters and was intimately familiar with both the Chinese and the China coast. He was also an ordnance and gunnery specialist with special expertise in mine warfare. Few other flag officers were more qualified to lead the naval forces in the war that was about to erupt.

It was America's good fortune that when Joy and Doyle sat over coffee, the Navy had put in place the two naval officers whose presence would be instrumental in preventing North Korea from taking and occupying South Korea by armed aggression. Yet, they were there not because of any prescience in the Navy Department, but because of MacArthur's understanding of the Navy's worth. CIA intelligence reports and his own staff had been predicting war in June. While MacArthur entertained doubts that Truman would allow the United States to become involved, he

Vice Admiral Joy was one of the most powerful and influential naval officers of the Korean War. He commanded and controlled all naval forces in the Korean theater and represented Navy and Marine interests within General MacArthur's headquarters. He strongly influenced MacArthur's decision to keep UN forces on the Korean peninsula during the Chinese attack of December 1950. (National Archives 80-G-427790)

nonetheless could take measures to be prepared. Publicly, however, MacArthur predicted a status quo in the Far East.

Still, his asking for amphibious training for his soldiers was not a whim. MacArthur's request had to have been deliberate and his thinking alone, for few on his staff had an inkling of the capabilities and intricacies of amphibious warfare. Had MacArthur not done so when he did, Doyle and his ships would have been in San Diego when the North Koreans attacked, and MacArthur would have been without means to get his troops from Japan to the Korean peninsula. North Korea would have occupied all of South Korea within weeks. Indeed, had Doyle not been in Japan, it is possible that Truman would not have ordered MacArthur to send troops into Korea, for certainly Sherman would have told the president there were no ships available. As we shall see, Doyle got the 1st Cavalry Division into Korea in the nick of time.

The fact that the Naval Forces, Far East command even existed was because MacArthur wanted naval ships under his direct control as CINCFE. While the Navy considered it as no more than a minor naval force to aid MacArthur in his occupation duties in Japan, the naval service ensured that a vice admiral was in command. Washington was determined that the ranking naval officer under MacArthur would wear the same three stars as MacArthur's senior Army and Air Force generals. As a matter of courtesy it would also have been customary for the Navy to have MacArthur's approval of Joy's assignment before cutting his orders. All in all MacArthur had good relations with the Navy; flag officers who knew him liked him, and he treated the Navy well.

Joy had a cruiser, four destroyers, and six minesweepers under his command, but a rear admiral looked after them as they undertook such nominal tasks as antismuggling patrols and showing the flag. His staff of twenty-nine officers and 160 enlisted men was organized for such peacetime administrative functions as coordinating Japanese-manned minesweepers clearing mines laid around the Home Islands during the war, facilitating the restoration of the Japanese merchant marine and shipbuilding industries, and supervising the naval stations at Yokosuka and Sasebo. The staff was neither organized nor prepared for a wartime emergency.

Joy and Doyle were old friends, so they quickly resumed their amiable relationship. When they went to MacArthur's headquarters, soon after Doyle's arrival in Japan, they encountered Secretary Johnson and General Bradley, who were touring the Far East. Bradley asked what Doyle was doing there.

"I am here," Doyle replied, "to give amphibious training to units of the Eighth Army at General MacArthur's request."

Bradley looked scornfully at Doyle and said nothing.

Doyle told MacArthur of the encounter, associating it with Bradley's earlier prediction that amphibious warfare was passé.

It was MacArthur's turn to be scornful: "Bradley is a farmer."

Doyle had agreeable memories of his first contact with MacArthur when both were in the Philippines before the war. He was pleased to see MacArthur once again, although he doubted that the general remembered him. MacArthur greeted Doyle warmly and explained his expectations for the training that Doyle had steamed the breadth of the Pacific to provide.

MacArthur's soldiers, the 35th Regimental Combat Team, first assembled with Doyle's training team on 25 June. The exercise was cancelled when word was received of the North Korea attack. Doyle went on four-hour standby, anticipating orders.

Struble was in Washington on 25 June, and his first reaction was to return to his diminutive "fleet"—its combatants were one carrier, a cruiser, eight destroyers, and four submarines—then in the Philippines and Hong Kong. Sherman told him to wait until after the CNO and the JCS met with Truman and his civilian advisors. The next day Sherman told Struble that American forces would be committed to Korea, although to what extent remained to be determined. Initially Washington authorized only such military action as was necessary to evacuate and protect Americans then in South Korea, and Secretary of State Dean Acheson warned that Korea might be a feint to mask a Chinese invasion of Taiwan and a Russian invasion of Europe. Whatever the Navy's eventual employment, Struble, as he returned to his command, knew the Seventh Fleet would be part of it.

Meanwhile General Cates, Commandant of the Marine Corps, was puzzled about how his Marines would be used. Secretary Matthews cancelled his regular conferences, and neither Matthews nor Sherman would grant Cates an audience. The general was convinced that the cold shoulder was intentional and that the administration meant to exclude the Marines from fighting in Korea, and he was not surprised. He had become accustomed to slurs and rebuffs. Truman was an avowed opponent of the Corps, and Bradley wanted to eliminate the Marines altogether.

By chance Sherman and Cates met in a Pentagon corridor on 29 June. Cates observed that things were looking grim. Sherman agreed.

"Why doesn't MacArthur ask for Marines?" asked Cates.

"What do you have?" Sherman replied.

Cates explained that he could immediately mount a provisional brigade comprising a regimental combat team and a Marine aircraft group from the 1st Marine Division at Camp Pendleton.

"Leave it to me," said Sherman after a pause. "I'll send a Blue Flag message to Joy."

Cates was puzzled for he had never heard of the private communication channel used by the Navy's senior flag officers. Several days passed until, on 3 July, Cates heard that, thanks to Joy's advocacy, MacArthur had requested the Marine brigade Cates had offered, and that the JCS would discuss it shortly. Cates went to Sherman and insisted that he be allowed to attend the meeting. The JCS reluctantly allowed him in, but agreed to send the Marines. Cates regarded the JCS decision as grudging because he felt they wanted to keep the Marines out of the war. Eventually MacArthur pounded on the JCS until it agreed to send the entire 1st Marine Division for the invasion of Inchon.

"Sherman didn't like the Marines," Cates later said, "but he was fair and square."

After Denfeld had been fired, Cates told Matthews that he hoped he wasn't considering Sherman as the new CNO. Matthews did not respond. The next day Sherman's appointment was announced.

"You certainly weren't my candidate," Cates told Sherman soon afterward.

"Well general," Sherman replied, "every man is entitled to his opinion."

Admiral Radford, Commander in Chief, Pacific, and Commander in Chief, Pacific Fleet, later recalled that he had gotten everything steaming westward as soon as he had heard about the attack in Korea. He pondered his and the Navy's role in the developing war, for it was unsettling that decisions from Washington seemed reluctant and hesitant and that forces were being committed piecemeal. Moreover, Radford was aware of the institutional hostility of the Office of the Secretary of Defense and the Army and Air Force members of the JCS toward the Navy and Marine Corps. He was also aware that the JCS, and especially the Army, were worried about a war in Europe and concerned that Korea was a diversion. In an early meeting with MacArthur he saw General Collins, Chief of Staff of the

BLUE FLAG
MESSAGES

THE PROLIFERATION OF TOP-SECRET messages particularly stressed communications resources because just a handful of people on communications staffs had top secret clearance. Only they could encrypt, decrypt, and route the flood of classified traffic, and the procedures were tedious. Before the Korean War top-secret messages were a rarity; now they had become commonplace. A special top-secret message category, called Blue Flag, which had been established solely for private communication among a small circle of flag officers, quickly began getting a lot of use. Not even Secretary of the Navy Francis Matthews was aware of their existence, nor were general officers of the other services. ("Blue Flag" referred to the traditional blue flags flown by Navy admirals.)

As the war entered its sixth month in December 1950, the secretary's aide, Capt. Harry B. Temple, spilled the beans to Matthews. Temple told Matthews he had drafted Blue Flags while he was in the Far East and was presumptuous enough to tell Matthews that he should see them. It was an embarrassing and awkward revelation that Sherman and his admirals had a private line that excluded Matthews, who naturally presumed he should know everything known by the admirals. When he asked Sherman for an explanation, the CNO agreed to show Matthews personally, "such Blue Flags as are appropriate." Moreover, Sherman ordered Radford and Joy to reduce the Blue Flags to a minimum and ensure that only flag officers drafted them, in effect closing the barn door. Nonetheless, top-secret messages flowed unabated, though fewer were Blue Flags. Temple, meanwhile, was promoted to rear admiral.

After the war, the CNO's top-secret message files were preserved on microfilm reels. Presumably, the originals were destroyed after the microfilming. Until recently the microfilm files remained classified and unavailable to historians. The standard Navy Department reason for refusing to declassify the Blue Flags was that retired senior flag officers did not want their private thoughts and communications to become public knowledge. In the late 1950s, the Director of Naval History contracted with James A. Field to write an official history of United States naval operations in Korea. As Field wrote in his explanation of source materials,

> The principal lacuna in the naval sources, and one that is reflected in the narrative, concerns the control and direction of the naval campaign. For Korea, as for the Second World War, information on such evanescent matters as the availability of intelligence, estimates of the situation, concepts of employment of own forces, and relations with the other services and with allies, must be sought in the dispatch traffic between the flag officers involved [i.e., Blue Flag]. But this remains an unexplored field. Although the availability of all pertinent naval sources was a condition of my undertaking this history, I have been unable to gain access to this material.

The Navy had denied Field access to all material classified higher than secret. By good fortune and the good offices of naval historians, the Navy Department declassified some of the Blue Flag files and made them available for this chapter on naval leadership. Work is under way to review the entire microfilm collection for declassification.

Army, tell MacArthur he would have to win the war with the troops available to him in Japan and Korea. MacArthur smiled. "Joe," he said, "you are going to have to change your mind."

Later MacArthur privately asked Radford what he thought the Marines might be able to contribute. A brigade almost immediately, Radford replied, and probably a full division by fall. MacArthur was already thinking about Inchon.

Realizing that Sherman was the voice of one crying in the wilderness, Radford wanted to give him some ammunition. Hence, once the

Admirals Sherman, Chief of Naval Operations, and Radford, Commander in Chief, Pacific, prepare to discuss the Korean situation at a July 1950 press briefing in San Diego. (National Archives 80-G-427791)

JCS had told MacArthur to fight the North Korean People's Army (NKPA), Radford counseled Sherman on 8 July in a way that reflected Radford's wisdom and broad strategic view, foretelling his eventual elevation to the JCS chairmanship. "I feel it is my duty," he wired Sherman, "to submit the following for your consideration in regard to my support of [MacArthur]."

> Over two thirds of the ships in the Pacific Fleet are either directly supporting [MacArthur] or are committed to his support. The remainder of my command is being made ready as quickly as possible to assist [MacArthur] as required. However, for the following reasons, the forces available in the Pacific Fleet are insufficient to provide the support which I believe is urgently required:
>
> The initial effects of the surprise attack on South Korea was countered to some extent by the resistance of South Korea and the surprise of the communists at the decision of the United States to fight if necessary to hold this area. The forces available to [MacArthur] are limited and

known to the communists. The forces in North Korea are greater in number and the reserve of Chinese communists in South Manchuria are reported to be about two hundred thousand troops, at least part of which can be moved to the battle area.

I consider that the importance of Korea to the communists (and the effect of its loss on U.S. prestige in the world) will require them to make every effort with the forces available in that area to defeat the U.S. forces. The United States cannot hope to hold Korea by number of troops but must depend upon mobility, mechanized forces, training and superiority of naval and air power at the point of conflict. I believe that the communists will continue to depend upon a superior number of troops, the mechanized equipment available in the general area, limited available air support and USSR advisors to the North Korean forces. Time and distance are on the side of the communists. We must make the most effective measures immediately to back up our presently committed forces. If we do not, we may ultimately be defeated in that area.

I believe that the American public will support any measures which may be required to insure victory in Korea. They have been told that new weapons and new methods of delivery will insure U.S. superiority in any area and their reaction should the U.S. be driven out of Korea would be great.

I recommend that immediate steps be taken to provide [MacArthur] with additional ground forces and air forces of the types needed for close air support [i.e., Navy and Marine aircraft]. That additional amphibious and other shipping be activated to carry and logistically supply these forces; that additional ships and aircraft squadrons ... be activated in order to provide adequate naval support; that the presently committed Marine [provisional brigade] be built up to full division strength as soon as practicable. Detailed recommendations for additional naval strength will follow by separate dispatch.

Meanwhile in Japan, Joy had conferred with MacArthur. Both were surprised that Truman intended to fight the North Koreans, although the rules of engagement were obscure and would remain so. MacArthur was also miffed that Washington had not consulted him beforehand. So unexpected was the attack and Truman's response to it that MacArthur and Joy had no contingency plans whatsoever. Accustomed to sleepy administrative tasks, Joy's staff was jolted overnight into emergency wartime planning for which it was wholly unprepared.

The most immediate question facing Joy was command and control of naval forces in the Far East. Any ship operating in Korean, Chinese, or Taiwanese waters would be in MacArthur's theater and hence under his unified command. This was a radical departure from the WW II arrangements, for Fleet Admiral King had never allowed the fast carriers to fall under MacArthur's direct control. During the Leyte campaign the lack of a unified command and the poor liaison between Adm. William F. Halsey and Vice Adm. Thomas C. Kinkaid, commanding the Third and Seventh fleets respectively, had endangered the amphibious shipping in Leyte Gulf. Halsey had commanded the fast carriers of the Third Fleet covering the amphibious assault and had reported to Nimitz; MacArthur had no say in their employment. Kinkaid, who reported to MacArthur, commanded the amphibious shipping and the close support warships. Consequently, Halsey had a free hand to do as he pleased and left the beachhead unprotected to chase a distant decoy force. A Japanese surface force entered the gulf and would have fallen on the transports had not the escort carriers and destroyers of Kinkaid's Seventh Fleet put up enough of a fight to discourage the enemy's advance.

This magnitude of split naval responsibility would not be repeated in Korea. (Although to a much lesser extent, personalities made the Navy command structure a contentious issue. Joy did his best to mediate and promote harmony such that, whatever the degree of naval command discord, it did not affect the Navy's performance at Inchon and Wonsan. In contrast, the appalling lack of a unified Army command and dispersion of forces on the Korean peninsula would complicate operations when the Chinese army attacked.) The JCS had some time earlier agreed that the Seventh Fleet would be placed under MacArthur's control in the event of an emergency in his area. Two days after the war began, Radford accordingly ordered Struble and his Seventh Fleet (centered around its fast carrier) to report to Joy for operational control. Since Joy reported to MacArthur, the general now had direct control—exercised through Joy—over the employment of the carriers. By fait accompli, Struble would report to Joy for orders, but as he was senior to Joy, a sacrosanct naval precedent was disregarded. Seniors normally did not report to juniors. In this instance there was no choice.

Joy's first order to Struble was to steam for Okinawa, for he had learned that the Seventh Fleet was headed to Sasebo, Japan, within range of Russian air bases. "I wanted to avoid another Pearl Harbor," he later explained. "I thought the Russians intended to start World War Three." The possibility of a larger war would weigh upon the minds of naval leaders in every decision they made.

In the hubbub of the emergency Joy had to make decisions and issue orders under conditions that often bypassed naval punctilio. As ship and aircraft reinforcements poured into MacArthur's theater, Joy had to decide how they would be organized. He and his staff were literally next door to MacArthur and his staff in Tokyo, and it was with them, and through them, that all naval operations had to be consolidated, negotiated, and coordinated. This could be done, and was done, through face-to-face contact and word-of-mouth between their respective staffs. Consequently, there was a lessened need for message traffic between them.

Joy next had to decide how to issue orders and plans to the forces afloat, whose numbers changed daily, if not hourly, and whose composition varied from aircraft carriers to yard craft. The basics of naval operational organization were practical and time tested: fleet > task force > task group > task unit > task element. Task organizations could be created or dissolved by the stroke of a pen. Administratively the Navy was organized more regularly into carrier, battleship, and cruiser divisions, and destroyer squadrons and divisions, with equivalent organizations for the amphibious and service forces. The commanders of the administrative organizations—by rank, mostly flag officers, captains, and commanders—would be assigned command of the task organizations as they were created for operations. As Joy and his staff wrote and released operation orders to carry out what MacArthur wanted done, the forces afloat were assigned to task organizations created by the operation order.

Early on, Joy knew he could not simply place everything afloat under Struble as components of the Seventh Fleet. That is, Struble could not operate as Kinkaid had in World War II. Struble's staff was too remote from MacArthur's CINCFE headquarters and too small to manage the complexity of the unfolding developments—within the first days naval forces had to evacuate American citizens under protection of air cover, take supplies to the ROK Army, blockade the North Korean coastline, patrol the Taiwan Strait against a possible Chinese invasion, prepare to transport American troops to the Korean peninsula should Truman so decide, and interdict North Korean forces with naval aircraft and gunfire. (When Truman ordered the Navy to attack targets in North Korea with carrier aircraft, he effectively refuted Bradley's congressional testimony the previous

October. Ironically, Bradley had testified "that he did not believe in using carrier aviation assets to attack land targets. Such a capability might be 'nice to have,' but it would not make a particularly important contribution in the initial stages of a war.")

Before the war began on 25 June, Joy and Struble had had little inter-action. Struble had reported to Radford in Pearl Harbor and had operated independently of MacArthur and Joy. Moreover, Joy may have heard the rumors from Washington that Struble was disliked and distrusted by some, and that Radford had a poor opinion of him. Joy's initial operation orders designated the task organization and composition for the Seventh Fleet, a move Struble would have considered a usurpation of his com-mand, seniority, and prerogatives. Sherman corrected Joy promptly by per-sonal message, each word carefully and tactfully chosen.

> Because the President has designated the "Seventh Fleet" to accomplish certain missions, out of consideration for a senior officer [Struble], and for reasons of naval prestige desire in drafting orders and in reports you designate as "Seventh Fleet" such forces as are under Struble's opera-tional control and leave to him the designation of component naval task forces.

Translation: Don't tell Struble how to run Seventh Fleet, as it might well be interpreted that the Navy lacks confidence in his ability as a fleet commander. Tell him what to do, but not how to do it.

Under no circumstances, in Sherman's estimation, could anyone question Struble's prestige as ranking naval officer in the Far East, for he had represented the Navy when Johnson and Bradley had recently visited the Philippines, and he would shortly represent the Navy in critical nego-tiations with Chinese Nationalist leader Chiang Kai-shek about defen-sive arrangements for Taiwan. In the following months, especially at Inchon, Struble would ensure that he was the naval officer most often seen in photographs with MacArthur, and that the public saw him as running naval operations in Korea. Flying his flag at sea and sporting the colorful nickname "Rip," he wanted the American public to perceive him as the Navy's counterpoint to MacArthur. Joy would operate in near obscurity in Tokyo.

The other major commander at sea reporting to Joy was Doyle, so for-tuitously on hand when the shooting started. It was self-evident that he would engage in amphibious operations from the moment that Truman committed American troops to the peninsula. Nearly every soldier sent to Korea from Japan, together with 99 percent of the logistical support, would go by sea. Doyle would get them there in his capacity as Commander Attack Force (CTF 90), operating at arm's length from Seventh Fleet. Without question, Doyle would command the specialized amphibious ships once an amphibious operation began, but concurrent command of the fast carriers and their escorts, as well as the warships providing naval gunfire support, was another matter. Joy had many issues to resolve.

Foremost was the fact that an amphibious assault was one of the most risky operations in war. Doctrine learned during World War II mandated that the attacking force take control of the sea and air before the landing began, so that no enemy ships or aircraft attacked the vulnerable amphibious ships and the troops exposed in landing craft and on the beaches. In the past war, the fast carriers had taken control of the sea and the air by attacking enemy ships and aircraft at their bases or en route to the landing area. Naval aviators in command of the fast carrier task forces preferred to steam unhampered, perhaps hundreds of miles from the landing area, to seize the initiative and attack the threatening enemy preemptively. In contrast, amphibious commanders normally wanted the fast carriers nearby, first to clear out the landing area and then to establish a barrier against any enemy attacks that might develop. This latter approach tied the carriers to the amphibious assault area, which the aviators dreaded because it compromised the mobility of the carriers.

Hence, the doctrine for how best to use the fast carriers during an amphibious assault had never been resolved. Moreover, should carrier air be in conjunction with, or separate from, Air Force tactical operations? (Navy–Marine tactical air doctrine and Air Force tactical air doctrine were so incompatible that joint air operations were to prove unworkable.) In Korea, especially in the first six months of the war, the nature of the threat was uncertain. North Korea had a miniscule navy and a weak air force, but the Navy worried that the Russians might oppose at any time an amphibious assault with their submarines and aircraft. China, too, was a dangerous threat because Beijing could try to invade Taiwan or attack American forces throughout the Far East. The fast carriers, together with their screen of cruisers and destroyers, had to be prepared accordingly.

In the beachhead area itself naval aircraft and warships had to attack and destroy enemy defenses ashore, especially those that would resist the landing. This posed another question: Who would command and control the naval forces engaged in this critical close support? Which ships did what and when and under whose command were complex issues that had to be resolved and understood by everyone beforehand?

Yet another complication was the participation of allied warships, especially those of the Royal Navy, which quickly arrived off Korea to augment the American fleet. To whom should they report? What tasks should they undertake? True, the Royal Navy and the United States Navy had been teammates first in the Atlantic and later in the Pacific during World War II, so in the summer of 1950 each was familiar to some extent with the other. Nonetheless, many details had to be worked out in the special circumstances of Korea.

Another great threat that could easily prevent an amphibious assault was enemy mines. Deployed in the waters transited by the amphibious assault shipping, they could delay, disrupt, and even defeat a landing operation. The Navy's minesweeping capability in the Pacific was very limited, but assuming more minesweepers could be made available, who would command them during an amphibious assault?

It was largely up to Joy to resolve these complex command and control issues almost overnight, so he relied upon doctrine, precedent, and his own judgment. The first test of Joy's operating policies materialized quickly. On 30 June, Truman authorized MacArthur to send troops to Korea. Joy's immediate task was to deploy the 1st Cavalry Division, then in Japan, to reinforce the disintegrating South Korean army and a few thousand soldiers of the 24th Infantry Division that had been airlifted to the peninsula. Doyle and his staff went to Joy's headquarters in Tokyo on 4 July to plan for the operation.

Unlike Joy's struggling staff, Doyle's staff contained some of the Navy's most expert amphibious planners, veterans of amphibious campaigns in the Pacific during World War II. With no more initial guidance than to land the division "somewhere in Korea," the staff went to work. At first the landing area was thought to be Inchon near Seoul on the west coast, but given the speed of advance of the NKPA the potential landing areas had to be moved to the south, a jump ahead of the North Koreans. Finally, Pohang-dong, a village on the east coast seventy miles north of Pusan, became the objective. It was chosen in the expectation the NKPA could not reach there by 18 July, the scheduled landing date. But given the fast advance of the NKPA down the peninsula, no one knew how close enemy troops would be to Pohang-dong.

Joy wanted the Seventh Fleet fast carriers to cover the landing in the event of enemy sea or air opposition, however unlikely. His request meant diverting the carriers from their immediate interdiction tasks and sending them to the waters off Pohang-dong. Trouble between Joy and Struble erupted when Struble learned that Joy had designated Doyle to command the aircraft carriers giving air cover to the landing. This move was unprecedented—not once during World War II had an amphibious commander ever given orders to a fast carrier. Struble predictably objected. The carriers should remain under his control, Struble argued. If Doyle wanted air cover, he should contact Joy who would order the carriers to give support. In other words, Struble would take orders from Joy but never from Doyle.

Sherman read Struble's objection and quickly responded in support. "I will not concur in placing carriers under command of [Doyle]," he wired to Radford, as one carrier admiral to another. "If naval command relationships cannot be worked out properly and harmoniously am prepared to consider your recommendations for changes in personalities." Radford was in Tokyo at the time, and he got the word to Joy. Struble retained control of the carriers.

Nonetheless, Joy and Doyle got what they wanted. Joy's operation order, with tacit approval of Sherman and Radford, directed Struble to provide close air support in the landing area as requested by Doyle. The latter would coordinate and control the operations of all aircraft in the objective area, and Doyle would define the objective area. Thus, while Struble would command the carriers per se, Doyle would decide when and where Struble's aircraft would be used. As it turned out the landing was unopposed. No air support was required, so the command relationship between Joy, Struble, and Doyle was not tested; however, it would be weeks later at Inchon.

Sherman and Radford continued to discuss the relationship between Joy and Struble. After a transpacific telephone conversation with Joy soon after the Pohang-dong operation, Sherman told Radford that he had considered an additional command echelon between Joy and Struble. He had rejected the idea because he did not want Struble to be subordinate to anyone junior to Joy. He was willing, however, to give Struble greater responsibilities that would allow naval aviator flag officers to take complete charge of the fast carrier forces. But for the moment Sherman was content with the status quo, and so matters remained.

Historian James A. Field later wrote about the growth and transition of Joy's staff as the war intensified:

[A]s his responsibilities and his forces grew, further difficulty was presented by the inadequacy of his staff and of those of subordinate commands. The total strength, officer and enlisted, of the NavFE staff at the end of June was 188; by November it would have reached 1,227. But in the first weeks, before reinforcements arrived, the job had to be done with what was on hand. Rarely in the history of twentieth century warfare can so many have been commanded by so few.

It was not done without effort. [Joy's] Plans Section went to heel and toe watches, 12 hours on and 12 off. The Operations Officer moved in a cot and did such sleeping as he could in his office; his people found themselves working a 12-hour day, with an additional four-hour night watch four days out of five. For Communications the situation became a nightmare as high-precedence traffic skyrocketed; in the first days the load of encrypted messages went up by a factor of 15, and was further complicated by great quantities of inter-service and U.S.-British dispatches.

Somehow they made do. Even as anguished requests were sent off to Washington for more personnel, the round the clock efforts of those on the spot were accomplishing the reorganization and redeployment of available naval strength. To Naval Forces [Far East] had now been added the Seventh Fleet and British Commonwealth units; with these accessions Admiral Joy had gained all that would be available until reinforcements could come from afar.

INCHON

MACARTHUR KNEW FROM the first shot fired by his troops on the Korean peninsula that, eventually, he would attack the NKPA from its rear with an amphibious assault. It was but a question of where and when, not whether. Even in the first days he had considered the immediate landing of the 1st Cavalry Division at Inchon, but the astonishing speed of the NKPA advance ended such thoughts. Within weeks the NKPA had forced the embattled Americans and the ROK Army into the Pusan Perimeter. MacArthur knew he could not possibly win the war if

TRUMAN AND
THE MARINES

IN AUGUST 1950, AS the North Korean People's Army steadily drove south, the 1st Provisional Marine Brigade kept the American line from disintegrating. Early one morning President Truman wrote a private letter to Congressman Gordon McDonough, a friend of long standing, who had recommended that the Commandant of the Marine Corps be made a member of the Joint Chiefs of Staff. Truman impulsively expressed his feelings toward the Marine Corps, a service he had criticized to varying extents over the years. It was, he wrote, "the Navy's police force" with a "propaganda machine that is almost equal to Stalin's." For unknown motives the congressman released the letter to the press, and it was published in the 18 September issue of *Time* magazine, coinciding with the Marines' victorious amphibious assault at Inchon.

The subsequent uproar rocked the White House with a deluge of phone calls, telegrams, and letters. Truman summoned his naval aide, Rear Adm. Robert L. Dennison, and his press secretary, Charlie Ross, and told them to do something "to get me out of this." Dennison recommended that Truman write a letter of apology to General Cates, Commandant of the Marine Corps, and ask him to publish it.

"The President of the United State can't apologize," Ross objected.

"I don't see why not," said Dennison, "if he's made a mistake, and I assume he has."

Truman agreed with Dennison and told him to draft the letter. Dennison phoned General Cates and asked him to come to the White House to help with the letter. "Hell no," replied Cates. Dennison wrote

President Harry S. Truman and General Cates, Commandant of the Marine Corps, enjoy an event at the Quantico, Virginia Marine base. Truman would anger Marine Corps leaders later in 1950 with an imprudent reference to the Marines as the "Navy's police force." (National Archives 127-N-A 407260)

the draft alone, Truman added his own twist, and it was quickly typed and signed.

"Wasn't I invited to some Marine Corps reunion here?" the president asked.

Dennison said he had been and regrets had been sent to the Marine Corps League.

"Well, I've decided to go," said Truman. It was to be held the next morning. The Secret Service worried about his security in light of the passions of the attendees, but Truman was adamant. "Ask Cates to meet me here and go with me," said Truman.

The next morning Cates waited outside while Truman met with his advisors in conference. Truman emerged accompanied by General Bradley.

"General Cates," said Truman, "we have decided I shouldn't go before the Marine Corps League." An awkward silence followed. Truman spoke again. "Well? What do you think about that? Are Marines afraid to speak up?"

"You never asked me," Cates replied.

"Well," Truman persisted. "What do you think?"

"I haven't told a soul about this, Mr. President," said Cates. "But I know that the Secret Service are already down there at the Statler, and the Marine Corps League must realize that you at least had the idea of going down to see them. Now, if you don't come, they'll think you are afraid to face them."

Truman banged his fist on a desk and said, "God damn it! I'll go!"

"Bradley's face was a study," Cates later said, for Bradley had attempted to dissuade President Truman from appearing.

Cates went on stage to great applause. When it became quiet, he said calmly, "Gentlemen, the President of the United States." The audience of Marine veterans was stunned and silent. Suddenly they erupted with cheers. "He gave a very simple but sincere talk," Dennison later said. "People were crying. A retired general on the platform removed a medal from his breast and pinned it on the President."

"You couldn't help liking Truman," said Cates long afterward, "even though he felt the way he did about the Marine Corps. Later he and I were talking over a glass of bourbon, and I told him he was absolutely right: the

Marine Corps did have a 'propaganda machine.' But we were fighting for our lives. What else would you do? Truman just grinned."

The two luckiest things that happened to the Marine Corps during his watch, said Cates, were the outbreak of war in Korea and the Truman letter. Cates observed: "They saved the Marine Corps."

the battlefield were confined to the Pusan area. He needed to widen the scope of UN operations.

The geographical characteristics of the Korean peninsula, as with any peninsula, begged for an amphibious assault behind enemy lines, the quintessential turning of the enemy's flank through sea power. As the NKPA had neither naval nor air forces left to protect its flanks and rear, its north-south lines of communication lay vulnerable and exposed to interdiction by naval guns, aircraft, and commando raids, and ultimately to an amphibious ground force slashing inland from a beachhead behind the enemy front. Deprived of supplies and reinforcements, the NKPA would be doomed.

As the United Nations army fought to survive during July and August, MacArthur saw not impending disaster, as did many in high places, but opportunity. The NKPA was exhausting its combat power at Pusan, and its flow of supplies over primitive roads was diminishing because of distance and naval and air interdiction. Banking that the Eighth Army could hold the perimeter, MacArthur reckoned that the time was near to counterattack with a massive amphibious assault. Getting it approved would be difficult. The JCS and the civilian leaders feared that Communist China was about to invade Taiwan and were concerned that Russia might be preparing to roll into Western Europe. Thus a third world war seemed imminent; and Korea, a diversion. Washington leaders were apprehensive and reluctant to take risks.

Then there was the matter of amphibious operations as a matter of principle. MacArthur, unlike some of his Army colleagues, believed in the utility of amphibious warfare. He had learned the art in the Pacific during World War II, from scratch operations in New Guinea to immense campaigns in the Philippines. In contrast, Bradley had publicly pronounced them obsolete, and the Air Force could hardly be expected to endorse what it had denounced as a matter of policy. And would Truman authorize the Marines to mobilize and lead an assault in light of his public excoriation of the Marines as an institution? If MacArthur prevailed, quantities of crow would be eaten in Washington.

The Navy as a matter of self-interest would of course have to support MacArthur in principle, but the details were another matter. Doyle first learned about Inchon in mid-July when MacArthur told him he wanted Doyle to land the 1st Cavalry Division there, even as the North Koreans were pushing the United Nations forces to the south. "I was 'slightly' upset," Doyle later said. "In fact I prayed, because the 1st Cavalry Division had no amphibious training whatsoever, and I had no ships to take them with. After the 1st Cavalry Division got to Pohang-dong . . . Inchon was moved again to the front burner."

Doyle and his staff began planning for the assault even though JCS approval was uncertain. When the Chiefs realized that Inchon violated every criterion for an amphibious assault area, they became apprehensive. The greatest incentive to press on was that, despite the risks, a landing there could reap considerable benefits. What MacArthur wanted, MacArthur ultimately would get.

Doyle was glad when Major General Smith, who would command the 1st Marine Division landing force, arrived on 22 August, three weeks before the tentative landing date of 15 September. Doyle had gotten to the point where he needed the troop commander's input to make the joint planning "fit together." After Smith met MacArthur that afternoon and listened to his pep talk, the Marine general, according to Doyle, "was no happier over the proposed landing area than I was."

The 15th of September had been chosen because it was the one day in the month when the tides would be optimum. "Twenty-four days remained," Smith later wrote, "in which to draw up plans, issue orders, reload the [1st Marine Division] in amphibious shipping at Kobe, forward to Korea the additional personnel and equipment to bring the 1st Provisional Marine Brigade up to strength; and then proceed to Inchon, rendezvousing with the units of the Brigade en route. On August 22nd the main body of the division was still at sea."

Smith's anxiety intensified when he met Major General Almond, MacArthur's chief of staff, who had been double-hatted as the commander of the combined landing force of Marine and Army troops, designated X Corps. (In this first meeting, Almond condescendingly addressed Smith as "son" although they were nearly the same age.) Almond and the Army planners had no amphibious experience and hence could not conceive the difficulties involved in getting ashore at Inchon against enemy opposition. "Almond considered an amphibious landing as a purely mechanical operation," Doyle later said, "which it might be if only the enemy would play dead. He was inclined to be arrogant and dictatorial and often confused himself with his boss." The Army planners thus considered the Inchon landing a fait accompli and concentrated on what would come later, the seizure of Seoul and the destruction of the NKPA.

Doyle was concerned that Almond and the Army staff were shielding MacArthur from the details of the planning and that MacArthur might not be aware of the risks. Almond, however, barred Doyle from MacArthur's door. "The General is not interested in details," Almond told Doyle.

"The General is making the decision," Doyle responded. "He must know what that decision involves, and I intend to see that he does so."

The opportunity to brief MacArthur came on 23 August when Sherman and General Collins, the Army chief of staff, arrived in Tokyo to consult with MacArthur on Inchon. As Collins later testified, he and Sherman had gone there "to find out exactly what the plans were. Frankly, we were somewhat in the dark, and as it was a matter of great concern, we went out to discuss it with General MacArthur."

Doyle and his staff were ready. In the inevitable discussion over the length and intensity of the prelanding bombardment, Doyle's gunnery officer illuminated the dangers by telling his audience that enemy shore batteries dominated the shipping channel and had to be eliminated. If all the emplacements in the reconnaissance photographs had guns and crews, he said, based on WWII experience it would take from four to five days to take them out. MacArthur commented that that length of time would take away the advantage of surprise and reveal allied intentions.

Sherman impulsively interrupted. "One or two days would be enough," he said. "I wouldn't hesitate to take a ship up off Wolmi-do after a day of bombardment."

"Spoken like a Farragut," MacArthur responded warmly.

Doyle was inwardly furious, for Sherman was a naval aviator, and Doyle felt he knew little, if anything, about amphibious operations. "Sherman was like the boxer's manager," Admiral Doyle later said, "who sends his tiger into the ring with the comforting words, 'Go in there, boy. He can't hurt us.' Admiral Sherman's remark was gratuitous, which I bitterly resented. We were never mutual admirers. However I held my tongue, and when I cooled off five or ten years later I called the episode the 'John Wayne Exchange.'"

As the briefing neared its end, Doyle spoke directly to MacArthur. No one had asked his opinion, said Doyle, but if he were asked his best answer was that Inchon "is not impossible."

"If we find we cannot make it," responded MacArthur, "we will withdraw."

"No, General," said Doyle. "We don't know how to do that. Once we start ashore we keep going." ("Now that may sound a bit 'John Wayne-ish' too," Doyle later admitted, "but the thought of our failure in an amphibious operation had never entered my mind, and it didn't then.")

In a lecture at the Naval War College in 1974, Doyle recalled MacArthur's closing pitch:

> MacArthur then began speaking, and he was superb. He gave his reasons for preferring Inchon to Posung-myon/Kunsan. Inchon was the closest point to Seoul, it cut the enemy's lines of communication to the south, and it had the element of surprise. The enemy would not believe that we would select Inchon, with all its hazards, as a spot to land. He compared Inchon to Wolfe's surprise landing and the capture of Quebec. He also said that a landing at Inchon was a 10,000-to-one shot and that for a five dollar bet he would win fifty thousand: he saw that Inchon and the capture of Seoul would end the war. He concluded with, "We shall land at Inchon and I shall crush them!" Now John Wayne couldn't top that, I'm sure. I have said of General MacArthur, many times, that if he had gone on the stage no one would have heard of his contemporary, another actor, John Barrymore.

Sherman was still worried about the hydrographic hazards and remained skeptical, despite his exclamation during Doyle's presentation. The next day, 24 August, Sherman spent better than an hour with MacArthur. When he emerged, Sherman had been convinced. "I wish I had that man's confidence," Sherman remarked to Joy.

Radford felt that the Navy and Marine Corps supported MacArthur and that the greatest opposition came from within the general's own staff. On a later trip to Tokyo Radford attended a somber planning conference and listened to a staff officer deliver an especially pessimistic assessment of the risks in a contemplated operation. "General," said MacArthur when it ended, "there is just one thing you've forgotten."

"What's that, General MacArthur?" the planner replied.

"My luck," said MacArthur.

Sherman and Collins returned to Washington to consult with the full JCS and Secretary Johnson, and the JCS approved Inchon on 29 August. MacArthur gave credit to Sherman for getting Washington's approval.

When Sherman returned to Washington, he summoned Burke into his office and told him about conditions in Tokyo. The Inchon invasion was going to be touch and go, said Sherman, and Radford had convinced the CNO that Joy's staff was not prepared to plan and coordinate wartime operations. Joy's chief of staff was Rear Adm. Albert K. Morehouse, a naval aviator a year senior to Burke. Although Morehouse had commanded an escort carrier in the last months of WWII, he was without wartime staff experience, and as an aviator, he was unfamiliar with amphibious operations. Hence, Joy desperately needed a staff flag officer with combat and staff experience to organize and direct its wartime responsibilities, especially for the immediate needs of Inchon. Burke was exactly the person Joy needed, for not only had he been a renowned wartime destroyer commander in the South Pacific, he had also become famous as chief of staff to Mitscher.

Having explained what Joy needed and why, Sherman asked Burke if he would go to Tokyo as Joy's deputy chief of staff, with the most immediate priority of directing the staff for the forthcoming Inchon assault. "Sherman still had misgivings," Burke later said. Sherman expressed his concern that Burke might be miffed that the billet would be of lesser stature than what he had held with Mitscher. Burke said he had no such reservations and would take the job, perhaps realizing he would be getting out of Washington and ridding whatever stigma remained from his role in the "revolt of the admirals." Burke's only immediate worry was that Joy's staff might resent his intrusion as the "expert" from Washington coming in to tell them how to run their business.

Sherman said it was possible but assumed Burke would quickly be welcomed. Sherman then introduced an additional role for Burke: to be his eyes and ears to apprise Sherman of unfolding developments through a super Blue Flag channel restricted solely to Sherman and Burke. For this purpose, he gave Burke a special set of encryption rotors. It was a preposterous idea for any number of reasons, the least of which was that Burke probably never had used a coding machine or the rotors that went with it.

Finding a communications specialist surreptitiously to decrypt and encrypt messages for him would raise suspicions within the staff. Then there was the moral issue: Would it be ethical for Burke to communicate directly with Sherman without Joy's knowledge?

Burke was in a bind, which he cleverly resolved. Anything he proposed to send to Sherman, said Burke, had to be shown first to Joy. Anything he got from Sherman he would also show to Joy. Sherman had to agree. As far as we know, not a single eyes-only message ever passed between Sherman and Burke. While Burke routinely drafted and often released Blue Flag messages to Sherman, they were always in Joy's name and had Joy's explicit or implicit approval.

As if Burke needed any incentive to go to Korea, Sherman gratuitously promised Burke any rear admiral's job he wanted once things were under control in Joy's bailiwick, perhaps within three or four months. Burke did not take the promise seriously, for even a CNO could neither predict nor control the conditions that influenced flag officer assignments. The upshot was that Burke proved invaluable to Joy through the crises of the last four months of 1950.

Joy summarized to Sherman and Radford in late January 1951 what Burke meant to him:

> Burke is my daily contact with top echelons GHQ where his influence is healthy for Navy. He is also staff coordinator for joint and combined operations as well as deputy chief of staff. Consider essential that flag officer with broad knowledge naval operations and experience in the service relationships fill this role. My 2 flag officers [Burke and More-house] cover contacts with 5 generals of Air Force and about 10 of Army on matters on which rank of conferees is important.

After periodic exchanges of messages between Sherman, Radford, and Joy, Burke finally got command of a cruiser division in May 1951. It would be a short tour, for he rejoined Joy in July as a member of the UN negotiating team for the fruitless armistice talks.

Doyle and Smith were still unhappy with the choice of Inchon, but while MacArthur orated and twisted arms and the JCS thought about it, their superb staffs pressed on with the planning. Within three days of Smith's arrival, they had completed a detailed plan for Inchon, and two days later they issued a preliminary operation order. Years later Doyle commented on the risks as he saw them at the time. "It has always been my conviction," he wrote, "that, given the enemy forces, an amphibious landing can be made anywhere if the commander is willing to accept the risk of the [estimated] losses. Naturally the commander would prefer the landing in a place where the losses could be minimized—which is all O. P. Smith and I were talking about."

Still to be determined was the command structure for the landing. Doyle would have preferred being in complete command at Inchon as he had been at Pohang-dong, where he had been responsible for planning and executing the landing of the 1st Cavalry Division. Struble, a fleet commander and senior to him by a full rank, had been left out of that operation; his sole task had been to provide carrier air support when and if Doyle asked for it, a role that in effect made him subordinate to Doyle. It would be different at Inchon: Struble intended to be in command with Doyle as his subordinate.

Indeed, in July Sherman, Radford, and Joy had discussed command relationships by phone and Blue Flag messages. While Joy had consistently advocated Doyle's position, Sherman refused to make Struble subordinate to anyone but Joy. More to the point, Sherman wanted Struble to have greater responsibilities under Joy and to delegate Seventh Fleet carrier operations to aviation flag officers. Hence, Joy had no choice but to appoint Struble the naval commander for Inchon.

On 25 August, presumably after conferring with Sherman during his visit to Tokyo, Joy informally told Struble he would command the Inchon operation. Joy made the assignment official when he issued his operation order and at Struble's suggestion designated him Commander Joint Task Force 7. The "joint" designation was intentional, for it gave Struble command and control over all the services in the landing. Thus, Almond would not take command of X Corps until he had established his command post ashore, in accordance with standard amphibious doctrine.

Neither of Struble's immediate subordinates, Doyle and Smith, was pleased at the prospect of working with him. When Smith had been Assistant Commandant of the Marine Corps, he had been assigned to work with the Navy establishing doctrine for command relationships in amphibious operations. The naval representative was Rear Adm. Jerauld Wright, who later became Commander in Chief, Atlantic Fleet. He and Smith got along well and were nearing agreement. Unexpectedly, Struble intervened in their discussions. "He put us back where we started," Smith later wrote. "About a year later he was overruled, and the present [1956]

DOYLE'S ARMY
PASSENGERS

THE INCHON TASK FORCE slogged up the west coast of Korea, and Vice Admiral Joy sent a final sitrep to CNO Sherman and Admiral Radford on D-day-minus-two: "General MacArthur and large staff now aboard *Mt. McKinley* in Sasebo after many changes prospective plans and dodging typhoon. Doyle has his hands full with all that staff and fighting a war too. Typhoon has probably made many Marines and soldiers appreciate the rigors of seagoing life but has had no other serious effect to date."

Doyle later recalled:

> [We] were rolling handsomely. After thirty minutes of that the orderly came from General MacArthur to the effect, "Couldn't the course be changed to eliminate the rolling?" It could be and I sent word to the captain. . . . He changed course just enough to ease the rolling, but, knowing that he had an appointment at Inchon, the captain soon came back to the uncomfortable course. Another message, another change, and finally we were in the lee of Korea. [The typhoon] was proceeding up the east coast and course was resumed for Inchon. It's helpful to be lucky.
>
> Breakfast the following morning was served in [the captain's] cabin. As was customary, my seat was at the head of the table, and I pointedly indicated a seat to my right when General MacArthur entered the cabin. Just as pointedly, he ignored the seat and took a seat at the far end of the table. An amusing thought came to my mind from an old story, and the punch line was, "Where Murphy sits is the head of the table." I didn't share my amusement.

Rear Admiral Doyle, Commander Task Force 90 and the Navy's premier amphibious expert, pauses on the flag bridge of *Mount McKinley* on the way to Inchon. Doyle had personally briefed his ship captains as to the vagaries of the landing sites and what he expected of the officers. (National Archives 80-G-423189)

Once the landing was under way, Major General Almond, commanding X Corps and embarked in *Mount McKinley* (AGC-7), asked Doyle to expedite the unloading of his communications van, so that it would be in place when he established his headquarters ashore and took command of the troops.

After Almond's inquiry, Doyle later wrote in a letter to Col. Robert Heinl:

> I asked the captain of the AKA [amphibious transport], which had the van, for the dope. The van was in fact Almond's living quarters and was loaded below the combat equipment. I informed the captain to let me know if further inquiry was made, and that I intended to tell Almond we'd cut a hole in the bottom of the ship to get it out. Apparently Almond did not follow up on the first inquiry.
>
> Several days later, Almond invited me ashore for dinner, and of course we spent the time over drinks before and after dinner in the van. It was a beautifully built and appointed small-size house trailer. Sturdier of course than those you'll meet on the highway. It had two couches which converted into beds . . . a head and a shower, ice box, desk, and a telephone which I suppose made it a communications van.
>
> It was my first look and I thought that war is not so tough for some soldiers. I contrasted that later at Hungnam when [Marine Maj. Gen.] Field Harris would come out to the ship for a hair cut and a bath.

doctrine of command relationships, almost identical with what Admiral Wright and I had agreed upon, was adopted and published."

Struble used his authority directly by not allowing the Air Force to participate at Inchon. "Like most naval commanders," Struble later wrote, "[I] was wary of the elaborate coordinating arrangements which always seemed necessary when Air Force units took part in invasions. As a veteran of Normandy [I] could well remember that despite all of the Air Force units present in England before the invasion, that the Air Force was unable to support the amphibious landing properly, and their efforts in this respect were practically nil." As Commander Seventh Fleet during interdiction operations, he had discovered that Air Force procedures were still cumbersome, if not unworkable. Knowing that having Navy, Marine, and Air Force planes in the same air space over Inchon would complicate coordination and control, Struble simply made Inchon a no-fly zone for the Air Force.

The Air Force was infuriated at its exclusion, as it wanted operational control over all aircraft flying over the Korean landmass, including carrier planes. More specifically, Lieutenant General Stratemeyer, commanding the Far East Air Forces (Joy's opposite number), wanted to control all aircraft operating from Korean and Japanese airfields, including Marine air and Navy ASW patrol and transport aircraft. Stratemeyer persisted in this demand well after Inchon, which Sherman, Radford, and Joy unreservedly opposed as yet another effort to unify the services, which had been a major feature of the "revolt of the admirals."

By late December Stratemeyer had gotten his proposal included in a comprehensive operation plan prepared for MacArthur's signature. MacArthur sent the plan to Joy for his review, and Joy told Sherman and Radford what he thought of it. It was an example, he said, of the continuing effort to make the Navy an auxiliary service. Sherman immediately responded. "You may quote me," he told Joy and Radford, "as having said that I will not accept any formula that puts naval aircraft under Air Force control merely because they are land based."

Radford had the last word. "As CNO states," he told Joy, "he will not accept any formula that puts naval aircraft under Air Force control just because they are land based. That particular question is settled. . . . It seems unfortunate but true that you have a continuing selling job to do where [MacArthur] is concerned and one which you have successfully accomplished so far. Good luck in your present efforts."

Sherman had returned to Washington, and JCS approval for Inchon, while likely, was still open. "Until that decision was received in Tokyo," Struble later wrote, "any planning had a preliminary and uncertain status about it." When JCS approval (albeit restrained) was received on 29 August, the invasion was on. Once assigned command of the Inchon assault, Struble stayed in Tokyo with a small staff and interjected himself into the planning already under way with Doyle, Smith, and their staffs. Most of their plans he approved, others he modified after discussion. Once he, Doyle, and Smith achieved an understanding, Struble got entree to MacArthur and informed him of the overall plan. (No CINCFE staff officer, even Almond, would refuse the imperious Struble admission to the inner sanctum!) "I told him what we were going to do," Struble later wrote. "I did not ask for any decisions." Struble issued his operation order two weeks before the landing, largely incorporating the detailed planning of the Doyle–Smith staffs. Operation orders from MacArthur and Joy authenticated Struble's order. The invasion force continued its preparations for Inchon.

The plans had assumed that the 1st Provisional Marine Brigade, then engaging the NKPA on the Pusan Perimeter, would be pulled out of line on or about 1 September and would rejoin its parent command, the 1st Marine Division, en route to Korea. Lieutenant General Walker, commanding the Eighth Army tenuously holding the perimeter, at first assented. But as the Marines began withdrawing, the NKPA broke through, so alarming Walker that he changed his mind and refused to release the brigade. The brigade had saved the perimeter, Radford later said, so it is understandable that Walker was reluctant to see it leave. Walker's apprehension was also predictable. When Radford, Sherman, and Collins had taken lunch with Walker at his headquarters near Taegu on 22 August, the headquarters had been set up to retreat on an hour's notice in the event the Communists broke through.

Almond was willing to leave the Marines with Walker and—presumably with MacArthur's approval—intended to substitute the 32nd Infantry Regiment to land at Inchon in the brigade's place. Such a change was preposterous. Smith and Doyle met with Joy on 2 September to express their dismay and seek resolution. The landing, they said, would be touch and go in any event. The experienced Marine brigade was essential to its success; the Army regiment had neither the training nor the experience for such a dangerous amphibious landing. Moreover, the Marines had been in combat; the soldiers of the 32nd had not been in action. It was madness to substitute raw soldiers for veteran Marines. Joy agreed and arranged a meeting with the Army commanders. Only two weeks remained before D-day.

Joy, Struble, Doyle, and Smith entered Almond's office the next day to confront Army generals Almond, Clark L. Ruffner, and Edwin K. Wright. Almond's attitude was that there was nothing to discuss. He confirmed his decision that the Marine brigade would remain at Pusan and that the 32nd Infantry would take its place in the first wave at Inchon. Joy expressed his objections and became infuriated that Almond had so little understanding of amphibious warfare and the dangerous consequences of excluding the Marine brigade. Hot words flared between Almond and Joy while the others watched the fireworks. Finally, Joy paused, turned to Smith, and asked for his opinion.

Smith explained the danger of last-minute substitutions. If the 32nd Infantry was forced upon him, he would not allow its soldiers to land in the first wave because it could not do what the Marine brigade could do. In effect, explained Smith, Almond was proposing to reduce unacceptably the combat power of the landing force to the point where the risk of failure would be unacceptable.

Almond was unmovable. "General Headquarters" would take that risk, he said. General MacArthur would be on Doyle's flagship and would take the responsibility for calling off the landing if necessary. Almond's inability to comprehend the impossibility of withdrawing once the landing was under way appalled the naval commanders.

Struble proposed a compromise: Use the Marine brigade at Inchon as planned, and station a regiment from the 7th Infantry Division as a floating reserve for Walker at Pusan. Almond agreed to think about it, and the meeting ended. An hour later the commander of the Marine brigade phoned Smith and said the brigade would be released to land at Inchon.

Joy was still worried that MacArthur might change his mind at the last minute and said so in a Blue Flag to Sherman and Radford summarizing the meeting. Joy reported:

> Made strong representations that without this brigade the success of the operation would be jeopardized beyond reasonable risk. Other units untrained in amphibious operations suggested by [MacArthur] staff to substitute for brigade in landing not considered acceptable substitutes by us. . . . Situation now clarified but lack of understanding of need for trained assault troops for amphibious operations plus Marines' demonstrated superior ability to prevent enemy advances has resulted in unwillingness of [Walker] to release brigade and reluctance of [MacArthur] to order it released. A new serious enemy breakthrough may cause Marines to be ordered not to withdraw. Believe [MacArthur] would continue forthcoming operation even without brigade. Will advise developments.

Radford replied in support: "Concur wholly with position you have taken regarding utter necessity inclusion of First Marine Brigade as part of assault force. Further consider that you are entirely justified in expressing view that without brigade the force will be deficient in qualified amphibious troops to a degree which renders operation as a whole unjustifiably hazardous."

Joy and Struble finally were able to confirm that the Marines would land in full strength. "The operation has a good chance of success," Joy reported a week before the landing. "The great benefits accruing if

Having watched the first wave of assaults on Wolmi-do, MacArthur takes time to relax on the flag bridge of *Mount McKinley* (AGC-7) with his senior advisors, left to right, Doyle, Wright, and Almond. (National Archives SC 348448)

operation successful warrant the great calculated risks involved.... Joy says go ahead—and pray."

Struble had much the same assessment a day later: "Consider that military, political and psychological advantages accruing if total operation successful warrants acceptance risks involved."

MAGGIE HIGGINS
AT INCHON

WE STILL WONDER TODAY why the Inchon invasion surprised the North Koreans, for the imminent assault was common knowledge. Some eighty-six correspondents, representing six countries, knew about it. They occupied some nineteen ships in the amphibious task force, and a platoon of public affairs officers, as Robert Heinl later wrote in *Victory at High Tide* (1979), were dispatched to "serve and yet curb this mettlesome crew."

On the day after the Inchon landing, correspondent Marguerite "Maggie" Higgins of the *New York Herald Tribune* asked to see Rear Admiral Doyle. The admiral had already heard of her. By tenaciously overcoming sexist obstacles she had landed with the fifth wave on D-day, had seen combat up close, and was becoming legendary for her extraordinary bravery and toughness. That morning she had gone ashore with MacArthur and had returned to Doyle's flagship *Mount McKinley* to file her story. "Naturally I agreed to see her," Doyle later recalled, "and she was brought to my cabin. Miss Higgins was tall and slender, she was dressed in a coverall, and her short, light brown hair was tousled and in ringlets. She had a smudge of dirt on her cheek. She was beautiful."

Higgins told Doyle she wished to remain overnight in *Mount McKinley*. Doyle, an officer and gentleman of the old school, had a problem. Joy had decreed that women correspondents had to be billeted in the hospital ship. Doyle not only was bound by this order, but there was no room on his flagship because MacArthur and his staff, as well as the Marine staffs, were living aboard. Thus if she remained overnight, explained Doyle, it would

Vice Admiral Struble and Major General Smith (in Marine battle dress) flank General MacArthur as they come ashore at Inchon, accompanied by staff and a gaggle of correspondents. Smith's Marines were already on the road to Seoul. Correspondent Maggie Higgins is among the crowd, having intimidated Rear Admiral Doyle into allowing her to remain in his flagship so she could see the action. (National Archives 80-G-421944)

deprive four officers of their room, and in addition it would tie up a head for her exclusive use.

Higgins dismissed Doyle's objections. She wanted to be treated the same as the male correspondents. If they could remain overnight, so could she, and that meant sleeping on the flagship. "Furthermore," she declared, "you'd be surprised how long I can go without using the head."

Doyle was momentarily flustered. "Interesting," he mumbled. He recovered his poise. "Nevertheless, you must go to the hospital ship tonight."

Weather intervened, preventing any boat traffic the remainder of the night. Doyle was stuck with Maggie Higgins. The admiral later recalled,

"I sent for the bull surgeon and learned that he could give Marguerite a cot in the dispensary and move the corpsman now occupying the space. So that crisis was solved. I was grateful that it made my inevitable defeat acceptable."

Doyle later met Higgins in Tokyo: "We had a pleasant visit and a few drinks at the former Imperial Hotel—a fond memory. She wrote well, and she had magnificent courage. Months later back in the states, one of my attention callers called my attention to an article in the *Ladies' Home Journal* which she had written. She had included a paragraph referring to the incident on the *Mount McKinley* and giving me my comeuppance but good."

The Inchon lancas indeed successful, and afterward in his action report Smith expressed his reasons why it went well:

> Under the circumstances . . . it is my conviction that the successful assault of Inchon could have been accomplished only by United States Marines. This conviction, I am certain, is shared by everyone who planned, executed, or witnessed the assault. My statement is not to be construed as a comparison of the fighting qualities of the various units of the Armed Forces. It simply means that because of their many years of specialized training in amphibious warfare, in conjunction with the Navy, only the United States Marines had the requisite "know-how" to formulate the plans within the limited time available and to execute those plans flawlessly without additional training or rehearsal.
>
> To put it another way, I know that if any other unit of our Armed Forces had been designated as the Landing Force for the assault on Inchon, that unit would have required many, many months of special-ized training, including joint training with the Navy, which is a regular part of the Marines everyday life.

TO THE YALU AND BACK

THE WAR SEEMED NEARLY OVER. The landing at Inchon, the recapture of Seoul, and the breakout at Pusan created a momentum that drove the

NKPA out of South Korea. The Truman administration and the JCS authorized MacArthur to cross the 38th parallel and invade North Korea. Exactly what MacArthur was expected to do there, and how he was to do it, became a contentious debate between MacArthur and Washington. Was he to advance to the Yalu—the China border—and then permanently occupy North Korea? Or was he expected to accomplish something less than that? The JCS directives were laden with qualifications and rules of engagement to reduce the risks of war with China, which would want neither MacArthur's army near its border nor North Korea permanently occupied by the ROK Army and its allies.

"Korea was the first war to be fought from Washington," Radford later commented. According to Radford, the JCS seemed incapable of planning or foresight. Once the Inchon invasion was a near certainty, it was obvious that American and ROK forces would have to cross the 38th parallel to exploit the victory, and in particular to close the trap on the NKPA. Not until 27 September, twelve days after the Inchon landing, did the JCS authorize MacArthur to enter North Korea to destroy the NKPA. Radford speculated that the delay in reaching this political decision might well have retarded operations after Inchon, enabling many North Korean troops and units to escape northward up the east coast because the Americans were unable to get across their line of retreat.

Enamored with the success of Inchon, MacArthur ordered a follow-up amphibious landing at Wonsan on the eastern coast of North Korea to block the retreat of NKPA forces there. Joy and his staff thought the idea wholly unnecessary. In their judgment, the X Corps could reach Wonsan faster and easier by simply marching overland from Inchon, compared to transporting it there by sea. Joy expressed his objections to MacArthur's acting chief of staff, Maj. Gen. Doyle O. Hickey, who was sympathetic but said that MacArthur had made up his mind and nothing would change it. Joy resignedly returned to his headquarters to make the necessary plans.

Joy and Burke had become increasingly aware of the threat of mines, the sole means by which the North Koreans could prevent amphibious assaults along their coasts. The Soviets, who were experts in mine warfare, were providing the North Koreans with an arsenal of mines and technical assistance. The North Koreans could deploy the mines in their home waters using small craft and could easily predict the most likely beaches on which the Americans would land next. Enemy capability became intention became fact. Reconnaissance planes sighted hundreds, then thousands of mines in the waters off Wonsan, forcing Joy and Burke to think about how to eliminate them. Otherwise, there could be no landing and an embarrassing admission that fishing boats had denied the United States Navy control of the sea. Joy had no intention of telling MacArthur that the Navy could not carry out his orders.

Because of postwar demobilization and institutional neglect, the Navy had but a handful of minesweepers, small ships with wooden hulls outfitted with paravanes and other special equipment. Many more would be needed for any hope of clearing the mines surrounding the approaches to Wonsan before the 20 October D-day. Responding to an early warning from Joy, Sherman recommended that Japanese minesweepers augment the handful of American minesweepers. Having received the CNO's implicit blessing, Burke set about getting Japanese permission.

Burke knew that the Japanese government employed perhaps a hundred minesweepers in a continuing program to clear the thousands of American mines, emplaced during the war, from Japanese waters. How was Burke to get permission and cooperation from the Japanese to send their minesweepers and expert crews (largely former officers and Sailors of the defunct Imperial Japanese Navy) to Korean waters? The legal, political, and moral obstacles seemed insuperable.

Burke decided to find a way without asking permission from higher authority because from past experience the answer would be no. "If you're going to do anything quickly," Burke later said, "then you've got to do it before you get permission to do it. But you must be sure it's the right thing to do."

Wanting to learn about the culture and the thinking of his former Japanese enemies, and Asians in general, Burke had already developed a good relationship with Kichisaburo Nomura, an Americanophile who had been Japan's foreign minister and later envoy to the United States at the time of Pearl Harbor. Burke liked and respected the old retired admiral and was accustomed to asking his advice and counsel.

Conditioned in the ways of the Japanese mind by Nomura, Burke contacted Takeo Okubo, the civilian director of the Maritime Safety Agency that operated the minesweepers. Burke met Okubo when the officer briefed members of the Japanese government. Burke went to Okubo's

The underwater demolition team from high-speed transport *Diachenko* (APD-123) pores over charts of a North Korean minefield off Wonsan. The operation to clear Wonsan would take fifteen days and claim three U.S. and two allied minesweepers. (National Archives)

office and laid out charts of Wonsan, incidentally revealing classified information to a Japanese civilian who was not cleared for such material, a risk that Burke took upon himself.

"This is where we are going," said Burke. "It's heavily mined, we have only twelve minesweepers, and we need more."

Okubo understood and agreed.

"The operation has begun, troops are loading into transports, and there is no turning back," said Burke.

Okubo understood and agreed.

"We need your minesweepers," said Burke.

Okubo again understood. Nevertheless, he explained, the Japanese constitution, imposed by MacArthur, did not allow Japan to go to war, which it would be doing if its minesweepers entered Korean waters in support of the American war effort. The problem was beyond Okubo's authority to resolve.

Burke attempted to counter Okubo's reservations. "You can do it," he insisted. The minesweepers were unarmed and would neither be committing an act of war nor harming any North Koreans. "You sweep mines," said Burke, "you get rid of mines. It's the same as having your own cargo ships there manned by civilian crews, as you do now."

"It's a greater problem than that," said Okubo. "I can't make a decision on that."

"Who can?" asked Burke.

Okubo said Japanese Prime Minister Shigeru Yoshida, whom Burke also knew from briefings. Burke said he would see Yoshida, knowing that Okubo would phone ahead saying Burke was on the way.

Burke audaciously set off to see the head of the Japanese government on a matter of the greatest delicacy, with neither the knowledge nor the permission of either MacArthur or the State Department. Had his mission backfired his career would have been over.

Yoshida received Burke and politely listened to him explain the urgency of his needs. No longer a blunt warrior but a subtle diplomat, Burke did not want to compel Yoshida to say either yes or no. Burke listened carefully to the nuances and intricacies of the Japanese language translated into English, and he sensed that Yoshida was expressing his implied assent to using the minesweepers. "I wish I'd had a tape recorder then," Burke later reminisced, "and could have recorded the exact wording, because he didn't agree and he didn't disagree."

Burke hustled back to Okubo to negotiate the details with him and his deputy, Kyozo Tamura, formerly a captain in the Imperial Japanese Navy, whom Burke discovered to be brilliant, pragmatic, and undoubtedly one of the greatest minesweeping experts in the world. Both Japanese leaders cooperated enthusiastically. The three men agreed that the Japanese would assign twenty minesweepers to Wonsan and pay double wages to the crews as an incentive.

Burke had gotten what he wanted, and MacArthur approved their use. Meanwhile Sherman scraped the barrel for other resources, and the combined American–Japanese minesweeping force began clearing the approaches to Wonsan.

Struble demanded of Joy that he be given direct control of the Wonsan minesweeping operations, both in light of his experience as Pacific mine force commander at the end of World War II and in his capacity as commander of Joint Task Force 7, as he had been at Inchon. Burke would not hear of it, for he trusted neither Struble's expertise nor his sensitivity in dealing with the Japanese. Consequently, the minesweeping operations came directly under Doyle as the amphibious task force commander.

As events were to prove, the mine clearing took longer than anticipated, and three minesweepers were sunk. Even though ROK forces had captured Wonsan by land, making an amphibious landing unnecessary, MacArthur would not scrub the operation. Hence, the Marines languished offshore while generals and admirals fumed and squabbled. Eventually mine-free lanes to the beach were cleared allowing the Marines to make an administrative landing on 26 October, six days after the planned D-day.

To what extent the Japanese minesweepers were used and what they accomplished at Wonsan is not to be found in open literature. Analysis of recently released Blue Flag messages between Struble and Joy indicate that ten were employed at Wonsan, ten in other harbors, and that one hit a mine in Wonsan. Their presence was diplomatically sensitive, so Struble directed the senior naval officers at Wonsan to ask the press not to report their employment. Cagle and Manson did not record their activity in *The Sea War in Korea* (1957); the book's description of the operation was in large measure based upon contemporary interviews with the participants who apparently did not talk about the Japanese, or if they did Cagle and Manson chose not to record it. *United States Naval Operations, Korea* (1962) by Field simply records that eight contract Japanese sweepers were employed at Wonsan, with no further details.

Burke later recalled the jubilation after Wonsan:

People were walking on clouds and were absolutely confident that the war had been won. There was not very much discussion about the possibility of North Korea pulling up her socks and being able to attack, because it didn't seem possible for that. But there was very little discussion about the Chinese possibility, or the Soviets' possible intervention . . . They thought this was too improbable. At the same time there was no discussion that I know of about the defense of South Korea.

As September evolved into October the Chinese government announced in various ways that it would not tolerate American troops in North Korea, yet the Americans remained skeptical. Burke went to his principal counselor, Admiral Nomura, to learn his opinion. "They mean it, they're warning you," said Nomura, "if you go north of the 38th

Parallel they'll come in. They'll have to do that to save face, to live up to their words."

Burke asked if, under the circumstances, Nomura thought the Americans should invade North Korea. Nomura said, "Yes. You've got to defeat them now. They started this war, so they have to be punished."

"That was my first indication," Burke later said, "that China would come into the war."

Despite China's verbal threats and reports of Chinese soldiers south of the Yalu River, MacArthur's huge intelligence staff continued to believe that the Chinese neither were in North Korea in numbers nor were they about to enter the war. Joy had but a handful of intelligence officers, who had to depend upon the Army for raw data, but they interpreted the data far differently—the Chinese were coming. His instincts conditioned by Nomura, Burke thought so as well. As they would throughout the Chinese offensive, Joy and Burke relayed to Sherman and Radford the manic-depressive atmosphere at MacArthur's headquarters tempered with their own steady assessments. Key messages (paraphrased) from Admiral Joy are summarized below:

> 3 October: MacArthur will issue ultimatum to North Korea in a few days.
>
> 8 October: MacArthur's staff working on plans for occupation of Korea (something of little interest to Joy). . . . Although end of war appears near, there may be enough strength left in North Korea to effect unpleasant resistance. They are beginning to fight as if they expect appreciable help from Manchuria, General Walker notwithstanding.
>
> 14 October: Herewith the future ground phases. a) Eighth Army will attack Pyongyang from the south and X Corps from the west. b) When they merge X Corps will be dissolved and return to Japan. c) Immediately when war is over Eighth Army will be withdrawn and United Nations occupation commander established. As many United States troops as feasible will be withdrawn leaving minimum military.

MacArthur's apprehension became evident in early November as more Chinese entered North Korea.

> 7 November [morning]: We estimate that the situation 10 days ago was not as rosy as pictured and now not as depressing as Army intelligence states, although it is not now good.

7 November [evening]: Discussed situation with General Hickey [MacArthur's acting chief of staff]. I believe recent dispatches from MacArthur may be misinterpreted as unduly alarming. My estimate of the situation follows: . . . There are quite a few targets in North Korea if we can find them and apparently the Chinese will send more over if we run short. The Army still has potential to knock hell out of as many Chinese communists as they want to push into the hopper. The Air Force and the Navy can help the Army do it.

11 November: Plans are being made for Eighth Army to attack on November 15th. Bridges over Yalu should be down by then. X Corps appears to us Sailors to be over-extended and with regiments so far separated in mountainous country they lack mutual support. Also no reserve. If enemy attacks any regiment with strength there will be great need for lots of air support for which Struble is prepared.

Struble and his Seventh Fleet carriers were indeed needed to support the Army. After discussions with the Army and Air Force, Joy told Struble what to expect.

Notified General Hickey that the carriers were going up to fight and not to act only as a reservoir if needed, which was concurred in. General Hickey stated not for dissemination that North Korea outside U.N. control was to be destroyed since back of enemy resistance must be broken quickly. I suggested however that power plants and dams not be destroyed without specific orders of MacArthur. More power to you.

Predictably the JCS ordered MacArthur not to attack the Yalu bridges, then relented after his outraged protests, with the provision that Navy and Air Force pilots were not to fly over Chinese territory nor fire on any targets on the north bank of the Yalu. Rear Admiral Ewen, commanding the carrier task force (Task Force 77), was furious, for Chinese antiaircraft batteries on the north bank could fire with impunity on his aircraft attacking the bridges. The suicidal rules of engagement remained in effect notwithstanding.

The need to take out the bridges seemed about to be overtaken by events, for by 23 November MacArthur and his staff had regained their confidence. The Eighth Army in the east resumed its offensive, and it would, they predicted, be at the Yalu in two weeks. The 2nd Infantry Division would be withdrawn early to the United States if, as Joy put it, "North Korea becomes a pushover." The Marines and the 24th Infantry Division

On 18 November 1950, Task Force 77 Skyraiders from carrier *Leyte* (CV-32) attacked the Yalu River bridges, dropping three spans of the highway bridge connecting Sinuiju, North Korea, with the Manchurian city of Antung. The JCS strictly prohibited pilots from penetrating Manchurian airspace, creating tactical problems for the aviators. (National Archives)

would follow shortly. The occupation plan was almost ready but not approved, for it was "subject to radical changes," Joy concluded.

"Army still buoyantly hopeful war will be over by Christmas," Joy reported on 26 November. "General MacArthur flew over North Korean Army and near Yalu and is optimistic, but there may be sneakers left in unpredictable oriental war. [Burke and I] have cautious but hopeful outlook." Burke prudently had begun to put transport ships in reserve, foreseeing the possibility that the troops and their equipment might well have to be evacuated if the Chinese struck in force.

Joy and Burke realized the next day that something was dreadfully wrong when, just past midnight on 28 November, they received a warning from a lieutenant commander attached to the 24th Infantry Division. "Big Ears report for your eyes only. Situation here becoming critical. Borders on desperate. Could result demand for evacuation plan Chinnampo [west coast of North Korea] or further north. Request for all Navy air may be made and needed. Not my business but you should know." Acting on the warning from the front, Joy and Burke immediately alerted Struble and Doyle. "Rumor may be unfounded," they concluded, "but be ready for drastic redeployment."

Army communicators in I Corps had encrypted and sent the message, so Joy and Burke had reason to believe that the front-line troops hoped that Joy would take the warning directly to MacArthur, which he did. Their concern was well founded: MacArthur's staff confirmed that the Chinese army had attacked in great force during the night of 27–28 November and assessed the situation as serious but not yet critical. "However," they advised Sherman and Radford, "we are preparing for drastic action nevertheless. Army should be able to hold."

Joy watched developments unfold throughout 28 September, and late in the day reported to Sherman and Radford that the ground situation was not good. MacArthur and his staff were depressed, he said, yet Joy saw no immediate danger of a collapse or need for evacuation, for he still had faith in the fighting ability of the Marines and soldiers. But the Eighth Army and X Corps were fighting separate and uncoordinated battles, and for them to survive Joy thought that the Army had to fix its command structure and corps boundaries.

Within the next forty-eight hours, Joy and Burke fully grasped the gravity of the unfolding disaster. General Hickey on the morning of 30 November called a conference of his chief staff officers, the Air Force, and Burke. He was not an alarmist, said Hickey, but there comes a time when facts have to be faced, and the things he feared might happen, had happened. It was apparent to him that the Chinese intended to commit all their forces to battle in an attempt to annihilate totally the United Nations forces. It was quite possible evacuations would be necessary on both coasts, and that some large troop concentrations might not be able to fight their way to the coasts.

He asked Burke about the rate of possible evacuations.

Burke replied that the Navy had already prepared an evacuation plan for either or both Inchon and Wonsan on short notice. Hickey warned him to keep the information concerning an evacuation in the highest secrecy, but to take preparatory steps without revealing their intentions. "Steady on," said Burke as he left the Army doomsayers.

Joy and Burke afterward pondered what Hickey had said and what they, in turn, had to pass on to their bosses in Washington and Pearl

Harbor. As naval officers reporting upon their Army counterparts engaged in a battle to survive, theirs was a ticklish role. Were they competent (or perhaps presumptuous) to judge what was happening in chaotic battles on Korean soil hundreds of miles away from Tokyo? And would they, if roles hypothetically were reversed, have felt that generals were privileged to judge the employment of naval forces engaged in a decisive fleet action?

But Joy and Burke did not have time for reflecting. They had to tell Sherman and Radford *something*, and soon, and what they ultimately reported had to be so phrased as not to cause Washington, already jittery from MacArthur's alarums, to over react. Well, Sherman and Radford were solid; they could handle harsh truths. With Joy beside him, Burke took a blank message pad and began to write.

It was clear to them, Burke wrote, that the mood in MacArthur's headquarters was defeatist. The Army wanted to cut and run to another Dunkirk. A hasty evacuation suggested by Hickey was possible, but what of those Army troops that Hickey had said were isolated inland? Were they to be abandoned? The Army could hold on, they reckoned, if there was but one overall commander (the dual command of Walker and Almond prevented coordination and cooperation), and if that commander concentrated his forces across the peninsula from Chinnampo to Wonsan where the Navy could provide flanking support through the ports. (Burke had suggested this earlier to the Army staff but had been ignored as being out of his realm.)

Now they made their most compelling point to Sherman and Radford. An evacuation of the peninsula would be disastrous to America's international interests.

If an evacuation becomes necessary the war from then on will be a purely naval war. If this happens our Army will be demoralized and it will be a long time before we again venture into land warfare. Realities dictate that the position of the United States in the Pacific from now on may be determined by the Navy's capabilities in a maritime warfare. [We] are prepared for this contingency but it is desirable that such forces as are trained and available be readied for onward routing in case this evacuation takes a long time or we lose much shipping in the process.

Parenthetically they added that the Air Force was planning to attack targets in Manchuria and had asked for naval participation. The Navy

A Corsair, barely visible through the rising smoke, has just struck enemy troops, permitting the exhausted Marines to continue their arduous march to the sea. Navy and Marine Corps close air support was critical to the Marines' reaching an evacuation port. (*Naval Aviation News*)

responded it would not be an appropriate use of carrier aircraft, which were needed to support the troops fighting for their lives. The chasm between the Navy and the Air Force on the proper use of tactical air could not have been more evident.

Even before reporting to Sherman and Radford, Joy had sent a "Flash" precedence message for admirals only, just before midnight on 30 November. It directed Struble and Doyle to put their ships on two-hour notice and otherwise prepare for probable troop evacuations, warning them to maintain secrecy in order not "to jeopardize the Army's present intentions." In other words, Joy knew that the Army was at the breaking point, and he feared they might bolt and run to the nearest port if they knew ships were on the way. All of the senior flag officers in contact with the Army shared this concern, and collectively they would try by various means to stiffen the Army resolve to fight it out on the Korean peninsula.

Joy revealed these naval preparations in a report to Sherman and Radford late at night on 1 December, which disclosed that the Army was ready to abandon Korea and withdraw to Japan. MacArthur was apparently in seclusion and no longer given to the histrionics that marked his performance before Inchon. "The Army has been informed," Joy reported, "that we believe they can hold the bridgeheads at both Inchon and Hungnam indefinitely with the help of naval gunfire support and naval air as well as Air Force air and Army tanks and artillery. They agree with us and they recognize the power we can provide."

Joy's next paragraph was stunning.

> The Army believes however that the Chinese communists have made a decision to throw in all the manpower necessary to overrun Korea regardless of the after effect this will have on a Third World War. The Army believes too that if the United States attacks Manchuria or China that it would not be advisable to hold a bridgehead in Korea but that it would be preferable to return our troops to Japan to defend the Japanese Islands. [Emphasis added. Apparently MacArthur felt that China was not unwilling to precipitate a third world war. He seems to have reasoned that bombing Manchuria and China, which he advocated, would not help the situation in Korea but would accelerate the start of a third world war, which he would fight out behind the barricades in Japan. The old general had lost his senses.]
>
> The success of establishing a dependable perimeter is dependent upon our ability to disengage some forces for sufficient time to establish defensive positions and supplies. So far this fundamental requirement had not been met by Eighth Army and may not be possible by X Corps. . . .
>
> Am holding 40 cargo ships in ballast as they become available. Used 25 for 2 divisions so 40 should do the trick.
>
> We do not want to be alarmist and for guidance this report is more optimistic than the outlook presented at Army headquarters. Army generals Hickey and Wright are conservative men who know their job and have a pretty good grasp of naval power. Their opinions are more pessimistic than this report but they too believe we can hold a beachhead with naval help.

Radford read Joy's reports and, taking a global view, believed the Chinese attack presaged even more serious attacks elsewhere, perhaps the third world war that MacArthur seemed to be accepting. Naturally, Joy focused solely on Korea and had requested that the attack carrier *Boxer*

(CV-21) and other ships be dispatched to the theater. The situation, he explained to Radford, was not as bad as the Army was reporting, and he did not intend to be alarmist; nonetheless, the ground forces needed all the air and naval gunfire support the Navy could provide.

Radford phoned Joy to assess exactly what kind of naval reinforcements were needed and when. Radford already had sent nearly everything he could to Korea; he could scratch for a few more ships, but if he did it would "aggravate the overall unsatisfactory readiness for a general emergency which is a major concern at this time. This readiness has progressively declined because of the continuing demand of the *limited emergency* [emphasis added] in Korea." After talking with Joy, Radford felt that the situation, while serious, was not as grave as he had first supposed. He told Joy he regretted he could not send reinforcements but "trusted that he would understand that the very emergency which caused him so much concern increased the probability of a general emergency for which the whole Pacific fleet must be prepared."

Radford's concerns of a war elsewhere ultimately proved unfounded, but at the time such perceptions conditioned the thinking of the top leaders. When Radford told Sherman of his conversation with Joy, Sherman directed the Pacific Fleet commander to keep *Bataan* (CVL-29) and *Bairoko* (CVE-115) available to Joy. The Chinese attack may have seemed a "limited emergency" to Radford, but Sherman saw clearly that the Navy had to do everything in its power to support MacArthur and keep the Army and Marine Corps in Korea. Moreover, Sherman had to ensure that whatever the outcome of the Chinese attack, no one could ever find cause to blame the Navy for not having done all in its power to support MacArthur. God help the Navy if MacArthur ever had reason to make that kind of accusation.

Burke saw first hand the defeatism shown by some elements of the Army. "[W]e could have held the Chinese ground forces," he later said, "but as it turned out we didn't, we couldn't."

> It got to be pretty desperate. The Chinese knocked the hell out of the Army on the west coast. The 2nd Infantry Division came back routed. They lost their elementary wisdom of how to fight a war. They kept to the road instead of putting out flanking detachments, and, of course, the Chinese overwhelmed them.
>
> I talked to the division commander as soon as he got back to Japan. He had been sent back in disgrace . . . he didn't know what had happened

to him. He cried, a major general, sat there and cried, telling me what he thought happened. He just lost command of his outfit. He lost his own ability to think, and the first thing a man's got to do when his force is knocked to pieces is to gather them together and get them to fight, or he loses them all.

He didn't do that. We just had the hell kicked out of us.

Joy had issued contingency plans on 13 November for emergency evacuations should they be necessary, and O. P. Smith had told Doyle he intended to slow the rate of advance as his 1st Marine Division neared the Yalu. Almond urged him to move faster, but Smith sensed a Chinese ambush and proceeded cautiously and deliberately. "Thank God he did," Doyle later wrote, "for on 27 November the Marines ran into massive Chinese Communist formations that would have gobbled up a dispersed division piecemeal. As it was, upon receipt of orders to return to Hungnam, the 1st Marine Division formed a legion which marched through the enemy like Caesar through Gaul, destroying seven Chinese divisions and ending the Communist offensive capability in eastern North Korea."

Once Doyle foresaw that an evacuation at Hungnam was probable, he went to Joy with furrowed brow and a presumptuous demand. "Doyle complained to me," Joy later wrote, "that at Inchon Struble was continually in his hair and interfering with his exercise of command." Doyle insisted that Struble, his nominal senior by a full rank, be kept clear of Hungnam and that Doyle have absolute command of the operation. Joy could have told Doyle to follow orders, but perhaps he was unsure whether Doyle would obey, so deep-seated was his antipathy. We will never know. Joy acceded to Doyle's demand. Joy later explained: "As Doyle was more valuable to the success of Hungnam than Struble I thought it best to keep them separated as much as possible." Struble would of course object bitterly, but such was the urgency of the evacuation that Joy was willing to take the heat.

This was the third time that Joy had denied Struble the command prerogatives he felt his rank deserved, the first at Pohang-dong at the beginning of the war, then over the Wonsan minesweepers. Joy's decision regarding Hungnam contradicted the policy he had received earlier from Sherman, who had insisted that Struble be in overall command of amphibious operations when carriers and fleet support were involved. But

Sherman, too, could not afford to affront Doyle, who was indispensable, and Struble was not. Doyle got his way, but Hungnam would be his last hurrah, and his finest hour.

When Joy met with Doyle at Hungnam to discuss the forthcoming evacuation, he was accompanied by Lieutenant General Shepherd, who commanded the Pacific Fleet Marine Force and was the senior Marine in the Pacific. Doyle was pleased when Shepherd remained with him when Joy returned to Tokyo. "Insofar as I knew," Doyle later wrote,

> Shepherd remained simply as an observer and to give whatever advice and assistance he could. Thus it was with considerable surprise that I learned 25 years after the withdrawal that [Radford] had directed that if the evacuation was not moving properly under me, command would shift to General Shepherd. This arrangement apparently had the agreement of both Joy and Shepherd.... [I]f I had known of Radford's instructions at the time, I would have been insulted, because to me those orders cast doubt on my competence to command the withdrawal. Fortunately, I knew nothing of the scheme. Certainly neither Turner Joy, who was my friend, nor Lem Shepherd, one of the Lord's own, would have ever taken advantage of the deal proposed.

The JCS ordered MacArthur to evacuate the X Corps at Hungnam in order to concentrate allied forces in South Korea. The evacuation began on 9 December under Doyle's command. In terms of military operations, a withdrawal from the battlefield while under attack from an aggressive enemy is hazardous and potentially disastrous. To prevent a rout the withdrawing forces must remain cohesive and disciplined, moving to the rear with measured steps. While some of the Army staffs were willing to leave equipment and supplies behind to expedite the evacuation, Doyle would not hear of it. Everything would be loaded at Hungnam and taken away.

The United States Navy had never evacuated such a large body of troops under fire, only landed them, so Doyle and his planners had no precedents. But it was clear that the Chinese had to be kept at a distance from the port so that the shipping could safely enter and embark passengers and cargo. Doyle employed Marine and carrier aircraft, naval gunfire, and artillery to saturate the approaching Chinese with overwhelming firepower, while rear guard troops fought off any enemy forces that got through the barrage. The payoff was an uninterrupted, systematic embarkation.

Marines board *Bayfield* (APA-33) for the evacuation from North Korea. In the fight to reach Hungnam, the Marines had badly damaged the Communists' capabilities, but the war would drag on for another three years. (Naval Historical Center)

The 3rd Infantry Division was still fighting as a rear guard when Almond came aboard Doyle's flagship with his headquarters on 19 December. Doyle greeted Almond and looked him in the eye. "You understand, General," said Doyle, "that those troops are now under my command."

Years later Doyle told this tale with wicked relish. "When I told Almond that," he grinned, "you had to hold him down?"

On Christmas Eve day the last of the troops boarded the ships and Doyle's force sailed. Timed demolition charges and naval gunfire then destroyed the port facilities. When the Chinese army finally entered Hungnam they found it a barren city. Doyle had taken out everything of value: one Marine and two Army divisions and a ROK corps totaling one hundred five thousand personnel; seventeen thousand five hundred tanks and other vehicles; and three hundred fifty thousand tons of cargo. In addition, ninety-one thousand Korean civilian refugees were rescued.

The Navy took the UN troops to Pusan, enabling them to survive and fight another day.

EPILOGUE

FORREST SHERMAN DIED OF a heart attack on 22 July 1951 at age fifty-four, while serving as Chief of Naval Operations. He had been CNO for only thirty-three months.

Arthur Radford continued as Commander in Chief, Pacific Command and Commander in Chief, Pacific Fleet until President Dwight D. Eisenhower appointed him chairman of the Joint Chiefs of Staff in June 1953. He received a Gold Star in lieu of a third Distinguished Service Medal for exceptionally meritorious service during the Korean War. Radford served two terms as JCS chairman before retiring in August 1957. He died in 1973 at age seventy-seven.

C. Turner Joy served as Commander Naval Forces, Far East until May 1952. In July 1951, he served concurrently as Senior United Nations Delegate at the Korean Armistice Conference at Panmunjom and Kaesong, a bitterly frustrating task that he wrote about in his book *How Communists Negotiate*. He received the Army Distinguished Service Cross and the Navy Distinguished Service Medal for exceptionally meritorious service in relation to the Korean War. He returned to the United States and served as superintendent of the U.S. Naval Academy before retiring in 1954 with a tombstone promotion to full admiral in recognition of his World War II combat awards. He died in 1956 at age sixty-one.

Arthur Struble was relieved as Commander Seventh Fleet in March 1951 and served in a variety of high command and staff positions on the U.S. East Coast. He received the Army Distinguished Service Cross and a Gold Star in lieu of a second Navy Distinguished Service Medal for exceptionally meritorious service in Korea. He retired in 1956 and received a tombstone promotion to full admiral in recognition of his World War II combat awards. He died in 1983 at age eighty-eight.

James Doyle was relieved as CTF 90 in early 1951 and received the Distinguished Service Medal for exceptionally meritorious service in Korea. He then served eight months as president of the Board of Inspection and Survey. For the final eighteen months of his active service, he chaired the Joint Amphibious Board, but to what extent he influenced the development of amphibious doctrine in that capacity is unclear. At his retirement on 1 November 1953, he was promoted vice admiral in recognition of his World War II combat awards. He practiced law in retirement and died in 1981 at age eighty-three.

Arleigh Burke continued as Deputy Chief of Staff on Joy's staff until he returned to sea as Commander Cruiser Division 5 off Korea. After a few short weeks in command he was appointed to serve with Joy in Panmunjom and Kaesong as a United Nations Delegate at the Korean Armistice Conference, a job he despised for its lack of success. He received a Gold Star in lieu of a third Legion of Merit from the Navy and an Oak Leaf Cluster from the Army in lieu of a fourth Legion of Merit, both for exceptionally meritorious conduct in Korea. He returned to Washington in December 1951 as the director of the CNO's Strategic Plans Division. He went back to sea as a cruiser division commander and then became Commander Destroyer Force, Atlantic Fleet. In August 1955, Burke bypassed ninety-one flag officers senior to himself when he was chosen to be Chief of Naval Operations. A four-star admiral, he served in that capacity for a record three appointments totaling six years before retiring in 1961. The Navy named a destroyer class in Burke's honor while he was living in retirement. He died in 1996 at age ninety-four.

THOMAS B. BUELL, *a retired Navy commander, is a distinguished author, scholar, and military historian. A graduate of the United States Naval Academy and the Naval Postgraduate School, he stood first in his class at the Naval War College. His writing began with professional articles for the U.S. Naval Institute* Proceedings *where he later served on the Naval Institute editorial board. While on the staff of the Naval War College he wrote* The Quiet Warrior: A Biography of Admiral Raymond A. Spruance, *which was copublished by Little, Brown and the Naval Institute Press. Following his command at sea, he taught military and naval history at the United States Military Academy and wrote* Master of Sea Power: A Biography of Fleet Admiral Ernest J. King, *also copublished by Little, Brown and the Naval Institute Press; it was a main selection of the Military Book Club.*

Both books received the Alfred Thayer Mahan Award for Literary Achievement and the Samuel Eliot Morison Award for Naval Literature. The Quiet Warrior *has been in continuous print for twenty-seven years, most recently as a selection of the Naval Institute's "Classics of Naval Literature" series, where it has been joined by* Master of Sea Power. *Buell's work* The Warrior Generals: Combat Leadership in the Civil War *(New York: Crown, 1997) was an alternate selection of the Military Book Club.*

Tom Buell has lectured and presented papers at universities, foundations, and such service institutions as the Naval Academy, the Naval War College, the National War College, the Army War College, the Army Command and Staff College, the Air War College, the Royal Military College of Canada, and the Marine Corps Command and Staff College. A former writer-in-residence at the University of North Carolina at Chapel Hill, he also lectured in history at UNC and Duke.

Naval Leadership in Korea *was his last published work. When Tom Buell passed away on 26 June 2002, he was writing a sea warrior trilogy about leadership under stress at the battles of Lake Erie, Hampton Roads, and Guadalcanal.*

CHAPTER 4

Fleet Operations in a Mobile War, September 1950–June 1951

JOSEPH H. ALEXANDER

THE UNITED STATES NAVY fought the Korean War on two distinct levels. In the operational sphere, the Navy attained command of the sea, established a surface blockade of North Korea, and supported United Nations Command ground operations with carrier air strikes, naval gunfire, coastal raids, and amphibious assaults, feints, and withdrawals. On the strategic level, the Navy protected Japan and Taiwan by vigilantly guarding against threats to these countries from two powerful and implacable enemies who shared a common cause with North Korea—the Soviet Union and the People's Republic of China. Each mission in Korean waters had to be executed with one eye on the real danger of superpower intervention, the possible onset of a third world war. The situation abided throughout the war but proved exceptionally stressful between September 1950 and June 1951. This was a time of great uncertainty in which the war escalated with the Inchon landing, the UN Command's subsequent invasion of North Korea, and the overland intervention by the Chinese Communists.

None of the armed services was prepared to fight a protracted, limited, conventional war on the mainland of Asia in 1950. After the defense cutbacks of the late 1940s, the United States was fortunate to have even a skeleton fleet available in Japan and the Philippines when the war erupted. The emergency restoration of full naval power to perform such daunting operational and strategic missions at a sustained operational tempo is a story of epic proportions in itself. The fact that Rear Admiral Doyle could assemble—cobble together, actually—a multinational invasion fleet of several hundred vessels for Operation Chromite at Inchon less than three months after the war began remains a phenomenal achievement.

All elements and communities of the Navy played key roles in the high-mobility phase of the Korean War that took place in the nine months from September 1950 to June 1951. A nation that so cavalierly dismissed the value of its minesweepers, amphibious ships, and escorts learned the hard way the price of its false economies. Vessels as diverse as aircraft carriers, battleships, and hospital ships were taken out of mothballs and recommissioned. They served with distinction throughout the war. The Navy entered the jet age—and the helicopter age. Yet old-timers like converted flushdeck destroyers served as high-speed transports for Navy commando teams on clandestine raiding missions.

The period of high mobility featured the spectacularly successful amphibious seizure of Inchon and the less well known but massive evacuation of nearly a quarter-million human beings from Hungnam. Ships trading fire with the enemy at point-blank range—for instance, the six destroyers anchored in broad daylight off Wolmi-do dueling with the island's hidden enemy gunners, and the little auxiliary minesweepers surging forward at Wonsan to pepper enemy gunners with 40-mm fire to cover the survivors of sunken fleet minesweepers *Pirate* and *Pledge*—reflected a naval heritage of earlier centuries.

Duty on board the ships, aircraft, and submarines of the Seventh Fleet during these multimission months was hazardous and exhausting. The pace never slackened, regardless of the fortunes or misfortunes of the forces ashore. The daily routine of flight quarters, bombardment missions, screening duty, Condition II watches, general quarters, and nightly underway replenishment operations continued unabated in good weather and in bad.

It has been said that the modern U.S. Navy stemmed from the "two-ocean navy" created in World War II. Yet it was the Korean War, with its professional application of sea power in so many forms in the Sea of Japan, the Yellow Sea, the Taiwan Strait, and the inner harbors of Inchon, Wonsan, and Hamhung that truly gave birth to the forward-deployed, global Navy of the Cold War and today.

INTRODUCTION

FEW HIGH-LEVEL MEETINGS in American military history have been as dramatic as the one convened in the Tokyo headquarters of General of the Army Douglas MacArthur on 23 August 1950. With the Korean War nearly two months old, and United Nations forces finally holding their own in the Pusan Perimeter, the time had come to use the mobility of the U.S. Seventh Fleet to open a new front behind the extended lines of the NKPA.

The senior officers gathered in MacArthur's conference room included two members of the JCS, Admiral Sherman and General Collins, and World War II veteran admirals Joy and Doyle.

While each officer favored the concept of Operation Chromite, an amphibious "end run" to outflank the NKPA and relieve the pressure on the beleaguered Eighth Army at Pusan, none supported MacArthur's proposed landing at Inchon, the nearly inaccessible port on the west coast that serviced nearby Seoul, the capital of the ROK.

Inchon's obstacles included notorious tides and mudflats, a serpentine approach channel, the fortified outpost island of Wolmi-do, and the seawalls around much of the city's perimeter. The 1st Marine Division would have to execute a forcible, daylight landing, and then fight its way through an industrial city the size of Omaha—all without benefit of prior rehearsal. Inchon's extreme tides would limit the opportunity to beach LSTs, with their 30-foot drafts, to two or three days each month. The next occasion would occur on 15 September—far too soon, it seemed to most of the naysayers, to plan such a complicated operation.

By contrast, many of the attendees preferred a landing at Kunsan, one hundred nautical miles south of Inchon, which they believed would retain the advantages of an end-run landing without the overwhelming hazards associated with Inchon.

Admiral Doyle would command the Attack Force (Task Force 90) for Operation Chromite regardless of whether the objective proved to be Inchon, Kunsan, or any other alternative. Doyle knew amphibious warfare. He had served as Admiral Turner's operations officer during some of the most desperate amphibious assaults of the early years of World War II in the Pacific. No naval officer on active duty in 1950 had a better grasp of the realities of executing an opposed landing from the sea. At this pivotal meeting Doyle intended to make sure MacArthur understood each of the formidable obstacles lurking at Inchon.

One by one, Doyle's staff officers briefed MacArthur and the two service chiefs on the problems involved with the forcible seizure of Inchon as compounded by the ambitious time schedule—D-day, set for 15 September, was then less than four weeks away. The senior visitors shifted uneasily when they heard the litany of dire predictions, but MacArthur sat impassively, smoking his trademark corncob pipe. Doyle had served with the enigmatic MacArthur once before and perhaps knew him better than the more senior officers gathered in the conference room. At the briefing's end Doyle added a gratuitous personal observation. "General," he said, "The best I can say is that Inchon is not impossible."

MacArthur considered that point; then said, "If we find we cannot make it, we will withdraw."

To this Doyle replied bluntly. "No, General, we don't know how to do that. Once we start ashore we keep going."

General Collins then spoke of his preference for an easier, simpler landing at Kunsan, far below Inchon. Yet this was no council of war. MacArthur patiently listened to every objection before standing to address the room. In a memorable, spellbinding discourse, he explained his vision of this bold strike at Inchon and subsequent seizure of Seoul. The landing force would then provide an anvil for the hammer of the Eighth Army attacking north from its Pusan trenches. As to General Collins's recommendation of Kunsan as an easier reach, MacArthur judged that option to be "ineffective and indecisive," observing that nothing in war was more futile than short envelopments. He continued: "The amphibious landing is the most powerful tool we have. To employ it properly, we must strike hard and deep."

MacArthur looked at Admiral Sherman. "The Navy has never let me down in the past," he said, "and it will not let me down this time."

The speech was vintage MacArthur: melodramatic, confident, lucid, and visionary. Seventy years old, a commissioned officer for the past forty-five years, he was—in the words of more than one awed junior officer—"senior to everyone but God." He would abide no further debate on the subject.

"We shall land at Inchon," he declared, "and I shall crush them."

The Joint Chiefs of Staff could find no grounds for overruling the theater commander, and five days after the Tokyo meeting they tepidly accepted the Inchon landing.

The Navy and Marine Corps had a lot at stake in this landing. The Truman administration had allowed the nation's immense amphibious assault capability of 1945 to atrophy sharply in the ensuing five years. Admirals Joy and Doyle would be hard-pressed to assemble even the minimum number of ships required to deliver, protect, and support the landing force. The Marines would find it equally difficult to provide an amphibiously trained division. Of the three infantry regiments in the 1st Marine Division, one was fighting for its life as the Eighth Army's "fire brigade" within the Pusan Perimeter, a second was en route from California, and the third was still being assembled from recalled reservists and a score of small regular units. Naval leaders already knew they could not deliver this third regiment to Inchon in time for D-day.

For these reasons Admiral Sherman requested one final audience with MacArthur. The general listened to Sherman's concerns but would change neither the objective nor the target date of 15 September. As Sherman admitted later to Turner Joy, "I wish I had that man's confidence."

Doyle's experts had not exaggerated the problems of an Inchon landing. The systematic "parallel and concurrent planning" process so essential to successful amphibious warfare went by the boards, replaced by nerve-jangling, helter-skelter improvisation.

And yet it worked. MacArthur had called this shot as infallibly as Babe Ruth once did by standing at home plate and pointing his bat at the centerfield bleachers. MacArthur landed at Inchon and indeed crushed the North Koreans. Inchon remains for its size the most boldly conceived and brilliantly executed amphibious assault in the nation's history.

The Inchon landing consequently dominates this phase of the naval war in Korea, but the period from September 1950 through June 1951 would also feature tremendous swings of fortune—embarrassing postponements of amphibious landings because of enemy minefields, the epic evacuation of a quarter of a million troops and refugees, and deployment of fleet elements throughout East Asian waters. At all times the Navy struggled to balance its response to the operational threat of the NKPA invasion of the Republic of Korea against the greater strategic threat of massive intervention by China or the Soviet Union. Future combat action in the Cold War would always invoke the threat of another world war, but in Korea in 1950, at the virtual onset of superpower rivalry, the threat was especially ominous.

COMMAND OF THE SEA

BY SEPTEMBER 1950 THE NAVY'S main role in Korea had changed from averting a catastrophic disaster—the forced evacuation of Pusan—to providing the principal means of seizing the offensive and winning the war. The planned landing at Inchon, for all its worrisome problems, promised no less a strategic reward.

The Navy's first concern was the threat posed by the Soviet Union. Tensions heightened dramatically in early September when Navy F4U Corsairs from *Valley Forge* (CV-45) intercepted a Soviet bomber approaching the carrier task force. The Russian pilot opened fire on the Corsairs, and they promptly shot him down. The Soviet Union responded angrily but did not retaliate.

Uncertainty over Soviet or Chinese intentions with regard to control of the seas in East Asia required the Navy to apportion a good number of frigates and scarce destroyers as protection for the daily convoys from Japan to Pusan against potential submarine or long-range bomber attacks. The convoys represented truly a lifeline to the Eighth Army in the early autumn of 1950, providing desperately needed reinforcements and heavier weapons. Ground forces especially required Pershing M-26 heavy tanks with 90-mm main guns to counter the Soviet-built Josef Stalin T-34 tanks that had proved almost unstoppable thus far in the war.

With so many ships committed to operational and logistic support missions, and in view of the even greater requirements for shipping to support Operation Chromite, the Navy began a crash program of reactivating mothballed combatants. As early as 25 July the Navy ordered the carrier *Princeton* (CV-37) pulled from the Reserve Fleet for service in Korean waters. By the time the sole operational battleship, *Missouri* (BB-63), sailed from New York on 18 August, the Navy had already decided to reactivate her three *Iowa*-class sisters.

Fitting out and recommissioning a ship involved a lot of grinding effort. When Cdr. Norvell G. Ward took command of the reactivated *Fletcher*-class destroyer *Yarnell* (DD-541) in January 1951, he and his largely reservist crew experienced "long hours, long days."

Ships newly arriving in the Far East were welcomed with unrestricted mission-type orders from Vice Admiral Joy, COMNAVFE. When Captain Thach, the renowned World War II fighter pilot (and inventor of the "Thach weave" tactic so successful against Japanese Zeros) left Yokosuka

RETURN OF THE
BATTLESHIPS

BY 1950 THE U.S. NAVY retained only one battleship in commission, the 45,000-ton *Missouri*, famous for her World War II role in the Japanese surrender ceremony in Tokyo Bay.

Her orders to proceed to Korea in the summer of 1950 followed an inauspicious beginning to the year. In early January she ran aground in Hampton Roads, Virginia, as she steamed seaward on a training mission. *Missouri* took two weeks to refloat and another two before she was able to assume training duty in Norfolk. The orders to Korea disrupted the summer schedule, forcing the abrupt removal of hundreds of Naval ROTC midshipmen assigned to the ship for eight weeks of training.

At first it seemed misfortune would continue to dog the ship. Her 11,000-mile transit from New York's North River to the Sea of Japan took a month and a day, her speed of advance slowed by close encounters with an Atlantic hurricane and then a Pacific typhoon. She would miss D-day at Inchon.

But *Missouri* immediately made known her arrival in Korea. Appearing dramatically out of the mists off Samchok on the southeast coast on 14 September, the battleship opened fire with fifty-two 16-inch shells, quickly demolishing one railroad bridge and damaging a second, seriously constricting the line of retreat of a North Korean division. Two days later *Missouri* fired nearly three hundred rounds from her main batteries to help a ROK division cross the Hyongsan River—nine miles inland. "The *Missouri*'s fire was really demoralizing to those Red troops," reported the

Missouri fires a salvo of 16-inch shells from number 2 turret, targeting communication lines at Chongjin, North Korea, just thirty-four miles south of the border with the Soviet Union. The battleship's massive shells greatly increased the destructive power of naval gunfire and provided several more miles of range, important for hitting enemy troops and equipment far inland. (National Archives)

U.S. shore fire control party officer with the 3rd ROK Division. "We practically waded across that river standing up."

In short order *Missouri* delivered long-range fire support to the X Corps's breakout from the beachhead at Inchon. Soon she became Vice Admiral Struble's flagship and harassed the enemy on the North Korean coast along the Sea of Japan. She began by giving the Mitsubishi Iron Works in Chongjin, thirty-four miles below the Soviet border, a vicious pounding. North Korean defenders of the port of Wonsan would know her silhouette well—and be uncomfortably familiar with the gigantic red-orange fireballs from her muzzles, the unmistakable roar of approaching rounds, and the concussive blast of a high-explosive shell as heavy as a small automobile.

In November 1950 the Navy recommissioned *New Jersey*. Sister ships *Iowa* and *Wisconsin* soon followed her out of mothballs. Each *Iowa*-class battleship served in the Korean War, often firing close enough to the hostile coast to suffer casualties from counterbattery fire. On one occasion Vice Adm. Harold M. Martin, who relieved Struble in command of the Seventh Fleet, invited Admiral Sherman to accompany him on board *New Jersey* during a fire mission off Wonsan. The ship engaged in a duel with mainland batteries. This was perhaps the first time a serving CNO had been under direct fire.

The battleships were universally welcomed by the ground troops. No Marine, Army, or ROK infantryman who ever fought within twenty miles of the coast would forget the gladdening experience of a battleship's legendary "earthquake salvos" fired in timely support against a stubbornly held enemy position.

in command of the escort carrier *Sicily* (CVE-118), he recalled that his orders "gave [him] complete freedom to go in where [he] could help anybody [he] wanted to." His orders from Admiral Joy read: "Proceed to Korea via Kobe. Render all possible support to ground forces. Direct air support of interdiction at your discretion. Keep COMNAVFE informed of actions, intentions, and position."

Admiral Joy was one of three highly experienced Navy leaders that good fortune brought to the forefront of the Inchon, Wonsan, and Hungnam operations in 1950. Joy, a native of St. Louis, Missouri, and a 1916 graduate of the U.S. Naval Academy, was then fifty-five years old. He had served often in the Far East, beginning in 1923 with the Yangtze River Patrol and later the Asiatic Fleet. He fought in the earliest naval battles in the Solomons in February 1942, commanded a cruiser during the Aleutians campaign, served as chief of the Pacific Plans Division in Washington, and returned to combat commanding a cruiser division in the Marianas campaign and the Battle of the Philippine Sea. A postgraduate ordnance engineer, Joy gained renown for the proficiency of his ships' gunfire support, especially at Guam, Okinawa, and Leyte. By the time of the North Korean invasion, Admiral Joy had commanded Naval Forces, Far East for ten months. Joy was comfortable in a joint command, enjoyed the confidence of MacArthur, and worked well with the two admirals who would shoulder the greatest responsibility for the landings and evacuations, Struble and Doyle.

Admiral Struble took command of the Seventh Fleet a month before the Korean War erupted. A native of Portland, Oregon, and a 1915 graduate of the U.S. Naval Academy, Struble was fifty-six years old at the time of Operation Chromite. In 1944 he had served on a staff preparing for the Normandy invasion, then commanded an amphibious group of the Seventh Fleet throughout the assault landings at Leyte, Ormoc Bay, Mindoro, and Corregidor. Like Joy, Struble inspired MacArthur's confidence. His experience in orchestrating massive amphibious landings would prove invaluable in 1950, as would his ability to maintain harmonious interservice relations. Struble's Joint Task Force (JTF) 7 at Inchon would include diverse Army, Navy, and Marine Corps components, as well as various allied naval and ground forces. Struble had been at sea during MacArthur's memorable "Sermon on the Mount" regarding the Inchon landing. By the time he returned to port and got the news of his assignment less than three weeks remained before D-day. "After a personal study of the problem, I could appreciate why General MacArthur had chosen Inchon," he said. "It was the prize gem if we could take it . . . and after the plans had been completed, I was convinced we *could* take it."

Admiral Doyle, Struble's principal subordinate as Commander Attack Force (CTF 90), was less sanguine than the fleet commander, but it was his lot to be concerned with details. Like Joy and Struble, Doyle had worked with MacArthur before. He was fifty-three years old, a native of Astoria on New York's Long Island, and a 1920 graduate of the U.S. Naval Academy. He earned a law degree from George Washington University during service with the Judge Advocate General of the Navy. Doyle had commanded several ships, but it was his service with Kelly Turner's Amphibious Forces, South Pacific Command in the Guadalcanal, Tulagi, and New Georgia campaigns of 1942-3 that distinguished the man. As Commander Amphibious Group 1, Doyle responded with alacrity in June 1950 to a request from MacArthur to bring a training team to Japan to instruct his Army occupation forces in amphibious warfare. On 25 June, the day the North Koreans swarmed across the 38th parallel, Doyle had just commenced the first day of training with the 1st Cavalry Division. The emergency canceled the training.

In the war's first days MacArthur directed Doyle to plan for a nontactical landing of the 1st Cavalry Division at Inchon to stiffen the resolve of the ROK forces still defending Seoul. "At this I said a silent prayer," recalled Doyle, "for the 1st Cavalry Division had no amphibious training, and I had no ships with which to land them."

Then Doyle concentrated on planning a tactical assault on the same port with the assistance of his counterpart, Major General Smith, who commanded the 1st Marine Division. Smith's amphibious assault credentials rivaled those of Doyle's— regimental commander at Cape Gloucester, assistant division commander at Peleliu, assistant chief of staff, Tenth Army, Okinawa. Intelligent and taciturn, Smith's combat leadership would blaze forth during the fighting withdrawal of his embattled division from the Chosin Reservoir later in the year.

Doyle and Smith pursued the critical missing elements of intelligence needed to execute the assault. Would the high tide on 15 September attain the minimum required twenty-nine feet of water needed to accommodate amphibious vessels? Which set of tide tables was the most reliable, those published by the United States or by Japan? How high were the seawalls at various tide stages, and would ladders be required to disembark troops from landing craft? How viscous were the mudflats at low tide?

Doyle kept his options open. While concentrating on the problems of seizing Inchon, he ordered a covert reconnaissance of the Kunsan area on the southwest coast of the Republic of Korea—just in case the Joint Chiefs or General MacArthur should change their minds at the last minute. He ordered the high-speed transport *Horace A. Bass* (APD-124) to reconnoiter landing beaches with her improvised special operations force of UDT 1 and advance elements of the 1st Marine Division Reconnaissance Company.

Tactical air support for Eighth Army units and long-range interdiction of NKPA supply routes by carrier-based F4U Corsairs, AD Skyraiders, and F9F Panthers continued daily while the Inchon invasion fleet slowly coalesced. Meanwhile, allied destroyers and cruisers pounded coastal and inland targets, often using target spotting provided by one of the larger ship's helicopters, a welcome innovation.

Shore bombardment against the invading NKPA divisions had commenced on 29 June when the antiaircraft light cruiser *Juneau* (CLAA-119) opened fire on enemy troops near Okkye. By September the number of ships available for bombardment had increased tenfold, and the battleship *Missouri* proceeded westward for Korea.

Those serving at sea in early September could sense the dynamics of a growing concentration of naval forces as combatants steamed from all across the Pacific into the Yellow Sea. Great events were in the wind.

COVERT
AMPHIBIOUS
OPERATIONS

AMPHIBIOUS WARFARE COVERS A broader spectrum than the familiar assault landing. The operational categories include amphibious feints, withdrawals, raids, and reconnaissance missions. Admiral Doyle would have the rare opportunity to execute each type of mission in Korea.

Initially lacking the means to execute a major amphibious assault, Doyle ordered a series of raids and reconnaissance missions from both the Sea of Japan and the Yellow Sea. On 6 August 1950 Doyle activated a Special Operations Group, designating Navy Capt. S. C. Small, commanding Transport Division 111, to lead the Navy Element and Marine Maj. Edward P. Dupras to command the Raiding Forces.

The ships of Transport Division 111 included high-speed transports *Horace A. Bass* and *Diachenko*, both converted *Rudderow*-class destroyer escorts with two 5-inch/38-gun mounts, turboelectric drives, and 24-knot speed. The ships also provided limited troop berthing spaces and four landing craft. They proved well suited for launching covert amphibious operations along the Korean coastline.

The raiding party on board *Horace A. Bass* in the first months of the Korean War consisted of about seventy-five men, two-thirds of them from Underwater Demolition Unit 1 and the others from the advance element of the 1st Marine Division Reconnaissance Company.

The assignment of Major Dupras to command this talented group was fortuitous. Dupras had been a company commander with Merritt Edson's Raiders (the 1st Marine Raider Battalion) in action at Tulagi and Guadalcanal, including the masterful raid at Tasimboko. Edson's Raiders

Carrying Navy underwater demolition teams and Marine reconnaissance units, *Horace A. Bass* joined fleet units off Korea in early August 1950 to begin vital amphibious raids against Communist supply lines. As UN forces prepared for a September offensive, the transport's raiding parties made daring forays scouting for possible landing sites. (Naval Historical Center)

had worked extensively at night debarkation from high-speed transports (APDs) into rubber boats, which were then towed shoreward by LCVPs and released just before the surf zone. Dupras taught these techniques to his combined raiding force in two nights of intense training.

Within a week after Doyle's letter of instruction, *Horace A. Bass* commenced a series of night amphibious raids from the Sea of Japan against railroad bridges and tunnels along the North Korean coast. Operating during the dark of the moon, the raiders rigged their demolitions ashore with 30-minute delay fuses, withdrew from the beach, and then observed the explosions from well offshore. In an operational pattern that became standard, the ship would recover the raiding force, disappear over the horizon, and then reappear at dawn to shell the repair crews already at work.

Ironically, on the same evening that General MacArthur spoke so eloquently in defense of his plan for a landing at Inchon, Doyle had his Special Operations Group busily at work conducting beach reconnaissance surveys in the vicinity of Kunsan.

One hour into the raiders' third consecutive nightly survey on 25 August, an enemy patrol spotted their activity in the bright moonlight and opened fire. The raiders returned fire, aborted the mission, and proceeded through the surf with their casualties to *Horace A. Bass*. Major Dupras reported nine Marines of the covering party missing. Captain Small put more boats in the water and shortly before dawn recovered the last of these men, steadfastly swimming toward the ship.

Both *Diachenko* and *Horace A. Bass* continued these clandestine amphibious missions throughout the period of high mobility.

THE ASSAULT ON INCHON

THE ENORMITY OF GENERAL MACARTHUR'S gamble at Inchon became more conspicuous to commanders and their staffs as the 15 September D-day for Operation Chromite neared. Yet the seizure of Inchon—as difficult as the amphibious assault might prove to be—represented merely the means to an end. The primary objective of Chromite was the recapture of Seoul, the capital of South Korea and current hub of most NKPA lines of communication to its forces assaulting Pusan. The advance by the landing force from Inchon to Seoul would require a dangerous division of forces along each side of a major river, with both flanks subject to NKPA counterattack for several critical days. Nor would MacArthur have any strategic reserves to deploy. Should the 1st Marine Division suffer a major setback, or should the Attack Force suffer the loss of key transports in the congested waters, the Far East Command would be unable to launch a new amphibious envelopment for months.

General MacArthur created an umbrella organization, Joint Task Force 7, under Struble's command, to accommodate the multiservice and multinational participants of the operation. All but a few of the units involved, however, were Seventh Fleet ships. Struble's task forces for Chromite included:

Task Force 90, Attack Force, Rear Adm. James H. Doyle, USN
Task Force 91, Blockade and Covering Force, Rear Adm. Sir William G. Andrewes, RN
Task Force 92, X Corps, Maj. Gen. Edward M. Almond, USA
Task Force 99, Patrol and Reconnaissance Force, Rear Adm. George R. Henderson, USN
Task Force 77, Fast Carrier Force, Rear Adm. Edward C. Ewen, USN
Task Force 79, Service Squadron, Capt. Bernard L. Austin, USN

Struble commanded 230 ships at Inchon, an impressive assemblage by a downsized navy so early in this unexpected war. While the total figure pales in comparison to the mammoth U.S. Fifth Fleet that invaded Okinawa five years earlier, the Inchon task force would nevertheless be the largest amphibious armada the world would see throughout the entire Cold War.

Doyle's Task Force 90 contained most of the ships, including vessels from the United States, Great Britain, Canada, Australia, New Zealand, France, and the Republic of Korea. Fully one third of Doyle's ships were Western Pacific cargo ships of the MSTS or chartered U.S. and Japanese merchant ships.

General MacArthur created the X Corps from two divisions scheduled to reinforce the Far East Command in September: the 1st Marine Division under Major General Smith and the 7th Infantry Division, commanded by Army Major General Barr. Augmented by two ROK regiments and the Tactical Air Command under Marine Brigadier General Cushman, the corps totaled 71,339 men. MacArthur placed Major General "Ned" Almond, his energetic and acerbic chief of staff, in overall command.

Smith served two masters. He took orders from Admiral Doyle during the assault on Inchon. Six days later, when General Almond moved ashore and signaled his readiness to launch the ground campaign against Seoul, Smith began operating under the X Corps commander.

Admiral Doyle reviewed the X Corps troop and cargo lists and concluded he would require 120 amphibious ships of different configurations to deliver Almond's force to Inchon—even when factoring in the noncombat landing of the 7th Division several days after D-day. The figure seemed staggeringly prohibitive. Although encouraged by the arrival of more than two dozen principal amphibious ships—APAs, attack cargo ships (AKAs), APDs, and LSDs— Doyle realized he lacked his total lift requirement by an order of magnitude. That he made good this deficiency in such short time reflected Doyle's skill as an amphibious warfare professional of the first rank.

Doyle needed four-dozen tank landing ships, the ubiquitous workhorses of World War II. These unglamorous, rough-riding ships were as much loved by force commanders as they were loathed by the seasick troops embarked. LSTs were the only amphibious ships that could deliver tons of combat cargo directly over Inchon's few "beaches" at high tide.

Unfortunately, the United States had decommissioned most of its LSTs at the end of World War II. The Navy resurrected seventeen for Doyle's use, although none was immediately seaworthy. Doyle then reclaimed thirty LSTs conveyed to the Japanese after the war for interisland trade. The so-called SCAJAP ships came with Japanese crews, some of whose officers had served in the Imperial Japanese Navy. The eight LSTs designated by Doyle for direct beaching at Inchon on the evening of D-day received patchwork American crews. The Sailors were appalled at the wretched condition of the ships.

Lt. Trumond E. Houston, newly assigned skipper of a SCAJAP LST, recalled the experience: "My ship, the *LST-799*, arrived about the same time in Yokosuka as I did. What a revelation! It was stripped, dirty, stinking, and generally in horrible condition." His executive officer, Lieutenant Hauber, described the ship as overrun with "rats bigger than footballs" and redolent with the "penetrating odor of fish heads and urine." Heroic efforts by the U.S. Naval Repair Facility, Yokosuka made the recommissioned ships minimally operational. "We were commissioned on 28 August, about 0930," said Houston. "At 1000 we had orders to get underway for a berth shift. I had never handled an LST before." Eighteen days later Lieutenant Houston guided his ship through the narrow passage of Flying Fish Channel toward burning Inchon.

Admiral Struble's Operation Plan 9-50 assessed the hydrographic conditions Lieutenant Houston and several hundred other ship captains would face in the approach to Inchon:

> The area for the landings experiences one of the largest ranges of tides in the world—over 31 feet. Waters are restricted with many off-lying reefs, shoals, and small islands. Due to the extensive mudflats surrounding the landing areas, plus the fact that in some cases the troops must land over existing sea-walls, a tidal height of 23 feet is necessary for landing craft

and a height of 29 feet is necessary for LSTs. These limitations restrict the number of days which are suitable for landing, and also restrict the time for unloading operations on any one day. The approaches to Inchon are narrow and tidal currents in the transport and gunfire support areas vary between 2 and 3 knots at maximum ebb and flood. The time of landing must be at or near high tide.

Tidal currents in the sixty-mile-long Flying Fish Channel proved to be even stronger than anticipated in the operation plan. Ships experienced 4.5-knot currents on a rising tide and nearly 7-knot currents during ebb tide. "You just can't imagine how fast that [tidal] current is," said Capt. Kleber S. Masterson, whose attack transport *Lenawee* (APA-195) nearly lost its anchor in a subsequent approach to Inchon. Kleber added, "If you come in there at low tide you've got a narrow little bay, [but] at high tide you've got a bay that looks like the Chesapeake."

Small wonder that commanders in both the attack force and the landing force began to clamor for updated intelligence information as September arrived. The dearth of readily available information and the confusion of conflicting data (the tide tables, for example) heightened the frustrations of the planning process. Commander in Chief, Pacific Fleet (CINCPACFLT) Interim Evaluation Report that assessed the major features of naval operations in Korea included this complaint: "Although South Korea was occupied by U.S. forces for four years following World War II, there was almost no intelligence available of the type required by amphibious forces. This should serve as a lesson for the future."

Doyle's dissatisfaction with the information available from the Far East Command headquarters led him to risk the covert deployment of Lieutenant Clark and his South Korean "buccaneers" to scout the upper channel and harbor for two weeks prior to the landing.

Operational security for Chromite seemed alarmingly slack. Correspondents in Tokyo called the pending campaign "Operation Common Knowledge." Far East Command counterintelligence agents arrested a Japanese national with North Korean ties who had in his possession a stolen copy of the operation order for Inchon. Admiral Struble tried to mask the obvious by conducting decoy raids and bombardments along both coasts, north and south of the 38th parallel. The North Koreans knew that they were vulnerable to a major amphibious operation somewhere on their coastline. But they clung to the belief that Inchon's notorious tides and shallows would prohibit the deep-draft American amphibious ships from launching a major assault on the port. The North Koreans may also have relied on the timely delivery of Soviet antiship mines, weapons that could make Inchon unassailable from the sea.

Struble and Doyle had based their respective operations plans on the assumption that the North Koreans possessed only limited mining capabilities. Here appeared a major failure in intelligence collection and analysis. Unknown to the Far East Command, the Soviet Union began shipping sizable quantities of antiship mines from Vladivostok to North Korea barely two weeks after the invasion of the South. On 17 July Soviet naval teams arrived in Wonsan and Chinnampo, the Yellow Sea port serving the North Korean capital of Pyongyang, to instruct their surrogates in mine warfare. By 1 August the North Koreans had gained enough proficiency to begin mining both ports. Similar plans materialized for Inchon, Kunsan, and even Mokpo in the southwest corner of South Korea. Soviet naval officers arrived in Inchon at some point during August, followed shortly by the first consignment of mines to be laid in the approach channels.

These surreptitious efforts by the North Koreans would challenge the near-total command of the sea enjoyed by the U.S. Navy and its allies. The coastal waters would never again be free from the threat of moored and free-floating mines, especially in the deeper waters of the Sea of Japan.

Not until the first week of September did Joy, Struble, and Doyle understand that they faced a mine warfare threat. On 4 September the destroyer McKean (DD-784) reported mines in the harbor of Chinnampo. On 10 September the ROKN vessel PC-703 sank a North Korean minelayer off Haeju and reported that the mouth of the bay had been mined. Haeju is less than fifty nautical miles from Inchon.

Doyle fretted over both reports, but there was little he could do other than urge a heightened vigilance among his task group commanders. The Navy had precious few minesweepers left in operation. A mere half-dozen of these vessels were currently under way to join Task Force 90, but they were small craft proceeding in rough seas and would not arrive before D-day. The exigencies of time and tide would prohibit effective minesweeping as a preliminary operation to the landing.

The mine threat however worrisome seemed manageable. Only a few mines had been reported near Inchon. Not until 23 September, after Inchon, did senior naval officers learn that the enemy had emplaced more than four thousand mines in Korea waters during July and August.

While Doyle worried about the mine threat and struggled to assemble the requisite LSTs and other specialized amphibious craft, General Smith and the landing force staff dealt with problems of their own. The outpost island of Wolmi-do presented the greatest concern. Here, too, the elements of time and the tides ruled tactical decisions. Smith's planners described the hilly, fortified island as "the cork in the bottle." There could be no landings at the port of Inchon until the guns on Wolmi-do had been silenced. Smith had little doubt that a Marine battalion landing team supported by naval gunfire and carrier aviation could seize the redoubt, but not simultaneously with the main force assault on Inchon. This situation meant a dangerous division of forces at the very onset of the assault. Because of the tides, the attack force would have to abandon the battalion on Wolmi-do and retreat to deeper water far down the channel. The naval force could not return until high tide in the late afternoon, twelve hours later. Moreover, the second H-hour, based on the Japanese tide tables, would occur so late and in darkness as to jeopardize the ship-to-shore movement and the critical beaching of eight LSTs loaded with supplies.

Other time and distance factors plagued Smith as D-day approached. The 1st Marine Division's units had never trained or rehearsed together for such a major amphibious and urban warfare operation. And the division was still incomplete. One reinforced regiment, the 5th Marines, remained heavily committed in combat at Pusan, and Lieutenant General Walker, the Eighth Army commander, was loath to release it for the assault on Inchon.

The absence of the "Fire Brigade" along the Naktong River would hinder Walker's operations, but its absence at Inchon might have doomed Smith's mission. Hence MacArthur ordered Walker to release the 5th Marines. Smith's third infantry regiment, the green 7th Marines, was still en route and not expected to reach Inchon until two days after D-day.

Smith also viewed with concern plans for the division's subsequent land campaign to recapture Seoul. Each of his regiments would have to force its way across the Han River under fire, then battle a tenacious enemy within the confines of a sprawling metropolis.

The Marines had not faced a river as broad as the Han since their 1918 crossing of the Meuse the last night of World War I. Smith knew he could deploy his riflemen across the tidal river at any point on board their LVT-3C Bushmaster amphibian tractors, but these forces would be at great risk without their accompanying M-26 Pershing tanks or artillery battalions. None of the bridges or ferries had survived the traumatic evacuation of the capital in the first week of the war. General Almond somewhat breezily assured Smith that a military bridging capability would be on hand by the time the Marines reached the river. Smith was less sanguine. He was grateful his engineer officer, of his own volition, had scrounged a pair of 50-ton pontoon sections on the way to Korea. If he could also scrounge some pusher boats from the Navy, the Marines might not need to rely on the problematic arrival of Almond's bridge trains.

Urban street fighting would present an unfamiliar scenario to Smith's men. The Marine Corps as an institution would spend much of the twentieth century deployed among the jungle islands and peninsulas of the Pacific—"the boondocks." The leathernecks had engaged in street fighting only sporadically—Peking, 1900; Vera Cruz, 1914; Garapan (Saipan), 1944; and Naha (Okinawa), 1945. Seoul would be a much more involved and bloody experience.

Preparing for these and other contingencies required an endless string of eighteen-hour workdays on the part of the attack force and landing force staff members, most of them located on board Doyle's amphibious force flagship *Mount McKinley* (AGC-7). "There never was or will be such an operation as Chromite for concurrent, word-of mouth planning," observed Colonel Heinl. Remarkably, in seventeen days the Navy and Marine staffs produced a coherent, balanced plan for the neutralization of Wolmi-do and seizure of Inchon, plus the follow-on non-combat landing of the 7th Division and X Corps troops. It began to look as if Doyle had achieved the impossible in assembling from all over the Pacific the hundreds of ships required for the job—even though one LST would have to be towed to the objective area. Punishing winds and waves from Typhoons Jane and Kezia made the task all the more difficult for the ships.

As Marines from Pusan to Kobe strove to combat-load their ships in between the typhoons, Admiral Doyle directed the first significant air strike against the North Korean outpost on Wolmi-do. On 10 September the escort carriers *Sicily* and *Badoeng Strait* (CVE-116) launched every available Corsair from Marine Fighter Squadrons 214 and 323, veterans now of a month's heavy fighting over the Pusan Perimeter. Each plane launched with a double load of napalm. As Captain Thach of *Sicily* described the mission, "We went up there and put 95,000 pounds of napalm on the west half of Wolmi-do and burnt it up so it looked real naked."

Admiral Struble tried to mask his intentions regarding Inchon. He ordered carrier air strikes against targets ranging from Kunsan to Pyongyang. On 7 September he ordered a diversionary landing by British Royal Marines and U.S. Army commandos against Kunsan, which many commanders junior to MacArthur still considered the most logical amphibious objective.

Struble and Doyle, however, decided to forego the feints and concentrate on reducing the threat posed by the NKPA guns on Wolmi-do. It was not clear where on the hilly island, even though denuded of vegetation by napalm strikes, the enemy had positioned their guns. Struble devised an aggressive plan—dubbed the "Sitting Duck" concept—that required a daylight attack on the island by a half-dozen U.S. destroyers anchored in the channel only a few hundred yards offshore. The ships would bombard the island with their 5-inch/38-caliber guns to goad the North Korean gunners into returning fire, thereby revealing their positions for counterbattery fire. The Fifth Fleet had employed similar tactics successfully before D-day at Iwo Jima, but no one denied the extreme risk to the "sitting ducks."

Rear Admiral Higgins's Gunfire Support Group provided the forces for the preinvasion bombardment of Wolmi-do. Two heavy cruisers, *Toledo* (CA-133) and *Rochester* (CA-124), and two Royal Navy light cruisers supported the mission with midrange fire. Admiral Struble accompanied the task group on board his flagship *Rochester*. Captain Allan, commanding Destroyer Squadron 9, led the six "sitting ducks"—*Mansfield* (DD-728), *De Haven* (DD-727), *Lyman K. Swenson* (DD-729), *Collett* (DD-730), *Gurke* (DD-783), and *Henderson* (DD-785). Allan intended to lead his destroyers up the channel and have them steam past the island, come about, and anchor facing the rising tide, broadside to the target, thereby allowing all guns to bear.

The plan was harrowing. The six ships would present inviting, stationary targets, arrayed at ranges as close as seven hundred yards to the enemy. While the North Korean coast defense guns comprised the principal threat, the destroyer skippers also took measures to repel boarders. A sudden sortie across the shallows from the island was considered not out of the question. Cdr. Frederick M. Radel prepared *Gurke* for all contingencies: towing, being towed, rescue operations alongside a stranded vessel, and arming his repair parties "to repel possible boarders." Commander Lundgren agreed to his crew's suggestion that the men fashion rag-filled dummies on *De Haven*'s forecastle to distract North Korean gunners.

Higgins's task group entered Flying Fish Channel at 0700 on 13 September just as the tide began to rise. Four hours later the cruisers anchored in their assigned fire-support stations. Then came an unsettling discovery. At 1145 *Mansfield* reported moored mines, barely exposed by the low water. Captain Allan ordered his ships to open fire and knock them out. Fire from *Gurke* detonated the first mine a minute later. Then the cruisers joined in, and the firing became general. "It got a little dangerous from your own folk," recalled Lt. John W. Lee in *Toledo*. "Everybody started popping away trying to explode the mines. Of course there were ricochets."

Captain Allan could not afford a prolonged diversion from his mission. He ordered cease fire, detached *Henderson* to remain on the scene to destroy as many of the mines as possible before catching up with the column at high speed, and then led the other five ships toward the island.

Navy AD Skyraider attack planes from Task Force 77 pummeled Wolmi-do as the destroyers approached. In a message intercepted by the flagship, the North Korean defense commander signaled his headquarters: "Enemy vessels approaching Inchon. Many aircraft bombing Wolmi-do. Every indication enemy will carry out a landing."

Less than an hour after their encounter with the mines, Allan's destroyers anchored just off Wolmi-do, guns trained to port, awaiting his signal. The tension was palpable.

"It was an eerie silence," recalled Cdr. Edwin H. "Harvey" Headland, commanding *Mansfield*. Then *De Haven* spotted a North Korean gun being slewed in her direction and opened fire. The other ships, lacking such targets of opportunity, responded to the commodore's flag hoist and commenced a steady probing of the island's topographic tucks and folds.

The North Korean gun crews endured this audacious pounding for a few minutes, then took the bait and cut loose. Associated Press correspondent Redman Morn, observing the island through binoculars from the bridge of *Toledo* several miles away, described the enemy fire as "a necklace of gun-flashes. . . . Soon they came so fast the entire slope was sparkling with pin-points of fire."

Gunfire from the island straddled several of the destroyers. "My God," cried Lieutenant Lee on *Toledo*, "they're sacrificing these guys."

For a solid hour Allan's destroyers engaged in an intrepid, point-blank gun battle. The Communists concentrated their fire on the three closest destroyers and registered telling blows. *Collett* sustained nine direct hits and *Gurke* three. An earsplitting near miss lashed the superstructure of *Lyman K. Swenson* with fragments, killing Lieutenant Swenson (no relation to the ship's namesake). Eight other crewmen on the three ships sustained injuries. Still, Allan's destroyers stood unflinchingly, firing 998 rounds from their main batteries into the smoking cave mouths that dotted Wolmi-do's exposed slopes. The enemy fire began to abate.

The tide at Inchon, however, dictated the battle more than enemy fire. Captain Allan kept an eye on the chronometer and the current. Around 1400 he ordered his ships to fight their way back down the channel. Emboldened, the surviving Communist gun crews fired parting shots. Commander Headland's *Mansfield*—first in, last out—ran a dangerous gauntlet. "I cranked up flank speed," he said. "From the wing of the bridge I actually saw shells flying over the ship." Worse, he discovered that he was so close to the island that his 5-inch/38 mounts could not depress their guns to fire. Headland ordered his 40-mm antiaircraft gunners to saturate the slopes. The cruisers pitched in, and another air strike materialized from Task Force 77. *Mansfield* raced unscathed through the plunging fire like a charmed water snake, her bow wave swamping several of the ubiquitous sampans that had gathered to watch the battle—akin to the citizens of Cherbourg, France, who took to the sea in 1864 to observe the epic duel between USS *Kearsarge* and CSS *Alabama*.

Admiral Struble had taken tremendous risks with this daylight bombardment mission, but another such operation was called for before he could order a Marine battalion-sized assault landing. He met with Higgins and Allan, reviewed the events and conditions of 13 September, and directed a return visit of the destroyers the next day, D-day-minus-one. The threat from enemy mines hung heavily over each man. They had been lucky their Sailors had spotted the initial mines exposed in shallow water. During the battle itself, *De Haven*'s Commander Lundgren, a mine warfare expert, had spied a pyramid of Russian contact mines stacked near Wolmi-do's causeway to Inchon. Would the North Koreans be able to lay these mines in the channel overnight?

The task group paused at daybreak on 14 September to bury Lieutenant Swenson's shrouded body at sea with full military honors. Then Captain Allan led his destroyers back up Flying Fish Channel, this time with five ships—*Collett*, hardest hit the previous day, was still nursing her wounds. Several mines remained in the string discovered earlier (the Navy would find it both difficult and time-consuming to detonate mines by gunfire). But there was no evidence of fresh mine laying. The ships anchored as before and resumed fire. This day the fight appeared to have been drained from the Wolmi-do gunners. Return fire seemed desultory and soon petered out. The destroyers departed in a more dignified manner this time. The cruisers and Corsairs then took their turns. The island smoked and burned, at last ready for invasion.

The drama of Wolmi-do played out against a backdrop of hundreds of ships laboring slowly through Typhoon Kezia's turmoil into the Yellow Sea. On board one of the heaving transports, Cdr. Glyn Jones, the thirty-five-year-old regimental chaplain of Colonel "Chesty" Puller's 1st Marines, sought to assuage the fears of his many green and seasick Marines. Puller had briefed the regiment thoroughly in advance. "We learned where we were going, about the seawall, and about Wolmi-do . . . and about naval gunfire and how the fleet would come in to land the 5th Marines, then go back out and wait for high tide [to land us]."

Chaplain Jones thusly described in a nutshell the D-day assault on Inchon. Admiral Doyle planned to seize Wolmi-do first, on the morning tide, with the reinforced 3rd Battalion, 5th Marines. The unit would land at 0630 over Green Beach on the island's northwest coast. The Attack Force would return on the late afternoon tide to assault Inchon at 1730. The balance of the 5th Marines were to storm Red Beach north of Wolmi-do, and the 1st Marines were to assault over Blue Beach well to the south ("beach" in both cases loosely defined). The big concern shared by Doyle, Struble, and Smith on 15 September remained the long interlude—would the North Koreans counterattack the battalion left guarding Wolmi-do in the absence of the Attack Force? It was a coldly calculated risk.

With L-hour at 0630, the naval task force had to make a night passage of Flying Fish Channel. The mission called for shallow-draft amphibious ships. Doyle assigned three destroyer transports and a dock landing ship to his Advance Attack Group commander, Captain Sears. These ships met the rigid operational specifications, but none had significant troop capacity. The veteran troops of Lieutenant Colonel Taplett's 3rd Battalion, 5th Marines would be shoehorned in like sardines—easily doubling the maximum capacity of the four ships—for a dangerous passage through waters known to be mined. The Marines would welcome Wolmi-do simply for the breathing room.

The same fire support group of destroyers and cruisers that had so valiantly dueled Wolmi-do's coast defense gunners led Sears's four ships into the channel just after midnight on 15 September. Admiral Struble accompanied the column in *Rochester*. Bringing up the rear was Doyle's amphibious command ship *Mount McKinley*, loaded to her gunwales, it seemed, with senior flag officers, their staffs, and various reporters. Not the least of the embarked brass was the Commander in Chief, United Nations

Command, General of the Army Douglas MacArthur, boldly accompany-ing the Advance Attack Group to observe the action at close range.

Later in the night, as Sears's column approached Palmi-do a few miles below the harbor, MacArthur noticed the navigation light in the local light house brightly lit. "We were taking the enemy by surprise," he recorded later. "The lights were not even turned off." Not even the supreme commander knew of Lieutenant Clark's secret mission among the channel islands, capped when he turned on the light on Palmi-do at midnight on D-day.

The history of the Korean War would have been written differently had the Advance Attack Group encountered significant minefields in the nar-row channel leading to Inchon that night. They did not. Whether the North Koreans lacked the required equipment to activate the mines on hand or the expertise to lay the mines in darkness and at high tide is unknown. Sears's force encountered no new mines (UDT frogmen inspected a suspi-cious area marked by wooden stakes and found it to contain merely fish traps). Sailors and Marines of the invasion force uttered a collective sigh of relief.

Marine Corsairs flying from *Sicily* and *Badoeng Strait* attacked Wolmido at first light, lashing the still-smoking island with bombs, rockets, and 20-mm cannon fire. Maj. Robert P. Keller led the "Black Sheep" element of Corsairs from *Sicily* "dropping 500-pound bombs on Wolmido, then strafing the landing beach." As Keller pulled out of his firing runs, he marveled at the size of the invasion fleet flowing up the channel toward Inchon harbor.

Admiral Doyle signaled "Land the Landing Force" at 0520, initiating the complex choreography of the ship-to-shore movement, painstakingly timed to meet the 0630 L-hour. Ten minutes later the destroyers and cruisers opened fire on Wolmi-do, their gun crews by now intimately familiar with the island's fire-port caves and bunkers. Their marksman-ship impressed the VIP observers crowding the flag bridge of *Mount McKinley*. Marine Lieutenant General Shepherd, commanding the Fleet Marine Force, Pacific, watched with the seasoned eye of one who had experienced the vagaries of naval gunfire support from Guadalcanal to Okinawa. "I have never seen any better shooting," Shepherd declared. "The entire island was smothered with bursting shells from the cruisers and destroyers."

Doyle's integration of all supporting fires—air strikes, surface bom-bardment, LSMR rocket ships—proved masterful this critical day. Seldom had any landing force been the beneficiary of such a concentrated forty-five-minute preliminary pounding. Nor did this umbrella of steel and smoke end at L-hour. As soon as Taplett's lead companies swarmed aggressively ashore from their sixteen LCVPs, the ships' gunners and Corsair pilots shifted their fire inland to the slopes of 351-foot Radio Hill or the small appendage islet, So Wolmi-do. On the heels of the LCVPs that delivered Taplett's infantry to Green Beach came three heavy lighters launched from the dock landing ship *Fort Marion* (LSD-22), bearing M26 Pershing tanks and an M4 Sherman flame tank.

The 3rd Battalion, 5th Marines—"The Darkhorse Battalion"—had fought half a dozen pitched battles against the best divisions of the *In Min Gun* (NKPA) the preceding month near Pusan. Taplett had proven adept at integrating his own supporting arms—tanks, recoilless rifles, mortars, and machine guns—with the heavier ordnance on call from his attached tactical air control party and the shore fire control party. His riflemen had fire in their eyes. They steamrolled the dazed second-rate troops defending Wolmi-do in less than forty-five minutes of violent close combat. The American flag flew over Radio Hill before 0700. By 0715 Taplett reported to Captain Sears the end of effective resistance on the main island. No Marine had been killed and seventeen had been wounded.

MacArthur smiled broadly at the sight of the American colors on Radio Hill and again upon hearing Taplett's reports. To Doyle: "Say to the fleet, 'The Navy and Marines have never shone more brightly than this morning.'" Then, surveying the circle of flag and general officers who had argued against his vision of Inchon, MacArthur said briskly, "That's it—let's get some coffee!"

The Advance Attack Group's quick and nearly bloodless victory at Wolmi-do and the muted response to the invasion from the Inchon defenders served to dissipate allied fears of a massive counterattack during the intertidal period. As Taplett watched the fleet withdraw with the receding tide he experienced much less anxiety than he had anticipated. "The day-long wait for Operation Chromite to resume seemed like sitting on the 50-yard line at halftime, waiting for the second half of a football game to begin," he said. His main concern centered on his casualties, dispatched in haste with Navy corpsmen in an LCVP to catch the departing ships. The small boat missed the connection by only a matter of minutes, and then became stranded high and dry by Inchon's incredibly shrinking tide. The wounded men were transported to safety when the fleet returned with the high tide.

Helpless to retrieve these men from the steaming gumbo of the mudflats, Taplett looked for other ways for his battalion to resume the fight. Later in the day, perhaps with residual adrenalin still pumping through his body, Taplett radioed for permission to launch a tank-infantry attack over the causeway into Inchon to seize a fortified lodgment on the south flank of Red Beach. Success would facilitate his regiment's subsequent assault. Doyle ordered him to stand fast.

The men of Taplett's Darkhorse Battalion may have been alone in Inchon harbor that hot afternoon, but they had plenty of company in the skies overhead. Rear Adm. Richard W. Ruble's Task Group 90.5 continuously cycled Marine Corsairs from the escort carriers *Sicily* and *Badoeng Strait* over the island as a modified combat air patrol. Farther at sea, Rear Admiral Ewen's Task Force 77 launched Skyraiders loaded for bear on patrol over the land and sea approaches to Inchon. All pilots maintained a special watch over the causeway to Wolmi-do. Ewen's fast carriers received a welcome reinforcement on D-day when *Boxer* (CV-21), completing her third high-speed, transoceanic shuttle since the war began, arrived from the United States to join *Valley Forge* and *Philippine Sea* (CV-47).

Doyle's increasingly confident Attack Force returned up the channel by mid-afternoon for the main event, the landings over Red and Blue beaches, which had now become for the Navy anticlimactic—the exact effect Doyle had sought by his exhaustive preliminary operations. Once again the ships, aircraft, and rocket boats opened fire in their carefully integrated sequence. Hitting targets in Inchon required more precision than on Wolmi-do. Admiral Struble had ordered careful control of fire missions to avoid collateral damage to civilians and nonmilitary facilities in the bustling city of two hundred thousand people. Yet the NKPA clearly occupied Observatory Hill and other high ground throughout the city, as well as trenches, bunkers, and gun emplacements just above the seawalls. The configuration of both beaches required the Marines in effect to attack into the center of a bight, leaving their flanks vulnerable to enfilade fire. "It really looked dangerous," said Captain Fenton, a rifle company commander in the 5th Marines. "There was a finger pier and causeway that extended out from Red Beach which reminded us of Tarawa, and, if machine guns were [there], we were going to have a rough time making that last 200 yards to the beach."

By contrast, Admiral Struble was by this time so confident of success that he invited General Almond to tour the harbor in an unmarked landing craft just seaward of the assault waves in order to educate the corps

commander in the fine art of amphibious warfare. Almond got an unin-
tended eyeful, as we shall see.

The main assault on Inchon proved to be a ragged affair, due in part to
complicated landing plans and lack of rehearsal. The enormous seaborne
assault represented the first amphibious experience under fire for the overwhelming majority of landing craft coxswains, LVT drivers, wave guides,
boat group commanders, and primary control vessel skippers. The day,
nearly spent, grew dark. Rainsqualls and smoke from burning buildings
obscured much of the waterfront. The results were not pretty.

Chesty Puller's 1st Marines had the longest distance to cover and the
largest force to control—fifteen waves of amphibian tractors and six of
LCVPs. Many of the craft bristled with handmade boarding ladders for
surmounting the seawalls. Confusion grew as wave commanders tried to
pick out their assigned landing points through the smoke. "No landmarks
could be seen in the grayish-green pall," wrote retired Marine Brig. Gen.
Edwin H. Simmons of his experiences as a weapons company commander
with the 1st Marines at Inchon. "The assault waves crisscrossed during the
run into the seawall, and all the sorting out wasn't complete before it was
pitch black." As Simmons searched for his landing point he asked his LVT
driver if the vehicle had a compass.

"Beats me, sir," the Marine shrugged. "A month ago I was driving a bus
in San Francisco."

As the 1st Marines scrambled to get their battalions ashore at Blue
Beach before dark, the unmarked LCVP containing Admiral Struble and
General Almond hove to a few yards from one congested segment of the
seawall. Almond was gaining valuable firsthand information about the difficulties of amphibious assaults, but the two commanders had unwittingly
moved into harm's way. A furious Marine sergeant yelled out from the
shallows, "BOAT THERE! GET THE HELL OUT OF HERE!" Almond
sputtered, but Struble ordered his coxswain to comply. Puller's combat
engineers had set charges to demolish a section of the wall, and Struble's
boat barely cleared the area when the charges blew, rocking the craft and
dusting its distinguished occupants with concrete fragments.

Chaplain Jones paid a higher price for the same explosion. "They blew
up the seawall too soon," he protested. "Huge chunks of concrete began to
come down . . . and one of those things landed on my communion kit!"

Chesty Puller, always at his best in chaotic situations, landed on Blue
Beach just behind the first assault waves and by the power of his bulldog
personality brought order out of rampant disorder. Meanwhile, just before

dark, the eight "kamikaze" LSTs commenced their desperate run to Green Beach under heavy fire.

Admiral Doyle admitted after the war that his greatest concern on D-day—once the Attack Force found no new mines in the channel and successfully overcame Wolmi-do—was the fate of his eight LSTs, the high-priority cargo ships earmarked to touch land on the heels of the Red Beach assault forces and remain deliberately stranded overnight. The ships would be sitting ducks at low tide. "I especially worried about having a United States Navy ship captured," he confided.

In World War II amphibious commanders rarely beached their LSTs until their assault forces had at least driven the enemy beyond direct fire range. Doyle did not have this luxury at Inchon. These cumbersome ships would be nosing ashore on an undeniably "hot" beach, subject to machine-gun, mortar, and artillery fire the final mile of their approach. Lt. Cdr. James C. Wilson commanded this unlikely flotilla, Task Element 90.3.2.1. "My orders were to get as many of the eight ships into the Red [Beach] area and unloaded as was humanly possible, no matter what the cost," he said.

North Korean gunners concentrated their fire on the approaching LSTs, hitting and holing several ships, setting one afire. Sailors on the weather decks returned fire indiscriminately, hitting more Marines ashore than enemy soldiers. Commanders conned their ships to plow into the quay wall with enough force to make space for the LST bow doors and ramps to function. "This was our first beaching," said Lieutenant Houston, skipper of *LST-799.* "We hit the seawall at about six knots. The ship shuddered and bounced for several minutes before hanging onto the quay. It was well that we had hit hard, for we shattered the quay wall, enabling us to commence immediate unloading."

Sailors and Marines worked all night to unload the beached LSTs and distribute the critical supplies to the front lines. From time to time a North Korean submachine gunner hidden in a nearby pile of rubble unnerved the Americans by firing. By dawn even these outbursts had ceased. The Marines, superbly resupplied by the exposed crews of the LSTs, had held their beachhead and were positioned to continue the assault on Seoul. Wilson awaited the high tide to extract his LSTs and make room for the fully loaded follow-on LSTs.

Many valiant ships contributed to the "Victory at High Tide" at Inchon during 13–15 September 1950, but only this task unit of eight do-or-die LSTs and the task element of six destroyers that stood and delivered fire against the guns of Wolmi-do received the Navy Unit Commendation.

MacArthur's surprise seizure of Inchon, executed so swiftly by Struble and Doyle, opened the back door to Seoul. X Corps troops and equipment poured ashore. In the next five days General Smith's 1st Marine Division seized Kimpo airfield and executed a forcible crossing of the Han River with the 5th Marines. The Corsair squadrons of General Cushman's Tactical Air Command deployed to Kimpo on one day and began flying close air support missions the next. General Almond assumed command of the X Corps on 21 September, officially ending the amphibious operation. Most maneuver elements had by then advanced beyond effective range of the naval gunfire ships anchored in the Inchon approaches. Heavy fighting lay ahead, especially among the tangled ridges just west of Seoul where the 5th Marines suffered Peleliu-like casualties, but by 25 September four regimental combat teams (three Marine, one from the Army's 7th Division) had crossed the river and were fighting within the city limits. Organized resistance by the North Koreans ended late on 27 September. Two days later, the X Corps bridge sections having arrived just in the nick of time, General and Mrs. MacArthur, President and Mrs. Syngman Rhee, and other dignitaries entered Seoul for the liberation ceremony.

The fact that the Red Chinese intervention later in the year resulted in the loss of Seoul, Kimpo, and Inchon should not diminish MacArthur's vision nor Joint Task Force 7's valor in executing an exceedingly difficult amphibious campaign that liberated an occupied capital in twelve days. Operation Chromite remains an amphibious masterpiece, an encouraging example of joint and combined teamwork, a jury-rigger's delight. Among the many miracles performed by Doyle and his Task Force 90 at Inchon, the rapid transformation of the wretched LSTs remains the most salutary. "It is phenomenal that the LSTs were able to perform their assigned missions only fifteen days after commissioning," observed the anonymous author of the Pacific Fleet Interim Evaluation Report. Doyle was also graced by phenomenal luck—from the typhoons to the mines, from the frail LSTs to Lieutenant Clark's near-suicidal intelligence mission—the kind of luck that sometimes comes to those unafraid of hard work and blind faith.

Retired Fleet Admiral Halsey sent MacArthur a congratulatory telegram after Inchon, calling the assault from the sea "the most masterly and audacious strategic stroke in all history."

MINE WARFARE AT WONSAN

IN MID-OCTOBER 1950, barely a month after receiving the news of the successful Inchon landing, Chief of Naval Operations Admiral Sherman received a candid admission from the Advance Force commander at Wonsan. Referring to the enemy minefields there, Rear Adm. Allan E. "Hoke" Smith observed that "we have lost control of the seas to a nation without a navy, using pre–World War I weapons, laid by vessels that were utilized at the time of the birth of Christ."

Smith would modify his characterization of the Wonsan minefields as subsequent intelligence reports arrived. Although the bulk of the mines encountered were indeed pre-World War I Russian contact weapons, Soviet advisors had also emplaced a number of sophisticated magnetic mines on the ocean floor. Further, the North Koreans used motorized barges much more often than their ancient sampans to lay the mines. Yet Smith's dire conclusion remained valid. Unlike at Inchon, Joint Task Force 7 faced minefields of significant proportion and lethality at Wonsan.

Naval analysts of the Cold War would later describe antishipping mines as "the poor man's amphibious defense." Mine warfare certainly became a nemesis to power projection from the sea in the Korean War, an efficient and affordable means for the North Koreans to offset the overwhelming naval power of the United States and its major allies. The lurking presence of enemy mines along both coasts hampered their ability to launch surprise amphibious assaults because preliminary minesweeping would tip off the Communists. Mines also forced gunfire ships to operate much farther out to sea and restricted the use of submarines and destroyers for inshore raiding missions.

These were heady days for the United Nations Command with first ROK Army and then other allied ground forces pouring across the 38th parallel in pursuit of the disintegrating NKPA. Giddy with success after Inchon, the allies changed their war aims from restoring the territorial and political integrity of South Korea to forcefully reunifying North and South Korea. The "Race to the Yalu" was on.

MacArthur and his staff wanted to repeat the success of the Inchon-Seoul campaign with another amphibious end run, this time a landing of X Corps on the east coast of North Korea at Wonsan. The choice seemed logical. Wonsan offered the finest port on either coast. The city was a rail

THE MINESWEEPERS

A LARGE SIGN GREETED the 1st Marine Division when the leather-necks finally landed at Wonsan after an unexpected three-week hiatus at sea: "THIS BEACH IS ALL YOURS THRU COURTESY OF MINE SQUADRON THREE." While impatient with their delay at sea, the Marines ruefully acknowledged the truth of the proclamation. The fact that they could now wade ashore at Wonsan was due entirely to the valiant efforts of a mere handful of minesweepers, the neglected orphans of the postwar Navy.

Few type commands sustained such draconian reductions as the mine warfare community did after the Japanese surrender. At the peak of World War II the Navy had in operation as many as 550 minesweepers of various configurations. Three hundred of these vessels served at Normandy in 1944; one hundred at Okinawa the following year. Yet only ten would be available to sweep a clear channel through the thousands of Russian mines at Wonsan.

By 1950 the Navy no longer maintained a mine warfare type commander and staff in the Pacific. In the Far East Command at the outbreak of the Korean War, Admiral Joy had nineteen mine ships in active commission: one steel-hulled AM fleet minesweeper, six wooden-hulled AMS auxiliary sweepers, and twelve Japanese minesweepers under contract. Their crews were uncommonly well trained, having spent the previous year sweeping WWII Allied mines from Japanese ports and harbors. In addition, Joy had ordered the activation of three other fleet minesweepers in a reduced operational condition. He placed an urgent request for the assignment to Korea of a handful of other mine vessels from elsewhere in the

Pacific, including several steel-hulled DMS destroyer minesweepers, then in equally high demand as substitute escorts for convoy duty.

Allied intelligence information on North Korean mine-laying capabilities and intentions proved sorely lacking at first. The fact that the North Koreans had strewn more than four thousand Soviet mines along both coasts in July and August was not reported until 23 September. Three days later the worst week of the war for the allied naval forces began. Five ships hit enemy mines. One sank; the others sustained heavy damage and many casualties. The unanticipated mine threat had changed the sea war.

The auxiliary sweeper *Magpie* became the first U.S. naval vessel sunk by enemy action since World War II. She had just arrived from Guam when she struck a mine in the Sea of Japan on 1 October and sank with the loss of the captain and twenty crewmen. Chief Boatswain's Mate Vail P. Carpenter, the senior man among twelve wounded survivors, reported the incident: "There was a tremendous explosion, . . . and the entire forward portion of the ship, forward of the stack, appeared to explode. The remainder of the ship immediately started to settle by the head." Carpenter and the other survivors barely had time to escape before *Magpie* went down.

Disaster struck the small mine force twice more on 12 October in Wonsan harbor when the fleet minesweepers *Pirate* and *Pledge* hit mines eleven minutes apart. Both ships sank, sustaining ninety-two casualties, including thirteen killed or missing in action. The loss would have been greater had it not been for UDT swimmers dispatched by the high-speed transport *Diachenko*. The frogmen extracted the living and the dead from *Pledge* just before she capsized and sank. Six days later mines destroyed first a Japanese sweeper then a ROKN craft in enormous explosions—further escalating the cost of a safe passage to Wonsan for the X Corps.

Considering the extent and lethality of the Soviet mines emplaced in Korean waters it is surprising that fleet losses were not higher. The deliberate process of sweeping channels through the approaches to Wonsan, Hungnam, and Chinnampo may not have met the ground commanders' timetables, but not one troop transport hit a mine during the war.

Ten Navy ships received the Presidential Unit Citation during the Korean War. All were minesweepers, including three that were sunk.

A magnetic mine claims the ROKN minesweeper *YMS-516*, conducting a sweep off the Wonsan invasion beaches on 18 October. The presence of magnetic mines slowed minesweeping operations, forcing a postponement of the landings until 27 October. (National Archives 80-G-423625)

Sweeping the Wonsan minefields, costly as it was, provided invaluable experience. One analyst concluded in 1954 that the Wonsan minefield operation provided "the foremost lesson of the entire naval conflict."

and highway hub, the site of a huge oil refinery and other heavy industries, and it could serve nicely either as the base for a flanking attack westward against the North Korean capital city of Pyongyang or for an advance farther up the east coast.

The success of the ground campaign ultimately frustrated MacArthur's plan. The general decided to disengage the X Corps divisions after the seizure of Seoul and concentrate them at Inchon and Pusan for reembarkation. This decision resulted in the loss of valuable time and created mammoth transportation bottlenecks. Both ports were overwhelmed by the accelerated logistic requirements of the Eighth Army as it surged out of the Pusan Perimeter. Meanwhile, the Capital Division of the ROK Army had advanced rapidly up the east coast beyond the parallel. Several naval officers began to suggest a logical alternative to the Wonsan operation: forego the second landing, keep the roads and ports clear for the Eighth Army, and advance X Corps overland to Wonsan in trace of the ROKs.

"The Tenth Corps could have marched overland to Wonsan in a much shorter time and with much less effort than it would take to get the Corps around to Wonsan by sea," said Admiral Joy. Rear Admiral Burke, Joy's deputy chief of staff, added: "We objected to an amphibious assault as being unnecessary. It would take a lot of troops out of action for a long time when the enemy was already on the run." Yet General Almond deflected these protests away from his boss, Douglas MacArthur, saying, "From a tactical point of view, it's cheaper to go to Wonsan by sea."

MacArthur's decision to execute an amphibious landing at Wonsan remained unchanged. Hence, Admiral Joy reestablished Joint Task Force 7 under the command of Admiral Struble. Both officers were aware of a mine threat in Korean waters. More than fifty mine sightings were reported to them during September alone. The mine threat to Struble's ships rose significantly between the time of MacArthur's warning order for the Wonsan landing and the date Admiral Doyle's loaded transports finally sortied from Inchon.

On 26 September the destroyer *Brush* (DD-745) struck a mine off Songjin, North Korea, that killed thirteen crewmen and wounded thirty-four. A skilled damage control party shored up her badly damaged bow, but the ship remained in danger of sinking during the next four days as she limped back to Sasebo, 470 miles away. The destroyer *Mansfield* passed the stricken destroyer and her escorts while steaming from Sasebo to the Sea of Japan. It proved to be an omen; *Mansfield* hit a mine on 30 September while searching for a downed B-26 pilot in the North Korean harbor of Chosen-ko. The explosion heavily damaged the destroyer's bow, wounded twenty-eight Sailors, and knocked the ship out of the war for several months. The next day, the auxiliary minesweeper *Magpie* (AMS-25) struck a mine off the east coast of South Korea and sank with heavy loss of life. *Magpie* was the first U.S. naval vessel to be sunk since World War II.

A PBM Mariner patrol plane of Fleet Air Wing 6 returns to *Curtiss* (AV-4) from mine-hunting patrols off North Korea. The Navy also used helicopters to spot enemy minefields at Wonsan. (Naval Historical Center)

News of these losses alarmed the Sailors throughout the blockade and escort forces.

James E. Alexander, a petty officer on the destroyer *John A. Bole* (DD-755), recalled his uneasiness after seeing *Mansfield* with her bow blown off: "My bunk was in the forward crew's quarters. That's where a mine would hit. If it happened in the predawn hours, casualties would be horrendous—a dozen dead chiefs and fifty dead crewmen. Assuming they were able to find and identify our remains."

Admiral Struble understood these unspoken concerns. His own operational background included experience in nerve-wracking minesweeping operations. After the Japanese surrender he had assumed command of Minecraft, Pacific Fleet with the responsibility for clearing mines throughout the Western Pacific.

Struble assumed the North Koreans would mine their prime harbor at Wonsan. If they had done as ragged a job as they did at Inchon, perhaps his few minesweepers could clear sufficient lanes by D-day, originally set for 15 October. He also had great confidence in his Advance Force commander, Admiral Hoke Smith.

Smith, Commander Task Force 95, the Blockading and Escort Force, was assigned the additional duty of commanding the Advance Force for Wonsan. Smith was fifty-eight years old at the time of Wonsan, the oldest of the senior line officers waging the war at sea that autumn. A Naval Academy graduate with the Class of 1915, he had been a battleship Sailor in both world wars. He served as a junior officer on board *New York* (BB-34) in the North Atlantic in 1918 and commanded *South Dakota* (BB-57) in the Central Pacific in 1944. More appropriately for the task awaiting at Wonsan, Smith had commanded a mine division and a 1,160-ton light minelayer. A man of uncommon courage well suited by temperament and experience for the responsibility, Smith would distinguish himself by his personal leadership of the minesweeping missions at Wonsan and Chinnampo.

The North Koreans began the war without a mine capability of their own. So as soon as the United States intervened, the Soviets wasted no time shipping thousands of mines across their Siberian border with North Korea. Some of the weapons arrived without the proper arming gear as at Inchon; others were laid hastily by inadequately trained North Koreans. But the Soviets took their time at Wonsan, creating multiple minefields, showing the North Koreans how to lay contact mines in patterns from open-decked barges, and emplacing the magnetic mines themselves. The

Soviet advisors departed Wonsan the first week of October, their job done, just before Admiral Smith's Advance Force arrived. By 10 October Smith realized he faced the monumental task of clearing more than four thousand mines covering four hundred square miles.

Smith already knew that minesweeping would be decidedly more difficult in the Sea of Japan than in the Yellow Sea. Most Korean rivers flow into the Yellow Sea, accounting in part for its unusual hydrography—shallow and opaque water, numerous offshore islands and estuaries, and extreme tides. The depth of the Yellow Sea remains around twenty fathoms as far as ten miles from the coast, but the 100-fathom curve in the Sea of Japan lies close inshore. Both coasts feature south-flowing currents, allowing the North Koreans to release free-floating mines, or "drifters," in hopes of sinking or damaging UN blockading ships farther down the coast. The North Koreans also covered their Wonsan minefields with coastal guns that were hidden on three harbor islands.

Capt. Richard T. Spofford, commanding Mine Squadron 3, began the mine-clearing task at Wonsan on 10 October with only six sweepers. Both Spofford and Hoke Smith adopted innovative methods to help spot and clear the enemy mines. The Advance Force made naval warfare history in early October by employing helicopters for the first time to locate an enemy minefield. "It didn't take long to discover the value of the helicopter as a mine-hunting platform," said the gunnery officer of the cruiser *Worcester* (CL-144), whose helicopter preceded Spofford's sweepers into the minefields. "If the sea was not rough, if the direction of the sun rays was right, and if the water was clear, you could see the mines very easily." *Worcester*'s helicopter confirmed the vast extent of the Wonsan minefield on 10 October.

Sobered by the breadth of the minefields, Spofford suggested to Smith that they use aerial bombing to detonate the mines. Smith agreed and requested Struble's help. Struble had tried this technique without success four years earlier but consented to the experiment. He ordered Task Force 77 to deploy AD Skyraiders and F4U Corsairs armed with 1,000-pound bombs for the mission. The results proved underwhelming. Few mines were exploded, even when the carrier aircraft used depth charges.

Smith also tasked the UDT swimmers from *Diachenko* (APD-123) with marking mines and searching for electrical wiring leading from the harbor islands that might indicate the presence of command-detonated bottom mines. The frogmen discovered no wiring but they did find many more

Underwater demolition team "frogmen" haul their rubber boat ashore at Wonsan after working to neutralize a North Korean minefield. (National Archives)

standard mines than they could possibly mark in a day. Minesweepers would have to do the job.

The 12th of October was a dark day for the Advance Force. Two of Spofford's workhorse fleet minesweepers, *Pirate* (AMS-275) and *Pledge* (AMS-277), struck mines within a span of eleven minutes. Both sank. North Korean shore gunners then opened up from Sin-do, severely hampering rescue operations. At the height of the crisis the fleet minesweeper *Incredible* (AM-249) experienced total engine failure. Only the spirited fire from the force's auxiliary minesweepers and a PBM Mariner seaplane of Patrol Squadron 47 prevented a general slaughter of surviving vessels.

Lt. Richard O. Young, commanding the ill-fated *Pledge*, reported the final minutes of his ship:

> The starboard side of the hull, just forward of the superstructure, was rent from below the waterline to the topside. The deck, at this location, was also sheared from gunwale to gunwale. . . . The silence that reigned

throughout the ship indicated that casualties were very heavy. I therefore gave the order to abandon ship.

Diachenko's ubiquitous UDT detachment came swiftly to the rescue in two small boats. The courageous Sailors ignored the shore batteries that bracketed the sinking hulks with shellfire, and saved many lives, including that of Lieutenant Young, hobbled by a broken leg.

The disaster sent shock waves throughout the fleet. Sherman admitted his frustration in a frank interview with columnist George F. Eliot:

> They caught us with our pants down. Those damn mines cost us eight days' delay in getting the troops ashore and more than two hundred casualties. That's bad enough. . . . Hoke's right; when you can't go *where* you want to, *when* you want to, you haven't got command of the sea. And command of the sea is a rock-bottom foundation of all our war plans. . . . Now we're going to start getting mine-conscious—beginning last week.

Hoke Smith directed Spofford to search first, then sweep—regardless of the time consumed. Spofford used his wooden hulled auxiliary sweepers, the UDT teams in their small boats, plus helicopters and PBM Mariners to search for and mark the mines. In this manner the task force designated an approach lane to the beach for sweeping by Spofford's "Chicks," the wooden-hulled auxiliaries. By 18 October it seemed to all hands that the worst was over and the revised D-day of 20 October could still be met.

Instead, 18 October became another dark day for the Advance Force. "Suddenly," reported the skipper of one of the auxiliaries, "the whole ocean started to erupt amidst the sweepers." The task group had encountered a string of bottom-laid influence mines. One weapon erupted under the keel of ROKN *YMS-516* and literally vaporized the small vessel. "Everything went into a tailspin," said the mine division commander. "We didn't know what type mine we had triggered—we didn't know where—we didn't know how many. We were back where we started." Admiral Smith reported to Admiral Joy: "Task Group 95.6, after fighting and cutting its way through for 25 miles, and within an arm's length of Blue-Yellow beaches, had three ground mine explosions."

Struble postponed D-day again, this time until 25 October, but at that point it was academic. The ROK I Corps had captured Wonsan by overland approach on 11 October. By 14 October, Marine Fighter

Squadron 312, the "Checkerboard Squadron," had landed at Wonsan's captured airfield. The Eighth Army captured Pyongyang on 19 October and rolled north toward the Yalu River. On 24 October occurred the ultimate indignity for the embarked Marine landing force—a Bob Hope USO show at Wonsan. Hundreds of appreciative ROK soldiers and Marine aviators enjoyed the show.

The Marines afloat had already renamed Operation Tailboard (the assault on Wonsan) "Operation Yo-Yo." The amphibious ships of Admiral Doyle's Attack Force steamed in monotonous rectangles, and their food supplies dwindled. Sailors and Marines suffered from dysentery, crowding, and boredom. "Never did time die a harder death, and never did the grumblers have so much to grouse about," stated the official historians of Marine operations in the fall of 1950.

The Marines would have atrophied at sea a lot longer were it not for the initiative of Lt. Cdr. Donald C. DeForest, a mine warfare specialist attached to Captain Spofford's staff. When the influence mines disrupted the final sweeping of the channel to Wonsan's beach, DeForest voluntarily went ashore and learned from some sympathetic North Koreans that the Soviets indeed had emplaced magnetic-influence mines in the final approaches. This confirmation enhanced Smith's ability to neutralize these weapons.

Clearing these last, dangerous influence mines took Spofford's depleted force an additional week's work, but by the evening of 25 October the coast was finally clear. The task of detecting, sweeping, and destroying the approximately 225 mines in the designated approach channel from the sea had taken fifteen days. Thousands more mines remained in close proximity, and in later months of the war these weapons and fresh ones laid by the North Koreans would continue to claim U.S. Navy ships and their crews.

The twenty-one transports and fifteen LSTs carrying the 1st Marine Division threaded their way fearfully through this narrow passage on 26 October. The leathernecks streamed ashore stiffly, ignoring the jibes of the Checkerboard aviators, and fanned out to their inland objectives, anxious to make up for lost time. Three days later Admiral Doyle's force landed the 7th Infantry Division at Iwon, north of Hungnam. Elements of this division would become the only U.S. forces to reach the Yalu River.

Admiral Smith received a few additional minesweepers to help clear Hungnam and Iwon on the east coast and—increasingly critical to the support of the Eighth Army—on the west coast at the port of

Chinnampo. As early as 21 October General Walker had signaled he could no longer supply his fast-moving forces by trucks and trains and needed seaborne resupply.

Smith dispatched two of his mine warfare experts to begin collecting intelligence about Chinnampo. The pair found a virtual intelligence gold mine in the ruins of Pyongyang—civilian tugboat and barge skippers who had been pressed into mine-laying service by the NKPA the previous summer. Hoke Smith would soon know with unusual precision the location of each string of mines in Chinnampo harbor, both contact and magnetic types. The mine force found their mission somewhat easier to perform on Korea's west coast, with its extreme tidal range and shallow waters. As a result, sweeping there proceeded at a much faster rate than had been the case at Wonsan, and this time the force suffered the loss of no men or ships to mines. "Like so many things in human life," observed naval historian James A. Field, "the opening of a mined harbor is easier the second time."

The U.S. Navy took a hard look at its mine warfare deficiencies displayed so graphically at Wonsan. "Mine warfare has long been a low priority training subject for general consumption in the Navy," concluded the CINCPACFLT Interim Evaluation Report. The experience sobered Hoke Smith. "The Russians apparently have everything we have and everything the Germans had in mining techniques," he stated. "The United States must put minesweeping on the same priority level as antisubmarine and carrier warfare." The Navy's mine-hunting and minesweeping capabilities would wax and wane throughout the next half-century, but never again would these capabilities become as deficient as those before Wonsan.

Meanwhile, an unseasonably cold wind from the Taebaek Mountains presaged the approach of an early winter. Far to the northwest, from the island-dotted mouth of the Yalu River, came a clandestine report from Navy Lieutenant Clark, the covert warrior of Inchon harbor. Clark had volunteered to wage another naval guerrilla war, this time by recruiting native Koreans among the islands in the Yellow Sea for raids and reconnaissance missions along the northwest coast. Clark then deployed his agents into the Yalu itself. They reported to him the alarming news that massive numbers of Chinese Communist troops were crossing the river each night from Manchuria. Clark relayed this critical intelligence by radio to MacArthur's headquarters in Tokyo. Considering the information unsubstantiated, the Far East Command chose to ignore the report.

FROM CHOSIN TO HUNGNAM

THE NAVY'S OPERATIONAL TEMPO during the month following the Wonsan landing ranged from bare steerageway to "flank speed ahead." The period abounded with rumors and blind optimism. The United Nations Command did little to analyze Red China's intentions on behalf of its reeling North Korean ally and instead perpetuated the stampede for the Yalu with promises of "Home by Christmas."

Some fleet activities never abated. Maritime patrol aircraft searched the distant horizons to provide early warning of Soviet or Chinese naval and air interventions. Frigates continued to escort convoys of MSTS ships and time-chartered merchantmen from Japanese to Korean ports. Submarines patrolled La Pérouse Strait for unusual Soviet naval activity, and destroyers, seaplanes, and submarines operated along the coast of China to discourage Chinese Communist or Nationalist military adventures.

The U.S. Navy began submarine operations in support of the Korean War as early as July 1950 with the deployment of *Catfish* (SS-339), *Pickerel* (SS-524), and *Remora* (SS-487) on reconnaissance patrols. Lt. Cdr. Paul R. Schratz, commanding *Pickerel*, led the *Tench*-class diesel sub into the Sea of Japan during 14–22 August to conduct a photoreconnaissance survey of Wonsan, a site already under consideration by MacArthur as a future amphibious objective. Schratz accomplished his surreptitious mission blithely ignorant that the Russians and North Koreans were laying the most extensive minefield of the war in proximity to the boat. "Only later did I learn the area was heavily mined," Schratz admitted. "Few Pacific Fleet submarines, including *Pickerel*, at the time had mine-detecting QLA sonar installed and none had mine-clearing cables."

The discovery of mines in Korean waters altered the special mission of *Perch* (ASSP-313), recently reconfigured as a troop carrier. Her conversion resulted from a discussion between Admiral Burke and Lt. Col. Douglas B. Drysdale, Royal Marines, who led 41 Commando. Drysdale requested a mission ashore for his battalion-sized force. Burke replied, "I don't know how the hell to use commandos—any ideas?" The two officers decided to conduct a series of submarine-based raids along the eastern coast of North Korea. "We got one of our subs [*Perch*] stripped it down, [and] put in some rubber rafts," said Burke. He observed that they "did a pretty good job."

Perch sortied from Japan on 25 September with Drysdale and sixty-seven of his Royal Marines embarked. Lt. Cdr. K. D. Quinn, the boat's commanding officer, received an urgent communication en route to

Recently reconfigured as a troop carrier, *Perch* carried Royal Marine commandos for the purpose of conducting raids along North Korea's eastern coast. (National Archives USN)

remain outside the 50-fathom curve because of the new mine threat. On 1 October, taking advantage of a brief window between the beginning of nautical twilight and the rising of a three-quarter moon, *Perch* surfaced four miles off the coast and launched eight rubber boats loaded with commandos. The Royal Marines spent the next seven hours planting explosives in two tunnels and a culvert under the coastal highway and fending off North Korean counterattacks. The raiders returned to the submarine by 0300, bearing the body of one Royal Marine killed in the fighting. The next day, well out to sea, Quinn surfaced and conducted a burial service with the crew and commandos standing at attention on deck. "Broke the United Nations' flag and lowered it to half mast," reported Quinn. "The deceased, covered by the British ensign, was . . . committed to the deep."

No one disparaged the boldness of the plan or the bravery of the commandos and submariners, but Admirals Joy and Struble decided not to repeat the raid. The enemy easily and quickly repaired the damaged tunnels and culverts, and Navy leaders weighed this fact against the considerable risks to the submarine from mines and coastal guns. Drysdale's 41 Commando then moved ashore and joined the 1st Marine Division in its advance through the Taebaek Mountains to a distant reservoir called by the Japanese *Chosin*. Near there, in November, Task Force Drysdale would gain international fame for its valiant but costly effort to break through encircling Chinese Communist troops.

Navy Lieutenant Clark and his scouts along the Yalu River had been correct. The Chinese Communists were crossing the border in enormous strength, executing one of the greatest secret deployments in modern military history. Biding their time until the Siberian winter unleashed its full fury in late November, the Chinese prepared to hurl half a million men against the scattered and largely unsuspecting United Nations forces slogging blindly northward.

By mid-November the UN ground forces had advanced well beyond naval gunfire range, and Admiral Struble began sending more and more ships to Japan for upkeep and liberty. Some of the overworked carriers became candidates to return stateside. The war seemed nearly over. Then came a call from General MacArthur for carrier aircraft to bomb the Korean half of the Yalu River bridges, the first indicator that the top command was beginning to accept the evidence that organized Chinese units were crossing the border.

For the carrier squadrons, bombing highway and railroad bridges along the 450-mile-long Yalu proved extremely dangerous—Chinese anti-aircraft batteries fired at Navy aircraft with impunity from the PRC side, and Chinese MiG-15 jets (as intelligence later discovered, many flown by Soviet pilots) swarmed out of their Manchurian sanctuaries. In two tense weeks Navy Skyraiders and Corsairs destroyed three bridges while F9F Panther jets shot down three MiG-15s, but it was all too little, too late. The Chinese troops hidden in the mountains sprang their trap, first over-whelming the Eighth Army north of the Chongchon River and then launching a massive attack against the 1st Marine Division and elements of the 7th Infantry Division around the Chosin Reservoir on a night when the temperature sank to twenty degrees below zero.

Of the twin disasters, the Eighth Army's plight was the most critical. So severe was the shock of the Chinese assault that the entire force retreated in disarray all the way to the Imjin River, more than one hundred miles south. As early as 28 November Admiral Joy warned Admiral Doyle to prepare for a redeployment of all United Nations forces from North Korea. Backloading of ships began at Chinnampo on 5 December. The Chinese pursuit of the retreating Eighth Army petered out north of

Pyongyang, however, so most of the surviving UN forces proceeded south via the main highway rather than risk the slower process of evacuation by sea. In the east, the 1st Marine Division had no such choice. The Marines and soldiers were surrounded and more than sixty miles away from the port of Hungnam. Joy and Doyle redoubled their efforts to extract all of Almond's X Corps and the ROK I Corps from the northern ports along the Sea of Japan, principally Hungnam.

First, though, naval aviation had to assure close air support for the Marines and soldiers in their fighting withdrawal from Chosin. Maj. Gen. Field Harris, commanding the 1st Marine Aircraft Wing, flew into beleaguered Hagaru-ri at the edge of the reservoir to coordinate air support for the two regiments surrounded at Yudam-ni. Harris sent an emergency message to Admiral Joy asking that the "main fast carrier effort be made in support of 1st Marine Division. Navy aircraft particularly desired by Marines."

The carriers and their air groups responded with ten days of concentrated close air support that rivaled similar operations in World War II. Time and again Navy and Marine Corsairs saved the day for one more embattled outpost, screeching down some fire-swept valley, strafing just ahead of the front lines, their empty shell casings raining down on the heads of Marines below. "It was like having artillery right over your shoulder," said Captain Thach of the escort carrier *Sicily*.

In desperate fighting the troops often requested napalm strikes at dangerously close ranges. "That really worried us," admitted Cdr. Horace H. Epes, commanding *Leyte*'s VF-33. "Sometimes napalm spreads for a block—we were afraid we'd burn up our own troops." "Napalm canisters were like overgrown fuel tanks," said Lt. (jg) Thomas J. Hudner of VF-32. "They would tumble when they hit, and you could not depend on their accuracy." Yet for the Marines on the ground, struggling with both the Chinese and the extreme cold, the risk was worth taking. "After the first Corsair's napalm dropped," recalled Epes, "the ground controller snapped, 'Move it closer.'"

The Chosin Reservoir crisis eased perceptibly when the 5th and 7th Marines fought their way back to Hagaru-ri, retaining their tactical integrity and bringing out their combat vehicles, wounded, and most of the dead. Field Harris, who would lose his son in the ground fighting still to come, flashed a message to Commander Task Force 77 from Hagaru-ri where he watched the two regiments stride into the perimeter, looking

F9F Panther fighters secured on *Philippine Sea*'s forward flight deck wait out a snowstorm off Korea in November 1950. The early winter brought heavy seas, snow, and ice, further complicating flight operations in support of the Marine breakout from Chosin Reservoir. (National Archives)

like ghosts but singing the Marines' Hymn. "They thanked God for air," he reported. "I don't think they could have made it . . . without air support. . . . Tell your pilots they are doing a magnificent job."

The ungodly cold continued to impose a terrible burden on the men trying to execute the breakout. Lt. Cdr. Chester M. Lessenden (MC),

During the Korean War a carrier's ready room was typically packed for daily mission briefs. (*Naval Aviation News*)

regimental surgeon with the 5th Marines, described his efforts to provide basic medical care to the many casualties:

> Everything was frozen. Plasma froze and the bottles broke.... We couldn't change dressings because we had to work with gloves on to keep our hands from freezing. We couldn't cut a man's clothes off to get at a wound because he would freeze to death.... Did you ever try to stuff a wounded man into a sleeping bag?

Survivors would later describe the winter of 1950–51 along the Manchurian-Siberian border as the coldest in fifty years. The cold proved especially hazardous to aviators during launch and recovery on icy carrier decks. Pilots feared even more having to abandon their aircraft in the frigid mountains of North Korea.

The destroyer crews that served as plane guards and antisubmarine screens for the carriers suffered grievously from the cold. Destroyerman

James Alexander provided this description of December operations in the northern Sea of Japan:

> Subfreezing temperatures at sea and winds exceeding forty knots were not uncommon. Salt spray was turned into four-inch-thick layers of ice on the decks and rigging of ships. High winds made work on the destroyers particularly uncomfortable. Topside tasks were arduous and dangerous.

Plane guard duty became especially critical in the extreme cold. Downed pilots could freeze to death within minutes. It became a tradition in Task Force 77 for the carriers to reward destroyers for the speedy rescue of one of their pilots by delivering the man's weight in ice cream, a dubious wintertime treat, yet one still welcome in the austere mess decks of the "tin cans."

At the onset of the crisis, Admiral Doyle ordered every ship of Task Force 90 to sea and once again augmented his force with an array of merchantmen. There was no sense of panic. The Seventh Fleet maintained complete control of the air and sea. The X Corps defended Hungnam and Wonsan in strength. Doyle began to question the wisdom of giving up these hard-won ports, especially Wonsan. He and other naval officers proposed establishing a line across the narrow neck of North Korea, from Wonsan west. Barring that strategic option, Doyle suggested the creation of a deep enclave around the port. "I still feel that with the Navy's surface and air power available we should have held the Wonsan area indefinitely," he said after the war.

General MacArthur would have none of this. The United Nations Command suffered from shock and dismay at its reversal of fortune, and some leaders feared that the massive Chinese intervention portended the beginning of a third world war. Doyle turned to his task at Hungnam.

The evacuation of Hungnam represents one of the Navy's finest hours, a little-known saga that closed the sad chapter of "the Race to the Yalu" with dignity. Hungnam was for Admiral Doyle as much a professional achievement as the much more celebrated landing at Inchon. The three-week epic evacuation involved other supporting heroes, including the Naval Beachmaster Group and the Army's port-handling 2nd Engineer Special Brigade. The enterprising Marine Col. Edward H. Forney, who had accompanied Doyle to Japan just before the war to instruct MacArthur's troops in amphibious warfare, became General Almond's assistant chief of staff for amphibious matters. He served brilliantly ashore at Hungnam as Doyle's redeployment coordinator.

Hungnam is often described as "an amphibious operation in reverse." While the evacuation did not technically fit that definition—the enclave defenders were reinforced and resupplied from the sea daily and the ships were not combat loaded—the principles of amphibious warfare certainly applied throughout. The emphasis on "detailed planning and violent execution" also applied at Hungnam. The trick for Doyle was to keep the Chinese hordes at bay while steadily contracting the perimeter to the lowest remaining tactical component.

The major elements of X Corps and ROK I Corps redeployed from Hungnam to South Korea by echelons. The 1st Marine Division reached the perimeter first, its troops frostbitten and exhausted, but proud. "Look at those magnificent bastards," exclaimed a Navy surgeon who had served with the leathernecks in their earlier battles. The Marines sailed for Pusan on 15 December; the ROK divisions reembarked on 17 December; the 7th Infantry Division, on 21 December; and the newly arrived 3rd Infantry Division, which provided the bulk of the perimeter defense, on 24 December. While U.S. Air Force Flying Boxcars and Marine R5D transports airlifted out some troops and equipment from nearby Yongpo airfield, ships evacuated the overwhelming majority of X Corps. The figures seem staggering: 105,000 U.S. and ROK troops, 91,000 refugees, 650 POWs, 17,500 vehicles, and 350,000 measurement tons of combat cargo. Doyle executed these redeployments using a heterogeneous fleet of six APAs, six AKAs, twelve MSTS transports, seventy-six time-charter ships, eighty-one LSTs, and eleven LSDs.

The Chinese, suffering tens of thousands of casualties to the Marines and their air support (and the extreme cold), probed the Hungnam perimeter nightly but without conviction. Doyle's gunships laid down a curtain of fire around the shrinking enclave, firing thousands more shells than the Attack Force had used at Inchon. The firing line at sea included the battleship *Missouri*, now serving as Admiral Struble's flagship, and cruisers, but much of the firepower came from the main batteries of the destroyers. "We could hold anything within range of a 5-inch/38 gun," said Admiral Burke, still proud of his destroyerman roots.

The presence of so many refugees seeking evacuation surprised Doyle and Forney. The two established camps, screened refugees for Communist infiltrators, provided emergency medical support, and fed the desperate people bread and rice from the bakeries and galleys of the fleet. Forney

Korean refugees crowd on board SS *Meredith Victory* in December 1950 as the merchant ship carries them from Hungnam to South Korea. The fourteen thousand Koreans in the ship were part of the ninety-one thousand refugees evacuated through Hungnam. (Naval Historical Center)

did his absolute best to evacuate as many of the refugees as possible, spooning more than five thousand on each available LST and more than fourteen thousand on a single merchant ship. The total of ninety-one thousand civilian evacuees did not include, said naval historian James A. Field, "children in arms, in knapsacks, or *in utero*." *Missouri* Sailors marveled at the sight of landing craft crisscrossing the harbor overloaded with "Korean civilians, goats, chickens—the damnedest collection of things you ever saw."

Although Admiral Doyle would say that "time was our enemy now," the real enemy at Hungnam remained the unremitting cold. The unsung heroes of the evacuation proved to be the coxswains of the landing craft, exposed to the wind and sea spray round the clock—many of them nearly frozen stiff at the end of each stint of shuttling troops and refugees to ships anchored in the harbor—and the Navy divers of salvage ship *Conserver* (ARS-39), who braved the frigid waters twice to unfoul the screw of a Korean LST laden with 7,400 refugees.

Doyle recognized the vulnerability of his enormous flotilla clustered around Hungnam. When intelligence reports indicated a buildup of MiG jets on Manchurian airfields, he dispatched a destroyer on early warning picket duty fifty miles north. But he refused to become distracted from the mission. He had the fleet carriers *Valley Forge*, *Philippine Sea*, *Leyte*, and *Princeton* of Task Force 77 on station, amply screened by thirty-two destroyers (including *Brush*, fully repaired and back in service after her near-disastrous mining incident). The presence of these combatants served to dissuade any airborne attack by the Communists.

Doyle's final concern was to ensure that not a single United Nations fighting man was left behind. Assured of this, and having directed his UDT force to rig the port with a massive array of explosive charges, Doyle sortied from Hungnam on Christmas Eve and ordered the demolition of warehouses and other military facilities.

The Hungnam waterfront disappeared in a wall of flame and smoke. Ens. Lee Royal watched in awe from *Missouri*: "The whole damned city of Hungnam was about two hundred feet in the air. They blew that place wide

Demolitions set by Navy and Army explosives teams destroy Hungnam facilities and abandoned allied supplies on the last day of the evacuation, 24 December 1950. High-speed transport *Begor* (APD-127) stands by. (National Archives)

open." Task Force 90 steamed southward to await another turn in the fortunes of war.

Hungnam was no Dunkirk. Not a life was lost. There was no *Luftwaffe* attacking the ships as they sortied. And unlike Dunkirk, the allies at Hungnam did not abandon a single usable piece of combat equipment. By virtue of Task Force 90's attention to duty and the mission, X Corps withdrew from North Korea in good order, with full unit integrity, and totally equipped and motivated to resume the fight in the south. This was Task Force 90's greatest contribution to the UN cause.

The amphibious evacuation of Hungnam was as formidable and potentially as dangerous as the assault on Inchon had been. Both demanded the highest professionalism in the application of sea power. In James Field's cogent analysis, "freedom to come and go depends upon control of the sea. The Athenians at Syracuse, Cornwallis at Yorktown, the Axis forces in North Africa lacked this control. In those armies no one escaped captivity."

SEA POWER ON CALL

THE YEAR 1951 BEGAN with the United Nations ground forces trying to establish a new front line well south of the 38th parallel. When General Walker was killed in a jeep accident, the JCS dispatched Lt. Gen. Matthew B. Ridgway to Korea to command and resurrect the Eighth Army. Ridgway later replaced MacArthur as the UN commander in chief, yielding the Eighth Army to Lt. Gen. James A. Van Fleet. The Eighth Army became a highly professional force under the superb leadership of Ridgway and Van Fleet.

The Navy's operational tempo did not slacken in the first half of 1951. In addition to its blockade, escort, and fire-support duties, the Seventh Fleet handled its strategic mission of preventing the Red Chinese and Nationalist Chinese from spreading the Far Eastern conflict. Aircraft carriers, cruisers, destroyers, and patrol planes operated off the long China coast.

The fleet also protected Japan and kept watch over the Soviet fleet. The Soviet navy based eighty submarines in and around Vladivostok throughout the Korean War. Joseph Stalin would have changed the course of the war had he unleashed these vessels against United Nations naval forces. The U.S. Navy lacked sufficient destroyers and destroyer escorts in the Far East to conduct an all-out antisubmarine campaign off

Korea while still executing its other operational missions. The sea-lanes between the United States and South Korean ports were especially vulnerable. More than 95 percent of all U.S. troops and combat cargo reached Korea by ship. Indeed, during the three-year war MSTS delivered five million passengers, more than fifty-two million tons of cargo, and twenty-two million tons of petroleum, oil, and lubricants to Korea. Since no one could predict Stalin's intentions, the Navy did its best with the limited number of destroyers available and instructed each skipper to regard any submarine contact as hostile. There were no restrictive rules of engagement in effect.

Allied navies helped carry the torch of sea power. In addition to the yeoman work provided by Japanese-manned LSTs and minesweepers, Admiral Joy benefited from warships deployed by Great Britain, New Zealand, Australia, Canada, France, Colombia, Thailand, the Netherlands, and the Republic of Korea. The ROKN displayed commendable professional skill. South Koreans proved to be tough seamen, and their exploits against the Communists in the countless islands off both coasts of Korea became legendary.

The Seventh Fleet spent the opening weeks of 1951 harrying the advancing Chinese Communist armies with a series of amphibious feints, raids, and heavy bombardments. One major feint took place during 29–31 January when battleship *Missouri*, light cruiser *Manchester* (CL-83), and their escorts in the Sea of Japan pounded Kansong and then steamed forty miles north to hit Kosong. On the third day at Kosong, an amphibious task force moved in, launched boats, and dispatched them shoreward under a deluge of fire from every vessel in the force, including rocket ships and the destroyer tender *Dixie* (AD-14). Engaging in a rare combat mission, the tender fired a prodigious 204 rounds of 5-inch/38 in the bombardment.

Missouri closed out her deployment to Korea with a week of furious bombardment of North Korea's east coast during 14–19 March. "Mighty Moe" blasted bridges, tunnels, and industrial plants in Songjin, Chaho, and Wonsan. As earlier at Hungnam and Kosong, the battleship used her own helicopters to spot for both her main and secondary batteries.

The North Koreans fought back, emplacing more and better coast defense guns adjacent to their ports, bridges, and tunnels. Enemy shore batteries scored their first hits of the war against the destroyer *Charles S. Sperry* (DD-697) off Songjin on 23 December 1950. From that date through the end of the war, eighty-one other U.S. Navy ships sustained damage from shore batteries. Enemy gunners hit the destroyer

Two captured Chinese Communist soldiers are kept under guard on board the transport *General J. C. Breckinridge* (AP-176) in January 1951. Unlike thousands of their compatriots, these men survived the harsh fight for northeastern Korea in December 1950. (National Archives)

minesweeper *Thompson* (DMS-38) on three different occasions. On 14 June 1951 off Songjin, the ship closed to 40-mm range. To the crew's surprise, NKPA troops wheeled four mobile guns out of hiding and began blazing away. *Thompson* returned fire and sped off, but not before sustaining thirteen hits, heavy damage, and the loss of three killed and four wounded.

The battleship *New Jersey* was recommissioned before Thanksgiving 1950, and arrived in Korean waters on 17 May 1951. Four days later, near Wonsan, the enemy welcomed her to the war with two rounds of counterbattery fire. The first shell hit one of her massive turrets dead center and bounced off. The other exploded close aboard, killing one Sailor and injuring three others.

While the bigger ships dueled North Korean shore batteries between Wonsan and Songjin, the high-speed transport *Horace A. Bass*, with UDT 1 embarked, conducted daylight amphibious surveys along likely landing beaches in the south. On 19 January 1951, while investigating the beaches around Kamak Bay on the southwest coast, one of the ship's LCVPs, filled with frogmen, came under heavy small arms fire from a band of North Korean guerrillas. The ship scattered the enemy troops with 5-inch/38 fire from four thousand yards offshore, but the survey team suffered two killed and three wounded. The boat's exposed coxswain, Boatswain's Mate Third Class Sidney A. Peterson, bravely kept his vessel in harm's way to recover swimmers. North Korean bullets hit him in the scalp and the left knee, but Peterson stayed at his helm until all swimmers were safely on board.

Navy leaders still regarded Wonsan as its hard-earned prize, so on 16 February 1951 Admiral Joy ordered the start of a naval siege of the key, ice-free port. The operation lasted 891 days, preventing the enemy from using the sea or coastal waters along the northeast coast of Korea and reinforcing North Korean and Chinese fears about the UN amphibious threat. The Communists took the threat to Wonsan and their heartland seriously. For the rest of the war, they maintained a defending force of eighty thousand troops around the port.

Besieging Wonsan constituted hazardous duty throughout the twenty-nine-month operation. UN naval vessels had to contend with minefields and enemy guns dug into caves in the hills that overlooked the inner harbor. The harbor became a veritable boxing ring in which U.S. ships and Communist gunners exchanged close-range fire night and day, week after week. The siege of Wonsan took place largely within the port's inner harbor. As recalled by Cdr. John Victor Smith, a Seventh Fleet staff

Aviation ordnance mates affix rockets to the wings of a VF-64 Corsair on *Philippine Sea*. (National Archives)

officer, Wonsan was "almost like operating in the upper Chesapeake Bay. They could shoot at us from all sides, but we still kept destroyers in there. This was a siege from the inside out." Enemy gunfire damaged forty-four U.S. ships at Wonsan, beginning with the destroyer *Ozbourn* (DD-846), hit by Sin-do shore batteries on 18 February 1951. The Communists' last victim was the heavy cruiser *Saint Paul* (CA-73), which sustained severe underwater damage from a 90-mm shell on 11 July 1953.

The siege of Wonsan was the brainchild of Admiral Hoke Smith, who retained a vested interest in the harbor by virtue of his ordeal with the minefields in October 1950. Smith knew the harbor islands had to be cleared of enemy gunners for the siege to succeed. He attacked Sin-do first. On 24 February 1951, the light cruiser *Manchester* and the ships of Destroyer Division 112 pounded the small island while South Korean marines stormed ashore from LCVPs furnished by the dock landing ship *Comstock* (LSD-19). The results proved to be a jewel of a pocket-sized amphibious assault. The Korean marines lost one man to drowning but none to enemy fire. They swept the island, then captured nearby Tae-do and Yo-do. Shortly afterward, an enterprising force of target spotters and sea raiders of all services and nationalities began operating from these and five other harbor islands. A North Korean attempt in mid-March to recapture Sin-do with motorized sampans failed. This action was the only unsuccessful amphibious landing by either side in the war.

The siege of Wonsan was barely a month old when Adm. M. Martin relieved Admiral Struble in command of the Seventh Fleet. Martin was fifty-five years old and a former star athlete at the U.S. Naval Academy, Class of 1918. Korea was his third war. An accomplished naval aviator, Martin commanded the *Independence*-class light carrier *San Jacinto* during the campaigns to seize the Marianas, Palaus, and Philippines, then led a carrier division during the invasion of Okinawa. He came to appreciate the value of the Wonsan siege for covert intelligence activities. "Our intelligence units occupied the harbor islands," he said. "One division of destroyers supported them by fire and also supplied them with materials useful for buying intelligence information ashore, especially wool socks and soap. Their secondary chore was to support the activities of the CIA."

The destroyermen on siege duty nicknamed the stealthy delivery of intelligence agents ashore "Comber Operations." The destroyer *Wallace L. Lind* (DD-703) conducted thirty-eight nocturnal comber missions in the Wonsan vicinity during 1 February–14 March 1951. Typically, the ship launched a clandestine party in a 26-foot motor whaleboat that towed a rubber raft. Seaward of the surf zone, the comber party boarded the raft. Each man was "provided with overshoes, rain gear, and life jackets— because of the clandestine nature of their activities ashore, [which meant] they must be dry when they get on the beach," explained the ship's captain. The combers paddled ashore, paying out a light line from the whaleboat. Safely ashore, they stuffed their incriminating foul-weather gear in the raft and tugged the line twice as a signal for the whaleboat Sailors to retrieve the raft and then return to the ship. The real danger to the combers came from counterintelligence forces sometimes deployed along the high-water mark of the beach. Not many combers survived these forays ashore.

Wallace L. Lind's final mission in this series proved the most bizarre. The two intrepid intelligence agents who had worked so successfully during the Inchon operation, Lieutenant Clark and ROKN Lt. Cdr. Youn Joung, reported on board with the senior medical officer on MacArthur's staff, Army Brig. Gen. C. F. Sams. ROK agents near Wonsan had reported an outbreak of bubonic plague among the local Chinese Communist forces. The United Nations forces had not been immunized against the plague, nor were large stocks of the vaccine available in the theater. "It became imperative," reported Dr. Sams, "that determination should immediately be made whether or not Plague existed in North Korea." Agents reported the presence of several suspiciously sick Chinese soldiers in a field hospital below Wonsan. Clark and his team suggested snatching one of these patients for a confirmatory diagnosis.

Wallace L. Lind's rubber boat put the Clark party ashore at about 0100 on 14 March. With great luck the men linked up with the South Korean who had filed the report, a former chemist at the Wonsan refinery. The man had remarkable powers of observation, and provided Dr. Sams with a complete description of the sick Chinese soldiers he had seen firsthand. Sams said, "he described eruptions on the face, arms, legs, and torso which could be nothing else but hemorrhagic smallpox," a disease that just before death tends to turn the patient "black." For Sams this knowledge obviated the need for the team to proceed to the field hospital, twelve miles distant, and abduct a patient. There was no bubonic plague epidemic, and all United Nations troops had been inoculated against smallpox. Lieutenant Clark led the party back to the beach, signaled the whaleboat, guided in the wary raft paddlers, and hustled all hands back through the surf to safety—thereby completing his third and last clandestine mission ashore.

The waters around the besieged ports of Wonsan, Hungnam, and Songjin remained extremely hazardous due to drifting mines that either broke loose from their original moorings or were released by the Communists. The auxiliary minesweeper *Partridge* (AMS-31) hit a mine on 2 February 1951 southeast of Wonsan and sank in less than ten minutes with the loss of eight killed and six wounded (the fifth and last U.S. vessel sunk by mines in the war occurred in August 1952). Two destroyers sustained major mine damage in 1951, *Walke* (DD-723) on 12 June and *Ernest G. Small* (DD-838) on 7 October. Twenty-six men died on the former; nine on the latter. *Walke* may not have been damaged by a mine. The ship, screening a Task Force 77 carrier, was steaming at twenty knots in deep water and on calm seas. At 0740 a heavy explosion on the port side aft jolted the ship, rupturing the hull and flooding two compartments. James Alexander, on the nearby *John A. Bole*, described the sight of *Walke* as "ghastly." She had "a horrendous hole twenty-six-feet long and fifteen-feet high gaping from her port rear quarter. Her main deck was buckled upward. She listed ten degrees to port and was down at the stern until the freeboard on the port quarter was one foot." The assisting destroyers classified several sonar contacts in the next three hours as a submarine—"target width about

LVTs filled with British Royal Marines depart *Fort Marion* for a commando raid against a North Korean railroad. (National Archives)

10 degrees, metallic echo, low Doppler." Depth charge attacks produced no convincing evidence of a kill. *Walke* limped back to Sasebo for repairs. Ten missing Sailors were never found.

Maintaining such a hectic and continuing operational tempo on station demanded inspired logistic support. Yet the immense logistic service organizations of World War II had suffered the same draconian cutbacks as the operating forces. In the beginning, the lack of a mobile replenishment group compelled the destroyers to return to Sasebo every three days, a lamentable drawdown of combat power. The piecemeal buildup of service ships continued to hamper operational support, though the situation improved after Inchon. "Underway replenishment as an art made great progress," concluded the CINCPACFLT evaluators. By the spring of 1951 the fleet had sufficient mobile assets on hand to permit daily resupply operations. The carriers and escorts of Task Force 77 rendezvoused with the service squadrons in the late afternoon and reloaded critical supplies—especially aviation gasoline and ordnance—until midnight, and then returned to their stations ready for flight operations the next morning. The system enabled each carrier of Task Force 77 to launch daily strike missions virtually without pause. The nightly underway replenishments (UNREPs), however, were dangerous, exhausting work for the deck crews.

For all of its initial shortfalls, the Navy logistic support system delivered the goods. There were few instances in which operational objectives could not be met for lack of critical supplies. Navy and Marine Corps aircraft, for example, flew more than a quarter-million sorties during the Korean War, and they dropped more than 178,000 tons of bombs and fired 274,000 aerial rockets. Likewise, Navy ships fired more than four million rounds at the enemy. All of the ordnance, fuel, and repair parts necessary to achieve such a huge and lethal output arrived at the right place and time thanks to an often improvised but usually dependable logistic support system.

At Hungnam, for instance, ammunition ships of the logistic group delivered critical ordnance on time, in the quantity needed, and despite ungodly winter conditions. Task Force 90 fired 21,731 shells of 5-inch/38-caliber and larger to protect the shrinking perimeter ashore during 7–24 December 1950. The logistic support forces, said Admiral Doyle, "did a magnificent job keeping us supplied with ammo."

The most significant logistic improvement of the war related to the use of helicopters for medical support. The rotary-wing aircraft could quickly evacuate critically wounded or injured men from ships at sea or embattled outposts ashore to one of the fleet's nearby hospital ships, *Consolation* (AH-15), *Haven* (AH-12), or *Repose* (AH-16).

The enemy's logistic support system proved equally resilient. Despite twelve months of interdiction and close air support strikes by Navy, Air Force, and Marine squadrons, the Communist logistic arm kept troops and supplies flowing to the front. Admiral Martin could only shake his head in frustration when talking about the meager results of these vigorous and repetitive interdiction missions. "Every bridge that was within reach of our gunfire or bombing planes had been destroyed," he said. "Yet the supplies continued to get through. This logistic achievement on their part was really little short of miraculous."

Hanson Baldwin, the distinguished *New York Times* war correspondent, reflected on the inability of the bombing campaign to cut off enemy troops from their sources of supply. "They couldn't possibly stop men with ammunition on their backs from filtering through the hills. You can't do it by air power."

With General MacArthur's star in decline (President Truman relieved him of command in April 1951), and the front stabilizing around the

38th parallel, the opportunities to use the fleet's amphibious capabilities declined as well. Admirals Joy and Martin continued to call for amphibious landings behind the enemy's line. Inchon had given the Navy renewed confidence in the amphibious art. With the availability of more numerous and sophisticated minesweeping assets, naval leaders believed the fleet could avoid another Wonsan. The CINCPACFLT Interim Evaluation Report extolled the value of amphibious operations as "incalculable," pointing out that Inchon "changed the entire aspect of the war," and claiming that the Hungnam evacuation had no equal in modern military history. "Korea has proved the necessity for our continued training and readiness for amphibious operations," the report concluded.

The irrepressible Admiral Doyle left the scene in January 1951, relinquishing command of Task Force 90 to Rear Adm. Ingolf N. Kiland. In late May Kiland assembled thirty-two amphibious ships for weeklong training exercises with the 41 Independent Commando in the Chigasaki Beach area of Japan. The task group experimented with night landings and daylight withdrawals under cover of smokescreens.

Marines and naval aviation units could not participate in the Chigasaki exercise because the Chinese Communists had just launched a 175,000-man offensive against the X Corps sector of the United Nations line. The ROK divisions on the seaward flank had collapsed, and allied leaders feared that Communist forces would once again push down the coast to Pusan. General Almond's forces, however, saved the day in ferocious fighting. The Chinese tide ebbed, and enemy troops struggled back toward the 38th parallel.

General Van Fleet, newly selected to command the Eighth Army, saw an opportunity to deliver a telling blow. He had commanded a regiment in the Normandy invasion, the greatest seaborne landing of all time, and he retained an appreciation for amphibious envelopments. He ordered the 1st Marine Division to embark in amphibious shipping at Kangnong, and on 6 June 1951 (the seventh anniversary of D-day) to execute an amphibious assault on the North Korean port of Tongchon. This attack would be followed by the seizure of Kumhwa, the Communist command and logistics center at the eastern edge of the Iron Triangle.

The plan appalled General Ridgway. The new allied commander understood that support for the Korean War, both in Washington and throughout the country, had declined sharply. Tongchon was sixty miles north of the 38th parallel, and an attack on that site would represent a major escalation of the war. Moreover, amphibious landings were inherently costly. The American public would no longer tolerate a spike in the casualty rate. The war was in transition from one of high mobility to one of static, limited-risk defense of the status quo. Ridgway overruled Van Fleet. There would be no more Inchons in this war.

Van Fleet remained embittered by what he viewed as a politically directed emasculation of his mobility. "The Navy could've shot us ashore and kept us ashore as we built up," he said. "We could have built up faster than the enemy could have managed. . . . We had the Chinese whipped."

The fact that the war had changed irrevocably became manifest in a radio announcement by Soviet UN Ambassador Jacob Malik on 23 June 1951. He suggested that now, in Korea, would be a good time to begin cease-fire negotiations. Most Westerners exalted at the prospect of an end to the bloodshed. Many Americans believed the war almost over. Yet in the Sea of Japan and the Yellow Sea, the U.S. Navy's operational work continued undiminished, day after endless day. No one then imagined that the shooting war in Korea would drag on for two more bloody years.

COLONEL JOSEPH H. ALEXANDER *served nearly twenty-nine years on active duty as a Marine Corps assault amphibian officer, including two combat tours in Vietnam and five years at sea. He was a combat cargo officer on an attack transport, the senior Marine on the staff of Commander Amphibious Group 2, and an echelon commander of the 31st Marine Amphibious Unit during its contingency deployment in the 1973 Yom Kippur War. As a colonel, he served as chief of staff in the 3rd Marine Division in the Western Pacific, director of the Marine Corps research and development center, and military secretary to the twenty-eighth Commandant of the Marine Corps.*

Alexander holds degrees in history and national security from the University of North Carolina (AB), Jacksonville University (MAT), and Georgetown University (MA). He is a distinguished graduate of the Naval War College.

A renowned author of military histories, Alexander has written five books and six monographs on U.S. Marine Corps amphibious operations. He received the U.S. Naval Institute's 1997 Author of the Year award for his book Storm Landings: Epic Amphibious Battles in the Central Pacific. *As chief military historian for Lou Reda Productions, he has helped produce eighteen documentaries for The History Channel and the Arts & Entertainment Network, including the 1999 special "Fire and Ice: The Korean War," an Emmy Award nominee. During 2001–6 he served as senior historian with the exhibit design team during construction of the National Museum of the Marine Corps.*

CHAPTER 5

Long Passage to Korea
Black Sailors and the Integration of the U.S. Navy

BERNARD C. NALTY

THE KOREAN WAR, like the other conflicts in the nation's history, challenged the Navy to make the most efficient and effective use of its resources, both human and material. Throughout all of its wars, the recruiting, training, and assignment of African Americans posed a recurring problem for the U.S. government in the employment of manpower because of slavery and the racial discrimination it spawned. As early as the undeclared naval war with France, 1798–1800, the Navy of the United States tapped the reservoir of free black fishermen and merchant seamen then available in northern seaports. Reliance on racially integrated crews survived beyond the Civil War and the abolition of slavery, only to succumb to the principle of separate but equal, validated in 1896 by the Supreme Court. As racial segregation took hold and the era of Jim Crow began, the Navy separated blacks from whites, a task completed by the outbreak of World War I in 1917, and paid the price in lost efficiency to maintain the policy during that conflict and afterward. The unprecedented demands of World War II, however, created pressure for a more rational use of human resources that eroded but did not destroy racial segregation in the Navy.

Secretary of the Navy James V. Forrestal, who took office in 1944, concluded that the training and assignments available to African Americans had to reflect their abilities and the needs of the wartime Navy, instead of being determined almost exclusively by race. By the time the war ended, the Navy had commissioned its first black officers, experimented with a few ships manned by African Americans, and begun integrating the races in the crews of fleet auxiliaries like oilers and ammunition ships, though not on combat ships where the only African American Sailors continued to be cooks or stewards.

After World War II ended, racial integration lost the headway gained during the last year of the conflict. Japan's surrender in September 1945 triggered the headlong demobilization of the armed forces of the United States. Many of the ships that had helped win the war were mothballed or sacrificed in tests of the new atomic bomb. Crewmembers went home, the African Americans among them returning to experience the humiliations of a society in which racial segregation still prevailed.

President Harry S. Truman challenged the existing racial policy on 26 July 1948, when he ordered the armed forces to integrate the races, but compliance proved uneven at best, with the Navy and Army lagging behind the newly established Air Force. When communist North Korea invaded South Korea on 25 June 1950, the smaller peacetime Navy had proportionally fewer African American Sailors than during World War II, and most of those still in uniform served in the Steward Branch where they performed housekeeping duties.

The outbreak of war in Korea launched another period of rapid growth for the Navy. The new recruits, reservists recalled to wartime active duty, and newly commissioned officers included African Americans who, thanks to the president's directive of 26 July 1948, often received better treatment and greater opportunity in uniform than they had encountered as civilians. The new policy of racial integration was in place, as were the Navy Department's directives to carry it out, but the naval service, despite its successful experience with racial integration as World War II ended, had not yet shaken off the dead hand of racism.

To its credit, the Navy that fought the Korean War made a determined effort to carry out President Truman's racial policy. This campaign had three major objectives: to increase the number of African Americans, especially officers but also enlisted men, and make full use of their abilities; to encourage black Sailors to choose specialties other than steward duty; and to mitigate the effects of racial segregation, which still prevailed by law or custom throughout much of the nation, on the Navy's African Americans in their contacts with civilian society. During the Korean conflict, the Navy demonstrated a commitment to equal treatment and opportunity, regardless of race, that took root and flourishes today.

INTRODUCTION

ON 4 DECEMBER 1950, the Iroquois Flight took off from the aircraft carrier *Leyte* (CV-33) to support U.S. Marines and soldiers then under fierce attack by Chinese troops in the snow-clad ridges and villages near the ice-covered Chosin (Changjin) Reservoir of northeastern Korea. Ens. Jesse L. Brown, one of the first African Americans to earn the gold wings of a naval aviator, piloted one of the six Vought F4U Corsairs in the flight. The formation crossed the North Korean coastline and searched for the enemy along the western shore of the reservoir, less than a thousand feet above the hostile terrain.

Near the abandoned village of Somong-ni, Lt. (jg) William H. Koenig saw vapor streaming from Brown's Corsair and radioed a warning. Koenig hoped that the plume resulted from a transfer of fuel from one tank to another, but Brown replied that he was rapidly losing fuel pressure and would have to crash-land.

Earlier that day, fire from the ground had damaged another F4U, and the pilot had chosen to make a belly-landing, a dangerous undertaking. Trying to land a damaged Corsair—some six tons of metal, ammunition, and volatile fuel—could be deadly. In this instance the attempt failed; when the aircraft hit the ground, it exploded, killing the pilot.

Brown nevertheless decided to risk a crash landing rather than parachute into the forbidding mountains. Lieutenant (jg) Hudner, his wingman, talked Brown through the checklist for an emergency landing as the Corsair lost power and altitude and its pilot searched for a reasonably level piece of ground free of boulders or other large obstructions. Brown guided the plane onto a snowy hillside, but as the Corsair skidded up a 20-degree slope, the fuselage broke just forward of the cockpit, pinning the pilot's right knee in a tangle of metal. Conscious but unable to free himself, Brown waved to the other members of the Iroquois Flight, signaling that he had survived.

Hudner's flight leader called for a rescue helicopter from the frozen Marine airstrip at Hagaru-ri. Then Hudner noticed two things: Brown was evidently unable to free himself from the cockpit, and smoke was now boiling out of the plane's engine cowling. "I decided that it was

On 4 December 1950, while on a close air support mission near the Chosin Reservoir, Ensign Brown's Corsair crashed in snow-covered mountains. Despite heroic efforts by squadron mate Lieutenant Hudner, who crash-landed his own plane, Brown could not be freed from the wreckage and died of his wounds and the cold. Ensign Brown was awarded posthumously the Distinguished Flying Cross. (National Archives)

worth it for me if Jesse was still alive to try and pull him out of his cock-pit," said Hudner, "so I made the decision to land close to his airplane." He lowered his flaps, circled slowly, and made a wheels-up landing in the snow. So far, so good.

Hudner found Brown dazed but alive. "I couldn't believe that he was as calm as he was with the circumstances so grim for him. I saw that the reason he couldn't get out was that his knee was jammed into the place where the fuselage had buckled. He had also taken his gloves off and his fingers were frozen solid." Hard as he tried, Hudner could not budge the man.

Hudner packed snow around the engine to reduce the fire hazard, then slipped and slid through the glaze ice back to his plane to radio the helicopter pilot to bring fire extinguishers and a cutting tool.

Ironically, Hudner's gallant attempt to save Brown had delayed the arrival of the rescue helicopter. The chopper pilot, Marine 1st Lt. Charlie

Ward, knew that his aircraft could barely lift three persons—himself, his crew chief, and Brown—in the thin air a mile above sea level. Now Hudner would also have to be picked up. Ward had no choice but to return to his base and drop off both the crew chief and the heavy tool kit that the helicopter normally carried. Ward landed at the crash site without the tools and thus had no way of cutting or prying apart the metal that trapped the pilot. Brown asked Hudner and Ward to amputate his leg, but they did not have a saw or a knife that could sever bone. Eventually Brown lapsed into unconsciousness from his injuries and the bitter cold. All they could do was stay with Brown until he died. Unable even to remove his body, they flew off into the gathering darkness.

Hudner's squadron commander nominated him for the Medal of Honor for his unselfish bravery in standing by his wingman. He would become the first Navy man to receive the award in the Korean War. A white pilot had risked his life to save a fellow aviator whom he respected and liked—a fellow pilot who happened to be black. Reality thus reversed a story line at the time often favored by Hollywood scriptwriters—the loyal African American willing to risk his life to save the white hero.

THE EARLY REPUBLIC

AS IN KOREA, BLACK AND WHITE Sailors fought side by side, but the road to full equality for African Americans, which began in the early days of the U.S. Navy, proved long and tortuous. During the American Revolution, African Americans served in the Continental Navy, in the state navies, and on privateers. Blacks from Maryland and Virginia, free men and slaves, proved especially helpful to the revolutionary cause. Their familiarity with the Chesapeake Bay and its tributaries enabled them to serve as pilots or skippers, taking small craft where few others dared to go.

Despite the varied and extensive contributions of African Americans, the new United States Navy, when it emerged in 1798 from the control of the War Department, barred "Negroes or Mulattoes" from enlisting. The Marine Corps adopted the same ban, though allowing black civilian drummers or fifers to attract whites to the recruiting rendezvous.

The Marine Corps retained its prohibition until World War II. Because of its small size, the Corps could be more selective than the Navy. Moreover, the role of Marines in maintaining order and discipline on board ship and at shore installations enabled the organization to invoke

Lieutenant Hudner receives congratulations from President Harry Truman, who presented him with the Medal of Honor for his heroic attempts to rescue Jesse Brown when his plane went down in North Korea. (Naval Historical Center)

the belief—which achieved the status of folk wisdom—that white men would not take orders from blacks. Not until 1942 did changing attitudes toward race in American society and the demands of the greatest war in the nation's history at last prod the Marine Corps into accepting African Americans.

In contrast, the ink had barely dried on the directive excluding blacks when the Navy found it necessary to recruit them. The reluctance among white Americans to endure the rigors of the naval service—harsh discipline, long voyages, a monotonous diet, and the possibility of violent death or severe injury from accidents or combat—caused individual captains to ignore the policy of the Navy Department and accept blacks. Although African American Sailors fought during the undeclared naval war with France, 1798–1800, they were not always welcome on board ship. Indeed, just three years after the fighting ended, Capt. Edward Preble and other officers warned subordinates "not to Ship Black Men."

THE IMPRESSMENT
OF BLACK SAILORS

GREAT BRITAIN, FIGHTING A long and costly war against Napoleon in the early years of the nineteenth century, invoked the time-honored practice of impressment to man its Royal Navy ships. At first the British sent press gangs to grog shops and brothels, as was the custom, but eventually stopped foreign ships on the high seas and took off any seaman who was a British subject or, all too often, could not prove that he was not. This practice angered American Sailors, black and white.

In 1807, the British warship *Leopard* hailed the American frigate *Chesapeake* and demanded permission to search for deserters. The American captain refused, but he could fire only one shot for honor before British cannon killed three Sailors, wounded another eighteen, and forced him to strike his colors. The British took off four men who claimed American citizenship, including Daniel Martin, a black Sailor from Westport, Massachusetts. Only one of the four men was definitely a British subject. Four years later, Martin and one of the other men were returned to *Chesapeake* in Boston Harbor; the fourth died during his service in the Royal Navy. The *Chesapeake* incident was not the only such occurrence involving African Americans, at least ten of whom were impressed into the Royal Navy from merchant ships. Two of the victims were freed by the frigate *Constitution* as a result of her victories over the British warships *Java* and *Guerrierre* in the War of 1812, caused in part by the issue of impressment.

The War of 1812 caused the Navy to accept officially and openly enlist free blacks, who were formally welcomed on board by an act of Congress in March 1813. African Americans had fought on warships and privateers, on the high seas and the Great Lakes, before the law took effect, so the act merely brought policy into line with existing practice. For example, when the privateer *Governor Tompkins* clashed with a British man-of-war months before the legislation took effect, two African American Sailors, John Johnson and John Davis, suffered mortal wounds. While they clung to life, the men refused all aid so their shipmates would not have to abandon their posts to help them. The privateer's captain, Nathaniel Shaler, declared that "while America has such men, she has little to fear from the tyrants of the ocean."

The presence of black Sailors became routine. In 1816, two years after the signing of the treaty that ended the War of 1812, the surgeon of a typical American warship, *Java*, estimated that African Americans made up from one-eighth to one-sixth of the crew. Without free black Americans and foreign-born Sailors, the Navy could not have manned its sailing ships.

The victory of any American frigate against a hostile man-of-war inspired appreciation among civilians and increased the solidarity within crews. When a group of New Yorkers sought to express their thanks by inviting the crew of such a victorious warship to a stage performance, roughly half the men that marched into the theater were African Americans. Harmony did not always prevail, however, for when danger abated, friction sometimes arose between the races on board ship.

Although years of effective service earned free African Americans the right to enlist, the Navy Department took pains to make sure that no slaves served on shipboard. And for a time, neither free blacks nor slaves were employed as civilian workers at navy yards. White laborers opposed such hiring not only out of fear of competition from unpaid slaves or low-paid free blacks but also because of a belief in their own racial superiority.

FILLING THE RANKS

THE NAVY OPENLY ACCEPTED free blacks who demonstrated a willingness to reenlist at a time when few whites would join up, even though the presence of black seamen aroused the wrath of Southern slaveholders. In the 1830s, the most striking feature of the service may well have been the large number of blacks in its ranks. For example, an American traveling in

Europe reported overhearing a conversation between two British tourists. They had concluded, after seeing American Sailors on liberty in Italy, that all Americans had black skin and that the white officers were recruited from the Royal Navy to exercise leadership. These views, absurd though they were, reflected the Navy's continuing dependence on black Sailors.

ESTABLISHING A RACIAL QUOTA   Acting Secretary of the Navy Isaac Toucey paid attention to the concerns of Southern politicians, even though he had commanded black Sailors on the Great Lakes during the War of 1812, and established a quota on the recruitment of African Americans. They could not exceed 5 percent of the men enlisting. This policy did not specifically address reenlistment and proved difficult to enforce in a time when communications moved at a leisurely pace and captains reigned supreme. The Navy's policy failed to satisfy people like South Carolina Senator John C. Calhoun, a champion of slavery and states' rights. Calhoun tried to banish blacks from the naval service, except as servants or cooks, but his attempt failed because the Navy of this era needed black Sailors.

To placate Calhoun and his like-minded colleagues, Secretary of the Navy Abel P. Upshur promised in 1842 that African Americans would make up no more than "one-twentieth part of the crew of any vessel," a pledge that depended on the primitive personnel accounting tools then in use—pen, ink, ledger book, and letter. Although difficult to enforce, the quota succeeded in reducing the percentage of African American new recruits to the desired level— 4.2 percent in 1850 and 5.6 percent in 1860.

None of the African American bluejackets could advance from forecastle to wardroom. As the British travelers observed, all naval officers were white. A number of blacks, however, served as masters of merchantmen or whalers. Indeed, the presence of black skippers in southern ports like Charleston, South Carolina, triggered complaints from local officials. As early as 1821, William Wirt, attorney general in the cabinet of President James Monroe, tried to bar African American masters from the coastal trade, explaining that they were not full citizens capable of executing the sworn statements required of a ship's captain. This legal opinion, which in effect restricted black skippers to whatever American ports would accept them and to whaling voyages, lasted until 1862; some eighty years would pass before the Navy commissioned its first black officers.

THE POOL OF BLACK MANPOWER EXPANDS   After secessionists fired on Fort Sumter, South Carolina, in April 1861 and the Civil War began, the United States Navy reacted by blockading the ports of the newly formed Confederate States of America. African American Sailors served with the blockading squadrons in the Atlantic and on the Gulf Coast. Closing the ports formed only one part of a Union strategy to isolate and crush the Confederacy. Operations ashore liberated thousands of slaves and encouraged still others to flee to Union-controlled territory. These men formed a vast pool of manpower to perform labor and, with appropriate training, to fight.

As early as September 1861, Secretary of the Navy Gideon Welles authorized the enlistment of "contrabands"—escaped or liberated slaves. Initially, they could sign on only as "boys," normally lads under eighteen years of age apprenticing to become Sailors, but, after December 1862, as landsmen, able-bodied adults without nautical experience. A boy received between $8 and $10 each month, and a landsman earned $12, four dollars less than a seaman.

The reservoir of contrabands proved especially important in the fighting on the Mississippi River and some of its tributaries, where the Navy in October 1862 assumed control of operations from the War Department. Acting Rear Adm. David Dixon Porter arranged for the conversion of river steamboats to armored gunboats, creating a force of a hundred warships. To help man them, he began recruiting former slaves. These men were readily available, accustomed to hard labor, and, he believed, naturally resistant to the illnesses that had hospitalized some four hundred white Sailors before the gunboat flotilla became ready for action.

Admiral Porter predicted a financial windfall for the Navy by recruiting contrabands. He advised the department that the substitution of lower-ranking blacks, either boys or landsmen, for higher-paid white seamen, especially in the engine rooms of the gunboats, could save exactly $112,608. Secretary of the Navy Welles put a crimp in this plan, however. He approved the enlistment of former slaves as landsmen and also agreed that a commanding officer might do what Porter recommended and employ them as ordinary seamen, seamen, firemen, or coal-heavers, instead of their usual blue-water duty as shipboard laborers or officers' servants. Welles eliminated the projected savings when he directed that the African American landsmen assigned to the work that Porter described receive pay appropriate to the new duties. For a landsman serving as a coal-heaver, the difference in pay amounted to six dollars each month. Although prohibiting the transfer of contrabands from one vessel to another except in the grade of landsman, the secretary decreed that when

ROBERT A. SMALLS

THE LIST OF BLACK HEROES of the Civil War begins with Robert Smalls, a slave who won his freedom and fought for the United States. Smalls served as pilot of the 300-ton side-wheel steamer *Planter*, which operated out of Charleston, South Carolina. Before dawn on 13 May 1862, while the white skipper and mate were ashore, Smalls and the African American crew fired the boiler, built up steam, and cast off. *Planter*—with nine men, five women, and three children on board—put out to sea. A Union blockading ship, *Onward*, intercepted her. The Union captain assured Smalls that all those on board had earned their freedom and turned over the steamer, with six cannon on board, to federal authorities. For seizing the ship and weapons, Congress passed legislation that awarded some $4,500 in prize money; Smalls received the largest share, about $1,500.

Planter entered the service of the United States with Smalls as its master. Ill-suited for blockade operations, *Planter* plied the coastal waters delivering cargo for the U.S. Army quartermaster department and sometimes landing troops. Smalls was eventually commissioned as an officer of the Army's U.S. Colored Troops. In January 1865, while the steamer was undergoing repair in Philadelphia, Smalls encountered northern racism. When he boarded a trolley in the city, a conductor ordered him off. This insulting treatment of a war hero pricked the conscience of the city's leaders who within two years ended the color ban on the city's transit system.

After the war, during the brief time that freed blacks dominated southern politics, Smalls served in the state legislature of South Carolina and then as the state's representative in the U.S. House of Representatives. He also served as a major general in the South Carolina militia until resurgent

Robert Smalls, naval hero of the Civil War. In May 1862, Smalls took control of the Confederate gunboat *Planter* in Charleston harbor, brought his family and other slaves on board, and made a daring escape. He turned the boat over to a Union blockading squadron. Eventually, Smalls was put in charge of the *Planter*, which served the federal government. After the war, Smalls won election to the South Carolina legislature and then to the U.S. House of Representatives. (Naval Historical Center)

whites expelled blacks from positions of authority. During World War II, African American Sailors trained at Camp Robert Smalls, a facility named in honor of the black hero, at the Great Lakes Naval Training Station, near Chicago, Illinois. Reflecting the times, the camp was segregated.

Racially integrated crews were the norm for USS *Miami* and most other warships of the Union Navy. (Naval Historical Center)

the enlistments of the former slaves expired they would be discharged in the highest grade attained.

The recruiting of freed slaves swelled the number of African Americans in the wartime Navy. Until recently, historians have had difficulty arriving at reliable statistics on the number of African American Sailors. An estimate made in 1902 suggested that African Americans might have accounted for thirty thousand of the one hundred twenty thousand men who enlisted during the Civil War. The African American Sailors Project at Howard University has identified twenty thousand black Sailors by name. The program has also documented that African Americans served on an integrated basis on board nearly all of the Union's seven hundred naval vessels.

FROM SLAVERY TO JIM CROW

THE DEFEAT OF THE CONFEDERACY and the abolition of slavery in the United States ended forever the need for the Navy to patrol off the coast of

Africa to prevent the importation of slaves, a mission first undertaken in 1843. Tensions with Great Britain, America's foe during the American Revolution and War of 1812, abated after the Civil War, so no potential enemy appeared on the horizon. The fleet would have to shrink. As the U.S. Navy declined in strength, the service needed fewer African Americans in its ranks. The proportion of blacks in the enlisted ranks fell from a maximum estimate of 20-25 percent during the Civil War to 13.1 percent in 1870. The Navy, moreover, played no role in Reconstruction, the reincorporation of the states of the former Confederacy into the Union, which proved the dominant political and social issue of the postwar years. As North and South came together, the Republican Party, with roots in the antislavery movement, lost its ardor for black freedom.

A wave of racism, fueled by competition for jobs between free blacks and white immigrants, swept the North after the Civil War. When the United States in 1876 celebrated the centennial of its independence, African American laborers were barred from working on the buildings in Philadelphia that housed the event. At the same time, the states of the South reduced African Americans living there to a status similar to the slavery that the Thirteenth Amendment had abolished.

The resurgence of racism caused some northern states to ignore laws enacted to protect the rights of African Americans. Meanwhile southern states erected legal barriers against their black citizens. "Jim Crow," the personification of this latest manifestation of racism, impeded or reversed the social, economic, educational, and political gains that blacks had made as a result of the Thirteenth, Fourteenth, and Fifteenth amendments to the Constitution. These amendments put an end to slavery and promised basic civil rights, regardless of race or previous servitude.

Jim Crow also affected the status of African Americans in the Navy. Black petty officers dwindled to a handful by 1870, and members of this race began gravitating from assignments that required a Sailor's skills to those usually performed by landsmen, like cooking and cleaning up or waiting on officers.

Whites enlisting in the Navy brought with them the hardening attitude toward African Americans, and white Sailors no longer willingly slung hammocks alongside blacks or ate beside them. Looking back on his service in the Navy, a white former Sailor declared that the presence of blacks on shipboard had become "one of the most disagreeable features of the naval service." This experience, he predicted, would extinguish any spark of sympathy for the African American and thus demonstrate the wisdom of segregating the races. By the end of the nineteenth century, racism had taken firm root in every aspect of American life; indeed, racial segregation became the law of the land because of the Supreme Court's decision in *Plessy v. Ferguson* (1896), which enshrined the principle of separate but equal.

Like the racial attitudes of white America, the needs of the Navy changed at the turn of the century. Sailing ships had placed a premium on the discipline, strength, and agility of their bluejackets. The new steam-driven battleships, with their larger crews, had different priorities, demanding of various crewmembers a working knowledge of electricity and optics, reciprocating engines or turbines, and wireless communication. Machines tended to compensate for physical strength and to some extent agility.

Moreover, instead of recruiting mainly at seaports, where large numbers of blacks had volunteered for the sailing Navy, the service now recruited nationwide. The Navy did not believe that African Americans could master the technical skills needed in the age of steam, steel, and electricity. Even if the Navy had not shared the common perception that whites were trainable and blacks were not, it needed too many men to risk alienating the white majority. Since white recruits often objected to serving alongside blacks, the Navy decided to segregate the races.

To make segregation work, the Navy selected specialties that blacks could perform while messing and sleeping separately from the rest of the crew. Many became messmen, a rating established in 1893, and operated as servants and housekeepers. The ranks of the messmen included John H. "Dick" Turpin, who barely escaped death when an internal explosion destroyed the battleship *Maine* in Havana harbor in 1898. Other African Americans, like Robert Penn, toiled in the heat of the engine room. He earned the Medal of Honor for risking death to shut down a leaking boiler in the battleship *Iowa* that was patrolling off the coast of Cuba during the Spanish-American War. A few African Americans retained the ratings they had earned before Jim Crow took hold in the Navy. Gunner's Mate John Jordan, for example, was in charge of the gun crew that fired the first shot at the Battle of Manila Bay, which broke Spanish naval power in the Philippines.

THE NAVY'S EFFORTS TO MAINTAIN RACIAL SEGREGA-TION   By the end of World War I, and during the two decades that followed, few blacks served in the Navy. Those who still wore the uniform tended to be mess attendants, though a few long-service petty officers, who

On numerous occasions before and after World War I, the United States deployed naval forces to the Caribbean and other regions of the globe to protect American interests and citizens threatened by political or social turmoil. Often, U.S. warships dispatched landing parties of Sailors and Marines, like these armed *New Jersey* (BB-16) bluejackets, to trouble spots ashore. (Naval Historical Center, Courtesy Lt. Col. Elton M. Manuel)

had earned their rank years earlier with gun crews or in engine rooms, were serving out their final years before retiring. In June 1940, when Adolf Hitler's Germany was overrunning France, only 4,007 African Americans served in the Navy, most of them as messmen, though at least one chief petty officer remained on duty.

Although the United States had begun to rearm by 1940, the Navy still had no interest in recruiting blacks except for an expanding Messman Branch, later redesignated as the Steward Branch. For example, the service called for 4,700 volunteers in July of that year, but only two hundred of them could be African Americans. Secretary of the Navy Frank Knox ignored the efforts of persons outside the Navy, whether politicians or champions of civil rights for African Americans, to persuade the service to recruit additional blacks and use them for naval rather than housekeeping duties. Knox insisted that his actions were for the benefit of African Americans, sparing them the embarrassment of having to compete against whites on equal terms. "I am convinced," he wrote, "that it is no kindness to negroes to thrust them upon men of the white race."

Legendary Sailor John Henry "Dick" Turpin was one of the Navy's first African American chief petty officers. Turpin, a crewman of USS *Maine*, survived the explosion that destroyed that warship in Havana Harbor, Cuba, in 1898. During the next decade he served in the boiler rooms and gun turrets of Navy gunboats and cruisers. Recognizing his abilities as a Sailor and a leader, in June 1917 the Navy promoted him to chief gunner's mate. After transferring to the Fleet Reserve in March 1919, Turpin worked at the Puget Sound Navy Yard, Bremerton, Washington, as a master diver. The Navy then sent the dynamic Sailor on recruitment drives around the United States. On 5 October 1925, Chief Gunner's Mate Turpin retired from the Navy after twenty-nine years of dedicated service. (Naval Historical Center)

THE MARCH ON
WASHINGTON

IN 1940, PRESIDENT FRANKLIN D. ROOSEVELT decided to run for an unprecedented third term as the United States rearmed to meet a growing threat from the Axis Powers—Germany, Italy, and Japan. A. Philip Randolph and other African American leaders believed that the national emergency and the presidential election afforded them a unique opportunity to attack racial injustice. If African Americans, who formed an important part of the electorate in some large northern cities, rallied behind Roosevelt and his program of national defense, a grateful administration might improve the treatment of blacks. Opportunities might also open up for blacks in the armed services and the burgeoning defense industries. To dramatize African American voting power, Randolph and his colleagues planned for an enormous march on Washington.

The mere threat of the march, which never took place, produced results. The president established a Fair Employment Practices Committee to persuade defense industries to make more jobs available to blacks, though it could not compel them to do so. The administration also appointed an African American, Judge William H. Hastie, as a special advisor to the Secretary of War, and promoted a black Army officer, Col. Benjamin O. Davis Sr., to the grade of brigadier general. The government also assigned an African American reserve officer, Col. Campbell C. Johnson, to help administer the Selective Service System, which was required by law to operate without regard to race. The Roosevelt administration's reforms, although modest at best, helped improve the lot of African Americans in defense industries and in the armed forces. Roosevelt earned the support and affection of African Americans, not only in the election of 1940 but thereafter.

The General Board of the Navy, which functioned like an advisory staff, suggested Knox respond to criticism of the Navy's racial policy by pointing out that "colored men are now enlisted in the messman branch . . . and given every opportunity for advancement to cooks and stewards." These grades enabled them to earn the same pay as petty officers though they could not exercise authority outside their branch. "Experience of many years in the Navy," the General Board observed, "has shown clearly that men of the colored race, if enlisted in any other branch than the messman's branch, and promoted to the position of petty officer, cannot maintain discipline among men of the white race over whom they may be placed by reason of their rating."

The threat of an African American march on Washington and the implied promise of the black community's support for President Franklin D. Roosevelt and his policies had a positive effect. Several prominent black leaders were appointed to positions of authority. The War Department also promised broader opportunities, including pilot training in the Army Air Corps, for black servicemen.

The Navy clung to its existing policy of segregation and restricted service, however. A panel with representatives from the Navy and Marine Corps met in July 1941 to review racial policy. At year's end it submitted two contradictory reports. The majority, consisting of all the uniformed panel members, endorsed segregation in its current form as the best means of preventing racial friction and thus ensuring efficiency. The minority report submitted by Addison Walker, a civilian special assistant to Secretary Knox, recommended assigning a small number of blacks on a few ships to duties other than those of messmen.

THE WORLD WAR II EXPERIENCE

NOT EVEN THE JAPANESE attack on Pearl Harbor could persuade the Navy to modify its racial policy and thus promote the more efficient use of manpower. Highlighting the absurdity of this policy, a black mess attendant, Doris Miller, helped carry the mortally wounded captain of the battleship *West Virginia* (BB-48) to cover, manned a machine gun, and earned the Navy Cross for heroism. Even after Germany and Italy joined forces with Japan, Secretary Knox continued to resist subtle pressure from the White House to change racial policy. He either ignored the president's wishes or responded with predictions of disaster if the status quo were changed. Those who advocated greater rights for blacks, including First Lady Eleanor Roosevelt, did not accept the secretary's arguments. In March 1942, President Roosevelt lost patience with Knox and told him that the Navy would have to accept black recruits in a proportion acceptable to the White House.

The Navy had no choice but to begin accepting black volunteers. But the number was limited to 277 each month, since only a few segregated training facilities existed. Similarly, the Marine Corps planned to train a separate defense battalion to absorb most of the one thousand African American volunteers it was being forced to accept; the remainder would serve in a Steward Branch modeled after the Navy's.

The Navy might well have maintained racial segregation by enlisting only as many African Americans as could be employed as messmen or assigned to separate, largely self-contained organizations like the new Naval Construction Battalions (Seabees). Global war, however, demanded the most efficient use of manpower. Roosevelt sought to ensure this efficiency when, in December 1942, he decreed that the War Manpower Commission, not the military, would decide how many black Americans the services would induct through the Selective Service System.

THE IMPACT OF SELECTIVE SERVICE ON THE NAVY Because of Roosevelt's action, African Americans entered the Navy by the thousands instead of the hundreds. The Navy increased the number of messmen, organized more construction battalions for blacks, and established base units in which African American Sailors served as stevedores. Indeed, most of the blacks serving in 1943 functioned as laborers at ports, bases, or ammunition depots in the United States or overseas. Most African American Sailors performed duties indirectly related to combat, and even the mess attendants on board warships functioned primarily as cooks, waiters, and housekeepers. Forced into a narrow range of specialties, black Sailors saw themselves as outsiders, excluded from the real Navy, serving as workers rather than as fighters.

The influx of African Americans into the Navy's enlisted ranks dramatized the absence of blacks in the officer corps. No black had ever received a commission, but in September 1943 Adlai E. Stevenson, an assistant to Secretary Knox, believed that the time had come to shatter precedent. Indeed, change had become all but inevitable. A dozen blacks—including a light-complexioned medical student, Bernard W. Robinson, apparently mistaken for a white—were already enrolled during 1943 and 1944 at various campuses in the V-12 officer-training program, the precursor of the postwar Naval Reserve Officer Training Corps (NROTC). Stevenson proposed accelerating the process by commissioning "10 or 12 negroes selected from top notch civilians." To prod the Navy into action, he pointed out that the Coast Guard had already commissioned two African Americans.

Instead, the Navy's Bureau of Naval Personnel decided to choose officer candidates from among the African American Sailors already on duty. Of the sixteen candidates who entered an accelerated program of training in January 1944, twelve became ensigns in the Naval Reserve on 17 March. The newly commissioned officers were: James E. Hair, Samuel E. Barnes, George C. Cooper, William S. White, Dennis D. Nelson II, Graham E. Martin, Phillip G. Barnes, Reginald E. Goodwin, John W. Reagan, Jesse W. Arbor, Dalton L. Baugh, and Frank E. Sublett Jr. Another of the candidates, Charles B. Lear, became a warrant officer, apparently because he lacked a college education. The group later came to be called the "Golden Thirteen." The twelve who received commissions broke the racial barrier, creating the opening through which Ensign Brown would enter pilot training and the naval officer corps.

The commissioning of the Navy's first black officers became the subject of a story in *Life* magazine and an inspiration to all African Americans, but it did not break Jim Crow's grip on the Navy. The handful of white officers who had helped shepherd Stevenson's proposal through the Navy's administrative hierarchy knew that something more had to be done. These officers—Capt. Thomas F. Darden and Lt. Cdrs. Charles E. Dillon, Donald G. Van Ness, and Christopher Sargent—formed the Navy Department's Special Programs Unit. The Special Programs Unit arranged for a leadership course at Great Lakes designed to prepare graduates for promotion to petty officer. To take advantage of the new course, the Bureau of Naval Personnel went so far as to permit the promotion of qualified blacks to petty officer even though specific openings for them did not yet exist.

Because Secretary Knox still favored separating the races, African American Sailors would have to serve on specific ships under the command of white officers and petty officers. As a result, the Chief of Naval Operations, Fleet Admiral King, in January 1944 ordered the assignment of 196 black Sailors and 44 white officers to the destroyer escort *Mason* (DE-529) and 53 black seamen and 14 white officers to the submarine chaser *PC-1264*. Another four submarine chasers later joined in the experiment. Gradually, black petty officers replaced their white counterparts and some black officers were assigned as they became available.

AFRICAN
AMERICANS IN THE
U.S. COAST GUARD

THROUGHOUT THE EXISTENCE OF the U.S. Coast Guard, an amalgam of the Revenue Cutter Service, Life Saving Service, and Light House Service, black Americans served with distinction, although often in segregated contingents. African Americans manned life-saving stations, tended lighthouses, and served in the Coast Guard messman's branch.

In January 1942, the Commandant of the U.S. Coast Guard, Rear Adm. Russell R. Waesche, enlisted five hundred African Americans into the service, which was under the Navy during the war. He assigned the black coastguardsmen to billets on small craft or in port security detachments and enabled them to compete for promotion to petty officer. The chairman of the Navy's General Board, Vice Adm. Walton R. Sexton, objected to this effort. He warned that the influx of even five hundred blacks might prevent the Coast Guard from maintaining racial segregation because of its small size. Nonetheless, the first of these African American recruits entered training at Manhattan Beach, California, in the spring of 1942, the Coast Guard's first attempt toward integrating the races.

By war's end, five thousand African Americans served in the Coast Guard. Although most blacks still functioned as stewards, the Coast Guard, as Admiral Sexton had predicted, could not maintain segregation; indeed, it chose not to. African American officers and petty officers exercised authority over whites on a racially integrated weather ship, an escort vessel, and some smaller craft.

The U.S. Coast Guard's first African American officers, Lts. (jg) Joseph C. Jenkins, left, and Clarence Samuels, brave winter weather in the North Atlantic during 1943 on board USS *Sea Cloud*, a Navy-chartered ship operated by the Coast Guard. The Coast Guard commissioned the two men a full year before the Navy took similar steps. The Navy's sister seagoing service employed *Sea Cloud* to test the feasibility of fully integrating the officer and enlisted ranks of a crew; the experiment was a success. (National Archives)

Concerns surfaced almost immediately that African American Sailors would not respect petty officers of their own race and that the petty officers would prove reluctant to discipline their fellow blacks. These fears never became reality, however. The Navy's *Guide to Command of Negro Naval Personnel*, published in 1945 and apparently intended mainly for white officers, declared: "Contrary to a fairly general belief, it has been found that Negro Naval personnel respond readily to good Negro leadership." Moreover, the guide continued, "Experience has taught . . . that colored personnel can be directed and disciplined with less likelihood of dissatisfaction by Negro than by white officers, provided the former are well selected and competent." Left unsaid was the fact that careful selection and competence were equally important for white officers in command of whites.

When Secretary Knox died suddenly on 28 April 1944, the President replaced him with Under Secretary of the Navy James V. Forrestal, a prewar investment banker who had been active in the National Urban League, a civil rights organization. The barriers separating the races had already been lowered to permit African Americans to become officers and petty officers and to serve at sea in a variety of specialties other than steward. The new Secretary of the Navy, however, faced a racially based crisis in morale. African Americans resented the narrow range of opportunity open to most of them, and white seamen objected to the prospect of repeated tours of sea duty and the likelihood of combat because black Sailors filled many shore-based billets.

An obvious solution would have been to assign trained African Americans throughout the fleet, but Forrestal knew that the bureaucracy had torpedoed such a broad proposal earlier. On 20 May 1944, the Secretary of the Navy therefore proposed the assignment of qualified blacks to large auxiliaries—oilers, ammunition ships, and transports—rather than to combat ships. In no case would African Americans exceed 10 percent of the total crew. Forrestal was making a concession to Vice Adm. Randall Jacobs, Chief of the Bureau of Naval Personnel, who remained convinced that "you couldn't dump 200 colored boys on a crew in battle."

President Roosevelt approved the idea. Admiral King set the measure in motion and Admiral Jacobs carried it out. What began as an experiment soon became policy, as the Navy routinely assigned African Americans to a lengthening list of fleet auxiliaries and ultimately to all such ships.

This measure coincided with an effort to desegregate support units after a tragic explosion of two ammunition ships being loaded at Port Chicago, California. The blast, on 17 July 1944, killed 320 Sailors, 202 of them members of an African American labor unit. When fifty of the badly shaken survivors, all of them African American, refused to return to the dangerous work, the Navy tried them for mutiny. Those believed to be the ringleaders were sentenced to prison, while most of the others received bad-conduct discharges. (After the war, the Navy took into account the effect of the death and destruction on those who survived and commuted the sentences and other punishment.) The Navy, in reaction to the public outcry over the affair, reduced the proportion of blacks in ammunition handling units.

Segregation survived in the new logistic support companies that replaced depot companies at advance bases overseas. There was at least one exception, however. When a segregated unit, totaling some four hundred black Sailors, arrived at a Pacific advance base in the spring of 1944, Cdr. W. Biddle Combs, the commanding officer, decided on his own initiative to create units with black and white Sailors. His innovation did not cause serious morale problems and raised efficiency.

Secretary Forrestal continued to advocate equal treatment and greater opportunity for black Sailors. In March 1945, he appointed an African

The Port Chicago disaster. On 17 July 1944, an enormous explosion at the Naval Magazine in Port Chicago, California, destroyed two ships and nearby buildings. The blast also killed 320 Sailors, two-thirds of them African Americans who had been loading ammunition onto cargo ships. (Naval Historical Center)

American, Lester B. Granger, as his civilian aide to monitor implementation of the Navy's racial policy.

By the end of the war, the Navy counted 164,942 African American Sailors (including about sixty enlisted women), 5.37 percent of the total enlisted strength. Although more than twice the prewar percentage, this was roughly half the proportion of blacks in the overall population. Moreover, some 40 percent of the African American enlisted men served in the Steward Branch. No one knew how many of these men and the sixty black officers, all of the latter reservists on active duty, would survive the demobilization of the wartime Navy and continue to serve in the smaller peacetime establishment.

INTO THE COLD WAR

AS WORLD WAR II drew to a close, Secretary Forrestal pursued the objective of providing equal treatment and opportunity for all races while causing a minimum of commotion in the ranks. A committee headed by Capt. Roscoe H. Hillenkoetter conducted a study that examined existing policy and changes proposed by Lester Granger, Forrestal's advisor on racial matters. The committee endorsed the conclusion that racial segregation resulted in inefficient use of manpower. The group called for a policy that would promote efficiency by assigning every Sailor according to his ability and the needs of the service, rather than on the basis of race.

Granger made an inspection tour in August 1945 that reinforced his belief that efficiency improved as a result of racial integration. Morale, he reported, tended to be low in those labor units manned mostly by African Americans. Granger was especially concerned that the Steward Branch, with its dominant African American representation, could well disrupt the integration process.

In the postwar Navy, African Americans were to be eligible for "all types of assignments in all ratings in all activities and all ships of the naval service." By 1 October 1946, African American Sailors, with the exception of the stewards at the Naval Academy, were reassigned so the proportion of blacks in any ship or activity would not exceed 10 percent.

After the war, Navy officer Charles F. Rauch Jr. reported to the cruiser *Huntington* (CL-107) and discovered that the Navy was indeed integrating the enlisted ranks. The crew included black petty officers whose duties had nothing to do with preparing or serving food. Although the stewards,

Lester B. Granger, a prominent figure in the African American community, inspects the working conditions of black Sailors at Naval Air Station, San Diego, in June 1945. To oversee racial matters in the Navy, President Franklin D. Roosevelt had appointed Granger to the staff of Secretary of the Navy James Forrestal. After the war, Granger led the National Urban League. (National Archives)

whether African American or Filipino, formed a distinct servant class, the young officer considered the black seamen simply as members of the crew. He did not realize that black Sailors were experiencing resistance to integration by some of their shipmates.

Despite Secretary Forrestal's intentions, African Americans continued to be clustered in the Steward Branch, with only a few men serving in other billets.

As the Navy drastically contracted in size after the war, it raised enlistment standards. Since blacks were more likely than whites to have graduated from substandard schools, African American recruits tended to make lower scores on general qualification tests. Thus, many black Sailors were unable to qualify for nonsteward billets. As late as 1948, of all the African Americans in the Navy (including about twenty enlisted women), 62 percent served as stewards.

During the war, two African American women, Harriet Pickens and Frances Wills, were commissioned in the Women Accepted for Volunteer

Emergency Service (WAVES), the Navy's wartime auxiliary for women. Although the WAVES became a part of the Navy, both officers returned to civilian life after the war. Four African American women—Edith DeVoe, Phyllis Mae Daley, Maxine Magee, and Eula Stimley—held reserve commissions in the Navy Nurse Corps. By 1951, however, only two black nurses served on active duty, Lt. (jg) Ellen Stricklin and DeVoe, also a lieutenant (jg), who had earned a regular commission.

The number of male African American officers declined dramatically after the war. From a wartime peak of sixty, the total dwindled by the end of 1946 to just three, all of them reservists on extended active duty. As Forrestal's successor Secretary of the Navy John L. Sullivan later explained, the service had slipped back into its comfortable prewar ways, with enlisted blacks waiting on white officers.

Not until 1947 did Ens. John Lee, commissioned in the reserves from the V-12 program during the war, become the first African American officer in the regular Navy. As Lee described it, his selection for a regular commission resulted from being in the right place at the right time. In 1947, when the only African American midshipman at the Naval Academy, Wesley A. Brown, was two years away from graduation, the Navy became disturbed by the lack of even one African American regular officer. Moreover, almost all of the black reserve officers commissioned during the war had left the service. One of the three men on active duty during the previous year, Lt. (jg) Samuel L. Gravely, had just left, since he was convinced that opportunities for an African American officer were severely limited. The other two reservists available for a place in the regular Navy were Lt. (jg) Dennis D. Nelson and Lee. The Bureau of Naval Personnel considered Nelson too old at age forty to receive a regular commission, but Lee was in his mid-twenties. Lee realized that he needed further training and duty at sea to complete a successful career in the Navy. Capt. Roland N. Smoot, the Director of Officer Personnel, after speaking with Lee, sent him to the General Line School at Newport, Rhode Island, and then assigned him to the aircraft carrier *Kearsarge* (CV-33).

Various obstacles hampered efforts to increase the number of black officers. Those commissioned in the reserves during World War II tended to be older than the typical newly commissioned ensign. Hence, they were older than most in the same pay grade, and the Navy hoped to retain mostly younger officers. The Navy's officer candidate program—which had produced the Golden Thirteen—contracted after the war. The NROTC at various colleges and universities became the normal source for reserve officers. Between 1946 and 1948, only sixteen blacks completed officer

On 8 March 1945, Commander Thomas Gaylord swears in five newly commissioned Navy nurses, including Phyllis Mae Daley, the first African American to join the ranks of the Navy Nurse Corps. (National Archives)

candidate school, and only fourteen African Americans (contrasted with 5,600 whites) graduated from NROTC programs.

Compounding the problem, the Navy excluded traditionally black schools like Howard University in Washington, D.C., from the wartime-V-12 officer training program, and that ban continued to apply to the post-war NROTC. Every college or university that participated in officer training agreed to accept anyone who had earned an NROTC scholarship in a competitive examination, but some ignored the pledge because of state law, local tradition, or school policy. As a result, African Americans who qualified for the program had to find an institution that would accept them. For example, Ensign Brown enrolled at Ohio State University and joined the NROTC program before leaving the school to enter pilot training.

A simple solution would have been to include black institutions in the list of schools offering NROTC training, but this option aroused scant enthusiasm, even among some Americans who favored racial integration. They feared that the black schools would attract too many African

American midshipmen and thus reinforce racial segregation in higher education at a time when barriers separating the races were beginning to come down. Not until 1965 did the Navy establish an NROTC unit at a traditionally black college—Prairie View A&M in Texas.

Although the Navy's racial policy had turned away from segregation toward integration, practice did not yet conform to policy. Numbers alone demonstrated that neither the existing officer corps, nor the NROTC, nor the Naval Academy, which had only five African American midshipmen in 1949, could claim meaningful integration. Similarly, the enlisted force was only 4.3 percent black in 1948. The trifling number of officers, and the continued existence of a predominately black Steward Branch, raised questions, especially in the African American press, about the Navy's actual commitment to equal treatment and opportunity.

Few outside observers knew, however, that the Bureau of Naval Personnel did attempt to correct those instances of racial discrimination that came to its attention. These largely unpublicized corrective actions dealt with specific incidents and did not alter the impression among African Americans that the Navy's commitment to racial integration had little substance. During his efforts to persuade blacks to take the examination for NROTC scholarships, Lieutenant Nelson learned of the depth of black disenchantment with the Navy. He and his special recruiting team addressed some seventeen thousand black high-school students in 1948 and 1949 but persuaded only ninety men to compete.

PRESIDENT TRUMAN ACTS   The Cold War that pitted the United States against the USSR grew dangerously warm in 1948 when the Soviets blocked access to Berlin in occupied Germany and took other hostile actions around the world. In this global confrontation, the United States could not afford to squander its resources, including manpower. Specifically, the nation could no longer relegate African Americans to nonessential tasks, in effect ignoring the potential skills of one citizen in ten, merely to maintain racial segregation. Not only did segregation waste manpower, it tarnished the image of the United States as the champion of the free world and offended African nations with resources that included oil and uranium.

Harry Truman, who had succeeded to the presidency in April 1945 when Franklin Roosevelt died, needed political support in the election of 1948 from African Americans and those in the Democratic Party who favored racial tolerance.

PRESIDENT TRUMAN'S EXECUTIVE ORDER 9981

DESPITE GROWING UP IN racially segregated Missouri, Truman revealed, while still a senator, a belief that African Americans should enjoy the basic rights guaranteed to all citizens. A wave of violence against blacks that swept the country after World War II strengthened the president's resolve. He seemed especially angered by an assault of South Carolina lawmen on Isaac Woodard, an Army veteran honorably discharged and still wearing his uniform as he returned home. After an unprovoked beating, the injured man was thrown in jail, where he suffered for hours without medical attention. When he was released, only an Army hospital would treat his injuries that left him blind.

Such brutality toward African Americans and the denial of their basic rights angered Truman. His commitment to the welfare of blacks did not include complete social equality, however, for he had not shaken off all the customs of his native state. Truman nonetheless pressed for an end to officially sanctioned segregation. In 1947 he convened a President's Committee on Civil Rights that recommended, among other things, the racial integration of the armed forces.

Truman's reaction to injustice helped prod him into action, but he also had political motives. Clark Clifford and other advisors warned him that the Republican Party could tip the balance against him in the 1948 presidential election by introducing legislation sought by African Americans—antilynching or fair employment practices bills, for instance. If these bills passed, or segregationist Democrats succeeded in torpedoing the Republican initiatives, blacks in the large northern cities might well desert the president. Something had to be done to ensure African American loyalty, especially since the likely Republican nominee, former Governor Thomas E. Dewey of New York, had been a strong advocate of civil rights.

At first, Truman's political instincts failed him. He did not heed Clifford's advice to bring blacks into a coalition with two groups the Republicans had alienated—farmers and organized labor. Even though the president moved warily, compromise proved impossible. The segregationist Democrats bolted from the convention and formed a new party, the Dixiecrats, who nominated a candidate of their own. When Truman issued Executive Order 9981 on 26 July 1948, the coalition envisioned by Clifford rapidly took shape. The votes of urban blacks, along with the support of blue-collar workers and farmers, enabled Truman to win a narrow victory in November 1948.

As a result, on 26 July 1948 Truman issued Executive Order 9981, which established a policy of "equality of treatment and opportunity for all persons in the armed services without regard to race, color, religion, or national origin." The president took the announced policy seriously, for the executive order also set up a committee to examine the response to the directive and to make appropriate recommendations to the commander in chief. When asked during a press conference if the executive order meant "eventually the end of segregation," Truman answered with one word, "Yes."

Capt. Herbert D. Riley, a naval officer on the staff of James Forrestal, now Secretary of Defense, warned that resistance to the racial integration of officers' clubs and wardrooms might result in mass resignations and early retirements. Riley even raised the specter of mutiny, but his fears did not reflect the views of the Navy as an institution. Policies designed to broaden opportunities for blacks already existed. Acting Secretary of the Navy (Air) John Nicholas Brown advised Forrestal in December 1948 that, as a result of these policies, most white officers and enlisted men had come to accept the principle of equal treatment and opportunity regardless of race. African Americans served in a variety of duties on board ship and ashore where they berthed and worked alongside whites.

Nevertheless, problems remained, especially with the continuing heavy concentration of blacks in the Steward Branch. By suspending the recruiting of African Americans to the Steward Branch, the Bureau of Naval Personnel hoped to improve the balance of blacks and nonblacks in the branch. After World War II, the Navy actively recruited Chamorros from Guam, and Filipinos. Even so, two out of three stewards were black.

THE REVIEW OF TRUMAN'S NEW RACIAL POLICY President Truman wasted no time in appointing the review committee called for in Executive Order 9981. In September 1948, he announced the formation of a panel headed by Charles P. Fahy, an attorney and former Solicitor General of the United States. The president and his advisors concluded that a committee dealing with so sensitive an issue as race relations had to have a white chairman. But Truman wanted someone who was sympathetic to the aspirations of blacks and could express his views in a way that did not grate on the ears of white Southerners. Fahy, a native of Georgia with a liberal attitude on questions of race, fit that description. The Fahy Committee—consisting of five whites and two African Americans—met for the first time in January 1949 to review the progress toward integration made by the armed forces.

After reviewing the Navy's program for providing equal treatment and opportunity to African Americans, the Fahy Committee asked why so few served in the Navy, and why so many of those who did were stewards. The Chief of Naval Personnel, Vice Adm. William M. Fechteler replied that blacks were not a seafaring people, which he thought answered the committee's question. Fechteler's explanation did not satisfy the committee, nor did the information that there were a number of African Americans training at Naval Reserve facilities and that Ensign Brown was undergoing carrier qualification.

During the committee's sessions, Lieutenant Nelson and other Navy representatives revealed that there were no programs to recruit or commission blacks. As a result, the Navy tasked Nelson with setting up such a special program. To carry it out, he chose five African American reserve officers, all but one who had been commissioned during World War II.

Lieutenant Nelson's success in attracting blacks to the naval service as officers or enlisted men, and the process of advising the Secretary of the Navy, had mixed effects on his Navy career. These activities kept him anchored to a desk, depriving him of the seagoing experience that counted heavily toward promotion or integration into the regular Navy. According to a fellow black officer, Samuel Gravely, Nelson made that choice regardless of cost to himself because he felt it vital to the future of black Americans in the Navy.

Gravely described Nelson as the sort of man "who did not hesitate to state his opinions and seek the support of the Secretary of the Navy," traits that did not endear him to his uniformed superiors. Nevertheless, Nelson received a regular commission and retired as a lieutenant commander, largely because of his valuable work for the secretary in connection with the Fahy Committee and its reforms.

After being recalled to active duty as a member of Nelson's group, Lt. (jg) John W. Reagan discovered that fellow African Americans were skeptical of his recruiting pitch. Some potential candidates for NROTC, despite the example of Reagan before them, doubted that a black man in the Navy could become more than an enlisted steward.

In the spring of 1949, as the Fahy Committee continued its deliberations, Ens. Wesley Brown became the first African American to graduate from the U.S. Naval Academy. A native of Washington, D.C., Brown had received his appointment from Representative Adam Clayton Powell, an African American whose congressional district in New York included the black enclave of Harlem.

Other African Americans, including George Trivers, who entered the Academy in 1937, had failed to graduate. Overwhelmed by hazing and forced isolation, they chose to earn a degree elsewhere. Brown, especially after he spoke with Trivers, feared the worst, but his experience at Annapolis was much less stressful. Most of Brown's fellow midshipmen, unlike many of Trivers's hostile classmates of the 1930s, for the most part just ignored him. A few men were openly friendly and two or three even offered to room with him. Brown chose to live alone, however, for he was concerned that a white roommate might face some form of retaliation. During his time at the Academy, Brown discovered that not every Northerner was liberal on racial matters, nor every Southerner a bigot.

Representative Powell, who frequently questioned the Navy's commitment to equal treatment and opportunity, insisted from the outset that Brown receive fair treatment. When Powell complained to Secretary Forrestal of a plot to grade Brown more strictly than white midshipmen, the secretary queried Vice Adm. Aubrey W. Fitch, Superintendent of the Naval Academy. Brown's surprised reactions to the commandant's own questions convinced the superintendent that there was no such plot. Powell had dreamed up the plot as a means of keeping pressure on the Naval Academy. Brown's graduation in 1949 broke the racial barrier at the Naval Academy, but not until 1953 did a second African American, Lawrence Chambers, graduate.

In the summer of 1949, the Fahy Committee proposed its solution to the Navy's racial problems. First, the service should launch a vigorous campaign to recruit blacks for both the general service and the NROTC.

In 1949, Wesley A. Brown overcame institutional and social prejudice to become the first African American to graduate from the U.S. Naval Academy at Annapolis. Brown entered the Civil Engineering Corps, rose to the rank of lieutenant commander, and completed a successful career in the Navy before retiring from the service in 1969. (Naval Historical Center, Courtesy D.C. Public Library)

To take the curse off the Steward Branch, the Navy should treat chief stewards like chief petty officers in all other specialties. In addition, the Navy should settle for the same mental standards required of recruits by the other services, instead of demanding higher test scores.

Senior officers of the Bureau of Naval Personnel objected to making the chief steward a peer of the chief petty officer and warned that uniform test scores for all the services would mean lower scores for enlistment in the Navy. Under Secretary of the Navy Dan A. Kimball, however, accepted the spirit if not the letter of the committee's recommendations. He intensi-fied the recruiting of African Americans, pledged that the Marine Corps would integrate recruit training as the Navy had done since 1945, agreed to enhance the status of chief stewards, and promised to undertake a study of possible assignments for recruits with lower test scores. The committee endorsed Kimball's plan, which Secretary of Defense Louis A. Johnson, who had replaced Forrestal in March, formally announced on 7 June 1949.

In August 1949, representatives of the Fahy Committee traveled to the Great Lakes Naval Training Station near Chicago. They also visited the technical training schools there, which provided instruction in electronics, communications, and other demanding subjects. The group reported that Great Lakes was "unquestionably following the policy of the Navy." The visit revealed "no segregation in either boot training or in the service schools." Clearly, "Negroes who are in the schools are there because they meet the qualifications of a particular rating. And meeting these qualifica-tions, they elicit the respect which craftsmanship deserves."

CHALLENGES TO BE MET   Although the Fahy Committee ratified the Navy's efforts to achieve equal treatment and opportunity for all races, problems remained. The question of social integration had to be resolved. Lieutenant Nelson believed that "personal relationships" in the Navy's enlisted force "were developing normally with a minimum of obstruc-tions." When these obstructions arose, such as racial segregation at barber shops or swimming pools, the Navy invoked a directive of 23 June 1949, which sought to achieve the goal of President Truman's policy by, among other things, prohibiting "special or unusual provisions"—in these instances racial segregation—in housing, messing, berthing or other facili-ties "for the accommodation of any minority race."

Problems surfaced most readily in the southern United States where a naval or military installation formed a racially integrated island in a sea of segregation, enforced by local law as well as custom. Nevertheless, by mid-1950 the Navy had integrated recreational and other facilities at bases in Jacksonville and Pensacola, Florida, and Corpus Christi, Texas.

Lieutenant Nelson enlisted the black press on behalf of the Navy's efforts to integrate the races. He also convinced his superiors to include African American journalists among those invited to join cruises meant to impress influential civilians with the importance of the Navy. In 1949, representatives of the black press went on board the battleship *Missouri* (BB-63) for a cruise to European ports. One of the African American reporters, Lucius Harper of the *Chicago Defender*, discovered during the cruise that some of the 104 black crewmen serving in the ship either were operating or learning to operate radar, manning gun turrets, or performing mechanical or engineering duties. He conceded that racial integration was not "perfect or fool-proof"—as the existence of the Steward Branch made up exclusively of blacks testified—but he believed that the stewards could be integrated racially through examinations and promotions. Nelson interpreted the article as evidence that the *Chicago Defender* and similar newspapers would continue to criticize actual instances of racial discrimination but "go more than half way in promoting and encouraging the aims of the integrated United States Navy."

Despite the signs of generally harmonious race relations within the Navy, misunderstandings sometimes arose with civilians when the Navy insisted on the racial integration of community-sponsored events for its officers and enlisted men. At Charleston, South Carolina, in the spring of 1950, the captain of the aircraft carrier *Saipan* (CVL-48) cooperated with the whites-only YMCA to hold a party on board the ship. Black crewmembers were not specifically excluded, and some did attend. The following night, the white YMCA and its black counterpart staged a separate party, exclusively for the African American crewmen, in the racially segregated city. The captain of *Saipan* played no part in planning the second party but accepted on behalf of his crew the invitation extended by the sponsors.

Learning of the racially segregated parties, which caught the eye of the *Chicago Defender*, Secretary of the Navy Francis P. Matthews, who had been in office since the summer of 1949, ordered an investigation. Based on this review he decided that *Saipan*'s skipper "did not knowingly sanction a segregated program," but he warned all commanding officers to avoid segregated events like those at Charleston. The Navy, Matthews also advised the Chicago newspaper, would not officially endorse, sanction, promote, or subsidize such activity.

The Navy's racial policy underwent another test the following year at an unlikely place, the city of Halifax in the Canadian province of Nova Scotia. *Missouri*, with black journalists again on board for a cruise, tied up there during the summer of 1950. The battleship's officers accepted assurances by a liaison officer from the Royal Canadian Navy that no color line existed at Halifax. When the local Colored Citizens Improvement League invited the ship's black Sailors to a party, *Missouri*'s captain assumed that this event would take place in addition to a similar event for the entire crew and promptly accepted on behalf of the African American crewmembers. Unfortunately, the captain was mistaken. In spite of the liaison officer's statement, racial segregation prevailed in Nova Scotia as it did in South Carolina. The sponsors at Halifax were planning two separate parties, one for whites and the other for blacks.

Once again, Secretary Matthews ordered an investigation. After weighing the evidence, he concluded that "the *Missouri* has enjoyed an excellent record in its efforts to achieve full integration and I am certain segregation of crew members at Halifax by special invitations was not intended or implied." He warned, however, that incidents like that at Halifax must not recur.

Lester Granger, formerly an aide to Secretary of the Navy Forrestal and now the executive director of the National Urban League, underscored the Navy's determination to put an end to segregated social and recreational events. He contacted B. A. Husbands, president of the Halifax Colored Citizens Improvement League, and pointed out that the Navy could not "insist upon the elimination of racial separation aboard ship and in any other service activities, and at the same time accept invitations which are restricted to Negro servicemen."

When war broke out in Korea during June 1950, Secretary of the Navy Matthews—a member of the President's Committee on Civil Rights—was systematically carrying out the reforms that Under Secretary Kimball had adopted to satisfy the Fahy Committee. Matthews in July 1949 issued an order banning discrimination on the basis of race, color, religion, or national origin in the enlistment, appointment, promotion, or assignment of Navy or Marine Corps personnel. He thus strengthened a policy of equal treatment and opportunity adopted in 1945 and reaffirmed in 1946.

Matthews then turned to the specific assurances given the committee by Under Secretary Kimball. On 25 July 1949, chief stewards became chief petty officers. Stewards first, second, and third class, however, remained in organizational limbo. Not until the end of August did the Bureau of Naval Personnel approve a recommendation from Lieutenant Nelson, now an officer of the regular Navy, to designate the lower-ranking stewards as petty officers in their appropriate grades.

A general perception that stewards were not real Sailors delayed the full acceptance of senior stewards as genuine petty officers. In the autumn of 1950, for instance, *All Hands: The Bureau of Naval Personnel Information Bulletin* printed a patronizing account of the work of some stewards at the Naval Air Station, Atlantic City, New Jersey. In their off-duty time they had planted and tended a garden that yielded a crop of vegetables that would have cost the Navy at least $1,000 to purchase from local farms. This accomplishment, however, remained buried amid the cuteness of a story that began: "Now that the frost is on the pumpkin and ruin reigns for the potato patch, the wardroom folks . . . sometimes sit back and reflect on the success of their 1950 garden plot." Although the headline referred to the stewards as "Men of the Sea," a reader could not help but conclude that they preferred "the memory of roasting ears and fresh green cucumbers" to the perils of the deep.

IMPACT OF THE KOREAN WAR

THE NAVY PERSISTED DURING the Korean War in its efforts to attract African Americans. The service dispatched recruiters to speak to black high school students. After a decline from 17,518 in 1949 to 14,842 in 1950, the number of African American Sailors reached 17,598 in 1951 and surpassed twenty-four thousand by the end of the fighting in July 1953. The number of blacks in the enlisted force had increased by seven thousand after establishment of the Fahy Committee in 1949. Equally encouraging was the fact that some 2,700 blacks applied during 1949 to enter NROTC, either by competing for scholarships or by joining units at colleges where they already were enrolled.

When African American officers, many serving as recruiters, were ordered to sea, they tended to be assigned as assistant communications officers on board ships. Indeed, over the years black officers were often first assigned to recruiting duty for one or two tours and then to an auxiliary vessel like an oiler, where they might well take charge of the radio shack. Assignments like these did not enhance an officer's chances for promotion. Not until the late 1950s did naval personnel officers, called detailers, make a conscientious effort to place officers, regardless of race, where their abilities best fulfilled the Navy's needs.

One of the officers brought back by Nelson specifically for recruiting duty followed the common assignment pattern of young black officers. Lieutenant Gravely proceeded from recruiting duty to communications school and then to an assistant communications billet on board a naval

Samuel L. Gravely Jr. accepts the congratulations of fellow officers in June 1971 on his promotion to rear admiral, the first African American to attain that rank. Gravely was commissioned through the Navy's World War II V-12 program. During that war he served in *PC-1264* and in the Korean War on board the battleship *Iowa* (BB-61). In 1976, Gravely was promoted to vice admiral and assigned command of the Third Fleet. (Naval Historical Center)

vessel, in his case the battleship *Iowa* (BB-61). He served in the mighty warship when she shelled targets in North Korea. He assumed that he had been selected for communications duty because he had been the communications officer in the submarine chaser *PC-1264* during World War II. But, he soon realized that "the Navy really didn't pick its best people" for this assignment. Gravely, however, was determined to succeed in the Navy. He earned a regular commission and fashioned a successful career path in surface warfare, taking command of destroyer escort *Falgout* (DE-324) in 1961. On 28 April 1971, in recognition of Gravely's superior leadership skills, the Navy selected him for flag rank—the first African American to become an admiral.

Lieutenant Lee, the first African American commissioned in the regular Navy, served in the cruiser *Toledo* (CA-133) during the Korean War as an assistant communications officer. The ship took part in the bombardment of enemy forces during the amphibious assault at Inchon, one of the most successful operations of the war.

The Marine Corps also recognized that it needed skilled men of all races to efficiently fight the difficult war in Korea. As a result, on 13 December 1951, Marine Corps headquarters issued a memorandum directing subordinate commands to fill all billets with qualified Marines, regardless of race.

The Navy Department's fight to end racial discrimination also proceeded on the home front during the war. In one instance, a group in Washington, D.C., which had previously sponsored social events for servicemen and government employees, arranged a cruise on the Potomac River exclusively for whites. Learning of the group's insistence on racial segregation, local commanders removed notices posted on government property advertising the event and pulled passes that would have enabled white Sailors to attend. The official response formally declining the invitation pointed out that the Department of Defense disapproved of the staging of racially segregated activities. On 10 November 1950, the Navy Department's Chief of Information, who monitored civilian-sponsored social events, issued a Navywide letter of instruction advising that "all commands should be guided by a policy of avoidance of official participation or in furtherance of the sponsorship of any entertainment which is racially discriminatory in nature."

Late in 1950, Clarence Mitchell, director of the Washington Bureau of the National Association for the Advancement of Colored People (NAACP), proposed two apparently simple actions designed to further equal treatment and opportunity within the Navy and also signal civilian communities that the service remained committed to racial integration. First, the civil rights organization wanted the Navy to stop using the standard racial identifiers—Caucasian, Mongolian, Negroid, Indian (Native American), and Malaysian—on personnel files; and second, to stop the housing and messing of recruits at racially segregated motels and restaurants while the new Sailors awaited transportation to a naval installation.

Although a strong advocate of equal treatment and opportunity, Secretary Matthews rejected Mitchell's recommendations. In some cities, especially though not exclusively in the South, there were no public accommodations that would serve blacks and whites equally. Unless a military or naval installation was near at hand, the Navy sometimes had no choice but to sign separate contracts to house and feed white and African American recruits. As for the racial labels, Matthews believed that the information was necessary to administer the program of racial integration and evaluate its results.

Even as the Navy struggled with segregation in the United States, L. Alex Wilson, a correspondent for the *Chicago Defender*, surveyed the state of racial integration with naval forces in Korea. Wilson found that the African Americans with whom he talked believed that the Navy was truly committed to racial integration and that the treatment they received was improving. Race relations, they said, were more harmonious at sea than in port, for ashore alcohol tended to dissolve personal inhibitions and the bonds of naval discipline. Despite the occasional brawl fueled by strong drink, a sizable number of whites seemed willing to associate with blacks and support equal treatment and opportunity—or at least not oppose the policy—and they served as a stabilizing influence on race relations.

The whites whom Wilson interviewed seemed to fall into three groups: a "fair percentage" accepted racial integration; a middle group was willing to go along with current policy; a minority felt that black Sailors were receiving unfair preferential treatment. Wilson believed that persuading this last group to accept, if not embrace, equal treatment and opportunity required strong leadership from officers and petty officers. Not every naval leader shared this commitment, Wilson reported, but even those who did not realized that they had to go along with Navy policy for the sake of their careers.

Another representative of the black press, Collins George of the *Pittsburgh Courier*, was much less optimistic than Wilson. In May 1951, he painted a discouraging picture of race relations at Camp Lejeune, North Carolina, and the adjacent town of Jacksonville. He described a "surface integration" beneath which "a deep core of old-fashioned segregation still festers." In his opinion, this ingrained racism influenced relations among Marines and affected the assignment of family housing.

After reviewing George's article, officers of the Division of Plans and Policies at Marine Corps headquarters responded promptly and vigorously. They disputed his assertion that black families lived in quarters inferior to those assigned to whites. They observed, "Negro Marines, white Marines, and their families have identical living quarters on a Marine Corps post or station." The officers acknowledged that segregation and

A USS *English* (DD-696) 40-millimeter gun crew prepares to bombard enemy installations on the Korean coast. (National Archives)

racial discrimination did exist, however, in the town of Jacksonville, where federally administered housing projects reflected local law and custom, which codified white supremacy.

The Marine leaders of the Division of Plans and Policies believed, moreover, that official policy could go just so far in governing relations between blacks and whites who wore the uniform. They observed, "The choice of friends, companions, and associates is an individual right of each Marine and cannot be directed by anyone." The racial prejudice that George discovered "can be eliminated only by the individual, which takes time. . . . Legislation and directives cannot do this job."

Despite the obvious problems, the Navy Department accomplished a great deal during the Korean War era. The policy of equal treatment and opportunity resulted in the more efficient use of manpower. Service men and women were being trained and assigned to specialties that fit their abilities. Refusing to cooperate with sponsors of racially segregated social or recreational events did not generate serious opposition from Sailors and Marines or from prospective sponsors.

EVOLUTION OF THE STEWARD BRANCH   One problem persisted—racial integration of the Navy's Steward Branch, the percentage of blacks having remained fairly constant throughout the war. Lester Granger, executive director of the National Urban League, called attention as early as the autumn of 1952 to the static racial composition of the Steward Branch. Granger asked Secretary of the Navy Dan Kimball to comment on "allegations"—which Granger knew were wildly exaggerated—that "90% of Negro personnel in the Navy" continued to serve in that specialty. When the Secretary of the Navy was tardy in providing accurate statistics, another request followed. This time, a search of Navy records revealed that 65 percent of the stewards were African American. "Although this percentage may appear high to you," Kimball conceded, "you must know . . . that a marked change has taken place since 1945." Then, Granger had served as an aide to Secretary Forrestal. Despite progress with integration, however, it was clear that the makeup of the Steward Branch was proving to be a difficult problem for the Navy.

The continued concentration of African Americans in the Steward Branch also caught the attention of New York Representative Adam Clayton Powell. "Will you be kind enough to advise me," he asked an assistant secretary of the Navy, "why your office continues to assign roughly one half of the Negroes in the United States Navy to work as messmen?" This apportionment of African American manpower, still taking place as the Korean War drew to an end, suggested to Powell that black Sailors were "fighting communism with a frying pan or shoe polish."

Powell's sarcasm not withstanding, there were several factors that influenced the racial composition of the Steward Branch. In addition to tradition, many African Americans gravitated to this branch of the Navy because of the potential for long-term employment and promotion. The fact that the Steward Branch reenlistment rate historically hovered around 80 percent at least partly reflected job satisfaction. In addition, the low test scores of many African American recruits, often the product of poor, underfunded primary and secondary schools, precluded their assignment to other job specialties in the Navy. This reality, however, clashed with the interests of a Navy trying to carry out a program, based on Executive Order 9981 and approved by the Fahy Committee, to broaden opportunities for blacks through integration into the other sectors of the service.

Besides embarrassing the Navy, the racial composition of the Steward Branch convinced many African Americans outside the service that the Navy would steer blacks away from nonsteward specialties. Attempts by the Navy to encourage stewards to qualify for other ratings had limited success during the war. Steward First Class Herbert Odom, who ranked first in his training class of electronics technicians, was an exception.

After the war, the Navy convened a special panel to study ways to better integrate the Steward Branch. The panel recommended against not offering special incentives to induce whites to volunteer for the branch, ending the practice of recruiting expressly for the Steward Branch, and focusing recruiting efforts in northern cities where integrated work forces were the norm. On 28 February 1954, seven months after the armistice that ended the Korean War, the Navy decided to end all first enlistments specifically for the Steward Branch. New recruits would be exposed to the range of opportunities in the service before they could join the Steward Branch. Recruits could not volunteer for steward duty until completion of boot camp, which gave the individual a better sense of the variety of training the Navy offered and his suitability for the different specialties.

This and other measures eventually resulted in a demographic change of the Steward Branch. More Filipino, Chamorro, and white Americans joined the branch so that by 1956, only 26 percent (the figure was never below 50 percent in the period from 1945 to 1955) of the Navy's stewards were African American. Moreover, between 1956 and 1961, roughly six hundred black Sailors transferred in grade from the steward billet to other ratings.

THE BLACK PIONEERS OF THE KOREAN WAR ERA The Korean War era was a watershed in the history of the racial integration of the Navy. In theory, if not always in practice, the Navy Department supported equal opportunity and treatment for Sailors of all races. At the same time, trail-blazing African Americans repeatedly demonstrated that they had much to contribute to the defense of the nation, including, as with Jesse Brown, their lives. When he died in the frigid mountains of North Korea in December 1950, he was the only fully qualified African American naval aviator and one of just twenty-one black male and female officers. But, other African Americans were ready to pick up the colors and move forward. Earl L. Carter pinned on his wings of gold in January 1951, earned a promotion to lieutenant (jg), and flew F9F Panther jets from the aircraft carrier *Bon Homme Richard* (CV-31) in combat operations over Korea. Ens. Albert Floyd became a naval aviator in March 1951 and served with the all-weather training unit at Naval Air Station, Key West, Florida. 2nd Lt. Frank F. Petersen Jr., the first African American Marine to become a naval aviator, earned his wings and his commission in October 1952. During the spring and summer of 1953, he flew sixty-four combat missions over Korea. Petersen retired from the Marine Corps as a lieutenant general.

As outstanding as was the service of black Sailors in the Korean War, it did not end discrimination against African Americans. The experience of Ens. Louis Ivey in the years after Korea was typical in many respects. A graduate of the NROTC program at Pennsylvania State University, Ivey was assigned in February 1954 to battleship *New Jersey* (BB-62), just returned to Norfolk, Virginia, from Korean waters. The night he reported on board, the black officer, the first ever to serve in *New Jersey*, shared a cabin with a white officer. For whatever reason, the next morning the white officer pulled rank and insisted Ivey find other quarters in the more spartan "ensign locker." Ivey gradually made friends among the other officers as he learned his duties in the boiler division and then in communications.

Lieutenant Carter, following in the footsteps of Ens. Jesse Brown, pauses for a photo in the cockpit of an F9F Panther jet before launching from the carrier *Bon Homme Richard* for another combat mission in Korea. (Naval Historical Center)

Social interaction ashore in the rigidly segregated Norfolk of the mid-1950s was another matter. The U.S. naval officer could not accompany his shipmates to the city's theaters, bars, and restaurants. He was compelled to spend much of his off-duty time on the naval base where he could not be denied access to the officers' club and other facilities, thanks to President Truman's directive of July 1948. When he did take liberty in town, he associated mostly with the few other black officers stationed in the area, carefully observing Norfolk's discriminatory racial laws and customs.

Only once during his tour of active duty did the civilian hosts of a social event make a special effort to put him at ease. The sponsors of a dance held in Mayport, Florida, asked Ivey if he wanted them to arrange a date for him, as they were doing for unmarried white officers. He agreed, and his date turned out to be a "very, very attractive, very elegant, very super" young African American. At other similar events, he remained a presence rather than a participant.

Overseas, Ivey discovered that he could move about freely in the company of other officers, whether white or black. For example, when *New Jersey* put in at Cherbourg, France, he joined two white ensigns in a four-day visit to Paris. There they experienced none of the complications that the interracial group would have encountered in Norfolk.

Ensign Ivey soon understood that African American enlisted men were proud that one of their own had become a naval officer. Ivey also realized that he was important to the black Sailors as a sympathetic listener and advisor. As an officer, he had frequent contact with African American stewards in the wardroom. He found that they served him promptly and courteously, as if to make it easier for him to cope with each day in the company of the mostly white officer complement of *New Jersey*.

Getting along with his fellow officers could be tricky, for the Navy still had a good distance to go to achieve genuine racial integration. Ivey had to endure snubs and thoughtless jokes. He remained open to overtures of friendship from whites but was wary of making approaches of his own. Thus did he pick his way through the minefield that was race relations in the Navy, which reflected American society in general. Ivey completed the tour of active duty required of a reserve officer commissioned through the NROTC. He returned to civilian life, entered medical school, and became a prominent surgeon.

Although the Navy in which Ivey served continued to reflect the racial prejudices of a society segregated by law and custom, the lot of the black naval officer had improved since World War II. When the single largest

BLACK SPORTS
HEROES OF THE
KOREAN WAR ERA

BLACK BOXERS ENJOYED REMARKABLE success during the Korean War period. Kenneth J. Bryant, representing the Naval Station at Kodiak, became the heavyweight champion of the armed forces in Alaska. In the Golden Gloves amateur competition at San Diego, two boxers from the Naval Amphibious Force—welterweight Felix Franklin and middleweight Nolan Davis—won titles in their weight divisions. At Helsinki, Finland, during the summer of 1952, Hayes Edward "Ed" Sanders became Olympic heavyweight champion, winning a gold medal by defeating Sweden's Ingemar Johannson, later heavyweight champion of the world.

African American Sailors also participated in team sports. In 1951, Baltimore police invoked the city's Jim Crow laws to prevent a game between a baseball team of black and white Sailors from *Ashland* (LSD-1) and a team of local blacks. More typical was the experience of the men of battleship *New Jersey,* which in 1950–1 fielded an undefeated basketball team that included one black player. The difference stemmed from the fact that the basketball team played at a naval installation. Racially integrated teams sometimes encountered problems in cities in the United States, but the Navy made it clear that it would not condone segregation in any form.

group of African American officers received their commissions in 1944, some white enlisted men refused to salute them. During the Korean War, a restaurant in Oxnard, California, refused to serve an African American officer unless he sat in isolation at a table near the kitchen; the owner did not relent until a white officer arrived and threatened to have the business declared off-limits to naval personnel. The Navy and the other armed forces, by carrying out President Truman's policy of equal treatment and opportunity, had moved ahead of a civilian society slowly inching toward racial integration.

The Navy made some progress in the racial integration of the service, made firm by Executive Order 9981, the work of the Fahy Committee, and manpower needs of the Korean War. During the decade following that conflict, the concentration of blacks in the Steward Branch at last ended. Blacks in the enlisted force totaled about 5 percent during the post-WWII period. The officer corps of the Navy of 1962 included 174 African Americans—men and women, regulars and reservists.

These figures represented definite improvement over pre-WWII and wartime totals, but they also demonstrated that the African American community remained a neglected national resource. Tragically, the United States would have to endure the legal wrangling, urban rioting, dissension in the armed forces, and other social and political upheavals of the 1960s and 1970s before African Americans could become full contributing members of the U.S. Navy.

BERNARD NALTY *spent almost forty years as a government historian, contributing during his career to the* History of U.S. Marine Corps Operations in World War II *and to the Air Force's official history of the Vietnam War. In the field of Black history, he collaborated with Morris J. MacGregor in editing the thirteen-volume* Blacks in the United States Armed Forces: Basic Documents *and its one-volume abridgement,* Blacks in the Military: Essential Documents. *He also wrote* Strength for the Fight: A History of Black Americans in the Military *and* The Right to Fight: African American Marines in World War II, *the latter a pamphlet in a series published by the Marine Corps to commemorate its contributions to victory in World War II. A graduate of Creighton University, he holds a master's degree from the Catholic University of America. He and his wife, Barbara, live in Woodstock, Maryland.*

CHAPTER 6

Attack from the Sky
Naval Air Operations in the Korean War

RICHARD C. KNOTT

INTRODUCTION

THE SPRING OF 1950 found U.S. naval aviation in an uneasy state of transition attempting to find its place in the challenging new world of jet aircraft and the atom bomb. So far for naval leaders it had been an uphill battle. The country was in a cost-cutting mood following World War II. Secretary of Defense Louis Johnson had canceled the construction of the world's first super carrier, the *United States*, a year earlier, not long after her keel laying. The Navy had counted on *United States* to help usher in the carrier jet age, as pundits questioned the suitability of jets operating effectively and safely from existing *Essex*-class ships or even from the three larger *Midway*-class carriers. With the cancellation of the *United States*, Secretary Johnson sent an unspoken but clear message to the Navy: make do with what you have or get out of the aviation business.

When the Soviet Union detonated its first atomic device in August 1949, the United States suddenly found itself without a monopoly on the nuclear option. The unsettling development was not expected for several years. While the United States was clearly ahead in nuclear weapons development no one knew how long it would take the Soviets to catch up.

Meanwhile, heated interservice debate over how best to spend limited defense dollars pitted the Navy against the newly created Air Force and carrier aviation against the intercontinental bomber, specifically the Convair B-36. Clashes between the two services increasingly spilled into the press and ultimately led to acrimonious congressional hearings at which senior officers and civilians from each side of the controversy gave vent to strongly held views.

While Navy supporters made a good case for their position, most observers believed the Air Force won the debate. Indeed, when the hearings ended, Chief of Naval Operations Admiral Denfeld, who had already been approved for another term, was summarily fired and the careers of other naval officers were threatened. The good news was that naval aviation had survived to fight another day. In any case, the "revolt of the admirals," as the press dubbed the interservice altercation, was over, at least for the moment.

Bloody but unbowed, the Navy turned its attention to integrating jet aircraft into the existing carrier force. Upgrading these ships was already well under way and there was even some hope that a big-deck supercarrier might ultimately be approved. Serious differences among the services over funding priorities and lingering disagreement over the question of roles and missions, however, continued to smolder.

Carrier aviation was also a difficult sell at the time largely because of an oversimplified public perception of the atom bomb and the way future wars would be fought. For one thing, the nation's leaders widely took for granted that the next war would be of the nuclear variety. Long-range strategic bombers were expected to bludgeon an enemy into oblivion in a matter of weeks, perhaps even days. In such a war there would be no role for aircraft carriers, said to be highly vulnerable to destruction and too expensive to build, man, maintain, and operate. Opponents alleged the money could be better spent on more useful weapons systems.

Naval aviation confronted another major problem: reasonable doubts by some longtime Navy supporters that newer, ever-faster, jet aircraft could operate safely from both existing and proposed carrier decks. There was even more skepticism over the idea put forth by naval aviation advocates that carrier aircraft could carry large, heavy, nuclear weapons. Even if they could, what was the point? The Air Force had won virtually exclusive rights to strategic bombing. In a nuclear war, the limited need for tactical air capability could be provided by the Air Force. These arguments were persuasive at a time of national economic retrenchment, and more than a few observers conceded that perhaps it was time for naval aviation and the aircraft carrier to pass quietly into history.

Then something entirely unforeseen happened.

AN UNEXPECTED WAR

ON SUNDAY MORNING 25 JUNE 1950, North Korea launched a well-planned and devastating assault on the ROK to the south. Although there had been some indication that the North Koreans were preparing to invade, Washington had expressed relatively little concern over this possibility. Indeed, the official U.S. government view was that war on the Korean peninsula was highly unlikely. As a result of that serious miscalculation, the United States became involved in a war for which it was largely unprepared. Not only had conventional American military forces atrophied to a shadow of their former selves, but the much touted nuclear option on which the United States had placed so much emphasis was ruled out for international and other considerations.

U.S. response to North Korean aggression was in keeping with the 1947 Truman Doctrine designed to contain the spread of Soviet-inspired Communist aggression throughout the world. The possibility, however, that war on the Korean peninsula might spark a wider and more serious conflict or adversely affect U.S. interests in other global hotspots preyed on the minds of U.S. leaders from the beginning and adversely influenced military operations throughout the war.

The NKPA took maximum advantage of the element of surprise. By the evening of 26 June strong forces were only seventeen miles from the ROK capital of Seoul. During the day American nationals were evacuated by sea from the port of Inchon. Still others were airlifted out on 27 June by U.S. Air Force C-54s and C-47s. Also that day the United Nations called upon its members to render assistance to the Republic of Korea. General MacArthur had already been authorized by President Truman to use U.S. forces against the North Koreans on 26 June. MacArthur would shortly become commander in chief of all United Nations forces in Korea, with the lion's share provided by the United States.

The North Korean air force was modest by the standards of the times, but its pilots were active in the very beginning, aggressively attacking Kimpo and Suwon airfields. The North Koreans were confident that they could overrun the peninsula in short order and present the world with a fait accompli. There was no attempt to tread lightly where the United States was concerned, and Yak fighters destroyed a U.S. Air Force Military Air Transport Service C-54 on the ground at Kimpo on the first day of strikes. The North Koreans had a number of propeller-driven fighter and attack aircraft, which included Ilyushin Il-10s, Yakovlev Yak-3s and -7Bs, and Lavochkin La-7s. The ROK Air Force, on the other hand, had no combat aircraft, its inventory essentially limited to a number of North American AT-6 trainers (U.S. Navy designation SNJ). By 29 June the North Korean army firmly held Seoul, including Kimpo airfield, and by the night of 30 June Suwon airfield just to the south had been abandoned to fast-approaching enemy forces. The poorly equipped, badly mauled, and demoralized ROK Army retreated southward.

During the first days of the war, no one knew whether the fighting would be limited to the Korean peninsula. Indeed, there was considerable concern that the People's Republic of China might use the occasion to attack Taiwan (Formosa), and on 27 June President Truman ordered the Seventh Fleet to prevent any such attempt.

It was a large order. The Seventh Fleet and Naval Forces Far East combined consisted of only one carrier, two cruisers, twelve destroyers, four submarines, two divisions of minesweepers, a small amphibious squadron, and some support ships. At the time of the attack, units of the fleet were split between the Philippines, Hong Kong, and Japan, and its commander, Vice Admiral Struble was in Washington, D.C. Fortunately, the acting commander, Rear Adm. John M. "Pegleg" Hoskins, a well-respected officer, moved quickly to bring his assets together to form a striking force designated Task Force (TF) 77. Hoskins's unusual nickname was derived from the prosthesis he wore to replace his right foot, which was blown off during the Battle of Leyte Gulf in World War II.

By June 1950 the active American carrier force that had numbered close to one hundred ships at the end of World War II had been reduced to fifteen carriers of all types. *Valley Forge* (CV-45), the only American carrier in the Western Pacific when the war began, sortied from Subic Bay in the Philippines on 27 June to rendezvous with other elements of Task Force 77 at Sasebo on the western side of the island of Kyushu, Japan. En route, Hoskins launched his planes to put on a show of force over the Taiwan Strait and the city of Taipei to reassure the Nationalist Chinese and to warn mainland China that the United States would not tolerate attempts to use the crisis in Korea to invade Taiwan. Truman also used the fleet to

On board *Valley Forge* (CV-45), the Navy's newest jet fighter, the Grumman F9F Panther, waits to resume flight missions. (Naval Historical Center)

restrain Nationalist actions that might widen the conflict throughout the Far East. Because Sasebo was vulnerable to attack by Soviet as well as Chinese Communist aircraft, *Valley Forge* and the other ships diverted to a new rendezvous site at Buckner Bay, Okinawa.

The five squadrons of Carrier Air Group (CVG) 5 embarked in the "Happy Valley," as the carrier was affectionately called, contained the total of all U.S. Navy tactical aircraft then available for combat in Korea. Fortunately, CVG-5 was also the Navy's most experienced, jet-equipped air group. Indeed, Fighter Squadron (VF) 51 was the Navy's first to qualify in jets (the squadron was designated VF-5A at the time) and had received its F9F-3 Panthers in May 1949. VF-52 was similarly equipped and well practiced while VF-53 and VF-54 flew the propeller-driven Vought F4U-4B Corsair, an exceptional aircraft design first used in World War II. Although the Corsair units were designated fighter squadrons (VFs), the missions they flew throughout the Korean War were almost exclusively of the fighter-bomber variety. Attack Squadron (VA) 55 rounded out the air group with propeller-driven Douglas AD-4 Skyraiders. Unlike the Corsairs, these aircraft had not been tested in combat during World War II but would turn out to be tailor-made for the job at hand in Korea and deliver a stellar performance throughout the war.

Martin PBM-5 Mariners of Patrol Squadron (VP) 47 based in Japan began patrols on 27 June, and VP-46 operating from a tender in Buckner Bay began patrolling the China coast and the Taiwan Strait on 6 July. By 18 July the latter squadron moved to the Penghu Islands where its planes flew from the tender *Suisun* (AVP-53) to provide increased surveillance of the sensitive passage that divided the mainland from Taiwan. Lockheed P2V-3 Neptunes of VP-6 began scouring the waters off the east coast of Korea, alert for enemy activity beginning 8 July, while VP-28 with Consolidated PB4Y-2 Privateers flying from Okinawa began patrols along the coast of China on 16 July. In mid-August PBMs of VP-42 began monitoring shipping in the Tsushima Strait.

The role of patrol aircraft in the Korean conflict was mostly one of surveillance and reconnaissance. Their presence in the Taiwan Strait also served as a continuing warning to mainland China that the United States was watching and would mount an aggressive response to any Chinese Communist attempt to invade Taiwan. Because of the Soviet Union's substantial submarine fleet, the task of patrol aviation necessarily included antisubmarine coverage especially in the vicinity of major fleet operations. Patrol-type aircraft like the PB4Y-2 collected intelligence information on enemy radar emissions. Toward the end of the war the new Martin Mercator P4M-1Q, powered by both jet and reciprocating engines and dedicated to the electronic reconnaissance role (VQ), was introduced.

Patrol aircraft even took on such tasks as spotting and destroying mines in coordination with surface units. Turret and waist guns were used to sink or detonate these moored or free-floating weapons while depth bombs with shallow settings were dropped in known minefields in hopes that the underwater concussion would set off several weapons at a time. Both techniques yielded limited success but, in the end, surface units accomplished most mine clearance.

Valley Forge and Task Force 77 left Buckner Bay on 1 July and headed for the Yellow Sea. Included in the combined fleet were the British carrier HMS *Triumph* and her escorts. British carrier and patrol aviation made important contributions to air operations throughout the war. Royal Navy carriers *Glory*, *Triumph*, and *Theseus* carried Supermarine Seafire, Hawker Sea Fury, and Fairey Firefly aircraft that racked up some twenty-two thousand sorties. The Royal Air Force provided two Sunderland flying boat patrol squadrons while the Royal Australian Navy contributed the aircraft carrier HMAS *Sydney*.

In the early morning of 3 July, *Triumph* launched twelve Firefly fighter bombers and nine Seafire fighters armed with rockets for an assault on the airfield at Haeju, located about sixty-five miles south of the North Korean capital city of Pyongyang. Minutes later sixteen Corsairs and twelve Skyraiders from *Valley Forge* were in the air and headed for Pyongyang itself, their objective to hit the city's airfields, railroad yards, and other targets of opportunity in the area. Because of their greater speed, eight Panther jets took off after the F4Us and ADs and, as planned, arrived first in order to deal with fighter opposition that might be encountered. This strike was the baptism of fire for the Skyraider and the Panther.

North Korean Yak-9 fighters rose to meet the jets and two were quickly dispatched by VF-51 pilots, the first by Lt. (jg) Leonard H. Plog and the second by Ens. Eldon W. Brown Jr. These were the Navy's first kills by jet aircraft. The Panthers also destroyed three enemy planes on the ground.

When the heavily armed propeller-driven aircraft arrived, they demolished hangars, fuel-storage tanks, and other facilities; cratered runways; and damaged a nearby railroad yard. *Valley Forge*'s planes returned to Pyongyang again that afternoon, this time concentrating on railroads, roads, and bridges. The next day it was more of the same with the Skyraiders dropping a bridge span over the Taedong River as well as inflicting considerable damage on locomotives and rail facilities that had survived the previous day's attacks.

Four Skyraiders were hit by ground fire during this action. One, which was unable to lower its flaps for a carrier recovery, bounced over the barriers and careened into aircraft parked forward. A Skyraider and two Corsairs were destroyed and several other aircraft were damaged in the accident. Such crashes were a constant hazard on board axial (straight) deck carriers of the period, and although the culprit in this instance was a propeller-driven aircraft, jets with their higher landing speeds introduced the potential for even more serious accidents of this type. The eventual solution to this vexing problem, the angle deck design, would not become a reality until after war.

Meanwhile, the ROK Army and American troops of the U.S. Army's 24th Infantry Division attempted to slow the advance of the North Koreans as best they could. The situation, however, was desperate. To shore up the troops, the fleet deployed the Army's 1st Cavalry Division ashore at

Pohang on the East Coast of the peninsula on 18 July. Task Force 77 got the job of supporting the landing that, as it turned out, was unopposed. As a result, the task force was released to make its way along the coast to an area off North Korea where aircraft from *Valley Forge* hit the enemy hard on his home turf.

During the day the planes made attacks in the Pyongyang area and that evening pounced on a large oil refinery at Wonsan. Ten Corsairs led the attack with high-velocity aircraft rockets (HVARs) and gunfire to suppress enemy defenses. Eleven Skyraiders loaded with 500- and 1,000-pound bombs as well as HVARs followed closely on the heels of the Corsairs to deal devastating blows to the refinery and its storage tanks. Thousands of tons of refined oil went up in smoke, which could be seen from sixty miles away. The plant was totally destroyed and burned for days, depriving the enemy of an important military asset.

On 20 July the highly mobile task force headed south and transited the Tsushima Strait for operations off the west coast. On the morning of 22 July, Skyraiders and Corsairs attacked targets in the vicinity of Haeju and Inchon before returning to Japan briefly to refuel and rearm.

CARRIER AIR COMES THROUGH

TACTICAL AIRCRAFT FLYING FROM carriers offer a unique advantage over their land-based counterparts. This air support was especially important during the early desperate days of the Korean War as allied ground forces held on precariously to a defensive perimeter around Pusan. The carriers could be positioned anywhere around the peninsula and their planes had to fly relatively short distances to target areas, arriving on station with full ordnance and fuel loads. Skyraiders, with two forward-firing 20-mm cannon (four in later models) could also mount thousands of pounds of bombs and rockets, earning them the well-deserved nickname "flying dump trucks." F4U-4 Corsairs mounted six .50-caliber guns in the wings while F4U-4B models had four 20-mm cannon and could carry smaller but still respectable quantities of bombs and rockets.

Napalm, which had been such a powerful weapon in World War II, turned out to be equally potent in Korea against a variety of targets, including T-34/85 medium tanks. Both napalm and fragmentation bombs worked effectively against troop concentrations. Skyraiders and Corsairs could spend about four hours aloft queuing up for target assignments or searching for and prosecuting targets of opportunity on their own before returning to the ship. From the very beginning to the end of the war, one could quite accurately say that no enemy target anywhere on the Korean peninsula was safe from a devastating attack by carrier aircraft.

Air support was critical to the defense of the Pusan Pocket in the early days of the Korean War. Because there were few suitable allied-controlled airfields from which land-based tactical aircraft could operate in any numbers, carrier air was critical. A handful of North American F-51 Mustangs manned by American and South Korean pilots and commanded by a U.S. Air Force officer operated out of the Taegu airfield known as K-2. Their efforts were courageous and they were kept busy trying to be in several places at once, but K-2 was a rough airfield made of earth and gravel, which turned into a muddy quagmire when it rained, and was often barely usable for sustained operations. Nevertheless, other F-51s from Japan frequently landed there to rearm, refuel, and make additional strikes before returning to home base across the Sea of Japan.

Although the airfield at Pusan was primitive by modern standards, it was sorely needed to support logistics flights critical to ground operations on the perimeter. Overuse by heavy cargo aircraft tore up the runways, making it difficult to maintain the field even for this supply purpose. Following the landings at Pohang, F-51s operated briefly from the airfield there, but on 12 August assaults by the NKPA forced these aircraft to abandon the base and return to Japan.

Air Force B-26s and F-82 Twin Mustangs flying from Japan provided what air support they could but transit time detracted from their time on station. The B-26s mounted .50-caliber machine guns, rockets, and as much as four thousand pounds of bombs as well as sizable fuel loads. They spent a respectable time on station and turned in creditable performances against North Korean troop columns and supply convoys. The problem was that there were simply not enough of them. Nor were there enough F-82s, and in any case, the pilots of these air defense fighters were not trained for tactical air strikes or close air support.

No airfield in the area held by allied forces could handle jets. Air Force F-80 Shooting Stars had no choice but to make the trek from Japan, arriving on station at the limit of their effective range. These aircraft had eight .50-caliber machine guns and could carry up to sixteen high-velocity rockets. With a full fuel load, however, their combat radius was only about 225 miles so that when the aircraft arrived in the combat area, their fuel states (levels) were so critical that they had only minutes to make hasty attacks before heading back to Japan. F-80s could carry two 1,000-pound bombs instead of wing tip fuel tanks, but this load reduced their effective radius to only about a hundred miles, not enough to reach the target and return home.

By 23 July the situation on the ground was so critical that the Eighth Army issued an emergency request that Task Force 77 provide close air support to troops attempting to hold the line on the shrinking Pusan Perimeter. The task force was ready and willing. On 25 and 26 July, planes from *Valley Forge* steaming off the east coast were in the air reporting to the Army/Air Force JOC at Taegu, which had been given control over target assignments.

Early attempts at coordinating Navy and Air Force strikes did not go well. Communications were poor, priority was given to Air Force aircraft because of their limited time on station, and procedural incompatibilities hampered the effectiveness of the interservice effort. The Air Force close air support concept was particularly irksome to Navy pilots whose own tried-and-true system they believed to be inherently superior to that of the Air Force. Urgent meetings took place to hammer out solutions to these problems.

As existing carrier forces did their best to slow the enemy advance on Pusan, efforts in the United States to bring more resources to bear moved into high gear. *Philippine Sea* (CV-47), originally scheduled to relieve *Valley Forge* in October, sailed on 5 July with Carrier Air Group 11 embarked. VF-111 and VF-112, the two Panther jet squadrons of this air group, which had just received their new fighter aircraft, resorted to training flights en route to bring their pilots up to speed.

As it became increasingly clear that the war in Korea might become a protracted affair, attention was given to bringing mothballed ships back into service. *Princeton* (CV-37), one of the last *Essex*-class fast carriers built during World War II, was at the top of the list and was first to be recommissioned on 28 August. The exigency of the unplanned war and the dire situation of UN troops on the ground made readying the ship an all-out effort. Some 80 percent of *Princeton*'s initial crew was from reserve units, many recalled on only twenty-four hours' notice. As the war progressed, other carriers and their air groups were manned almost entirely by reservists. The "weekend warriors" responded well to the call and some reserve squadrons even volunteered as complete units, the first being VF-781 from Naval Air Station Los Alamitos, California. By the end of 1951, reservists were flying more than half of all U.S. Navy carrier air strikes in

A DIFFERENCE
OF CONCEPTS

DIFFERING IDEAS OF CLOSE air support hampered allied air operations in the beginning and, to some extent, throughout the war. The Air Force concept developed in Europe during World War II depended largely on targeting by Air Force controllers in the air or a Tactical Air Control Party (TACP) on the ground but usually operating independently of ground combat forces. A typical scenario might involve the TACP initiating a call for close air support, which was routed through the ground force involved, and then on to the next-higher Army echelon. From there the request went to the Joint Operations Center, then to an Air Force TACC, and finally to the supporting aircraft. The pilot of the aircraft then contacted the TACP on the ground or an airborne controller over the target for further instructions. The entire sequence could take as long as forty minutes before air support was actually delivered. It was almost never made closer than a thousand yards from friendly forces and was frequently made at much greater distances.

The Navy/Marine Corps method, on the other hand, was a product of the Pacific Islands campaigns of World War II where the ground war involved Marines fighting for footholds on beachheads or in other situations in close proximity to the enemy. Marine tactical air controllers serving with troops on the ground directed the air support, calling in fire against entrenched enemy forces sometimes as close as fifty yards away. Under this concept, the pilot delivering the support dealt directly with the people on the ground. In most cases, an urgent request could be acted upon instantly.

High on a Korean mountainside, a Marine forward air controller calls in an air strike on an enemy-held ridge. (U.S. Marine Corps)

The problem of land-based aircraft having to transit from Japan hampered early interdiction as well as close air support efforts by Navy aircraft. Navy pilots, their planes bristling with rockets, bombs, and napalm, were often frustrated when more lightly loaded F-80 Shooting Stars from Japan were given targeting priority because of their limited time on station. On occasion, Navy planes that had orbited for hours waiting for a target assignment had to jettison their ordnance loads in the sea before returning to the ship. Still, despite vexing coordination problems and conceptual differences among the services, carrier aircraft were able to get in their licks supporting troops on the ground and wreaking havoc on enemy troop columns, trucks, and rail lines. As the war in Korea moved on, communications and coordination between the Army/Air

Force JOCs and fleet aircraft would improve, but conceptual differences concerning the most effective way to provide close air support would remain. When the situation demanded it, Navy and Marine pilots did what was necessary to support troops on the ground.

Korea. This important national asset proved critical in mobilizing naval aviation to an acceptable force level.

Boxer (CV-21) was pressed into emergency service as an aircraft ferry and made a hurried Pacific crossing carrying 145 F-51 Mustang fighters. Also on board were some one thousand Air Force support personnel and two thousand tons of equipment. The planes had been commandeered from the Air National Guard to bolster critically needed Air Force tactical aircraft in the combat arena. *Boxer* left Alameda, California, on 14 July and arrived in Japan on 22 July, a record crossing of eight-and-a-half days.

Philippine Sea, with Air Group 11 embarked, arrived at Buckner Bay on 1 August and on 5 August joined *Valley Forge* in combat operations off the Korean coast. The touch-and-go situation along the Pusan Perimeter made close air support a top priority. Navy tactical air controllers in Navy planes joined Air Force controllers over the front lines to direct the activities of carrier aircraft. This procedure helped to eliminate some of the problems previously experienced, particularly those involving communications. Carrier aircraft also renewed their efforts against enemy supply and troop columns working their way toward the front and further hindered enemy movement by destroying roads and bridges.

During this early period carrier operations were, of necessity, interrupted periodically so the ships of the task force could return to port for replenishment. Carrier aircraft expended enormous quantities of aviation fuel and ordnance during combat operations and accompanying destroyers required refueling every three days. With two fast carriers on the scene they were able to stagger these replenishment periods to allow the aircraft of one ship to be constantly available for sorties against the enemy. Nevertheless, the necessity of returning ships to port every few days detracted from the total early effort.

The drawdown of fleet assets following World War II had hobbled the Navy's service squadrons even more severely than its combat units;

Reserve Fighter Squadron 783 Corsairs of *Bon Homme Richard*'s Carrier Air Group 102 fly in formation over Korea. The F4U Corsair, a well-tested combat veteran of World War II in the Pacific, proved just as effective in Korea. (National Archives)

consequently, UNREP was unavailable on a sustained basis at this stage of the war. Oilers and supply ships were increasingly available toward the end of the year, however, and by the spring of 1951 there were enough service ships to permit UNREP scheduling daily or as required. Carriers were then able to launch their strikes during the day, take on aviation fuel and ordnance in the late afternoon or even after dark, and remain at sea for extended periods.

Two escort carriers were hastily dispatched to the Western Pacific. *Sicily* (CVE-118) left San Diego on 4 July, put in at Guam to offload her antisubmarine aircraft, and proceeded to Yokosuka, Japan, where she took on board F4U-4B Corsair fighter-bombers of Marine Fighter Squadron (VMF) 214. The planes engaged in combat for the first time on 3 August with a rocket and bomb attack on Chinju near the Pusan

Oiler *Ashtabula* (AO-51) refuels *Boxer* to port and a destroyer to starboard in heavy seas off Korea. Carriers in the Korean combat zone typically operated around a geographical reference point called Point Oboe, about 125 miles east of Wonsan. They retired another fifty miles east to receive underway replenishment. (National Archives)

Perimeter. *Badoeng Strait* (CVE-116), known affectionately as the "Bing-Ding," sailed from San Diego on 14 July with part of Marine Aircraft Group (MAG) 33 on board, arriving at Kobe, Japan, on 31 July. She launched Corsairs of VMF-323 in combat on 6 August.

In early August General MacArthur directed all air assets to concentrate on close air support and related interdiction. Marine Corps aircraft from *Sicily* and *Badoeng Strait* joined in, their planes using the Navy/Marine Corps concept of close air support. They were permitted to depart from Army/Air Force close air support practices because their main function was to support the recently arrived 1st Provisional Marine Brigade now holding a hotly contested portion of the Pusan Perimeter. General MacArthur was persuaded that Marine pilots were trained to work directly with their own troops on the ground using Navy/Marine Corps doctrine and that to require them to do otherwise would be to disrupt a well-established and highly effective procedure.

The war continued with both sides launching heavy attacks and counterattacks along the Pusan Perimeter. Aircraft from both the fast and escort carriers were heavily engaged. By 10 August it seemed clear that the Pusan Perimeter would hold. The support rendered by carrier aircraft had been critical to preserving this precarious foothold.

THE TIDE TURNS AT INCHON

NOW IT WAS TIME for a decisive move against the enemy. That initiative came in the form of a brilliantly planned and executed amphibious landing, a daring stroke that was the brainchild of General MacArthur himself. The idea was to insert UN forces into North Korean held territory well north of the Pusan Perimeter and drive inland to cut the enemy's overextended supply lines, liberate Seoul, and retake the city's all-important Kimpo airfield. The assault would also divert enemy attention and reinforcements allowing the U.S. Eighth Army and ROK forces to break out of the Pusan Pocket and move north to join invasion forces and crush or trap the North Korean army in the middle.

It was MacArthur's choice of the west coast port of Inchon as the invasion site that gave the Joint Chiefs of Staff and other senior military leaders cause for concern—and with good reason. The Marines, who over the years had refined amphibious assault to a science, were to go ashore in shallow-draft small craft. Supplies and equipment, however, would go in on LSTs that needed at least twenty-nine feet of water to reach the landing sites. Low tide rendered the Inchon harbor a huge mudflat with a tortuous, snaking channel just twelve feet deep. Even at high tide the water was deep enough for the LSTs on just two days, 15 September and 11 October, and even then there was limited time to make the beach. Once they grounded, the ships had to remain beached overnight off-loading critical supplies. Should Marines ashore become overwhelmed by enemy troops, the immobile LSTs could be destroyed or seized and their crews killed or captured.

It was an immense gamble, but one that offered the important advantage of surprise. The North Koreans were well aware of the hazards involved in an Inchon landing and the Americans hoped the enemy would completely discount the idea as being too risky for consideration. False intelligence and increased allied operations at other locations might catch the North Koreans unprepared to defend against an Inchon assault until it was too late. The Joint Chiefs were also very much aware of the risk and the potential for disaster, but MacArthur remained confident. Finally, on 28 August the Joint Chiefs of Staff approved the amphibious landing at Inchon code named Operation Chromite. It was clear to everyone that air support would be a critical element.

Planners were concerned about how the Soviets and the Chinese might react to the invasion. Combatant ships and aircraft of both Communist countries were too close for comfort. Antisubmarine efforts thus became an important part of the operation, a situation calling for the specialized capabilities of multiengine patrol aircraft.

During the first days of September the planes from the fast carriers continued to support troops on the Pusan Perimeter as before, particularly in the Naktong River area. Then, on 4 September, radar on board the light cruiser *Worcester* (CL-144) picked up an unidentified aircraft to the north heading for Task Force 77. Four airborne VF-53 Corsairs, the combat air patrol from *Valley Forge*, were sent to investigate. They intercepted a twin-engine Soviet aircraft only thirty miles away and coming on fast toward the fleet. When the plane opened fire on the VF-53 flight leader, the Corsairs made quick work of the intruder. No Soviet counteraction resulted from the incident.

To divert attention from the Inchon invasion site, Air Force bombers began hitting roads and bridges serving the port of Kunsan, a very plausible landing site further south, on 5 September. Aircraft from *Badoeng Strait* and HMS *Triumph* bolstered this deception by cutting supply routes—roads and bridges—running into the area from the north. Planes from *Valley Forge* and *Philippine Sea* hit targets from Seoul to Pyongyang further diverting the enemy's attention from the real landing site. Meanwhile, ships from nine nations were assembling in Japanese ports to form the Inchon invasion task fleet under Admiral Struble, Commander Seventh Fleet.

Corsairs from *Sicily* and *Badoeng Strait* began pounding targets in the Inchon area on 10 September, especially Wolmi-do, an island commanding the approaches to Inchon Harbor. The attackers dropped large amounts of napalm to neutralize the island's defenses before the invasion began.

Further softening-up of the targets took place on 13 and 14 September when cruisers and destroyers bombarded the island and fast carriers and escort aircraft carriers (CVEs) launched more air attacks. Marine

Corsairs took off at first light on 15 September to give Wolmi-do a last minute pasting before the 3rd Battalion, 5th Marines stormed ashore. Meanwhile, other planes from *Valley Forge* and *Philippine Sea* prevented reinforcements from reaching the beleaguered enemy troops to whom fell the unenviable task of defending Inchon.

The Inchon invasion involved 230 ships of nine nations and some seventy thousand men. *Boxer* arrived off Inchon at noon on 15 September bringing to three the number of fast carriers on the scene. Her Air Group 2 was equipped with four squadrons of Corsairs and one of Skyraiders, an ideal mix for support of troops making an amphibious assault.

The primary assault forces at Inchon were Navy and Marine Corps units. Planes from the three U.S. Navy fast carriers and the two escort carriers provided air strikes and close air support while P2V and PBM patrol aircraft performed patrol, escort, reconnaissance, and antisubmarine duties. Seafires and Fireflies from the Royal Navy's HMS *Triumph* contributed air cover for UN naval forces while two squadrons of RAF Short Sunderland flying boats joined in the patrol and reconnaissance effort.

At 0633 the Marines went ashore on Wolmi-do and by 0800 they had secured the island. That afternoon heavy naval gunfire and air strikes on the city by carrier aircraft paved the way for the main event. The Marines made their first landing on the mainland at Inchon about 1730 during high tide and accompanied by plenty of air support. Corsairs and Skyraiders that had spent much of the day pummeling the shore now came in low over the landing craft to keep enemy heads down during the shore approach. By midnight some thirteen thousand Marines were ashore and Inchon was in UN hands. General MacArthur's magnificent gamble had succeeded beyond expectations. Senior officers in Washington breathed a sigh of relief.

With mopping up operations still in progress on the morning of 16 September, the 1st Marines headed toward Seoul while the 5th Marines went for Kimpo. The airfield fell the following day, and on 18 September an advance party of Marine Aircraft Group 33 arrived to ready the field to receive aircraft. In the following weeks Corsairs of VMF-212 and VMF-312 as well as two-place, twin-engine Grumman F7F-3N Tigercat night fighters of VMF-542 arrived from Japan. With four 20-mm cannon in the wings and the ability to carry up to a thousand pounds of bombs under each wing, the Tigercats were ideal for ground support missions and welcome additions to the combat inventory in Korea. These radar-equipped aircraft, which could see in the dark, functioned in a variety of missions, but their forte was night attack, especially interdiction, bomber escort missions, and combat air patrol.

The morning after their arrival Tigercats were in the air flying close air support for Marines on the ground. That night they were aloft again hitting the enemy's supply lines into Seoul. On 21 September F4U-4Bs of VMF-323 from *Badoeng Strait* joined in concerted attacks on North Korean troops at Yongdung-po on the outskirts of Seoul. Fighting was especially heavy here as the enemy tried desperately to halt the 1st Marines. By this time the city of Suwon and its important airfield had been retaken with the help of Skyraiders from the fast carriers. Air Force cargo aircraft were now able to off-load supplies and equipment for the rapidly advancing Marines. The situation was changing by the hour, and it was not long before UN forces from the south linked up with invading troops from the west sending large numbers of the enemy fleeing.

By 27 September, following a bloody, hard-fought action by the Marines, Seoul was again in friendly hands and the battered enemy was retreating north. Of the seventy thousand North Korean troops, which had driven the ROK Army south into the Pusan Pocket, only about thirty thousand recrossed the 38th parallel into North Korea. The rest had been killed or captured. The situation on the ground had changed so rapidly that aircraft from the fast carriers soon found it increasingly difficult to find worthwhile targets. By 3 October, Task Force 77 had departed station in the Yellow Sea for Sasebo, Japan.

Despite concern in Washington over the possibility of provoking a Soviet or Chinese response, General MacArthur was given the go-ahead on 27 September to pursue what was left of the North Korean army across the 38th parallel and destroy it. Leaders hoped the peninsula could be quickly unified under the government of South Korean President Syngman Rhee. Even as the order to cross the 38th parallel was given, however, Chinese troops were massing on the border just north of the Yalu River. Neither General MacArthur nor others in Washington believed the Chinese would intervene but they knew it might happen and that speed of advance was all-important. With the North Korean army in total disarray the UN planned to accomplish its goal to destroy the army quickly and present the world with its own fait accompli.

MacArthur, fresh from his incredible success at Inchon, now called for another amphibious assault at the port city of Wonsan on the opposite coast. The North Koreans, however, had learned an important and painful lesson at Inchon and applied their newfound wisdom at Wonsan. They heavily seeded the harbor and approaches with moored mines that required extensive clearing before an amphibious landing could take place. Naval aviation was recruited to assist in the effort.

On 3 October an HO3S-1 helicopter from the light cruiser *Worcester* was assigned to assist minesweepers clearing the area. The mission was one of the first efforts to use the new aerial asset for mine clearance. Skyraiders and Corsairs with 1,000-pound bombs dropped their loads on known minefields. As it turned out, aircraft—particularly helicopters—proved quite useful for mine hunting, but less so for mine destruction.

Patrol aircraft searched for mines and, to the extent possible, assisted in destroying them with gunfire and depth bombs. On one occasion a lumbering flying boat even engaged the enemy in support of U.S. Navy surface vessels under fire. On 12 October minesweepers *Pirate* (AM-275) and *Pledge* (AM-277) both struck mines during a sweep just offshore and began to sink. Enemy shore batteries opened fire on the stricken vessels to administer the coup de grace. A PBM Mariner flown by Lt. Cdr. Randall Boyd radioed information for rescue operations while spotting naval gunfire from the destroyer minesweeper *Endicott* (DMS-35). The PBM even brought its own .50-caliber waist and turret guns to bear at close range receiving return fire in the process. Despite the big plane's vulnerability Boyd remained overhead until Corsairs from *Leyte* (CV-32) arrived to rake enemy positions, suppressing fire so rescue operations could be completed.

Meanwhile, the three fast carriers of Task Force 77 steamed from the west coast around the peninsula to conduct prelanding bombardment of Wonsan. They were joined by the carrier *Leyte*, which had arrived in the combat area on 9 October with Air Group 3. CVG-3 contributed two Panther jet, two Corsair, and one Skyraider squadrons to the mix. For the first time in the Korean War there were four fast carriers in Task Force 77. Their planes attacked targets along the east coast north of Wonsan preparing for the amphibious assault that was scheduled for 20 October. By the morning of 10 October, however, the ROK Army's I Corps was already on the outskirts of Wonsan where they met only residual North Korean resistance. Aircraft from *Leyte* flew in to hit stubborn enemy armor and artillery and by afternoon the ROK Army was in control of the city.

Marine Corsair squadron VMF-312 was operating from the Wonsan airfield by 14 October while VMF (N)-513, a Corsair night-fighter squadron nicknamed "The Flying Nightmares," arrived three days later. The two Marine squadrons now provided land-based air support to the rapidly advancing ROK Army that was now moving north beyond Wonsan. Because the port was still closed by mines the Marine squadrons ashore were supported logistically by an Air Force airlift that flew in aviation fuel in 55-gallon drums. The mines were cleared a few days later and Marines landed unopposed at Wonsan on 25 October. As they came ashore they were cheered on good-naturedly by members of the ROK Army and the 1st Marine Aircraft Wing already there.

The fast carrier task force was reduced again to three carriers on 22 October when *Boxer* left for the United States with propulsion problems. With the enemy in full retreat the carrier could well be spared. Air operations from both the fast carriers and the CVEs, as well as from tactical aircraft now land based in Korea, continued. Worthwhile targets, however, were becoming hard to find. Indeed, as UN forces pushed steadily north toward the China border, it was increasingly clear that for all intents and purposes the North Korean army had been defeated. There was a feeling that the war was all but over and General MacArthur himself predicted that some UN troops would be home for Christmas.

REVERSAL OF FORTUNE

THE EUPHORIA WAS PREMATURE. By mid-October 1950 the Chinese were already in North Korea and by early November their presence was detected in significant numbers. Even at this late date, however, the full extent of the Chinese threat had not yet become apparent. What's more, it was hoped that air power could halt further Chinese troop movement and logistic support via the Yalu River bridges. On 5 November, Task Force 77 sortied from Japan. Carrier aircraft and land-based planes of the Air Force now began a belated and somewhat futile attempt to destroy the critical spans between China and Korea, seventeen bridges in all.

Under the best conditions bridges were difficult targets. The most effective technique to destroy them was to orient air attacks along the axis of each structure. But for diplomatic reasons, the Joint Chiefs of Staff directed that pilots would have to make their attacks perpendicular to the spans. The results were almost always disappointing although on numerous occasions pilots did beat the odds and score hits.

To make matters worse, the Chinese sent up a barrage of antiaircraft fire from their side of the river while UN aircraft were prohibited from responding in kind. Allied fighters accompanying the attack aircraft were not even allowed to penetrate Chinese territory in hot pursuit of enemy air-craft making quick combat forays into Korea. Enemy planes could thus climb to altitude on the Chinese side, position themselves for advanta-geous overhead attacks on UN aircraft, and then dive for safety across the river.

During this phase of the Korean War American pilots met their first challenge by the Mikoyan-Gurevich MiG-15, one of the most advanced fighters in the world at the time. Mounting one 37-mm and two 23-mm cannon, this aircraft was fast, lightweight, and highly maneuverable, achieving its best performance above twenty thousand feet. It was superior to U.S. Navy and Marine Corps jet fighters but had some undesirable char-acteristics, not the least of which was a tendency to collapse into an uncon-trollable spin during violent maneuvers at lower altitudes. Less capable American jet aircraft piloted by well-trained aviators did remarkably well when pitted against the MiG-15s. On 8 November, Air Force F-80 Shoot-ing Stars escorting B-29 bombers tangled with several of these high perfor-mance enemy fighters. Air Force Lt. Russell J. Brown shot one down before the others scurried across the Yalu to their sanctuary. The next day the Navy was introduced to the fast swept-wing Soviet-made jets.

Skyraiders, Corsairs, and Panthers were launched from the carriers *Valley Forge* and *Philippine Sea* steaming in the Sea of Japan. Their targets were rail and highway bridges across the Yalu at three widely separated points along the border including Sinuiju, a city way over on the western side of the Korean peninsula. The Skyraiders carried 1,000-pound bombs as well as HVARs and full loads of 20-mm ammunition. Corsairs each carried a 500-pound bomb as well as HVARs and plenty of rounds for their guns.

Panther jets were on hand overhead to deal with enemy fighters that might attempt to interfere with the propeller-driven aircraft. Primed and ready for an encounter, the Navy pilots were not disappointed. As expected, MiGs attacked the formation, and the covering Panthers engaged them. Lt. Cdr. William T. Amen, skipper of VF-111, got one in his sights and shot it down. This was the Navy's first kill by a jet pilot; it would not be the last.

Attacks on the bridges were conducted between 9 and 21 November. Navy planes were able to take out the highway bridge at Sinuiju, although the railroad bridge remained standing despite great effort, and destroyed two more bridges at Hysanjin. Planes made hits and inflicted damage on

The propeller-driven Douglas AD Skyraider, on order by the end of World War II, proved to be an excellent aircraft for the war in Korea. The "Spad" could stay in the air for an hour and a half and drop an enormous amount of ordnance—as much as a B-17 bomber. (*Naval Aviation News*)

other bridges that stubbornly refused to fall and remained in use. On 18 November during an assault on the bridges, Panthers flown by Lt. Cdr. William E. Lamb and Lt. R. E. Parker of VF-52 from *Valley Forge* shared a MiG kill while Ens. F. C. Weber of VF-31 from *Leyte* accounted for another on the same day.

Miraculously, with no losses during these November attacks, carrier aircraft flew almost six hundred sorties against the bridges. By this time, however, most of the Chinese troops had already crossed into North Korea. As the Korean winter closed in, the river froze over and the enemy was able to walk across on the ice.

By 25 November the Chinese in Korea began their assault on ROK Army and U.S. Eighth Army units in the western part of the peninsula, and by 27 November it was evident that UN troops were in serious trouble. The next day General MacArthur notified the United Nations that his forces now faced more than two hundred thousand Chinese troops. In fact, the number may have been more than two hundred fifty thousand.

Driving snow, sleet, and unusually heavy weather on 25 and 26 November kept Task Force 77 aircraft from doing much to help UN forces in the west. On 27 November, however, the bad weather was simply ignored as aircraft launched from the fast carriers in the Sea of Japan and flew across the Korean peninsula, joining planes of the Fifth Air Force to provide desperately needed air support to beleaguered ROK units and the U.S. Eighth Army. The weather was so bad that some Navy aircraft diverted to Wonsan after making their attacks.

A bad situation grew worse. On the night of 27 November, Marines at the village of Yudam-ni on the Chosin Reservoir came under heavy ground attack, as did the nearby U.S. Army and ROK Army forces. Enormous numbers of Chinese troops threatened to envelop and overwhelm them.

By this time *Valley Forge*, which had been involved in combat operations since the war began, had departed for the United States leaving *Philippine Sea* and *Leyte* as the only fast carriers on station. What's more, *Sicily* had off-loaded its Marine squadron and was in port in Japan leaving *Badoeng Strait* the only CVE in position to immediately respond to the new situation. Planes from these three carriers as well as land-based Marine aircraft from the Yon-po airfield just south of Hungnam took to the air to support the Marines on the ground.

The Marines had already suffered a number of casualties and an air evacuation was desperately needed. The harsh Korean winter foiled an imaginative plan for seaplanes to splash down on the reservoir to pick up the wounded. Two Martin Mariner PBMs arrived on the scene only to find the reservoir covered with ice.

On 2 December an ambitious breakout to the coast began. Marines and allied units, carrying their wounded with them, began a fighting withdrawal through rugged mountain terrain in bitter cold weather with the Chinese exerting maximum effort to surround and destroy them. The allied goal was to reach the coast at Hungnam where they would be under the guns of the powerful Seventh Fleet. Carrier and shore-based Navy and Marine aircraft pounded the Chinese unmercifully while Air Force cargo planes dropped tons of ammunition, food, and supplies.

Valley Forge, which only five days earlier had returned home from Korea, was hurriedly recalled on an emergency basis. Air Group 2, which had just arrived in the United States on board *Boxer*, was hastily taken aboard the Happy Valley at San Diego. The ship sailed for Korea on 6 November.

Meanwhile, the fast carrier *Princeton* with Air Group 19 embarked had arrived in the combat area on 5 November. *Sicily* took VMF-214 aboard again, and the Corsairs were in the air over the embattled Marines on

7 November. After delivering a load of aircraft to Japan, the light carrier *Bataan* (CVL-29) picked up VMF-212 and joined *Sicily* and *Badoeng Strait* on 16 November. It was an all-out effort, as everyone understood the gravity of the situation.

As the Marines fought their way toward the coast, Navy and Marine Corps aircraft kept up a steady rain of fire from the sky leaving an enormous toll of dead and wounded Chinese along the route. Suicidal efforts on the part of the enemy slowed but failed to halt the march to the sea. Flying in miserable, sub-zero temperatures from carriers crusted in ice and snow, planes maintained determined, unrelenting pressure on the enemy.

Close air support using the Navy/Marine Corps concept was applied with spectacular success. Marine controllers on the ground sometimes called in low-level strikes so close that on occasion shell casings from a supporting aircraft's guns fell on friendly troops below. As the planes poured fire into enemy positions, Marines moved forward beneath them taking out remaining opposition.

The situation on the ground changed so quickly from hour to hour it was sometimes hard for the pilots to distinguish between friendly and enemy units. One morning Corsairs mistakenly attacked Marines in an area that had been in the hands of the enemy only hours before. The battery of the Marines' only radio had frozen during the night and they were unable to advise the pilots of their error. Marine Cpl. Walter "Scotty" Blomley who always carried a Confederate flag in his helmet—a gift from his girlfriend—fastened the flag to his rifle and began waving it at a low flying Corsair that had just begun its strafing run. The pilot quickly grasped the situation, waggled his wings, and flew off to engage more appropriate nearby targets.

By Christmas day all UN ground forces including the 1st Marine Division, the ROK I and II Corps, and the U.S. Army 7th and 3rd Infantry Divisions, along with their equipment, had been evacuated from Hungnam. Naval gunfire from ships offshore and attacks by some four hundred planes from seven carriers covered the weeks' long loading aboard ships and the departure from the area. More than a hundred thousand troops and ninety thousand civilians were sealifted from the area. The fighting withdrawal to the sea prevented what might have been an unparalleled American military disaster and enabled allied forces to fight again.

Now, in the face of the overwhelming Chinese offensive, UN forces on both sides of the peninsula retreated southward. Wonsan had already been evacuated by 7 December denying Marine aircraft further use of the

U.S. NAVY CARRIERS IN THE KOREAN WAR

FAST CARRIERS*	LIGHT CARRIER	ESCORT CARRIERS
Essex (CV-9)	Bataan (CVL-29)	Rendova (CVE-114)
Boxer (CV-21)		Bairoko (CVE-115)
Bon Homme Richard (CV-31)		Badoeng Strait (CVE-116)
Leyte (CV-32)		Sicily (CVE-118)
Kearsarge (CV-33)		Point Cruz (CVE-119)
Oriskany (CV-34)		
Antietam (CV-36)		
Princeton (CV-37)		
Lake Champlain (CV-39)		
Valley Forge (CV-45)		
Philippine Sea (CV-47)		

* The fast carriers designated CV were redesignated CVA on 1 October 1952.

Bataan begins her second Korean deployment in January 1952 transporting VMF-312, known as the "Checkerboard Squadron," and its Corsair fighter-bombers to the combat theater. (National Archives)

airfield there. On the west coast the U.S. Eighth Army and South Korean forces moved with deliberate speed out of the North Korean areas they had so recently taken from the enemy. Early in the month U.S. and ROK Army units were evacuated from Chinnampo, the port city for Pyongyang, and by the last day of the year all UN forces with their equipment had abandoned Inchon. So much for hopes of being home by Christmas.

TARGETING SUPPLY LINES

THE WAR ENTERED A new phase. All that had been gained in North Korea had now been lost, as was some territory south of the 38th parallel. Even Seoul changed hands once again before UN forces were finally able to dig in and hold. Chinese and North Korean logistics lines, however, were now stretched to their limits. By January 1951 the front stabilized just south of the city of Wonju.

UN ground forces began to push north again against fierce opposition. The fighting was slow going and brutal. By 14 March Seoul was retaken, and by June the front had moved just north of the 38th parallel where it stabilized again. The conflict amounted to a continuous give and take with no clear and sustained advantage to either side. On 11 April President Truman replaced General MacArthur with General Ridgway, the U.S. Eighth Army commander. The first armistice negotiations took place on 8 July with the UN contingent headed by Commander Naval Forces, Far East, Vice Admiral Joy. The talks, however, produced little progress.

During this period shore-based Marine squadrons, which had been forced to move to Japan during the Chinese offensive, reestablished themselves in Korea south of the 38th parallel. At Pusan in late January, VMF-311, the first Marine squadron to fly Panther jets in Korea and the only Marine squadron that had remained on the peninsula during the Communist drive south, was relieved by VMF (N)-513. By mid-February VMFs 214, 312, and 323, and VMF (N)-542 had also returned. The tempo of shore-based air operations increased accordingly.

During the early days of 1951, Navy and Marine Corps aviation focused primarily on close air support, but in February the disruption of enemy logistics took on increased importance. Now Task Force 77 began an assault on supply lines in earnest. Indeed, the majority of offensive strikes by aircraft from the carriers were concentrated on interdiction of roads and rail lines until the end of 1952. It was a tough, frustrating assignment with a paucity of encouraging results.

In the first place, Chinese and North Korean forces could be maintained in the field with considerably less support than that required by the UN's mechanized and equipment-heavy units. This advantage meant there would have to be an almost complete shutdown of supply lines to significantly affect the combat ability of enemy forces on the front lines. That, of course, was impossible to accomplish.

The Korean transportation system was primitive but easy to maintain and repair, and in this regard it served the enemy well. Roads were either dirt or gravel. Trucks, wagons, carts, and all sorts of pack animals, including camels, were used to move large quantities of supplies over these roads and trails. Rail lines were mostly single-track affairs that wound through mountain passes and canyons, making them hard to target from the air. When aircraft cut the roads and railways, an army of men and women—tough,

Both the primary railroad line and an alternate route constructed by the enemy show clear evidence of Task Force 77 attacks. (*Naval Aviation News*)

hardened peasants with picks and shovels—swarmed over the afflicted area at night and quickly restored the supply line.

Railroad tunnels were especially hard to damage from the air and enemy supply trains often holed up inside, completely safe while attacks were in progress. Lt. Frank Metzner, a reserve officer in charge of a Composite Squadron (VC) 35 detachment, has been credited with selling the idea of skipping bombs with delayed-action fuses into the mouths of the tunnels to Rear Adm. Ralph A. Ofstie, Commander Task Force 77. An accurately placed 2,000-pound bomb could collapse a tunnel, damaging or trapping trains inside. The enemy countered with antiaircraft traps near tunnel openings. Corsairs provided flak suppression for low-level, tunnel-busting runs by Skyraiders.

The technique worked best when a Skyraider pilot lowered his flaps and flew slowly along the tracks releasing his bomb at the last minute. Then he poured on power to the plane's big Wright R-3350 engine and pulled up to clear, often by a matter of feet, the mountain housing the tunnel. It was a hairy business but it sometimes worked. Of course the slow, low-flying aircraft were juicy targets for enemy gunners. For the most part Skyraiders were the aircraft of choice to deliver the weapons into the tunnels, but Corsairs were also used in this manner, scoring a few dramatic successes of their own.

Bridges were somewhat more vulnerable but hardly easy targets. Even after inflicting major damage on bridges, American pilots often discovered that they had been quickly restored to service. Planes had to return to the sites again and again to keep the bridges out of service. A barrage of flak was always waiting for them.

As with the tunnels, the enemy concentrated antiaircraft guns at key bridge points. Battle damage to planes was heavy and many aircraft were lost. Flying into deep, rocky canyons through withering antiaircraft fire became daily fare for carrier pilots. Despite superb airmanship there was a considerable degree of luck involved and no one knew when his luck might run out. Although Task Force 77 planes kept some enemy transportation routes shut down for short periods, too many roads, rails, bridges, and tunnels demanded their attention and they could not sustain an effort against any one particular structure or area indefinitely. Even when a rail line was cut for a time, the enemy moved war material across the gap on the backs of hundreds of peasants to a waiting train at the other side of the break. An ancient and ingenious device known as the A-frame enabled each human mule to carry enormous amounts of

THE BRIDGES AT TOKO-RI

DURING THE KOREAN WAR author James A. Michener was a war correspondent filing stories from the carriers *Valley Forge* and *Essex*. Some of the material he collected was fictionalized to become the widely acclaimed Korean War novel *The Bridges at Toko-ri* about a Naval Air Reservist called back to active duty as an F9F Panther pilot. The book was subsequently made into a motion picture starring William Holden, Grace Kelly, Mickey Rooney, and Fredric March. The name of Holden's character was apparently taken from real life, Lt. Donald S. Brubaker of VF-194, a Skyraider pilot who flew from *Valley Forge*. The story, however, is a composite adapted from the hair-raising experiences of more than one naval aviator.

One of Michener's sources was probably Cdr. Paul Gray, commanding officer of VF-54, who shared his considerable expertise with the author in a dinner meeting on board *Essex* along with three other squadron skippers. It was the night before a major attack on some heavily defended railroad bridges in central North Korea. Gray described how the target area was bristling with some fifty-six radar-controlled antiaircraft guns that would make the mission especially hazardous. The next day Gray and his squadron dove through heavy fire to silence the guns and destroy the bridges. Michener was on hand in "Vulture's Row" to watch the squadron's return to the carrier following the successful strike.

Another source might be the tale of Carlson's Canyon in which VA-195 pilots from *Princeton* repeatedly attacked a railroad bridge, engaging not only in a running duel with North Korean antiaircraft gunners but with

A railroad bridge in "Carlson's Canyon" shows evidence of North Korean efforts in the early months of 1951 to shore up the bomb-damaged structure. (National Archives)

repair personnel who put the bridge back in service almost as fast as its spans could be destroyed.

In the novel the fictional Brubaker is shot down in enemy territory and is joined on the ground by a helicopter pilot and crewman when their chopper is also downed during an unsuccessful rescue attempt. Professor Emeritus Richard F. Kaufman of California State University, Sacramento studied the author's notes and journals. Writing in the March-April issue of *Naval Aviation News* he suggests that this part of the story was fashioned from an actual and somewhat similar situation that took place in February 1952. In this case, Skyraider pilot Ens. Marvin S. Broomhead was shot down in enemy-held territory as was an HO3S rescue helicopter flown by Navy Lt. Edward Moore and Marine Corps 1st Lt. Kenneth Henry. All three men were thought to have been killed by the enemy but were actually captured and were repatriated after the war. Michener's Brubaker and the helicopter crew that tried to rescue him were not so lucky and perished at the hands of the enemy.

The same railroad bridge after an April 1951 visit by carrier aircraft of Task Force 77. (National Archives)

It is not clear why Michener put his fictional hero in the cockpit of an F9F Panther instead of a Skyraider, but jet aircraft were still relatively new at the time, and perhaps the author thought it would have a more dramatic effect on his readers. The actual flying scenes used in the movie were flown by Panther pilots of VF-52 who had just returned to the United States following a combat tour in Korea. Cdr. James L. Holloway III of that squadron flew in the role of Lieutenant Brubaker and was reminded of his own Korean War experiences. Holloway became an admiral later in his career and was Chief of Naval Operations from 1974 to 1978.

material on his back for a considerable distance in a relatively short period of time.

Interdiction became more hazardous as enemy gun crews gained experience. An increasing number of antiaircraft weapons took their toll of allied aircraft. The enemy had learned early that truck convoys survived best when they moved at night and remained hidden by day under trees or in village buildings. Camouflaged antiaircraft guns sometimes scored hits on low-flying aircraft searching for signs of these vehicles.

On 21 March, two Panther jets of VF-191 flying from *Princeton* scoured the east coast looking for trucks. Ens. Floryan "Frank" Soberski was making a low-level pass, checking out a possible target hidden in a building, when his canopy was suddenly shattered by ground fire, and he was struck in the face by broken Plexiglas. Rendered unconscious for a moment, he came to and realized that except for a dim gray light, he couldn't see. Making his plight known to his wingman, Lt. (jg) Pat Murphy, the two discussed what to do next. Initially they thought Soberski's best chance was to return to the sea and for Murphy to talk him down to a ditching in the ocean near the carrier where he could be retrieved by a helicopter or a boat. The water, however, was only 33 degrees and immersion meant death in a matter of minutes. They decided to attempt what seemed impossible—a "blind" carrier landing.

Murphy flew his plane next to Soberski's on the trip back. He gave the wounded aviator course corrections and pumped him up psychologically for the difficult feat ahead. A carrier landing under the best conditions is a precise maneuver for a skilled pilot with 20/20 vision. Soberski and Murphy were aware of the odds against a successful trap on board the ship. Murphy continued to fly off Soberski's wing as they neared the ship and coached him through the landing checklist. The landing signal officer now became a critical part of the equation, talking the injured pilot onto the pitching deck. It was a phenomenal piece of flying—on everyone's part. The young pilot was evacuated to a medical facility ashore. Following surgery in Japan he was flown back to the United States. Soberski ultimately regained full vision in both eyes.

On 1 April 1951 Panther jets of VF-191 flying from *Princeton* attacked a railroad bridge near Songjin. It was an unusual flight because, for the first time, the jets were employed as fighter-bombers dropping 100- and 250-pound bombs. This new flexibility enhanced the jet contribution to interdiction efforts. It also highlighted a problem that would have to be remedied soon if the new heavier jet aircraft were to become effective as carrier-based attack aircraft. The hydraulic catapults on the fast carriers of the period were not sufficiently powerful to launch jets in light- or no-wind conditions. The ships could make thirty knots top speed, but because of their weight the jets needed at least thirty-five knots across the deck to get airborne. For this reason Panthers were used primarily for strafing attacks or as fighter protection in the early days of the war. When employed as fighter-bombers, however, their heavier ordnance loads increased their weight. In low- or no-wind conditions planes were sometimes obliged to remain on deck while their propeller-driven brethren flew off to battle.

SWEDE CARLSON'S
BOMBS AND
TORPEDOES

ONE STORIED INTERDICTION ASSAULT involved a railroad bridge spanning a deep ravine south of Kilchu and the determined efforts of VA-195 pilots flying from *Princeton*. On 2 March 1951, the bridge was attacked resulting in superficial damage, but on 3 March, eight Skyraiders led by squadron commander Harold G. "Swede" Carlson knocked out one span and did serious damage to two others. Four days later, they attacked the bridge again, dropping another span. North Korean construction crews went to work, and by 14 March, it was apparent the bridge would soon be in service again.

Night attacks designed to keep workers from making repairs failed to significantly slow the work, and soon the bridge resumed funneling supplies south. Braving withering fire, the carrier planes hit the structures with napalm, setting the wooden framework afire but failing to prevent its repair and continued use. The Navy pilots refused to be dissuaded, and in early April the Skyraiders again made concerted attacks that completely demolished the bridge leaving little but pilings. Eventually the North Koreans built smaller bypass bridges to replace it, but the site became known as Carlson's Canyon in honor of the dogged determination of the squadron skipper and perseverance of his pilots.

By the end of April 1951, UN forces had dug themselves in along the Pukhan River to hold against the Communist offensive. The North Koreans meanwhile had closed the sluice gates of the Hwachon Reservoir Dam just north of the 38th parallel, allowing them to lower the water level to a point where troops could ford the river for an assault. If, on the other hand, UN forces elected to mount an attack, the enemy could open the

April also brought a spectacular precision attack on the Hwachon Reservoir Dam by Swede Carlson and his band of Skyraiders using a novel weapon for the mission: torpedoes. Artist R. G. Smith captures the famous torpedo attack that broke two floodgates, sending torrents of water down the canyon. The exploits of VA-195 earned them the nickname "Dambusters." (Navy Art Collection)

gates and flood the area. B-29s had made bombing attacks on the dam without effect. Carrier air was called upon to execute a torpedo attack.

On 30 April, while torpedoes were being readied, six of Carlson's Skyraiders attacked the dam with 2,000-pound bombs but were also unable to effect a break. On 1 May Carlson and his ADs, eight aircraft in all, led by Air Group Cdr. R. C. Merrick, tried again, this time with aerial torpedoes. Twelve Corsairs from VF-192 and VF-193 accompanied the attack aircraft to suppress antiaircraft fire as the highly vulnerable torpedo planes made their approach.

The Skyraiders came in over the hills, dropped down low to the water, and headed straight for the sluice gates. Each plane released a torpedo, six of which ran true, breaching the dam and releasing the flood. All aircraft returned to the carrier safely. It was the first and only time that torpedoes were used in the Korean War and it was a spectacular performance.

Steam catapults and more powerful jet engines would ultimately resolve the problem but, like the angled deck, this development would have to wait until after the war.

There was relatively little chance for aerial combat by Navy and Marine Corps pilots because their assignments were in areas where they were unlikely to encounter enemy fighters. Nevertheless, there was occasional contact. On 21 April 1951 two Corsairs of VMF-312 led by Marine Capt. Philip C. DeLong were checking out an area near Chinnampo when they were jumped by four Yak-9s. DeLong shot down two of the enemy propeller-driven aircraft while his wingman, Lt. H. Daigh, destroyed a third and damaged a fourth.

Interdiction continued throughout the spring of 1951, but Task Force 77 was obliged to take time out to provide close air support to UN troops during the Communist spring offensive, which began on 22 April and lasted until the end of May. The enemy made good use of the interdiction hiatus to repair roads, bridges, tunnels, and rail lines and to fortify key points with antiaircraft guns. When the planes returned to interdiction the task was harder and more hazardous. What's more, they had to start their campaign from scratch.

By 5 June, Navy and Marine aircraft were involved in Operation Strangle, a concentrated interdiction effort against roads, bridges, and tunnels in a coast-to-coast swath, one degree wide above latitude 38° 15′ N. The Fifth Air Force took the westernmost portion, the 1st Marine Aircraft Wing the easternmost, and Task Force 77 the middle.

In addition to cratering roads and destroying bridges, aircraft laid delayed action and antipersonnel bombs in hopes of killing or discouraging workers and slowing repair work. Carrier planes went so far as to drop leaflets warning of unexploded ordnance. Marine Corsairs and Tigercats of VMF(N)-513 flying from Pusan kept up the attacks at night as did night-flying Corsairs of VC-3 and VC-4 and Skyraiders of VC-35 flying from the carriers. Navy, Marine Corps, and Air Force Skytrains (R4Ds for the Navy and Marines and C-47s for the Air Force) and Navy PB4Y-2 Privateer patrol aircraft turned night into day with flare drops.

Marine Corps Capt. Albert A. Graselli remembers flying his R4D on these night hops. He could often spot the lights of a truck convoy from some distance, but the enemy drivers quickly doused their lights at the sound of his approach. Making his flare drop as quickly as possible, the night fighter with whom he was working took over and made his attack while Graselli circled nearby to "enjoy the fireworks."

Despite the allies' best efforts, however, the interdiction campaign failed to stop enemy supplies. The North Koreans accepted casualties as inevitable and their logistics personnel and repair crews kept the line of communications open. While the air assault undoubtedly caused difficulties for the enemy, the essential flow of supplies to North Korean and Chinese troops on the line was never cut for very long. Operation Strangle failed to achieve the desired result. In February 1952 it was replaced by a similar operation called Saturate that faired little better.

THE HELICOPTER DEBUTS

ALTHOUGH VIETNAM HAS BEEN dubbed "the helicopter war," these unique machines were first used during the Korean conflict. Even before the war, military planners had investigated wartime uses of the helicopter.

When the war broke out, Navy Helicopter Utility Squadron (HU) 1 headquartered at North Island, San Diego, was providing detachments for the carriers at sea. The helicopters were assigned as plane guards during flight operations. Their primary function was to retrieve pilots who went into the water during launch or recovery. The rotary wing aircraft were also used to rescue fliers downed on land in enemy territory. Not only did helicopter rescue often save a highly trained pilot but also boosted the morale of his fellow naval aviators.

The Marine Corps put the helicopter to good use during the desperate days of the Pusan Perimeter defense in August 1950. Within three days of arrival, a helicopter assigned to Marine Observation Squadron (VMO) 6 picked up its first downed pilot. These versatile machines also carried top-level commanders between key positions, evacuated the wounded, and delivered essential supplies to defensive outposts. The Marines quickly realized the advantages provided by the helicopters and hastily assigned more of them to Korea.

One rescue provides good-natured interservice humor. In January 1951 Marine Capt. Russell G. Patterson's Corsair flying from *Bataan* was damaged near Suwon. The pilot bellied his Corsair to a stop in a snow-covered rice paddy. He was soon picked up by an Air Force helicopter from the 3rd Rescue Squadron flying out of Pyongtaek. His Air Force hosts informed Patterson that he would be held hostage until his CO agreed to send ten gallons of ice cream, fifty pounds of boneless steak, and one bottle of Scotch in exchange for his return. A dispatch from *Bataan* quickly agreed to the terms, and Patterson was soon back at his job on board the carrier.

Several LSTs were fitted with miniature flight decks and pressed into service as helicopter carriers. Intended for use as mine spotters, the LST HO3S helicopters added the rescue function to their repertoire. In

A Sikorsky HO3S rescue helicopter hovers astern of *Boxer* as Corsairs prepare to launch from the carrier. Plane guard helicopters such as this one saved the lives of many naval aviators whose aircraft failed to get airborne or to recover on board. (Naval Historical Center)

March 1951, *LST-799* set up for business off Wonsan as the Navy's first helicopter carrier with a detachment of two Navy HO3S-1 choppers from HU-1. Although the enemy held the city and surrounding territory, at least one LST was continually assigned offshore at Wonsan, usually in the vicinity of Yo-do Island. UN pilots were told to head there if their aircraft were disabled. With luck they could ditch in Wonsan Harbor where they would be picked up quickly by an LST-based helicopter. On 5 April an HO3S-1 made *LST-799*'s first rescue when it fished Ens. Maurice A. Tuthill out of the water unhurt. It was Tuthill's second time to be rescued by helicopter and he was suitably impressed by this new capability. In all, *LST-799* aircraft rescued twenty-four fliers from the sea or from land in Korea.

A few old LSTs that had been turned over to the Japanese and converted into cargo vessels were commandeered and reconverted into helicopter carriers. The *Q-007*, crewed by forty-five Japanese civilians under contract to the U.S. government, served as one of these vessels off the coast of Korea. The pilots of the helicopter detachment conducted rescues, spotted naval gunfire, and assisted surface minesweepers by tagging discovered mines with dye-markers. They also destroyed mines with rifle fire. On one occasion, Lt. (jg) Earl R. Bergsma's chopper was almost knocked out of the sky when it got too close to a floating mine that exploded throwing a plume of water two hundred feet into the air. After that, naval leaders restricted the helicopters to mine hunting.

On 3 July 1951 Navy Lt. (jg) John K. Koelsch and crewman Aviation Mate George M. Neal took off from *Q-009* in their HO3S escorted by four Corsairs. Their mission was to rescue Marine Capt. James V. Wilkins who had been shot down behind enemy lines. As was frequently the case in Korea, weather was considerably less than ideal with low-lying clouds preventing fighter cover during the extraction.

Arriving at the designated location, Koelsch descended through the overcast and quickly located the downed pilot. As he lowered a sling to make the pick-up, his helicopter was hit by ground fire and downed. Neither Koelsch nor Neal was hurt in the crash but their situation was serious. Wilkins, they discovered, was badly burned and unable to walk. Refusing to abandon him to the enemy, Koelsch and Neal rigged a litter to carry him out of the area. They were able to elude the enemy for nine days but they were captured. Koelsch, who died in captivity, was posthumously awarded the Medal of Honor for the courageous rescue attempt and for inspiring his fellow prisoners.

The war also enabled the Marine Corps to evaluate the new technology in the combat environment. On 21 September 1951, for instance, Sikorsky HRS-1s airlifted several Marines to a hilltop northeast of Kansong where they were lowered to the ground to clear a landing area. That accomplished, more choppers brought in troops and tons of equipment. In no time there were 228 Marines on the ground at this isolated outpost. Without the helicopters they would have had to make their way over a dangerous mountain road where ambush was an ever-present danger. It was the first time that a large contingent of combat troops had been transported in this manner.

Helicopters demonstrated their many uses during the Korean War. In addition to rescue and medical evacuation functions, they served as troop carriers, utility and supply vehicles, reconnaissance aircraft, and gunfire spotters for artillery and naval gunfire, sometimes at night. They flew from cruisers and battleships as well as from aircraft carriers and LSTs. These early choppers were not instrumented or approved for night operations but were often so employed when necessity dictated.

JOINT RAIDS, INTERDICTION, AND SPECIAL MISSIONS

THE COASTAL CITY OF Rashin is only about thirty miles from the North Korean border with China and even closer to the border with the Soviet Union. It had one of the finest ports on the east coast of Korea and shipments of war material poured in by sea and by rail from the Communist giants to the north. Because Rashin had been off-limits to UN aircraft since August 1950, the Communists believed it was immune from attack. As a result, the city had become a major material storage point and rail center for transshipment of supplies to Chinese and North Korean troops at the front. In the summer of 1951 the JCS decided that the enemy perception of immunity had to be changed.

The mission was assigned to Air Force B-29s, which carried an enormous bomb load. Because of the proximity of Rashin to airfields in both China and the Soviet Union, American leaders considered the probability of MiG-15 opposition high. The heavy bombers needed fighter escorts, but Air Force planes were too far away to accomplish this mission. Once again, the special capabilities of carrier aviation were called upon to deliver air support.

The fast carrier *Essex* (CV-9), first ship of that illustrious class, checked in with Task Force 77 in the Sea of Japan off the northeast coast of Korea on 22 August 1951. Air Group 5 was embarked with two jet fighter squadrons. VF-51, on its second Korean tour, flew Panthers while VF-172 introduced the McDonnell F2H-2 Banshee to the Korean War. In addition, there was one Corsair squadron, VF-53, and one Skyraider squadron, VF-54. Although Skyraiders were attack aircraft, the VF fighter designation for this latter unit was probably left over from a relatively recent aircraft changeover in that squadron from F4Us to ADs.

Three days after arrival, planes from both jet squadrons, twenty-three in all, rendezvoused with the B-29s and headed north toward Rashin. The Panthers flew level with the bombers, and the Banshees, which functioned best at higher altitudes, were positioned above. It was a clear day and, curiously, the Communists did not challenge the force. The B-29s had a field day, laying waste to storage facilities and rail yards. It was an especially successful operation and one of several such joint missions flown against enemy targets in the north. While interdiction remained the focus of carrier operations during this period, special missions occasionally offered a change of pace. One of these, made possible by information provided by Korean guerrillas, took place in October 1951.

Eight Skyraiders of VF-54 led by Cdr. Paul N. Gray heavily bombed the meeting place of Communist leaders with 1,000-pound bombs and napalm. An intelligence evaluation of the effort indicated that hundreds of Communists were killed in the attack. (The aggressive Commander Gray also holds the distinction of being shot down three times during the Korean War.)

Naval aviators gained experience in Korea that would season them for future combat. Some would go on to national and even world acclaim for other aerial achievements. On one occasion during the Korean War a low-flying VF-51 Panther jet took a hit that sent it plunging toward the ground. Just as the pilot regained control the aircraft struck a utility pole tearing off three feet of wing. Keeping a clear head and calling on all of his skills he carefully nursed the damaged jet up to a somewhat safer altitude. Then he found that his landing gear was jammed in the up position. With no other choice, the pilot ejected from his damaged plane. In a short time he was back on board *Essex*. This skilled but lucky aviator was Neil Armstrong who later piloted the lunar module *Eagle* to a safe landing and became the first human to walk on the moon.

U.S. NAVY AND
MARINE CORPS
JET FIGHTERS

THE GRUMMAN F9F PANTHER was a straight-wing jet fighter, the first to be used by the U.S. Navy in combat. It was also the aircraft that bore the major burden of U.S. Navy jet fighter operations in Korea. Straight-wing jets with lower approach speeds were better suited to carrier operations.

Mounting four fixed 20-mm guns in the wings, the Panthers were initially used strictly as fighters for combat air patrol and for suppression of enemy antiaircraft fire in support of propeller-driven attack aircraft. They also engaged in strafing attacks against other ground targets. Later in the conflict they were configured to carry modest numbers of bombs, and in this capacity were employed as fighter-bombers.

The Panther was inferior in both speed and maneuverability to its jet fighter competition in Korea, the swept-wing Mikoyan-Gurevich MiG-15. It was able to hold its own with the Soviet-designed fighter during the relatively few engagements between the two aircraft, largely because of the superior training of U.S. Navy and Marine Corps pilots.

The McDonnell F2H Banshee, nicknamed Banjo, was a twin-engine jet fighter designed to replace the FH Phantom, the U.S. Navy's first pure jet carrier aircraft. Like the Panther, it had a straight wing, which enhanced carrier compatibility but reduced its aerial combat capability. Employed as a fighter-bomber, it performed well against bridges, railroads, and other ground targets and as a fighter was more effective than the Panther at higher altitudes. The Banshee mounted four 20-mm cannon in the fuselage and, like the Panther, could carry relatively modest underwing bomb loads. The F2H-2P version of the Banshee fitted with

F2H-2 Banshees of Fighter Squadron 172 head home after a mission. The twin-engine McDonnell fighter was the second type of jet aircraft to join Task Force 77 off Korea when *Essex* arrived in August 1951. (National Archives)

cameras in an elongated nose section proved to be an excellent photo-reconnaissance aircraft.

The Douglas F3D Skyknight was a large, twin-engine, two-place, straight-wing, jet night fighter that played an important role in the development of all-weather tactical aviation. Nicknamed "the Whale" because of its size and appearance, the Skyknight had side-by-side seating for a pilot and radar operator. It mounted four 20-mm cannon, but because the aircraft was used strictly as a night fighter it carried no other armament. Its unique design allowed it to carry three on-board radars including one in the tail to detect enemy fighters approaching from the rear. While slower and less maneuverable than its jet adversary, the MiG-15, its sophisticated radar system gave it a distinct advantage over the higher performance Soviet aircraft.

The Skyknight's most important mission in the Korean War was that of protecting B-29s from enemy fighters during night bombing operations. In this capacity, it flew barrier patrols between the big bombers and

The Douglas F3D Skyknight, the Navy Department's third type of jet aircraft deployed to Korea, proved to be an excellent escort for Air Force B-29 bombers conducting nighttime missions. (Naval Historical Center)

the MiG-15 threat emanating from Chinese airfields to the north. The Skyknight also took on and destroyed enemy propeller-driven aircraft employed in night harassment missions. F3Ds shot down six enemy aircraft including five confirmed or probable MiG-15s.

As harsh winter weather came on again in Korea at the end of 1951, operations settled down to grueling, day-after-day, track breaking, bridge and tunnel busting, and interdiction missions. Most strike groups were met by increasingly heavy antiaircraft fire. After every attack, the North Koreans made repairs that kept their supplies moving. From October through December 1951, sixty-five Navy and Marine Corps aircraft fell to enemy gunners, most of them while engaged in interdiction. During the Korean War more than 650 Navy and Marine Corps planes were lost to ground fire and only a few to aerial combat. Many Task Force 77 pilots considered the interdiction campaign an exercise in futility, and maintaining morale was a constant challenge for air group and squadron commanders.

In January 1952, operations code named "package" and "derail" focused missions in the northeast. While aircraft attacked Operation Package targets, naval gunfire, zeroed in by aircraft spotters, concentrated on Derail targets along the coast. These attacks disrupted rail traffic and reduced enemy supply operations in the region during February. Still, the U.S. effort was not enough.

Imaginative ideas on how best to neutralize the North Korean rail system blossomed. One suggestion evolved into a night operation code named "moonlight sonata" that began in January 1952. It took advantage of the illumination qualities of the moon on the snow-covered Korean landscape to locate trains and tracks. Pilots of night-flying aircraft scoured the rail lines for trains trying to work under cover of darkness. When they found one, they bombed the tracks in front and in back of it. Early the next morning naval aircraft would pound the immobilized target into rubble.

During the spring of 1952 several trains were isolated and destroyed in these operations. Operation Insomnia, begun in May, continued the tactic but varied nocturnal flight schedules to confound the Communists who had observed flight patterns and adapted their railroad activities accordingly.

Despite Herculean efforts by Navy aircraft, the results of interdiction efforts were less than the allies had hoped for in terms of stopping the flow of enemy supplies. The lack of progress in the truce talks at Panmunjom was equally disappointing. Something was necessary to get the enemy's attention. Allied leaders decided to concentrate UN air assets in a massive assault on thirteen North Korean power-generating plants, previously off-limits. Navy, Marine, and Air Force squadrons teamed up for a joint air assault on the most important power plant, the Suiho hydroelectric facility on the Yalu River. Planes from all four fast carriers of Task Force 77 on station, *Boxer*, *Princeton*, *Bon Homme Richard* (CV-31), and *Philippine Sea*, took part. Opposition from MiG-15 fighters based at the Antung airfield across the river in Manchuria was fully expected.

On the afternoon of 23 June 1952, planes laid waste to the Suiho facility in a coordinated assault. While Panther jets conducted suppression runs on antiaircraft emplacements, Skyraiders hit the powerhouse, transformers, and sluice gates of the dam with ninety tons of bombs. Air Force F-80s and F-84 Thunderjets followed close behind to make it a clean sweep. For whatever reason, the expected MiG opposition failed to materialize. Other planes made similar strikes on power plants that day and the next, and the Air Force wrapped it all up with attacks on the last two targets on the list on 26 and 27 June. These attacks caused extensive and sustained blackouts in North Korea and over the border into China. Some areas were without power for months. A massive joint attack on industrial targets in and around Pyongyang took place on 11 July. On that day planes from *Princeton*, *Bon Homme Richard*, and the British carrier HMS *Ocean* joined Marine, Air Force, and Royal Australian Air Force aircraft to plaster targets in and around the North Korean capital. A similar attack in August pounded what remained of the Pyongyang industrial complex into rubble. The devastation was enormous.

Throughout the war Royal Navy carrier aircraft engaged in interdiction efforts and attacks on industrial targets along with their Navy and Marine Corps counterparts. They too had little opportunity to engage in aerial combat until 9 August 1952 when British pilots on an armed reconnaissance patrol got a chance to show their stuff. On that day four propeller-driven Sea Furies unexpectedly encountered eight MiG-15s near Pyongyang. Engaging in head-on attacks with the enemy jets they managed to shoot one down. The remaining MiGs exited north. It was the first kill of the war for the Royal Navy's Fleet Air Arm. Although flight leader Lt. Peter Carmichael was credited with the shoot-down, he was quick to point out that all pilots in his flight had fired at the enemy aircraft and had a part in the incredible victory.

A particularly interesting development of the war occurred on 28 August 1952, when Guided Missile Unit 90 on board *Boxer* launched a pilot-less, radio-controlled Grumman F6F-5K Hellcat fighter against a target ashore. The plane loaded with 1,000-pound bombs was guided to a bridge at Hungnam by a controlling AD-4N Skyraider of VC-35. Five more of these early "guided missiles" were launched between 28 August and 2 September resulting in two hits and one near miss. They were the first guided missiles to be launched from a carrier in actual combat.

A major fuel supply center for the enemy was the large oil refinery located at Aoji less than ten miles from the Soviet frontier and even closer to the Manchurian border. As with the raid on Rashin, the site was beyond the range of land-based fighters. It was determined that this was an ideal mission for carrier-based tactical aviation, so on 1 September 1952 more than 144 planes from *Essex*, *Princeton*, and *Boxer* carried out the attack, the largest carrier strike of the Korean War. Attacks on industrial targets at Munsan and electric plants at Chongjin were made that same day. The missions were successful and all planes returned to their ships safely.

Now Task Force 77 was ready for another joint venture with the B-29s, this time against the big enemy rail and supply center at Kowon. *Kearsarge* (CV-33) had joined Task Force 77 on 14 September with Air Group 101 embarked. On 8 October, twelve F2H Banshees of VF-11 rendezvoused with the big Air Force bombers and escorted them to Kowon where they relieved themselves of tons of ordnance. Minutes later eighty-nine aircraft from *Princeton, Essex,* and *Kearsarge* finished the job by plastering the area with rockets and bombs. These three ships and, indeed, all U.S. Navy carriers with the designation CV and CVB had been reclassified CVAs on 1 October 1952. The added letter A signified that they were attack carriers. The Kowon raid seemed a fitting confirmation of the new designation.

In October, Task Force 77 aircraft began a series of attacks on enemy supply concentrations near the front. Cherokee strikes, as the new assaults were called, were initiated by Vice Adm. J. J. "Jocko" Clark, Commander Seventh Fleet, and were intended to deplete stores that had already made it through the interdiction gauntlet and were stockpiled behind the front. These supply dumps were spread across the area but well back beyond the range of UN artillery. They were sometimes located from the air when aerial spotters observed trucks or personnel concentrating at a site. Because of several early successes, the Cherokee strikes accounted for about half of Task Force 77's effort by mid October. Much of the material near the front was in the form of ammunition, and TF 77 pilots were frequently rewarded with the sight of huge secondary explosions. Cherokee strikes, named in honor of Admiral Clark's Native American origins, continued until the end of the war.

AIR-TO-AIR COMBAT

THE NEWLY DESIGNATED attack carrier *Oriskany* (CVA-34) was an *Essex*-class ship built for World War II but had never seen service in that conflict. Numerous improvements remade her into a virtually new class of carrier by the time of her commissioning on 25 September 1950. Two years later, on 28 October 1952, the carrier arrived in the combat area with Air Group 102 consisting of four reserve squadrons—two flying Panther jets, one equipped with Corsairs, and one with Skyraiders.

A NAVAL AVIATOR'S RECOLLECTIONS

■ *Adm. James L. Holloway III, USN (Ret.)*

ON 7 JULY 1953 I was a lieutenant commander, executive officer of Fighter Squadron 52, flying Grumman F9F-2 Panthers from USS *Boxer* operating with Task Force 77 off Korea. My flight was the first of the day from TF 77 and the weather was lousy. We launched at 0615 and almost immediately off the catapult I went into the overcast, breaking into the clear at three thousand feet on top. The entire Sea of Japan was covered solid by low-level stratus, and we could see the mountains of Korea some six to seven thousand feet high pushing up through the cloud cover more than seventy miles away. I called the ship to report the weather. *Boxer* suspended the rest of the launch, and Commander TF 77 put a hold on further flight operations.

I rendezvoused the flight on top, climbed to ten thousand feet, and crossed the coastline into North Korea just south of Wonsan. I checked in with the Tactical Air Control Center in Seoul and reported a solid overcast. The TACC confirmed these conditions from ground observation and said that none of their forward air controllers was available. All were socked in with rain and fog. Our flight was directed to drop its bombs—each plane was carrying four 260 frags and two 100-pounders—through the overcast on radar. We were switched to MPQ control, similar to ground control approach (GCA), and unloaded in formation over a reported Chinese troop marshalling area in North Korea.

With bomb racks empty, I headed for home. Checking out with the TACC, I was informed that CTF 77 had directed all Navy aircraft to land in Korea. The carriers were in zero visibility conditions and the entire task

Lt. Cdr. James L. Holloway, executive officer of Fighter Squadron 52, whose Panthers were based on board *Boxer* during the Korean War. (Naval Historical Foundation)

force was moving east in search of better weather. They were already well beyond our range. In succession I called every jet-capable airfield in Korea: Pusan, Taegu, Pohang, Kunsan, Kimpo, Suwon, and Kangnung (K-18). Responses were the same: field closed, less than a quarter-mile visibility in rain and fog.

I checked back in with the TACC at Seoul to see if they had any emergency fields open. "Everything is shut down below minimums. Looks grim. Sorry, buddy," was the response.

We were getting low on fuel and a decision had to be made. I now had six planes. Two F9F-2 Panthers from *Philippine Sea* had joined us because they had taken off before CTF 77 cancelled flight operations.

There was no alternative except to bail out.

I didn't want to parachute the flight into unfriendly territory so I got a radar vector to a safe area in South Korea, as much of the south was in the control of guerrillas. I placed the flight in a right wide echelon and instructed each pilot to eject in succession three seconds after the man on his left. I would go first.

As the controller vectored us in a wide turn to our final course, I looked down to see a hole in the overcast and at the bottom of the hole about five hundred feet of runway. It was the end of K-18 at Kangnung, a South Korean F-51 Mustang base. I recognized it from a previous emergency landing.

I told the flight I had sighted K-18 and to form a column. We were going to try to get in. I chopped the throttle, popped the speed brakes, and in a 40-degree dive headed down the hole for the landing end of the runway.

When I called the K-18 tower, I was told we couldn't land. The field was closed due to fog and rain. I replied, "Clear the runway. If you don't, we will, because we're coming in." It was Marston matting—pierced steel— so we slowed down quickly after touchdown. We had all six jets on the runway before the first jet turned off. We had made it. But just barely.

When the weather broke two days later, CTF 77 messaged us to return to the carriers. I taxied my six-plane flight to the takeoff end of the runway with some difficulty. The rain had washed out areas under the Marston matting. As I was turning onto the runway for takeoff, my left wheel got stuck and I had to apply a lot of power to the jet engine to break loose.

Suddenly a bevy of ground handlers appeared, waving their arms and giving me the "cut engine" signal. I wasn't about to abort our flight home, so with an extra shot of power, I broke clear.

As I lined up on the runway I looked over my shoulder and saw the source of concern. A C-47—an Air Force version of the DC-3—was parked behind me, tail first. I noted two things: the rudder was dangling loose on the vertical fin, broken off by my jet blast, and the C-47 had a large blue flag with two stars painted on the fuselage.

It was an Air Force general's personal plane. I applied full power for takeoff and, with my five Panthers behind me, never looked back until we had Task Force 77 in sight.

What did I learn from this experience?

The immediate lesson learned was that a carrier deck is the only sensible landing field for a Navy pilot. Second, and more serious, tactical air power was the supporting arm in the Korean War that prevented the UN forces from being driven off the Korean peninsula by the Chinese and North Koreans. Yet air power alone could not defeat the enemy for two principal reasons: lack of an all-weather capability and the limited accuracy of air-delivered weapons.

Fifty years later, naval aviation has overcome these shortcomings. Carrier operations in Operation Iraqi Freedom are unhindered by night or weather conditions, and precision-guided munitions provide a kill-per-weapon ratio approaching unity. There is now no limit to the capabilities and effectiveness of carrier-based tactical aviation.

Admiral Holloway is the former Chief of Naval Operations and Chairman of the Board, Naval Historical Foundation.

For the most part the naval air war in Korea was an air-to-ground affair, but naval aviators got an occasional opportunity to demonstrate their prowess in aerial combat. They performed well even against the highly touted MiG-15, despite the superior qualities of the Soviet-made aircraft and the added advantage of operating from convenient sanctuaries just over the Chinese or Soviet borders.

In November 1952 the *Oriskany* air group concentrated its efforts against industrial targets in northeastern Korea. Because of the task group's proximity to Soviet fighter assets, eight F9F-5 Panthers of VF-781's Pacemakers were in the air as combat air patrol. The first of the newer model Panthers to be employed during the Korean War, the F9F-5s, like their predecessors, the F9F-2s and -3s, were outmatched technologically by the fast, agile, swept-wing MiG-15s. But confident of their training and professional skills, Navy pilots never hesitated to tangle with the enemy.

Early in the afternoon of 18 November, the carrier's radar detected a number of unidentified aircraft heading her way. Four of the combat air patrol Panthers led by Lt. Claire R. Elwood were dispatched to intercept them. As they closed the enemy formation, Elwood's aircraft developed engine problems that put him out of the action. He detached a two-plane section under Lt. E. Royce Williams to climb to altitude and engage what turned out to be seven MiGs.

Four of the swept-wing aircraft made an unsuccessful attack on Williams and his wingman, Lt. (jg) David M. Rowlands. Williams scored a hit on one of the MiGs and sent it into a spin. Rowlands followed the MiG down before it splashed into the sea. Williams and Rowlands then mixed it up with the remaining three enemy planes. Rowlands scored a hit that left his MiG smoking. Williams's aircraft was hit and damaged but he was able to take cover in a cloudbank accompanied by Rowland, who was now out of ammunition.

At this point the action was joined by Elwood's wingman, Lt. (jg) John D. Middleton, who shot down another MiG. All the Panthers returned safely to the ship. Williams and Middleton were each credited with a MiG kill and Rowlands with damaging a third. It was a good score for pilots flying the much-less-capable Panthers. While the MiGs were almost certainly flown by Soviet pilots in this instance, the superior training of the Navy pilots was enough to make the difference.

MiGs were a greater danger to propeller-driven aircraft, but U.S. naval aviators—like their Royal Navy counterparts—did quite well when attacked by the enemy jet. On 10 September 1952, Marine Capt. Jesse G. Folmar and his wingman flying Corsairs from *Sicily* were attacked by MiG-15s. While the Marines maneuvered to avoid becoming combat statistics, one of the MiG pilots got careless and Folmar, seizing the opportunity, shot him down. Several MiGs now joined the fight against the two Corsairs, and Folmar's plane took a mortal hit. The Marine captain bailed out and was soon plucked out of the ocean while his wingman made it safely back to the ship. Folmar's remarkable MiG kill was the only one of the war by a Corsair.

The only American aircraft comparable to the MiG-15 was the swept-wing, North American F-86 Sabre in which U.S. Air Force pilots chalked up a very creditable kill ratio in air-to-air encounters. Naval aviators on exchange duty with the Air Force also flew this aircraft in the vicinity of the Yalu River where they had several opportunities to engage MiG-15s and show what they could do with the more competitive Sabres. Several became MiG killers. Maj. John F. Bolt topped the list, scoring six kills to become the Marine Corps' only ace of the Korean War. Maj. John Glenn, who later became the first American to orbit the earth, was credited with three MiG kills. Navy Lt. Walter "Wally" Schirra had one confirmed MiG kill and another probable. (He, like Glenn, became one of America's first seven astronauts, the men whom author Tom Wolfe immortalized in his book *The Right Stuff.*) Navy and Marine Sabre pilots accounted for at least twenty-four MiG kills during the Korean War.

In the latter part of 1952 the Marines of VMF-513, flying Tigercats from K-8 at Kunsan, received a new jet fighter, the Douglas F3D Skyknight. Sometime later the Marine Skyknights moved to the K-6 airfield at Pyongtaek. Two Skyknights were kept airborne nightly and patrolled the sky under radar control from Cho-do, an island off the west coast of Korea. An especially important part of the F3D mission was the escort of B-29s during night air strikes. The F3D was big for a fighter and it would be a considerable understatement to say its speed and maneuverability were not comparable to the enemy jet fighters it challenged. The F3D did, however, have a state-of-the-art radar system while the MiGs had none and were obliged to rely entirely on information from Ground Controlled Intercept (GCI) sites. The Skyknight's airborne radar along with its trained radar operator sitting side by side with the pilot went far to compensate for the plane's deficiency in flight performance characteristics.

On 3 November 1952 an F3D flown by Maj. William T. Stratton Jr. and his radar operator M.Sgt. Hans C. Hoglind shot down a jet aircraft which they identified as a Yak-15, but which may have been another type of enemy jet. It was the world's first combat encounter of jet aircraft at night. A few nights later Capt. Oliver R. Davis and Warrant Officer Dramus F. Fessler bagged the squadron's first MiG-15. Altogether, five enemy jet fighters, including four MiG-15s, would fall to the Marine Skyknights between November 1952 and January 1953.

THE BEDCHECK
CHARLIES

BY THE SPRING OF 1953, the situation at the front had become a stalemate, with each side attempting to move the line into territory held by the other before the war ended. During this period, the North Korean Air Force undertook a stepped-up harassment campaign using trainers and other slow, low-performance aircraft to drop light weapons along the battle lines at night. While most of these raids did little damage, they caused disruption and loss of sleep, adding to the exhaustion factor among UN personnel on the ground. Well-placed concern over the possibility of a lucky hit on an ammunition dump or a fuel storage facility added to the stress.

Seoul was another favorite target of these nocturnal hecklers. The raids may have been partly a form of psychological warfare intended to remind the South Korean populace of the capital city, as well as UN defenders, that the North Korean army had twice overrun the area and were even now just a few miles away. The small aircraft, some of which were no more than light, open cockpit biplanes, were known as "Bedcheck Charlies." In June 1953, a multiplane raid of these aircraft dropped several bombs on the city, one of which hit dangerously close to President Syngman Rhee's residence. Another incursion did substantial damage to a petroleum storage facility at Inchon. Something had to be done.

Jet fighters were, for the most part, too fast to be effective against the slow, maneuverable Bedcheck Charlies although one Marine Skyknight had managed to down a Polikarpov Po-2 biplane trainer in December 1952. These light enemy aircraft could turn on a dime to deny a jet a good firing position. Perhaps more important, they could also be inadvertently overrun by the much faster pursuing jet. Indeed, one Air Force fighter is known to have collided with its slow-moving target. Propeller-driven fighters, although still much faster than these enemy aircraft, were more suited to the task. Marine night-flying Tigercats and Corsairs had already managed to bag three Po-2s and a Yak-9.

In June 1953, Admiral Clark sent two Navy F4U-5N night fighters of *Princeton's* VC-3 detachment ashore to K-8 (Kangnung) airfield from which the Marines operated Corsairs and could provide maintenance and servicing. The field was only some thirty-five miles south of Seoul and close to the front line, making it an ideal basing location for the operation.

On 29 June Lt. Guy P. Bordelon shot down two of the hecklers. He got two more Bedcheck Charlies on 30 June and another on the night of 17 July to become the Navy's only ace of the Korean War. Bordelon was awarded the Navy Cross for his contribution.

During the next few months of 1953, Task Force 77 aircraft were employed in a variety of tasks, including close air support, attacks on enemy supply lines and storage facilities, and strikes against industrial targets. The port city of Chongjin on the northeast coast of North Korea was plastered by the air groups from *Philippine Sea* and *Oriskany* on 13 April. Other targets on the northeast coast were hit by aircraft from *Oriskany* and *Princeton* on 21 April.

On 26 April, armistice talks that had been stalled resumed with a discussion of the difficult matter of prisoner exchange. In early June, with the repatriation problem largely agreed upon, the Communists launched attacks to gain territory to their south that would be recognized in the truce. On 6 June, Admiral Clark ordered the maximum effort of his fleet to prevent this from happening. Aircraft from four fast carriers—*Boxer, Lake Champlain* (CVA-39), *Philippine Sea*, and *Princeton*—pulled out all stops to provide close air support to UN troops. On 16 June the terms of the armistice were agreed to but fighting continued until the last moment.

A Navy detachment of Composite Squadron 4 headed by Lt. Gerald G. O'Rourke arrived at K-6 on 21 June, having been transported to Korea by way of the attack carrier *Lake Champlain*. The Skyknights were ill suited to carrier operations, however, because of their canted tailpipes. If the planes sat in one spot for a brief time with engines running, they were likely to set fire to teak decks, a phenomenon that did not endear O'Rourke's detachment to the carrier skipper. In addition, the planes' heavy weight taxed the underpowered hydraulic catapults. As a consequence, the Skyknights were sent ashore to operate with the Marines of VMF-513 who were glad to receive the extra planes, pilots, radar operators, and crewmen.

Although it was now late in the war, O'Rourke's Detachment 44N was immediately put to work, and the VC-4 pilots were able to get in a number of nocturnal combat air patrols and B-29 escort missions. They made several contacts with enemy night fighters. One Navy Skyknight was credited with a possible MiG kill but, unfortunately, was lost to another MiG in the same engagement. With the war now coming swiftly to a close, naval aviators made sure that their presence was felt until the very end. Planes from the four attack carriers positioned off the east coast of Korea were constantly in action with records broken for numbers of sorties set on 24, 25, and 26 July. Almost all of these sorties were flown in support of ground forces at the front. Planes from the escort carrier *Bairoko* in the Yellow Sea and Marine aircraft ashore made major contributions.

The Armistice Agreement was signed at 10 AM Korean time on 27 July 1953.

EPILOGUE

AT WAR'S END THE U.S. NAVY had thirty-four carriers in commission, more than twice the number that had been in service just over two and one-half years before. There were fourteen *Essex-* and three *Midway*-class attack carriers (CVAs) as well as five light carriers (CVLs) and twelve escort carriers (CVEs). The Korean War experience reaffirmed the role of naval aviation as an essential element of the U.S. defense arsenal. It breathed new life into this proven asset and inspired the development of a whole new family of U.S. naval aircraft, weapons systems, and ordnance. Among the superb tactical jet aircraft designs that appeared over the next ten years were the supersonic Vought F-8 Crusader, the Douglas A-4 Skyhawk, the McDonnell Douglas A-4 Phantom II, and the all-weather Grumman A-6 Intruder. Even more sophisticated and powerful aircraft would follow.

Carriers, too, underwent important postwar changes. The angled deck eliminated the problem of landing aircraft jumping the barrier and crashing into planes parked forward. It also allowed a pilot to take off again safely if the aircraft failed to catch a wire. Powerful steam catapults replaced their hydraulic predecessors. Pilots of new, heavier, jet aircraft launched from carrier decks knowing they would be tossed into the air with the kind of energy required to keep them flying even when the wind across the deck would have kept a Korean War jet on board. The mirror landing system gave aviators more precise approach information that enhanced both efficiency and safety during the recovery of heavy, high-performance jets.

Big-deck supercarriers soon appeared on the scene. Their size not only increased the landing area but provided greater stability for recovery in high seas. The first of these, *Forrestal* (CVA-59), was commissioned on 1 October 1955. Others followed: the first nuclear-powered carrier *Enterprise* (CVAN-65) and then the powerful *Nimitz*-class ships of today.

Americans and their leaders had changed their perceptions of what future military conflict might be in the nuclear era. The United States still had to deal with the sobering possibility of nuclear holocaust but Korea had introduced the limited war with conventional warfare challenges that suggested a pattern of future limited conflicts. It was evident that these challenges would require hard-hitting, highly mobile, forward-deployed forces able to project the power of the United States anywhere in the world in a timely fashion. Naval aviation and carrier task forces represented one of the best means of providing that capability.

RICHARD C. KNOTT *writes on the subject of naval aviation from the broad perspective of a long and varied career. Enlisting at age seventeen, he served as an aviation machinist's mate in one of the Navy's early Panther jet fighter squadrons and was a "plank owner" on board USS* Oriskany. *He left the Navy to attend college and later was commissioned, completed flight training, and was designated a naval aviator. His operational squadron tours were in antisubmarine warfare where he flew Martin Marlin P5M flying boats and Lockheed P-3 Orions with a tour in Vietnam.*

Knott's shore duty included an assignment with the United Nations Command component of the Military Armistice Commission in Korea. He was a member of the original three-man negotiating team that met with the North Koreans in an attempt to secure the release of USS Pueblo *and her crew. Later he served as a politico-military analyst in the office of the Chief of Naval Operations, as an exchange officer with the Department of State, and as a law-of-the-sea specialist in the office of the Joint Chiefs of Staff.*

In his final tours of duty, he served as editor of Naval Aviation News *magazine and headed the Naval Aviation History and Publications Division of the Naval Historical Center before retiring in 1986 after more than thirty years of naval service. Captain Knott holds a master's degree and is a graduate of the Naval War College. He has written four books on naval aviation, edited a fifth, and has authored numerous magazine articles on the subject. His latest book,* Fire From The Sky: Seawolf Gunships in the Mekong Delta, *is a hard-hitting history and true adventure story of the U.S. Navy's only attack helicopter squadron of the Vietnam War.*

CHAPTER 7

Sea Power On Call
Fleet Operations, June 1951–July 1953

MALCOLM MUIR JR.

INTRODUCTION

THE INITIAL STAGES OF the Korean War confounded the prophets of the late 1940s who had seen wars of the future conducted against the Soviet Union on the European subcontinent and decided by strategic bombers dropping nuclear weapons. Instead, the Korean conflict, fought in a totally unexpected theater, in its first year had much more closely resembled World War II with blitzkrieg-like warfare on the land and amphibious operations from the sea.

For the first six months of the war, the front had surged from the 38th parallel south to the Pusan Perimeter, then north to the Yalu River. The Communist Chinese intervention in the fall had saved the North Korean regime of Kim Il Sung from total defeat. At this point, both sides had identical political objectives: to unify Korea by military force. But as the renewed Communist offensive during the bitter winter of 1951 lost steam along the 38th parallel, the armies settled into stalemate. With the support of the Joint Chiefs of Staff, President Harry S. Truman overruled General of the Army Douglas MacArthur's requests for military action against

Communist China and scaled back UN objectives. When the president relieved the recalcitrant general on 11 April 1951, he formulated more limited aims: "to repel attack, to restore peace, to avoid the spread of conflict."

The next month, the Soviet government announced that the Communists would consider a negotiated settlement. When actual truce talks started on 10 July 1951 at Kaesong, the ancient capital of Korea, correspondents made bets as to how long the war would last; pessimists thought six weeks.

Instead, the struggle dragged on for more than two years as the UN and Communist delegations met 575 separate times. The sessions

American delegates to UN truce talks share a light moment on the steps of "UN House" at Kaesong in July 1951. Left to right, Vice Admiral Joy, Army Maj. Gen. Henry I. Hodes, and Rear Admiral Burke. Despite early optimism, the UN allies found the Chinese and North Korean Communist negotiators dogmatic and unbending. The negotiations would drag on for another two years before all sides reached agreement on a cease-fire on 27 July 1953. (National Archives)

produced 18 million words of argument, acid hard feelings, and finally on 27 July 1953 an armistice—but no peace treaty. As of 2005, the armistice continues in force.

As the negotiators talked, troops on the front lines entrenched. The UN forces dug in to compensate for their numerical weakness; the Communists, to escape a blizzard of UN bombs and shells. As the armies remained locked in position, the defensive systems grew ever more elaborate. When British Field Marshal Lord Alexander visited Korea, he observed at once that the trenches brought back his days as a junior officer in Flanders during World War I.

In support of UN ground troops, air power proved a major asset. For striking deep behind the front at strategic objectives, cutting enemy supply lines, and providing close air support to embattled ground troops, air power was simply invaluable. But however useful, it could not by itself force a decision.

Strategic bombing once again yielded mixed returns. The U.S. Air Force scorched North Korea as it had Japan, burning to the ground virtually all the North Korean cities—without discernible effect on the Communist leadership. At the operational level, the U.S. campaign to destroy the North Korean war economy and to cut Communist supply lines also proved an exercise in frustration. Profitable targets were soon scarce. Aircraft carrier *Boxer* (CVA-21), for example, reported after a strike in 1953: "Jets . . . set a coal dump ablaze in northeast Korea and killed eighty sheep."

In this attrition warfare, so different from that envisioned by prewar planners, the U.S. Navy also played a variety of major, often essential, roles. It blockaded the enemy coast, diverted the enemy's attention with amphibious threats, swept up enemy mines that interfered with UN sea power, and supported the troops in the trenches with close air support and naval artillery. In this strategic milieu, the Navy experimented with new equipment such as helicopters and faced potential new threats in jet aircraft and high-speed submarines. But much of the hard work was done by equipment only recently derided as obsolete: the landing craft, the little minesweepers, and the destroyers, cruisers, and battleships of the surface navy.

The Navy's war in the last two years of the Korean conflict has not been well documented, in part because it lacks the mighty drama of Inchon and Hungnam. Although there is certainly excitement in this story, for many Sailors the war combined tedium and hard work. As one surface warfare officer remembered, "on the cruisers and destroyers, it was monotony and boredom, a lot of gunfire and stuff but no running battle and no spectaculars—no submarines."

At the end of the war, Pacific Fleet evaluators, searching for lessons from the bitter stalemate, drew a number of pointed conclusions. Given what was to occur little more than a decade later in Vietnam, their dissection of the Korean War lessons seems remarkably deft. That the war ended in a stalemate, despite the complete UN air and sea superiority, emphasized "the dominant role of the ground forces in this war." The Navy's bottom line read: "The front line rifleman has been the central figure in the Korean War. All other forces support him."

Yet the war had revealed inadequate cooperation between air, ground, and naval forces. The evaluators suggested: "The United States could well again be involved in a series of wars similar to that in Korea. Joint doctrine and procedures should be adopted for the most effective integrated employment of Army, Navy, Marine and Air Force forces in limited or total war. The need, at all times, for a balanced team of sea, air and ground forces cannot be over emphasized."

In looking at the UN attempt to starve the Communist forces at the front of supplies by air and sea bombardment, the evaluators concluded, "Primitive transportation systems combined with masses of coolie labor successfully defied a colossal effort by modern machines of war." Adding to the debit side of the ledger, the assessment continued: "Certainly the value of the UN aircraft lost alone is greater than that of all the enemy's vehicles, rolling stock, and supplies destroyed. While the cost of the war assumes fantastic proportions to the US, the enemy largely offsets our efforts by the use of his cheapest and most useful asset, mass manpower." In looking to the future, Navy evaluators cautioned, "These conditions may not be peculiar to Korea; some or all may well be repeated in similar types of fringe warfare in the Far East. . . . Thus the lessons of Korea cannot be disregarded with the thought that Korea is not typical; no war is typical."

Many of these comments strike the historian as remarkably prescient. And, yet, little was learned from the experience by the broader defense establishment. The theoreticians of the following administrations, hoping to buy security on the cheap, regarded Korea as an aberration. The rifleman might have been the central figure of that conflict, but he was soon relegated to the budgetary outposts of the Cold War. Limited war capabilities

BLOCKADE
DUTY

WITHIN TWO WEEKS OF the beginning of the war, President Harry Truman charged the U.S. Navy with blockading the coast of North Korea. Effective early, the blockade was nonetheless subject to unending challenge by the enemy, who employed small craft to smuggle supplies and ordnance down the peninsula. During the final two years of the war, patrolling UN warships occasionally captured or sank—mainly at night—such vessels. Supplementing the efforts of the UN cruisers and destroyers to good effect were small, armed craft and even ships' whaleboats for inshore patrol work.

The haul, if never spectacular, was continuous. During the last seven months of 1951, patrolling UN forces sank or damaged an estimated two hundred junks and sampans. On the night of 14 May 1951, the Canadian destroyer HMCS *Nootka* captured several sampans and twenty-eight prisoners off the western coast of North Korea. In May 1952, *Douglas H. Fox* (DD-779) snagged twenty-six enemy fishing sampans. Unsurprisingly, radar proved a key asset in night interceptions, as the destroyer escort *Lewis* reported on 13 October 1952 when she engaged five sampans using radar ranging on the water splashes of her 5-inch/38 gunfire. These successes forced the enemy to sneak materials south on wooden barges. The primitive nature of some enemy craft proved a positive advantage. As one U.S. naval officer remembered, "We had weapons that were effective against warships, effective against aircraft; but how do you sink a wooden barge, a log?"

Following the war, Pacific Fleet evaluators concluded, perhaps optimistically, "The blockade of North Korea by UN forces was virtually 100%

effective throughout the war." Certainly the quantities of materials slipped south by sea were minute compared to those sent overland. Had air interdiction clamped as tight a hold on enemy logistics as did the seaward blockade, the Communist fighting machine at the front would have shuddered to a halt.

slipped. After hardly a decade, the Korean experience might as well have been the War of Jenkins Ear for all the relevance it held for most planners.

THE CHALLENGE OF THE MINE

MINE WARFARE—UNGLAMOROUS, dangerous, and incessant— epitomized the U.S. Navy's larger fight during the stalemate years of the Korean War. Victory over the mines, while never final, was utterly essential for the larger Navy to do its job, which in turn was a fundamental precondition for the success of both the Army and Air Force.

Early in the war when Communist mines frustrated the planned amphibious envelopment at Wonsan in October 1950, minesweepers had quickly moved from the wings to center stage. As one expert remarked, "The Wonsan mine scare . . . brought mine warfare to the attention of a public which, if it had ever heard the term before, vaguely supposed it might have something to do with John L. Lewis [the controversial labor leader of coal miners]. If submarines composed the silent service in World War II, minecraft comprised the unmentioned service."

Mine warfare had atrophied in the U.S. Navy during the post-WWII years. Scarce money went elsewhere; the few minesweepers that remained in service worked at miscellaneous duties. For instance, the two sweepers based in Guam spent their time towing targets or dumping surplus ordnance; they had to fight to get time to practice their specialty. The Communists, following up on their successes at Wonsan, continued their mining campaign, using mostly Soviet contact mines. Some of these dated to czarist days, but were nonetheless lethal. Once the sweeping gear had cut their mooring cables, these antiques bobbed to the surface where they

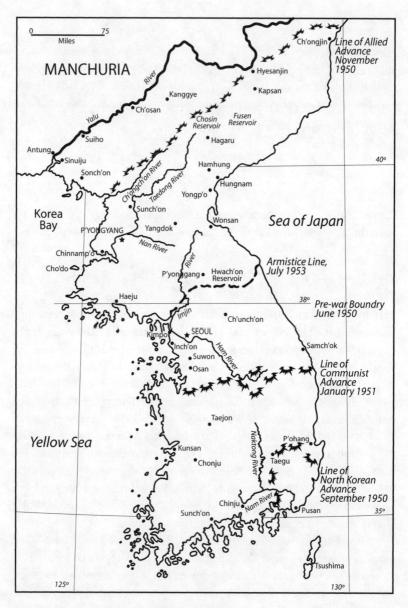

The War in Korea, 1950–1953. (Steve Karp)

proved remarkably tough, often taking fifty rounds or more of .30-caliber machine-gun fire before exploding. The Soviets, reluctant to give away their most recent technology, provided their allies with only a few magnetic mines, and no pressure or acoustic mines. The vessels that placed the underwater weapons were as primitive as the czarist mines. Facing overwhelmingly superior UN naval forces, the Communists countered with stealth: sampans, junks, or barges laid most of their mines. Emblematic of the enemy effort was the minelayer captured off Cho-do by the Canadian destroyer HMCS *Nootka*: a sampan measuring twenty-five feet in length and powered by oarsmen.

Rudimentary as the Communist mining effort might have been, it forced the UN command to major exertions. The U.S. Navy established a new command: Mine Force, Pacific Fleet. Most of its personnel learned on the job, given the paucity of career Sailors trained in mine warfare. The operational command, Task Group 96.5, grew rapidly. By December 1951, it numbered forty-one vessels (thirty-one U.S.; ten ROK) on permanent assignment with others attached as events dictated. These forty-one minecraft accounted for one-quarter of all the warships in the UN Blockading and Escort Force (Task Force 95), an index of the seriousness of the menace.

The largest of the warships were two destroyer minesweepers (DMS) favored for their ability to check sweep rapidly large areas of coastal waters for moored mines. Later in the war, *Thompson* (DMS-38) also enjoyed some success in locating mines with her sonar. However, the destroyer minesweepers were too big to operate in constricted waters, and their magnetic signature kept them well out to sea when the presence of magnetic mines was suspected. For these reasons, the destroyer minesweepers spent much of their time performing normal destroyer duties.

More valuable were the specialized minesweepers—the minesweeper (AM) and the auxiliary motor minesweeper (AMS) of which the command had eighteen—and the small craft of a minesweeping boat division consisting of twenty-one LCVPs and 40-foot motor launches converted to sweepers. The command also began using helicopters for minesweeping duty. Perhaps the command's most unusual asset was a hapless ex-Japanese merchantman called in official reports "the Guinea Pig vessel." She tested waters in southern Korean ports for residual U.S. influence mines implanted in those waters late in World War II. Fortunately for her crew, she found those waters clean.

The challenges confronting the minecraft were Sisyphean. The enemy "freshened" his minefields frequently, compelling the Mine Force to check sweep the east coast waters at least biweekly. Stretched for resources, the command limited its efforts on the west coast to major ports such as Chinnampo and Haeju.

A most insidious challenge was the modern Soviet magnetic mine. Although only nine were found in the last seven months of 1951, their very existence forced "the sweeping of vast areas of water less than thirty fathoms deep, which otherwise could have been declared safe after sweeping for moored mines had been completed." Complicating the challenge was the ship counter, often a feature in magnetic mines. Because the counter could be set to tally as many as twelve ships before the mine exploded, the sweepers were forced to comb the same waters a dozen times over before the area could be classified as secure.

As a further difficulty, minesweepers often worked close to enemy shores where they made good targets for coastal artillery, especially because the vessels crept slowly along certain preset tracks. Without significant armament with which to retaliate, they came under fire so often that they were repeatedly forced to resort to night sweeping. But this offered its own hazards: accurate navigation was tougher; helicopters, an increasingly valuable adjunct, stayed on deck; moored mines were thus much more difficult to find; and black swept mines bobbing in a black ocean made for an unnerving menace.

Given the nature of the Communist mining campaign, the sweepers could not restrict their operations close inshore. International convention required that a moored mine be automatically disarmed if the mooring cable was severed. Because the enemy disregarded such strictures, drifting mines threatened vessels well to seaward. By the fall of 1951, more than three hundred mines had floated as far as Japanese shores.

With plenty of opportunity to practice, the UN minesweeping forces became adept at their work. They learned to differentiate between the lethal mines and the flotsam of a war zone, such as aircraft wing tanks and empty fuel drums. The Sailors soon learned to approximate the date when a mine had been put in the water by the marine growth on its case. And they certainly harvested a bounty of mines. In just one day (14 June 1951), the little motor launches working at Wonsan brought up forty-one mines. During the last seven months of 1951, sweepers cleaned 683 mines out of Korean waters, including 186 from the harbor of Hungnam alone.

Another index of the proficiency of the minesweepers was their own casualty rate. Before May 1951, five sweepers were sunk in exchange for two hundred mines swept. In the next seven months, no mine vessels were lost

Ernest G. Small, minus her bow, which an enemy mine and heavy seas tore from the destroyer in October 1951, heads for repairs in Japan. (National Archives)

in neutering more than triple the number of mines. Not that mines had been rendered completely innocuous. During the same period, mines sank two ROKN vessels and severely damaged two U.S. destroyers. On 12 June, *Walke* (DD-723) hit a floating mine, which flooded two living compartments, damaged the port shaft, killed twenty-six enlisted men, and wounded thirty-five more. *Ernest G. Small* (DDR-838) got off more lightly when, on 10 October, the ship strayed outside the swept channel at Hungnam. Twenty-seven of her crew were casualties, including nine dead. Three days later while limping toward Japan, her bow began to work loose. Her crew rigged a watertight bulkhead aft of the break, a repair that enabled the destroyer to make Sasebo.

These distressing episodes aside, it was clear that the U.S. Navy had come a long way from the Pacific Fleet staff assessment in the first half-year of the war that antimine operations ranked as "a major deficiency." By the end of 1951, naval evaluators could rank minesweeping materials, procedures, and techniques as "adequate." True, improvements were still needed, especially in night techniques and in communications between sweeper and helicopter. Also, the specter of more sophisticated mines, especially pressure and acoustic types, caused continuing concern.

While the mine struggle lasted until the end of the war, its pace ebbed and flowed. For the first half of 1952, the increasingly proficient minesweepers found only 107 mines—all contact—compared with six times that number in the preceding half-year. On the other hand, enemy gunfire grew as a nuisance, sometimes forcing the sweepers to cut their gear and retreat under the cover of smoke. In hotly contested areas like Wonsan, the minesweepers reluctantly turned to night operations with all the accompanying drawbacks.

In the end, UN persistence paid dividends. Losses to mines late in the war dropped even further. As one example, during the period July 1952 to January 1953, the minesweeping group scoured an area of about 270 square miles; not one UN ship struck a mine in those waters. Mines scored in all waters against only two ships during this period: the fleet tug *Sarsi* (ATF-111) was sunk at Hungham; and the destroyer *Barton* (DD-722), heavily damaged. Both were outside swept zones (indeed, *Barton* was ninety miles east of Wonsan) and probably were victims of floaters torn loose from their moorings by Typhoon Karen.

In its final Korean War report, Pacific Fleet could conclude with justified satisfaction, "Mine countermeasures in Korea have been developed to a high state of efficiency and effectiveness." More specifically, the Pacific Fleet staff paid tribute to the work of the minesweeping Sailors who, in hazardous conditions, "made a magnificent contribution to the Naval effort" by keeping the sea-lanes cleared for blockading and bombarding ships.

Pacific Fleet evaluators also cautioned that the minesweepers had not confronted acoustic or pressure mines, against which the United States lacked satisfactory sweeping techniques. Citing the enormous effort expended in countering mines, they pointed to the "urgent need for the improvement of our capability in this field." In fact, the Navy had begun a major program of minesweeper construction during the war. Of three basic types, the largest was the *Agile* class of sixty-five ships. Built to sweep magnetic mines, these oceangoing vessels featured wooden hulls and engines made of special nonmagnetic stainless steel alloys. Orders for the similar coastal *Bluebird* class eventually totaled twenty-two ships for the U.S. Navy and 267 for NATO navies. This extensive construction program that continued to mid-decade seemed to vindicate the evaluation team,

WORKING WITH
THE ALLIES

THE KOREAN WAR WAS that rara avis: a successful coalition war. Although the contributions made by the many allies of the United States to the ground war are reasonably well known, less visible has been the participation of other UN navies.

Their assistance was substantial, both in quantity and quality. For example, in the spring of 1953, ninety-three UN warships ranging in size from frigates to attack carriers were operating in Korean waters. Of this total, sixty-two flew the United States flag, and thirty-one hoisted pennants of other nations.

The British Commonwealth nations of Great Britain, Australia, Canada, and New Zealand provided the largest number of combatants. Operating mostly off the western coast of North Korea, the Commonwealth detachment, usually commanded by a British flag officer, commonly included a light carrier, one or more cruisers, several destroyers, and smaller warships.

Among the notable accomplishments of the Commonwealth force was the pressure it put, by operating in the Han River estuary, on Communist negotiators in the fall of 1951. On 3 October, HMS *Black Swan* made a foray up that river to force Communist troops and artillery to reveal their positions. Attacked by enemy aircraft, the frigate suffered substantial damage, but her gunfire gave lie to the enemy negotiating position that the Han estuary was under complete Communist control.

As another example, the Royal Navy helped recover a MiG-15 swept-wing fighter that had crashed in shallow water near Cho-do in

Bataan crewmen, at least one manning a twin-mount 40-millimeter gun, watch as the British light cruiser HMS *Belfast* moves smartly alongside in waters off Korea. (National Archives)

northwestern Korea. The light cruiser HMS *Kenya* and the frigate HMS *Cardigan Bay* covered an American landing craft fitted with a special crane while it recovered the pieces of the aircraft in July 1951.

Some of the Commonwealth ships took an active part in the campaign to interdict enemy supplies by bombarding railroads running near the coasts. In December 1952, for instance, the Canadian destroyer HMCS *Haida* shelled an eight-car train and was later credited with a second train. Her sister HMCS *Athabaskan* also wrecked two enemy trains. The most successful member of the "Trainbusters' Club" was HMCS *Crusader* with four trains to her credit.

Besides the Commonwealth contribution, warships from Colombia, Denmark, the Netherlands, South Korea, and Thailand took part in the Korean War. They shared with their coalition peers a host of missions:

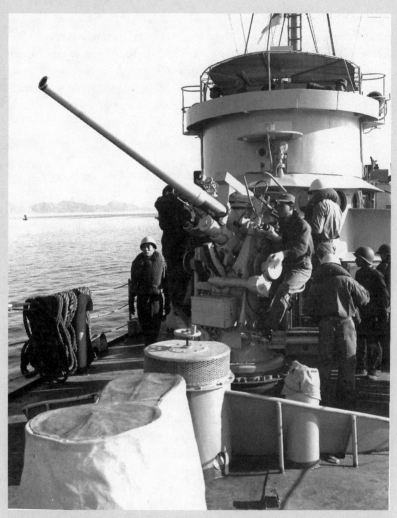

ROKN Sailors man a 3-inch/50-caliber gun on board *Sam Kak San* off Korea's west coast. The submarine chaser, formerly a U.S. Navy warship, operated throughout the war along Korea's coasts and among offshore islands. (Naval Historical Center)

blockade, shore bombardment, patrol, and escort duties. Given the disparate languages, lack of common codes and maneuvering procedures, differing materiel requirements, and incompatible communications, these warships worked in harness remarkably well. Smoothing the way were liaison officers and interpreters. One analyst identified the most intractable problem as that of surface-to-surface identification, a problem never truly conquered and one that caused several friendly fire casualties.

The ROKN was the youngest of the UN navies that fought the Korean War but also one of the hardest-fighting outfits. At the outset of the war, the ROKN of seventy-one naval vessels and 13,700 men aggressively sought out enemy supply craft on both sides of the peninsula, sinking numerous coastal sampans. After helping defend the Pusan Perimeter, the ROKN worked north alongside the UN ground advance, clearing mines, patrolling the coast, recapturing islands, and landing guerrillas behind enemy lines. ROKN units paid the price for their boldness with enemy mines sinking several vessels. In an accident at sea, the ROKN frigate *Apnok* collided with the American ammunition ship *Mount Baker* (AE-4), killing twenty-four South Korean sailors. But in one success story, South Korean motor torpedo boats worked closely with the American destroyer *Diachenko* in "Fly Catcher" patrols bent on capturing North Korean fishing craft.

The ROKN was hard pressed to fight effectively since the naval service had been provided with older American submarine chasers and mine warfare vessels, which were prone to mechanical breakdown, and its Sailors were inexperienced. The poor health of many South Korean Sailors, insufficient training of junior and midlevel officers, and language barriers also hampered ROKN operations.

Despite these shortfalls, the ROKN added its considerable weight to the allied effort to control the seas off Korea. At the end of 1951, the ROKN contributed 66 of 152 naval vessels that formed the allied blockading and escort Task Force 95. Through hard fighting and the development of naval skills, by the end of the war the ROKN had become a valued member of the UN naval contingent.

In a broader sense, the UN effort in Korea represents a case study in successful coalition warfare at sea. There was friction, but on the whole the integration of warships from ten disparate navies proceeded with marked success. Pertinent was the observation of the Pacific Fleet staff when the Colombian frigate, after fourteen months in theater, sailed for home: "The ... *Capitan Tono*, which made a splendid reputation for herself and crew, departed WESTPAC on 27 Jan 1953."

which stated emphatically of the Navy's entire record in the Korean War, "Need for minesweepers was the major Naval lesson learned."

Sadly, this lesson learned was forgotten almost immediately. After the armistice, many of the new ocean minesweepers (MSOs) and smaller coastal and inshore minesweepers were quickly transferred to allied navies. One mine specialist, Lt. Cdr. Gordon Hogg, attended the Naval Intelligence School. He wrote, "What bothered me then, fairly fresh from the Chin-nampo, Korea sweep ... was that an important subject like mine warfare rated only a one hour treatment by the most junior member of the instructor staff." Hogg's was a voice in the wilderness. As one of the careful historians of mine warfare has concluded, "The Navy had not taken to heart the main lessons learned by the MCM [mine countermeasures] force throughout its history, namely, that minesweeping is tedious, mine hunting is more tedious, and countering mines cannot be made easy, cheap, or convenient."

THE GATOR NAVY

IN THE LAST TWO YEARS of the Korean War the spotlight moved away from the amphibious forces. Having proved essential in the Inchon invasion and the Hungnam evacuation, while being frustrated at Wonsan, the resurrected amphibious elements by 1952 resembled more a paper tiger than the big stick of the early war months. Twice the command, officially Amphibious Forces, Far East (Task Force 90), menaced the rear of the enemy but never made another major landing. Nevertheless, the amphibs performed during the whole period a full slate of unappreciated, albeit essential, duties.

The first of the major ruses came in August 1951. In conjunction with a UN ground offensive on the eastern side of the peninsula, an amphibious force threatened Changjon. The effort was a large one with three attack transports and one attack cargo ship backed up by a powerful bombardment force including a battleship, a heavy cruiser, four destroyers, and one LSMR. For three days prior to the "landings," these warships shelled the Communists in the area, and minesweepers set about their work. Finally, on 30 August, the transports put their landing craft in the waters—and then repeated their feint the next day.

Despite the smoke and mirrors display, enemy reaction was disappointingly meek. American evaluators concluded that the UN efforts lacked sufficient realism to cause the enemy any great alarm. As one planner noted, the continued presence of the 1st Marine Division on the front denied any credibility to an amphibious threat. Given the spare Marine force structure in Korea, that formation could not be relieved of its duties as line infantry; hence one of the great advantages conferred by the sea services was forestalled.

Following the disappointing Changjon ruse, the "gator navy" hardly lapsed into a coma; rather it became a jack-of-all-trades in the theater. With no landing in the offing, the force was now "available for many tasks foreign to its mission," as one evaluation noted. And availability equaled employment. Landing craft soon found themselves ferries, helping in the latter part of 1951 to lift elements of the 45th Infantry Division from Hokkaido to Inchon. In January 1952, the amphibious force assisted in switching the 40th and 24th Infantry divisions, the former arriving in Korea, the other leaving. Two months later, much of the heavy equipment of the 1st Marine Division rode the landing craft, not in a leap-frogging advance behind the front, but rather from the east coast to the west coast in a large-scale tactical redeployment of the unit. Some Korean refugees also benefited from the lift provided by the landing craft, as in the winter of 1952 when three LSTs evacuated civilians from offshore islands to safer ground. A similar, but much larger effort came in 1953 at the approach of the armistice when the amphibious vessels helped remove the remaining 19,425 civilians from the west coast islands north of the truce line.

For the amphibious Sailors, the transport of enemy prisoners proved a task of major magnitude and lengthy duration. Throughout 1951 and the winter of 1952, Task Force 90 carried 170,229 prisoners and their guards to Koje-do, south of the peninsula. Then the massive riots at that camp in the spring of 1952 jerked the machine into reverse. Beginning on 19 April, eleven landing craft separated 80,225 anti-Communist POWs and civilian internees from the enemy diehards. Hard-working amphibs transported the diehards to smaller, more secure camps in an operation aptly dubbed "spreadout."

Amphibious Sailors found themselves further employed in helping the Army's 2nd Logistical Command meet its requirements. The landing craft carted so much water for troops that one evaluator complained, "Unless resupply employment of TF 90 is guarded against, this force would find itself constantly in the water transportation business, to the detriment of assigned primary tasks."

Farther afield, the command was obligated to keep one of its larger vessels (an attack transport or attack cargo ship) within two days' steaming of Hong Kong in order to rescue U.S. nationals there should Chairman Mao Tse-tung decide to expand the conflict at the expense of the British Crown Colony. Closer to Korea, one LST or medium landing ship (LSM) found occasional work as a tender for the Japanese Coastal Survey Project.

The landing craft assisted in charting poorly marked Korean waters, a task that held its own perils. In this duty, two of the invaluable LSTs ran aground during the first half of 1952. *LST-819* was helping map the coast at Cheju-do when she broached on the beach. The ship repair yard took thirty days to fill the many holes punched in her hull. *LST-1068* ran onto a sandbar on Amma-do; her repairs occupied five weeks.

Besides surveying, landing craft found work in other unfamiliar roles. One LSD acted as flagship and tender for a minesweeping squadron. Supporting the development of experimental technology, another LSM at Sasebo launched experimental drone aircraft, and an LST served as a pad and support base for mine-hunting helicopters.

Certain missions carried a more distinctly martial tone. LSMRs, an integral component of Task Force 90, often fired their rockets in shore bombardments, especially on the west coast. Other landing craft put ROK troops ashore in raids behind enemy lines. In a more defensive mode, the landing craft backed up island garrisons exposed to enemy attack and helped construct the emergency airfield on Yo-do in Wonsan harbor.

These myriad duties entailed costs. Because employment "in almost every conceivable task" invariably meant skimpy upkeep, the amphibs fought a losing battle against material deterioration. Especially worn were the ex-SCAJAP LSTs, recommissioned for the Inchon landings in September 1950. At that point in bad shape, their condition by 1952 required the unremitting efforts of their crews to keep them operational.

Obviously, the Sailors were stretched thin as well. Although manning of the amphibious forces stood generally at a satisfactory level for the last two years of the war, some serious shortages arose in key ratings and ranks, in part because of the constant churning of personnel through the rotation system. For example, in the middle of 1952, Amphibious Forces, Pacific Fleet reported that it enjoyed 110 percent of its personnel allowance, but only 65 percent of its allotment of petty officers. Especially troublesome was the shortage of communications personnel. High-speed transport *Diachenko* (APD-123) in early June 1952 was unable to get under way except in an emergency because of unfilled billets in this key specialty.

The many important, but ancillary, duties foisted on the landing craft led to doubts about the ability of the command to execute its primary mission if the UN resorted again to an amphibious assault. Following a careful study, one assessment optimistically contended: "TF 90 can be quickly assembled for a major amphibious operation or emergency." But the landing craft were themselves only part of the equation. An amphibious attack would also require that the assaulting Marines and the covering aircraft squadrons be honed to a sharp edge. It was the readiness of these elements for such possible employment that was suspect.

Partly to remedy this shortcoming, UN planners ordered a sham landing at Kojo in October 1952. An important objective was to prod the enemy into action, thereby drawing his troops into the open for punishment. To make the charade as convincing as possible, only those at the very top of the planning process were conversant with the true nature of the "landing."

On 12 October, while UN troops to the south increased pressure at the front lines, the gunnery ships and aircraft began their preliminary bombardment at Kojo. Fire support was substantial: the battleship *Iowa* (BB-61), two heavy cruisers, five destroyers, and three LSMRs. Minesweepers went into action, but accurate enemy shooting by their shore batteries forced the minecraft to carry out night work.

After three days of setting the stage, including executing a mock paratrooper assault, the attack force arrived off Kojo. The weather was wretched as winds gusted from thirty-five to fifty knots and low clouds scudded across the horizon. More than one hundred ships stood off the beaches. At 1130, the time-hallowed command "Land the Landing Force" set in motion the amphibious craft from twenty-three thousand yards offshore. Given sea conditions, it was a blessing that no troops were embarked in the boats. As the landing craft ran in toward the shore, they drew a few desultory rounds from the shore artillery, but overall, the enemy reaction was feeble, and the last wave of amphibs turned away from the beach at 1435. Recovering the boats in the heavy seas was dangerous

The battleship *Iowa*'s 16-inch guns open up on enemy coastal defenses at Kojo in October 1952. (Naval Historical Center)

and slow work that took almost two hours, but was accomplished without casualties. Under covering fire that went on into the next day, the attack force withdrew.

Measured by its objective of hammering the enemy's troops, evaluators ruled the Kojo feint a flat failure. An early indicator that the enemy was not following the script came on the night of 13–14 October when a U.S. intelligence agent went ashore only to report that the enemy beach defenses were unmanned and that he had seen only a few enemy troops at any point. Following the feint, the report of the Striking Force (Task Force 77) commander claimed that from 12 to 18 October air attack had killed ten enemy soldiers! Pacific Fleet evaluators concluded dryly, "If the operation brought any large numbers of enemy troops into the open, it was only at night." On the positive side, the same headquarters rated the operation as "highly successful" for the experience it gave planners. Lower ranks displayed markedly less enthusiasm, with the bogus nature of the exercise drawing pointed complaint. Perhaps the most judicious assessment of the whole affair came from James Field's official history of the war: "Of Kojo, as of earlier and smaller demonstrations, it seems proper to conclude that an enemy incapable of quick response cannot be very profitably hoaxed."

Following this stratagem, the amphibious command returned to its earlier diverse activities. Although training in landing techniques for both the Marines and the Army remained high on the priority list, the employment of those troops at the front and the shortage of amphibious craft rendered any large unit exercises impossible. Indeed, the 1st Marine Division could not train even at the regimental level, and in their final report, Pacific Fleet staffers asked, "Should both services merely dabble in amphibious operations or should the Marines be maintained at the peak of amphibious assault efficiency?"

The multifarious tasking of the amphibs from the pre-Kojo days continued to the end of the war. Task Force 90 continued to support

American naval personnel provide cigarettes to North Korean and Chinese POWs as they board a U.S. Navy utility landing craft at the UN prison camp at Koje-do off southern Korea. When the vessel reached Inchon, the POWs were exchanged in Operation Little Switch for UN prisoners then being held by the Communists. (Naval Historical Center)

helicopter and minesweeper units. It gave relief to flood victims in Kyushu, laid nets at Pusan, engaged in various salvage and rescue operations, and supported the French in Indochina by transporting smaller landing craft to Saigon. Hauling prisoners became once again a prominent mission when, during Operations Little Switch and Big Switch, the command assisted in the exchange of 101,756 POWs and internees.

In reflecting on the place of Task Force 90 in the Korean struggle, evaluators concluded that the unit played a "characteristically unglamorous, yet indispensable role, in support of other forces, particularly the Army." By their estimate, the amphibious command helped tie down perhaps two hundred fifty thousand troops, or twenty-five Chinese divisions, along the coast. Such numbers totaled almost one-quarter of all enemy troops in North Korea at the time of the armistice. In light of the perdition to which national planners had assigned landing capabilities prior to the outbreak of the war, the amphibious force certainly had confounded their critics. Orders for larger, more capable LSTs and LSDs went out to shipyards immediately after the war.

CLOSE AIR SUPPORT AND SUPPORTING THE CARRIERS

DURING THE LAST TWO YEARS of the war, Navy and Marine aviation provided intermittent backing for the troops at the front. Until the fall of 1951, one of the main missions for Task Force 77 aircraft was close air support. However, beginning in September, the Navy somewhat reluctantly directed its carrier aircraft to bolster the interdiction efforts of the Air Force for ten months. In June 1952, the focus of the air war shifted to strikes against the North Korean industrial and power infrastructure. Not until the spring of 1953 did carrier aircraft again devote any significant percentage of their effort to the close air support mission.

From the very beginning of the war, two themes proved constants in executing this task. First, aircraft demonstrated repeatedly their great military power when used effectively in direct support of troops. Second, the Air Force preferred a system of close air support that differed markedly from that favored by the Navy and Marine Corps. In brief, the Marines with their relatively light organic artillery relied more heavily than did the Army on close air support. Thus, the Marines preferred air units tightly controlled from the ground; indeed, whenever possible, Marine aircraft engaged in continuous patrols above troops on the ground—the "on-call" method. The Air Force, with its predilection for strikes deep behind enemy lines and interdiction of enemy communications, regarded such Marine practices as wasteful of resources and preferred close air support strikes scheduled well in advance or, at the most, for tactical aircraft to be held on strip alert until called to action.

A 1951 Pacific Fleet comparison of the two systems over a six-month period found the Marine-Navy system superior in a number of important ways. It could result in the drop of ordnance on target within an average of ten minutes of the ground forces' request. The time lag usual for the Air Force procedure was forty-five minutes. Air Force strikes were also less precise. Air Force planes delivered strikes an average of three miles from the friendly forces whereas the Navy-Marine planes dropped their bombs on average closer than one mile from the troops. As the Pacific Fleet assessment concluded: "The Marine-Navy system is more reliable; it interferes less with other functions; it costs no more; and, it produces superior results."

Notwithstanding, the Air Force view prevailed for most of the war, and aircraft from the carriers and the 1st Marine Aircraft Group usually flew subject to Fifth Air Force operational control. To the frustration of Marine ground commanders, they found that their advance requests for close air support were rarely even acknowledged. Consequently, the ground commanders simply stopped submitting such requests. The Air Force did, in the end, bend slightly by trying to dispatch Marine aircraft to support Marine ground units needing help, but the improvement proved only marginal.

As the truce approached and fighting intensified, close air support became a high priority once again for Task Force 77, which backed not only the Marines but also the Eighth Army. In July, while the war approached its conclusion, the four carriers on station mounted a maximum effort, averaging 170 sorties daily, the highest sortie rates of the war. Despite being hampered by low ceilings and fog, *Princeton* (CVA-37) alone delivered 184 sorties in one day. But because the close air support system remained as centralized as ever, many of these strikes arrived late—sometimes by as much as seventeen hours, and found the mobile targets long since departed, compelling the aircraft to jettison their ordnance.

The controversy over close air support has remained a hardy perennial among issues dividing the services. Bitter as this matter became,

A 1,000-pound bomb dropped by naval aircraft flying a close air support mission explodes in the "Bunker Hill" area near the 38th parallel of Korea. (National Archives)

interservice relations were generally harmonious in the theater. As James Field's official naval history notes:

> The evacuation of casualties and the allocation of air and sea lift crossed service bounds. Joint planning for amphibious operations was effective. Logistic cross-servicing was generally satisfactory, as Marine aviation was provided with scarce engineering talent by the Air Force, deficiencies in marine transport were made up by the Army, and aviation materiel was traded back and forth between the Air Force and the Navy.

The Navy's close air support missions came, of course, from the carriers. High-value units, they were accompanied by surface warships that gave protection against air or subsurface attacks by Communist forces. Of substantial concern to the Navy during the war was the threat of jet aircraft attack. The thousands of World War II veterans in the fleet recalled the deadly Japanese aerial thrusts at Leyte Gulf and Okinawa.

The warships off Korea steamed near hostile coasts, sometimes for weeks on end. Navy leaders understood that the much higher speeds of jet aircraft would give them little advance warning. To enable defensive fighters to intercept a piston-engine bomber, the fleet needed to detect the enemy aircraft within eighty miles of the carrier formation. A MiG-15 jet fighter demanded about twice the distance. Fleet exercises showed that the most menacing planes were those at extreme altitude or, conversely, low-flyers, especially tough to pick up on radar. The close proximity of enemy coasts further confused the radar picture and slowed reaction times. Combat information centers, noisy and congested, were incapable of processing data quickly enough.

If enemy aircraft evaded the carrier's combat air patrol, escorting cruisers and destroyers were charged with providing a last-ditch defense. Doctrine called for the defending fighters to break off action ten miles out, at which point the surface warships would pick up the attacker with their antiaircraft guns.

Whatever doctrine dictated, prospects for success seemed slim. For their close-in antiaircraft armament, most warships still carried the 40-mm Bofors, a mainstay of the World War II fleet; some vessels still operated the 20-mm Oerlikons. The Bofors, a fine weapon in its day, was now judged too light and of too-limited range, and the old weapons frequently malfunctioned. Marginally superior to the 40-mm was the heavier 3-inch/50, developed at the end of World War II especially to shatter those kamikazes that had "gone ballistic"; that is, which continued on a ballistic course to their target even though damaged. Unfortunately, the 3-inch/50 also suffered from recurrent breakdowns. For example, in the fall of 1952, the heavy cruiser *Los Angeles* (CA-135) reported electrical shorts, which rendered several of her mounts out of commission for much of the deployment.

On the positive side, electronic countermeasures offered promise for fooling enemy aircraft. The introduction early in the Korean conflict of an automatic tracking radar (the Mk 25) quickened reaction time and substantially improved the effectiveness of that old stand-by, the heavy 5-inch/38 antiaircraft guns common throughout the fleet.

Given the sheer number of radars and gun barrels in any task force as well as the high quality of the Sailors, some Navy men viewed the jet aircraft menace with a certain degree of optimism. One Pacific Fleet evaluator noted that the concentration of antiaircraft gunnery in Task Force 77 exceeded substantially that usually encountered by U.S.

aircraft over North Korea. He hardly needed to add, "Enemy flak has been very effective."

Still, surface warships found too few opportunities for antiaircraft practice. Perhaps fortunately, Communist aviators did not challenge UN warships in any sustained way. Incidents were not, however, unknown. In October 1951, enemy aircraft struck at HMS *Black Swan*, a Royal Navy frigate operating up the Han River, and did significant damage to the ship. In 1953, aircraft attacked without effect *LSMR-409*.

In September 1952, several MiGs came within seven miles of the destroyer *Bradford* (DD-545), although they retreated when she opened fire. Two months later, the heavy cruiser *Helena* (CA-75) detected seven MiGs closing the carrier *Oriskany* (CVA-34). Navy fighters intercepted the Communist jets only thirty-five miles from the warship and claimed five of them.

Events like these coupled with fleet exercises against friendly aircraft underscored the need for a drastically improved air defense capability for the fleet. As one report concluded, "Fleet anti-aircraft defenses have improved slightly since World War II, but have not kept pace with the marked advances in aircraft performance." Guns no longer had the range or lethality to deal effectively with the new high-speed menace. The Navy accelerated work on its guided missile program.

Another great uncertainty throughout the Korean War was the danger posed by Communist submarines. In capability, high-speed snorkeling submarines based on the late–WWII German Type XXI offered a challenge analogous to that of the jet aircraft: a major leap in performance that threatened to overwhelm state-of-the-art defenses. The Soviets had under construction, and analysts feared had completed, numbers of these potent craft (dubbed the "Whiskey" class) at Vladivostok. Naval intelligence officers ranked them as "a serious and continuing threat." American planners were concerned about a Spanish Civil War scenario when Italian submarines, operating anonymously, had torpedoed Republican shipping.

The first line of UN defense lay in the long-range U.S. Navy aircraft patrols over the Sea of Japan and the Yellow Sea. On several occasions, these aircraft surprised Soviet submarines on the surface. The Pacific Fleet also maintained in the Far East a submarine hunter-killer group composed of an escort carrier with accompanying destroyers.

While on guard against an attack by Soviet submarines, this unit served as a test bed for antisubmarine techniques and as a training force for destroyers, which were cycled through the command to hone their antisubmarine warfare (ASW) skills against "tame" U.S. submarines. Some ASW exercises demonstrated graphically the capabilities of modern undersea craft. For example, in one test in October 1951, two high-speed U.S. submarines penetrated the destroyer screen repeatedly and fired notional and exercise torpedoes with great success. On another occasion in that same year, submarines seven times got through the escorts—in every case completely undetected. Not surprisingly, the task group commander confessed "great concern" at this state of affairs.

Part of the problem was that destroyers lacked training time with a "live" submarine—less than a single day in forty-five at one point in the war. Exercises showed that cooperation between air and surface ASW forces proved difficult to effect. ASW equipment was only marginally up to the task, if at all. Older sonar lacked range, and the rubber domes on the newer sets tended to rupture in severe seas. ASW weapons lacked lethality against tough, deep-diving submarines whose acoustic homing torpedoes represented an urgent threat to the surface warships. The hunter-killer groups were built around the escort carrier, which was too slow and small to operate efficiently the newer antisubmarine aircraft.

The harsh cold of the Korean winters tried men and equipment alike. Guns remained dependable, but ASW ordnance fell victim to severe icing. One February 1953 report from an escort division called attention to typical conditions aboard its destroyers when the side throwers for depth charges were incapacitated about one-half the time and the stern racks were unusable. The Hedgehogs, which gave surface warships ASW firepower ahead, were frozen solid. For the ships of this escort division, the only reliable weapon in such conditions was the antisubmarine torpedo. The author summarized, "Some better method of keeping ASW armament ice free must be found if we are to hunt subs in Arctic weather."

A few bright spots relieved this generally bleak picture. Two embryonic developments looked promising: electronic countermeasures (ECM) and helicopters. The former gave a means of pinpointing the location of enemy submarines. The latter looked useful for that purpose as well, but also offered the potential for extending the killing range of the destroyers. A Pacific Fleet report remarked with some prescience of ASW prospects immediately after the Korean War: "The techniques of electronic interceptions and helicopter operations advanced rapidly and these proved that they would henceforth be prominent features of antisubmarine warfare."

Nonetheless, analysts postwar breathed a sigh of relief that the Communists had not challenged the allied fleet with modern submarines. One

SUBMARINE OPERATIONS

EARLY IN THE KOREAN WAR, U.S. submarines—the only UN undersea craft in the theater—searched for missions. One submariner remembered, "Here we were just sitting on the line and starving fast. I begged to be allowed to go to Tokyo and perhaps explore and find somebody who would be acceptable for using a submarine for anything. If we could just get them into the action, perhaps something would develop." Beginning in February 1951, a command entitled "Submarine Group, NAVFE" stood up at Yokosuka. Supported by a small staff and a submarine rescue vessel, four submarines operated from that base.

Their principal duties were to make reconnaissance patrols and to provide ASW training opportunities for U.S. destroyers and escorts in the Far East. The normal rotation had one submarine out on patrol, two honing the ASW skills of their surface comrades, and one boat in upkeep status.

Submarines patrolled the waters around Hokkaido with special attention to La Pérouse Strait separating that Japanese island from the Soviet island of Sakhalin. Occasionally transiting the strait on the surface, the subs kept the naval command advised of ship movements: *Blackfin* (SS-322) in little over a month in the spring of 1952 made 106 contact reports; and *Caiman* (SS-323), an even one hundred during the same period.

Wintertime operations were less productive. With Communist shipping traffic much curtailed, the subs patrolled one week out of four in 1951. For the boats, the severe weather presented special challenges.

U.S. Navy submarines conducted patrols not only off the coast of Korea during the war but also along the littorals of the USSR and the People's Republic of China. (Naval Historical Center)

Constant fogging of periscopes handicapped search, and condensation within the submarines made for difficult living conditions. Submarine *Charr* (SS-328) reported in August 1952, "This entire patrol was characterized by a constant battle against fog and fogging periscopes. Of 31 days on station visibility was restricted a total of 23 days."

As the war dragged on, submariners found work in new areas and roles. When in December 1952 weather conditions caused a suspension of the Hokkaido area patrols, one of the submarines, *Scabbardfish* (SS-397), conducted a special reconnaissance patrol off the coast of southern China. In the next year, submarines became more active in special operations, carrying out an amphibious raid and several other clandestine missions.

Realistically, the war allowed for little active participation by the submarine arm. Its boats did their best work testing—and often showing up—their surface cousins in ASW trials.

evaluator noted that UN ASW efforts would have been "barely adequate" in response. Another concluded that such a challenge would have "necessitated a considerable revision of the pattern of operations in the Western Pacific." Throughout the war, the UN forces had taken the calculated risk of operating at slow speeds in the same area for days running. The situation helped push the Navy to greater efforts in the ASW arena in the war's aftermath.

NAVAL GUNFIRE SUPPORT

IF THE CARRIERS OPERATING off North Korea became floating air bases, the battleships, cruisers, and destroyers steaming along the coasts became floating artillery batteries. For both the aviators and surface warriors, their principal duty was to support United Nations troops ashore. Such backing, whether from bomb or shell, could assume several forms, to include deep strike against enemy resources, the interdiction of enemy supply lines, and the bombardment of enemy troops close to the front lines.

KOREAN WEATHER:
A SPECIAL
CHALLENGE

NOT LEAST AN ENEMY of the UN naval forces was the operating environment close to the Korean peninsula. Along the western shores of North Korea, shallow waters and wide tidal swings marked the rugged coastline. During the winter months, icing, rough seas, high winds, and Siberian cold plagued vessels and crews alike. Minesweepers especially found their efforts stymied by drifting pack ice. Naval gunfire support vessels were similarly frustrated, with an extreme example of the *LSMR-527* caught in ice two feet thick. The ship dragged anchor for more than two miles before it could break free to clear water.

Winter conditions at the end of 1951 were so severe that they forced the suspension of submarine patrols in La Pérouse Strait. High winds, severe cold, ice, and heavy seas hampered the submarines. The amphibious forces similarly found that winter made execution of their primary mission virtually impossible, principally because the low temperatures and freezing spray handicapped the smaller craft.

Summer, following hard on the spring rains, brought other challenges. Dense fog and heavy precipitation hampered operations while high humidity and elevated temperatures made living difficult for Sailors. The great majority of warships lacked air conditioning.

Summer and early fall also brought typhoons. Ruth in October 1951 disrupted operations from Taiwan to Korea and damaged ships and aircraft alike. The next August, when *Iowa* passed through the fringe of Typhoon Karen, the massive battleship took so much water topside that fifteen of her nineteen 40-mm antiaircraft mounts shorted out. The

The frozen gun mount on board attack carrier *Oriskany* is no winter wonderland to this gun captain who faces a deicing job in January 1953. (Naval Historical Center)

heavy seas that came with Karen tore communist mines from their moorings and forced, for the first and only time, a suspension of the siege of Wonsan.

Changeable conditions brought upswings too. Korean falls with their crisp air and cool temperatures could be beautiful; dropping humidity offered a distinct relief from summer conditions. And the Korean coastal landscape presented scenic delights, especially along the east coast where the rugged Taebaek range came practically down to the sea.

Corsairs from light carrier *Bataan* (CVL-29) saw these small boats as targets of opportunity and burned them with napalm. No means of transportation was considered too primitive for the Communist logistics network, which coerced the North Korean civilian masses into moving war supplies and food to the front lines. (*Naval Aviation News*)

Secure command of the air enabled warships to close enemy coasts for sustained periods; on the other hand, ships could help planes by shelling antiaircraft batteries. In contrast to naval aircraft, which were usually limited to daytime operations in fair weather, the seaborne artillery could render fire support to troops night and day and in virtually all weather conditions. Beneficiaries of naval gunfire support were, naturally, troops stationed closest to the coast, during the last two years of the war usually from the ROK Army I Corps and the U.S. 1st Marine Division.

Gunnery support warships came in a variety of sizes and types. A modified landing craft, the LSMR, could lay down a blanket of rocket fire in short order. For example, on 23 May 1951, two of the warships shot 4,903 rockets near Wonsan in just thirty-five minutes against enemy gun emplacements. Unfortunately, the LSMRs, like the landing craft from which the variant was derived, were slow and clumsy. Lacking armor and laden with rockets, they presented a tempting target for enemy coast defense artillery. After duels at Wonsan during the summer of 1951, during which the LSMRs escaped with only slight damage, naval leaders restricted their operations to night surprise attacks or shoots with heavier warships.

The destroyer escort was also of problematic utility. Here the issue was not so much the vulnerability of the warship but its lack of offensive punch. Part of the problem lay in the elementary fire control equipment on board these vessels. The gear was incapable of laying precise fire on indirect targets or of engaging accurately while the ship maneuvered at speed. Worse, the light 3-inch guns on many destroyer escorts were usually outmatched in range and destructive effect by enemy coastal batteries. One analyst concluded,

> The employment of the 3-inch gun DE in the Songjin area, except as an emergency measure, is not recommended. The willingness of the enemy shore batteries to open fire against bombardment ships appears to be inversely proportional to the caliber and number of the gun battery of UN bombardment ship.... The 5-inch battery is the minimum which will command the respect of the enemy shore batteries.

The 5-inch/38 with a good crew could, in a minute, get off twenty rounds, each weighing about sixty pounds. Presented with lucrative targets, the gunfire of a destroyer could be enormously destructive. For example, the destroyer *Orleck* (DD-886) firing on the east coast on 11 May 1951 claimed three hundred enemy casualties.

Some destroyers shot vast quantities of ordnance. For instance, four ships of Destroyer Division 52 during June 1951 expended in just two weeks 8,269 rounds of 5-inch. Despite its many admirable qualities, the 5-inch did have a wickedly sharp blast, which opened cracks in welds and fittings. It also played havoc on Sailors' hearing and worse. For example, the commanding officer of *Mackenzie* (DD-836) "was knocked down twice and temporarily blinded and deafened during the peak of the action by the number two 5-inch mount firing at the maximum limit of train." Regardless, Pacific Fleet evaluators concluded, "The versatility and capability of the modern high-speed destroyer [in shore bombardment] is outstanding." In numbers, the "tin cans" constituted the most important element of the bombardment force. During the last four months of the war, the bombardment group was composed of forty-eight destroyers, one battleship, three cruisers, and four destroyer escorts.

Surpassing destroyers in weight of ordnance were the light and heavy cruisers, all of WWII vintage and armed with 5-, 6-, and 8-inch guns. Although shore bombardment had not been a prime mission when these vessels were designed, it became their principal duty in Korea.

Like the destroyers, the cruisers shot vast quantities of projectiles. For instance, the heavy cruiser *Rochester* (CA-124) in the first week of January 1953 expended 642 8-inch projectiles and more than 1,200 5-inch rounds. A sister ship, *Helena*, had fired ten thousand major caliber rounds by June 1951—after less than a year of war. Not surprisingly, her entire battery was replaced in December of that year at Long Beach, the California naval shipyard.

As with destroyers, cruisers were not immune to damage from their own weapons. *Los Angeles* reported on 29 January 1953 that she suffered "repeated blast damage" in part because of the necessity to shoot directly ahead and astern in the confines of Wonsan harbor. Concussion wrecked one gun director.

Accidents ranged from the trivial to the deadly. On 15 October 1952, the identification bracelet of one Sailor working in a 5-inch mount on the heavy cruiser *Toledo* (CA-133) dropped into the loading tray just as projectile and charge were being rammed. The bracelet fell between the breech plug and gun chamber, necessitating work with a crow bar to extract the offending ID.

Toledo's sister, *Saint Paul* (CA-73), a ship that made three Korean War tours, suffered a far more serious accident on 21 April 1952 when an explosion wracked turret one. Survivors attempting to escape breached turret security, and about seven seconds after the first explosion, more powder ignited. All thirty men in the turret died.

This sad episode aside, the 8-inch gun cruiser with its 250-pound main battery round was particularly valued for its effectiveness. As one example, *Los Angeles*, striking at Kojo in July 1951, caught a train and a battalion of troops in the open. Naval officers estimated that the ship's fire killed seventy-five of the enemy and wounded fifty and destroyed twelve boxcars laden with ammunition.

Unfortunately, the most capable U.S. Navy cruisers never got into action. The three ships of the *Des Moines* class were equipped with a new rapid-fire 8-inch gun mount. One of the three, *Salem* (CA-139), was fitted with a specialized shore-bombardment fire control system, the only such equipment in the entire Navy. *Salem*'s retention in the Mediterranean demonstrated the global concerns of the Truman administration, but these quick-shooting precision weapons were missed on the Korean bombline.

Battleships, when available, more than compensated. Roundly denounced by air power enthusiasts as antediluvian relics, battleships had almost disappeared from the U.S. Navy's active duty rosters. By June 1950, only *Missouri* (BB-63) remained in commission and this largely because of President Truman's personal interest in the relatively new but already historically important warship.

In the summer of 1950, *Missouri* had rushed to Korea, just missing the Inchon invasion but participating in the UN advance up the peninsula in the fall. Her contribution had been so valuable that the Navy brought out of reserve her three sisters, *Iowa*, *New Jersey* (BB-62), and *Wisconsin* (BB-64). Their renewed presence in the fleet led the Navy in October 1952 to redesignate the Cruiser Force as the Battleship-Cruiser Force. For the rest of the war, one battleship was usually in theater.

A battleship brought singular qualities to the fight. Its thick armor enabled the vessel to approach enemy shore batteries with relative impunity. The main battery of nine 16-inch guns provided unequalled firepower. Each 16-inch shell weighed almost a ton. For certain missions, the projectile of choice was the armor-piercing shell, which tipped the scales at 2,700 pounds and could penetrate thirty feet of reinforced concrete. With their protection and firepower, the battleships frequently closed the coast to blast North Korean railroad tunnels. One battleship skipper remarked that he welcomed enemy gunfire "because then we could locate shore batteries and dig them out with our 16-inch guns."

The relatively spacious command areas of a battleship ensured its fre-quent use as a flagship. While a valuable attribute, flagship duties occa-sionally conflicted with the bombardment mission. At no time was the conflict between the two tasks more evident than when Vice Admiral Clark commanded Task Force 77 from *Iowa*. An aviator, Clark preferred to be out with his beloved carriers. Because they usually operated about eighty miles off the coast, Clark would order *Iowa*, if she had no fire mis-sion immediately scheduled, to rush out at thirty knots to join the carri-ers. When the battleship did shoot, Clark was, in the words of *Iowa*'s commanding officer, Capt. William R. Smedberg III, "certainly bored with our role of bombardment. . . . He wanted to go duck-shooting instead of knocking out tunnels and railroad trains." In pursuit of a good night's sleep, Clark ordered Smedberg to fire only with the after turret. This eccentric directive forced the battleship Sailors to move the one-ton pro-jectiles from the forward shell flats to the aft barbette—an onerous job.

In the hands of gunnery experts, the 16-inch/50 Mk 7 proved a most effective weapon. One officer later remembered, "We had the best guns I suppose the Navy has ever produced or put in a ship. They were accurate. They were equally good at direct range, at point blank range of a couple thousand yards or at a twenty mile range." The extreme range of the 16-inch rifles represented a unique asset. When *New Jersey* was on station in 1952, almost half of all her shooting was to a distance beyond the reach of the next best gun—the 8-inch on the heavy cruisers.

The battleships certainly got a thorough workout. During her six-month tour in 1951, *New Jersey* fired 423 missions, thus averaging more than two a day. In her second deployment to the theater, *Missouri* shot 1,600 rounds, resulting in deep scoring of her 16-inch rifles. The one-ton ammunition and the proximity of Japan led the Navy to direct the battle-ships to Sasebo to replenish ammunition, thereby saving time and averting the danger of at-sea replenishment. Over the course of the conflict, the four *Iowas* fired more than twenty thousand 16-inch projectiles, many more than the class had expended during World War II when their princi-pal mission had been the escort of fast carriers.

With few exceptions, performance of Navy ordnance met the test of combat. During twenty-one months of combat, heavy cruiser and battle-ship guns experienced seventeen premature detonations of 8-inch and 16-inch ammunition. Given the tens of thousands of rounds fired, this failure rate was very low. The Bureau of Ordnance tracked the problem to a thin washer allowing propellant gases to leak through the base fuse and set off the round.

More troublesome were proximity-fuse shells used against land targets; these rounds experienced a large percentage of premature bursts. Especially prone to failure were the 5-inch white phosphorus (WP) incendiary projectiles. Fired by battleships, cruisers, and destroyers, the 5-inch WP garnered a ranking of "disappointingly poor" and a dud rate swinging wildly from 25 to 90 percent.

Also important to naval gunfire was aerial spotting. In the words of one Pacific Fleet evaluator: "It must be emphasized once again that good spotting is essential to high quality naval gunfire." A variety of aircraft types engaged in this task: high-performance jet fighters, carrier propeller aircraft, Army and Marine light planes, and helicopters. The bombarding ships found some of the best work done by helicopters. With its hovering ability, the helicopter made a stable platform for observers as long as enemy antiaircraft fire was minimal. Some analysts preferred the light airplane because it could carry out the low-level observation and better evade enemy guns.

In either helicopter or light plane, the pilots and observers won frequent praise for their skill and courage. A typical accolade came from an officer who remembered,

> Our principal difficulty and actually the only difficulty we had was in keeping them and restraining them against going too far inland and away from support that we could give them against hostile fire. We frequently would see machine gun ammunition streaking up toward them, but they were very shifty and they did magnificent work for us.

Spotting did not always go smoothly. Occasionally too many ships drew on the services of too few aircraft. Air spotting often resided well down the list of priorities for carrier aircraft, many of whose pilots lacked training in target identification or in the specialized communications procedures. For reasons of fuel conservation, some fighters operated at higher altitudes; others rocketed over the target area at great speed. Neither practice was conducive to careful observation of the fall of shot. Jet aircraft also lacked endurance and maneuverability at low altitude. After the amphibious Kojo feint of October 1952, the heavy cruiser *Toledo* submitted a report that encapsulated many of these problems:

> The air spotters varied in proficiency from poor to unsatisfactory. . . . Spotting planes often arrived late and departed early. The planes frequently had ordnance to unload, and that occupied from 20 minutes to

HELICOPTERS
AT SEA

ALTHOUGH VIETNAM HAS BEEN dubbed the "first helicopter war," the rotary wing aircraft really came into its own in Korea. During the war, the U.S. Navy experimented with helicopters in a variety of missions. Their usefulness, whether potential or realized, became so clear that they moved from a curiosity to an essential element in the naval force structure—a place that they have retained ever since.

From their embryonic state in World War II, helicopters had advanced sufficiently in the immediate postwar period to replace floatplanes on board cruisers and battleships. Shortly after North Korea crossed the 38th parallel, helicopters proved their value, flying their first combat sorties in August 1950 from the heavy cruiser *Helena*. Spotting gunfire was initially their principal task, and in this they enjoyed marked success. *Helena* the next year found her spotting helicopters especially valuable against precise targets like rail and highway bridges.

Encomiums for the new aircraft soon filled the action reports. Heavy cruiser *Rochester* noted that her helicopter "can easily maintain a good position and the spotter can watch the target with binoculars to evaluate damage." The captain of the heavy cruiser *Toledo* wrote: "The helicopter proved to be a highly versatile and valuable weapon . . . the best air spot or spot of any kind available to the cruiser in the Korean theatre." Pacific Fleet evaluators concluded, "HELO spot gives by far the greatest chance of observing fall of shot."

Part of the reason for this success was the steadiness of the platform, but part was owed to the integrated nature of the entire weapon system.

A helicopter lifts off hospital ship *Consolation* (AH-15). By quickly evacuating wounded personnel to hospital ships or medical facilities ashore, helicopters dramatically improved the survival rate for UN troops. (Naval Historical Center)

The ship "owned" the helicopter, and thus its spotters could be thoroughly briefed on the terrain and targets. In contrast, most carrier pilots were not especially interested or expert in improving surface ship gunfire. One surface warfare officer remembered that helicopters gave cruisers and battleships "a good self-contained system for doing our own spotting over coastal targets." Helicopters were also detailed to mine spotting. Early on, helicopters proved able to spot mines that were invisible to Sailors on the surface.

They also quickly demonstrated their worth in the search and rescue mission. They plucked so many downed pilots from the ocean that the job became almost routine. Never humdrum was the rescue of fliers downed behind enemy lines. In October 1951, the helicopter from the battleship *Iowa* darted ten miles inland to effect the daring rescue of a pilot from *Bon Homme Richard* (CVA-31). In an even lengthier mission a year later, *Helena's* helicopter flew an ultimately unsuccessful 105-mile night rescue mission, often under heavy enemy antiaircraft fire. The enemy tried to jam the helicopter's communications with *Helena* and built fires to lure the helicopter closer to antiaircraft guns. A few days later, *Helena* countermanded Air Force instructions to the helicopter to search for a downed pilot in an area thick with antiaircraft defenses. The Navy informed its sister service that "the helicopter was not to cross the front lines until the downed pilot had actually been located by high performance planes, and there were sufficient flak suppression planes present."

Helicopters demonstrated their value in a host of other roles, to include the medical evacuation of wounded and transport of personnel and supplies. Helicopters also began testing their capabilities in antisubmarine warfare. Naval aviators quickly became proficient in the execution of these missions. The Korean War was the nursery for the most important functions of naval helicopters today.

one hour of the plane's scheduled time on station. Some spotters were not familiar with spotting procedures. *None* of them exhibited much skill in locating targets and spotting the fall of shot on the target. It is believed that most of this trouble was due to inadequate pilot training in naval gunfire spotting, and the remainder due to the poor visibility from the plane and high aircraft speeds.

Despite these drawbacks, cooperation between ship and aircraft could yield dividends—and not just for the bombardment vessel. One demonstration of how ships could help aircraft occurred on 6 June 1951 near Wonsan. The destroyer *Joseph P. Kennedy Jr.* (DD-850) located a convoy of nearly two hundred trucks and then illuminated it for night bombers that destroyed many of the vehicles. Ships gave even more direct aid by suppressing enemy antiaircraft batteries, enabling aircraft to bomb more accurately and with less risk.

SPECIAL
OPERATIONS

SUBMARINES AND SURFACE WARSHIPS supported clandestine operations north of the front line. Naval vessels landed raiding parties, intelligence agents, and underwater demolition teams; supported them ashore; and picked them up when circumstances dictated.

Clandestine operations included large raids behind enemy lines. Most of these operations were mounted on the west coast where numerous small islands proved ideal as listening posts or bases for guerrilla raids. In 1951, these operations typically involved British or U.S. warships supporting ROK naval units. For example, on 27 June a raid at Chong Ye-Ri inflicted casualties on the enemy and blew up two of his ammunition dumps. In early September, two hundred ROK guerrillas supported by UN naval gunfire stormed ashore in a raid. In late November, the pattern was repeated with a raid on Ka-do.

Meanwhile, near Songjin on the east coast in late May, the destroyer *Stickell* (DD-888) and the frigate *Burlington* (PF-51) landed a raiding party, which destroyed three steel-decked junks. On 7 June, the destroyer *Rupertus* (DD-851) dispatched a raiding party, which grabbed several North Korean prisoners. Toward the end of 1951, destroyer transport *Herbert A. Bass* (APD-124) twice put ashore Royal Marine commandos who tried unsuccessfully to sever enemy communications.

Overall, these raids were successful enough that in the next year, the several covert agencies operating on the west coast were unified under one

An ROK naval officer and a U.S. Navy officer question a captured North Korean fisherman in September 1952 about the location of fishing nets off the enemy coast. The allied naval officers were conducting Operation Fishnet, part of the UN effort to cut food supplies to enemy troops. (National Archives)

umbrella organization: Covert Clandestine and Related Activities, Korea, known as CCRAK. On the other side of the peninsula, the Navy cooperated with a similar organization under the Army (called T. F. Kirkland) in sponsoring guerrilla activities. These friendly personnel ashore occasionally spotted the fall of naval gunfire.

In support of these hit-and-run raids, the UN command seized coastal islands off northwestern Korea. These positions proved valuable for intelligence collection and guerrilla support. Additionally the islands provided forward radar installations for the Air Force against the MiG bases just across the Yalu as well as refuges for UN fliers in trouble.

All these UN activities proved so galling to the Communists that they mounted amphibious operations to recover the islands, beginning in November 1951. On 30 November, Chinese Communist troops, traveling in wooden boats propelled by outdoor motors and supported by mortar fire from junks, attacked Taehwa-do in the Yalu Gulf. UN forces, covered by gunfire from the destroyer HMS *Cockade*, evacuated the island. Next to be overrun were Ung-do and Changyang-do.

By the end of the year, most of the bases on both coasts were in enemy hands. The Navy now undertook responsibility for the defense of those islands remaining under UN control—and set up a special command, the Island Defense Elements, built mainly around garrisons of ROK marines. The tide swung back. In late February 1952, an enemy force of about 245 men attacked Yang-do off Songjin on the east coast. The ROK garrison repulsed it. Action reached intense peaks, with the fate of islands seesawing back and forth. Yongwi-do on the west coast changed hands four times in May 1952.

During the period, U.S. Navy UDTs operated against various enemy objectives, the most unusual being enemy fishing nets. UDT platoons equipped with heavy cable cutters and saw-toothed knives destroyed the nets. For example, in the summer of 1952 the high-speed transport *Diachenko*, with elements of UDT 5 embarked, and two ROKN motor torpedo boats (MTBs) conducted six missions during which they destroyed two large nets, three sampans, and various buildings. They also took five prisoners. Another such success occurred when the destroyer transport *Weiss* (APD-135), UDT 3, and two ROKN MTBs undertook nine missions along the northeast coast of Korea where they destroyed five nets and an equal number of sampans as well as bagging forty-four POWs.

Four raids in the first half of 1952—two by the high-speed transport *Wantuck* (APD-125) and two by her sister ship *Horace A. Bass*—sought to capture prisoners and collect documents with the subsidiary mission. Despite the effort devoted, the Pacific Fleet concluded that some of the landings "failed completely. . . . Actual accomplishments have not been impressive considering the time and effort devoted to planning. Enemy vigilance, early detection and opposition forced early withdrawal of the raiding party in some cases."

As the war continued, these efforts at fostering war in the enemy's backyard grew ever tougher and less productive. The enemy's security was very tight, and friendly agents operated ashore only at terrible risk. Still, some observers concluded after the armistice that a good chance to harry the enemy had been largely wasted. The commander of Task Force 95 remarked: "It is possible that the advantages available through Task Force 95's complete control of the sea were not fully exploited in a positive sense. Only in the last few weeks was a start made in carrying out raids along the east coast by the Partisan Command."

One of the more unusual employments of ships in the bombardment role was on the Han River in support of the UN negotiators in the summer and fall of 1951. The ships engaged in a "naval demonstration" operated only a few miles southwest of the negotiating table at Kaesong. Communist negotiators had asserted that their troops occupied the Yonan and Ongjin peninsulas; if sustained, the claim would give the enemy control of the seaward approaches to Seoul. Following the intervention by air and surface forces of several UN nations, a Pacific Fleet report concluded: "The naval gunfire, within hearing distance of the conference table, nullified Communist delegates' contentions that they controlled this 200 square miles of land area south of 38°N." The UN command cancelled the Han River demonstration when the Communists agreed in November to a provisional armistice line.

Apart from supporting the UN negotiators, the gunnery ships found work in a host of missions. They fired to support friendly troops ashore, minesweepers, and commando and guerrilla raids. They also interdicted enemy supply routes and harassed enemy garrisons along the coast, especially at Hungnam, Songjin, and Wonsan.

The naval missions of the interdiction campaign aimed at cutting the Communist logistical lifelines were dubbed Operations Package and Derail. These naval air and surface efforts focused on chokepoints in the Communist transportation net, especially along the coastal railroad. The Navy committed major resources to this campaign. For example, in January 1952, warships delegated to bombardment duties included one battleship, three cruisers, thirty-nine destroyers, and eight frigates. On rare occasions, these ships scored major and visible successes, as when the destroyer Orleck in July 1952 caught a train between tunnels and wrecked its ten boxcars loaded with ordnance.

The bigger the naval gun, the more effective at cutting the rail lines. In 1952, New Jersey fired thirty-one times at bridges, expending an average of twenty-five rounds per shoot. Her performance was rated as effective on a majority of occasions. In March of that same year, *Wisconsin* went north to strike against the railroad at Songjin. She closed three tunnel entrances—and consequently the coastal railroad itself—for three days. This shoot was considered "extremely gratifying."

Naval gunfire proved equally valuable in backing UN ground units at the front. Marines, soldiers, and ROK troops all expressed gratitude for the effective support they received. Extracts from action reports and assessments included such accolades as "The devastating effect of 16-inch fire against the enemy's dug-in troops and enemy MSR [major supply route] was repeatedly demonstrated and attested." "Battleship NGFS [naval gunfire support] was valued most highly by Ground Force Commanders." Late in the war, when bitter fighting raged all along the front, naval observers believed that "naval gunfire support, particularly by the battleship, was highly effective at the eastern terminus of the battle line."

Cruiser and destroyer gunfire was equally welcome, not least by ROK units that often lacked the amount of artillery support accorded U.S. ground forces. On 24 November 1952, *Helena* backed up units in the hard-pressed ROK 5th Infantry Division. After the action, the heavy cruiser claimed to have destroyed or damaged five 76-mm guns, four mortar positions, several enemy buildings and shelters, and twenty bunkers. Following a November 1951 bombardment by destroyer *De Haven* (DD-727), the commanding general of the ROK I Corps extended congratulations to the warship for her illumination and fire support which contributed to the death of 608 enemy soldiers, including twelve officers. In May 1951, a shore fire-control party reported officially that *Helena*; the destroyers *Orleck*, *Fiske* (DD-842), and *Buck* (DD-761); and the British destroyer HMS *Cockade* "saved ROK Army units in area from complete annihilation."

Naval gunfire support proved particularly lethal against enemy soldiers in the open, whether on the attack or in retreat. U.S. Army troops valued naval gunfire support for its two advantages over their own organic artillery. First, warships could move north of the front and then fire at enemy forces on the reverse slopes of ridgelines. Second, by going up the coast, warships were able to reach well beyond the range of Army artillery. The principal—sometimes the only—complaint that ground troops made about naval gunfire support was that there was not enough of it.

In the last two years of the war, bombardment kept pace with the ebb and flow of combat. Numbers are sometimes telling, and the scale of gunfire support can be partly gauged by ammunition expenditure figures.

In one week in October 1951, *Toledo* alone fired 850 rounds of 8-inch while supporting the 1st Marine Division. When this level of support is calculated for many ships over many months, the gunnery effort takes on extraordinary proportions. From May 1951 to March 1952, UN warships undertook about twenty thousand gunfire missions in which they fired more than 414,000 projectiles, the large majority 5-inch.

On the grading scale for the effectiveness of the missions, the top rating was "highly successful." Broken down by caliber, the battleships scored at this level with two-thirds of their 16-inch projectiles; the heavy cruisers with one-half of their 8-inch; and all vessels with one-third of their 5-inch rounds. Surprisingly, the lowest score went to the light cruiser 6-inch, of which only one-fifth of the missions ranked in the top category. Occasionally ships got so close to shore that they opened up with their antiaircraft batteries, as in early August 1951, when several units fired 11,703 40-mm and 1,946 20-mm into the Songjin-Chongjin area.

Some ordnance experts calculated that the Navy shot more rounds in the Korean War than in World War II. Little wonder, given that the gunnery warships operated on one bombardment station around the clock for weeks on end. This practice led the Sailors to become familiar with the terrain and enemy dispositions and, in the opinion of some officers, resulted in greater effectiveness. Such employments were routine and arduous at the same time. Occasionally breaking the tedium, a task group formed around a battleship or cruiser would dart forward to shell a high-value area such as Hamhung. Whether on such a strike or on a more routine gun-line deployment, ships came to general quarters at dawn and dusk to guard against potential Communist aircraft attack. Facing the more tangible danger of enemy coastal artillery fire, UN ships shot more than half their missions at night.

Following a September 1952 deployment off Wonsan, an unusually detailed action report from the destroyer *Barton* revealed many of the human realities that prolonged bombardment duty entailed:

> Detrimental to morale was the necessary requirement (in the heat of summer) that all idlers remain off the weather decks during daylight hours and that topside work be held to a minimum, as in any part of the harbor the ship was well within range of enemy fire. Also very difficult was the problem of sleeping in the CPO [chief petty officer] quarters and in the large after living compartment during night bombardment because of the noise and shock from firing of Mounts 51 and 53, respectively. These problems were hardly susceptible to correction.

Another, remedial problems quickly developed. The incessant firing shortly began shaking loose fine particles of fiberglass insulation from the overhead, which continuously blanketed the upper tier bunks in [the after living compartment] and many bunks in other living compartments on the first platform deck, rendering them uninhabitable. The only solution was in "hot-bunking," which is in itself a demoralizing practice. The predicament was accentuated by the continuous receipt on replenishment days of more men assigned to the ship for duty so that upon departure from Wonsan there were onboard for duty, including staff, 377 enlisted men and 25 officers, with total authorized berthing for 333 persons. With regard to the problem of the fiberglass insulation it is interesting to note than in the report of operations made by the *Barton* covering the entire Okinawa Campaign of World War II involving 2 months of strenuous shore bombardment, the greatest single factor detrimental to morale was stated emphatically by the Commanding Officer to be the fiberglass dust.

Crew morale normally held up well despite such difficulties, with one destroyer division commander assessing his Sailors as "generally eager and capable." Relief from the bombardment routine came when the gunnery ships joined the carrier task force or screened high-value units like troop transports or replenishment ships. The captain of *Helena* remembered that his cruiser would spend a month lending her 8-inch guns in fire support, then steam with the carriers for a month, and finally head for Yokosuka where the crew would enjoy a deserved leave, and the ship would receive needed upkeep and battle repair. But the demand for gunfire support vessels was so great that maintenance periods were frequently cut short, often below the fleet minimum requirements.

Many naval leaders wondered if all this effort paid corresponding dividends. While the expenditure of ammunition was prodigious, hard intelligence about its effects was meager. Surface warriors complained frequently of the paucity of resources allocated to the collection and interpretation of intelligence. On-the-spot assessment frequently proved impossible because of the craggy terrain or the blanket of night. Photoreconnaissance was rarely made available to the gunnery ships. Sailors voiced their frustration with such comments, as "Commands responsible for target selection cannot intelligently exercise that function without accurate intelligence." Or, "Paucity of intelligence prevents accurate assessment and evaluation of results obtained from naval gunfire." The lack of hard data coupled with the routine and never-ending nature of the bombardment missions eroded the confidence of many Sailors in the value of their contribution to the war effort.

Especially suspect was unobserved "harassing" and interdiction fire. The expenditure of "huge quantities of all calibers of ammunition" in these missions led one Pacific Fleet report at the end of 1951 to conclude that "the results obtained are considered to be but a fraction of what might have been possible with observed fire." Troops on the ground were more sanguine on this issue, attesting repeatedly to the value of unobserved shellings. In counterpoint, some Navy officers considered that even allowing for the psychological benefits accorded soldiers and Marines, ammunition expenditure for this purpose was too lavish.

Given that the enemy avoided moving during daylight, late-war evaluations stressed the need for better night interdiction techniques. Responding to the requirement, some ships experimented with using their radars to detect vehicles and trains, a technique that seemed to hold great promise. In 1952, the heavy cruisers *Toledo* and *Los Angeles* had on board specially trained radar operators who attempted to track moving objects against a land backdrop. Their radars sometimes picked up contacts but could not lock on them long enough for a fire control solution.

By 1953, some ships were doing better. The escort destroyer *Taylor* (DDE-468) reported in March that the operators of the 3-inch/50 gunfire control radar were able to pick out and track trucks, trains, and even individual soldiers moving close to the shore. The ship took many of these targets under fire and thereby considerably reduced enemy activity in the area.

These experiments aside, the commander of one cruiser division spoke for many Sailors shortly after the war when he noted that significant targets of opportunity appeared only rarely. Many observers expressed grudging admiration for the Communist repair capabilities. As Pacific Fleet evaluators noted late in the war, the coastal railroads were bombarded by projectiles of all sizes from 40-mm to 16-inch in "unbelievable" quantities, but the enemy continued to operate his trains.

Of course, the enemy devoted considerable resources to countering the heavy UN interdiction effort. The U.S. Navy late in the war calculated the size of the enemy railroad repair organization at twenty thousand workers, with an equivalent force dedicated to fixing the roads.

However, by stockpiling repair materials along the lines (and roads), "very determined" repair crews patched railroad cuts in a few hours. The obvious counter was to shell the repair crews. By one U.S. calculation, destroyers needed to stand offshore and fire at least ten shells per hour to stymie repair parties.

As these work gangs became more efficient, so did the Communist coastal defenses, which grew in number and capability. Early in the war, enemy coastal artillery pieces were few and relatively passive. By 1952, U.S. naval commentators had noted a marked transformation. Backed with Soviet equipment and advisors, the enemy placed in caves tanks, self-propelled guns, and artillery pieces on railway flat cars. This equipment would roll forward to the cave mouth, fire a shot, and quickly reverse to escape the inevitable hail of counterbattery fire.

Some of the Communist guns were radar controlled and capable of firing accurately on UN warships at ranges up to ten miles. As early as 1951, the coastal artillery began employing proximity-fuse shells to give airbursts over naval vessels. Moreover, the gun emplacements, originally unconnected, were stitched together into a coherent and effective system by 1953.

Even in 1951 the enemy guns could sting. The destroyer minesweeper *Thompson* on a 14 June gunfire mission near Songjin moved to within three thousand yards of the beach in order to use her 40-mm. Seizing the opportunity, the enemy wheeled out from under camouflage four 3-inch batteries. As *Thompson* reversed course and withdrew, North Korean guns hit her fourteen times. The warship suffered damage to her radars, communications gear, and one gun director. Worse, the enemy killed three of her crew and injured four others. Two months later, the destroyer *Uhlmann* (DD-687) returned the favor when she got into a fierce half-hour duel with seven enemy guns. The enemy fire was so heavy that the U.S. Sailors counted 117 splashes, but the Communist gunners scored no hits. *Uhlmann* did better in retaliation, getting off 240 rounds of 5-inch and claiming destruction of five of the enemy pieces.

Such duels continued until the armistice. The destroyer *Southerland* (DDR-743) fought seven shore batteries in July 1952 and took four direct hits. Even single shells could occasionally achieve a "mission kill" on a ship. For instance, on 13 August 1952, the destroyer *John R. Pierce* (DD-753) took a direct hit on the starboard after signal searchlight. The ship's action report graphically recounted the damage: "It was this hit that sprayed shrapnel over the starboard side of the signal bridge and air defense platform, severed antennas, waveguides, cables, halyards, and after starboard stay of the mast, wounded the 40mm control officer, and resulted in loss of all high frequency communications due to the fallen antennas."

Even more serious was a hit on *Alfred A. Cunningham* (DD-752). On 14 October 1952, the destroyer was struck directly on the stern. The enemy shell blew a depth charge to pieces and scattered burning explosive over the starboard side and fantail. Crewmen rushed aft and, by hand, threw overboard a second depth charge that had caught on fire.

While covering minesweepers, the destroyer escort *Lewis* (DE-535) was put in mortal peril by a 76-mm coastal artillery piece that hit her twice on 27 November 1952 off Umi-do. Although a relatively small projectile weighing only about fifteen pounds, the first shell punched through the hull into the engineering plant where it penetrated the steam drum of a boiler. As superheated steam rushed into the engineering spaces, the engine room crew attempted to shut down the plant. They were only partially successful before six died at their posts, overcome by the extreme heat and suffocated by the carbon dioxide released automatically from the fire-fighting system. Steam then filled the pilothouse, forcing the transfer of steering control to the aft position. Compounding the peril, *Lewis*'s speed dropped off. As fires burned in the engine room, the surviving Sailors there managed to crossconnect the plant. Despite severe damage, the destroyer escort made smoke and covered successfully the withdrawal of the minesweepers she was protecting.

Larger ships occasionally attracted the attention of enemy artillery. The heavy cruiser *Bremerton* (CA-130), while backing a ROK regiment, came under fire from enemy 76-mm guns, which showered the heavy cruiser with shell fragments. One of these, a nose fuse stamped with Soviet markings, ended up on the deck by turret two. Not even battleships were immune, as the hits on *New Jersey* at Wonsan and a second on *Wisconsin* at Songjin showed. The last victim of enemy shore batteries was *Saint Paul*, holed under the waterline off Wonsan on 11 July 1953. With a certain poetic justice, that heavy cruiser fired the last projectile of the war on 27 July.

It is worth reflecting on the fact, however, that despite hitting a number of UN naval vessels with shellfire, Communists failed to sink even one warship during the Korean War. In summary, interdiction occupied much of the attention of the surface navy during the last two years of the war. The gunnery ships thus complemented the efforts of the carrier navy and the Air Force. As was the huge endeavor mounted by the aviation arms, the scale of the surface warfare effort was by any index—numbers of ships committed, ammunition expended, time spent on the line—most impressive. And yet, many naval leaders evaluating the campaign, whether during the war or after, found the payoff incommensurate with the effort.

At the end of 1951, Pacific Fleet assessors concluded that naval gunfire combined with air attack had broken some enemy supply lines, but the "enemy had built up his forces all along the battle line and maintained an adequate flow of logistics to these forces." In early 1952, Operations Package and Derail more closely focused UN air and surface efforts on key chokepoints. Pacific Fleet concluded, "In spite of the combined air and surface interdiction efforts of all the Services the enemy succeeded in strengthening his forces and defenses along the coasts and battleline." By January 1953, Communist forces were, in the estimation of Pacific Fleet, in the best shape ever regarding equipment, supplies, and food.

In drawing major lessons from the Korean War, the Navy concluded pointedly, "Primitive transportation systems combined with masses of coolie labor successfully defied a colossal effort by modern machines of war."

THE SIEGE OF WONSAN

ON 16 FEBRUARY 1951, 210 South Korean marines, backed by U.S. destroyer gunfire, landed on the tiny island of Sin-do in Wonsan harbor on the eastern coast of North Korea, thus beginning the longest naval siege of the twentieth century. Maintained for 861 days (with but one short break) until the suspension of hostilities on 27 July 1953, the effort reflected in many ways the larger war: UN firepower, technological sophistication, and dogged determination to prevail matched by Communist numbers, low technology, and dogged determination to persevere.

In the fall of 1950, Wonsan had been the target of General MacArthur's hard right punch to trap the North Korean forces fleeing his left hook thrown at Inchon. This second amphibious operation, however, went awry, frustrated by enemy minefields. The invading fleet had cruised back and forth for days off the port, while minesweepers cleared lanes for the amphibious craft. Seasick Marines dubbed the affair "Operation Yo-Yo." By the time they went ashore, UN troops driving up from the south had flushed the Communists from the city. Chinese Communist entry into the conflict in the following months prompted MacArthur to withdraw from the port on 7 December.

In early 1951, Rear Adm. Allan E. Smith proposed an operation against Wonsan to regain the initiative and to bring sea power to bear on the land battle. Smith envisioned putting several hundred ROK troops on islands in the harbor to hold those until the front flowed north and to impede Communist remining of the bay, so laboriously cleared the preceding fall.

And what a harbor it was! Relatively tideless, ice free, and protected from storms, the 300-square-mile body of water had been called by the Japanese the "Harbor of Refuge." The city of Wonsan, an industrial center prior to the war, had a population of about a hundred thousand and served as a nexus for railroads and roads running both north-south and across the peninsula. Its importance seemed mirrored by its great beauty, with islands dotting the harbor and the Taebaek Mountains framing the gentle curve of the shoreline.

Soon after landing on Sin-do, UN troops occupied six more islands in the bay. Initially conceived as a temporary expedient, UN presence on the islands and in the waters of the enemy harbor turned out to be prolonged as the front stabilized south of Wonsan. UN troops on island tours of duty generally lasting four months lived a troglodyte existence under Communist mortar and machine-gun fire during the daytime from Hodo Pando and Kalma-gak. Landing craft delivering food, water, and ammunition came in during the night.

As the battle front stabilized near the 38th parallel, advocates of the siege advanced a host of reasons (critics said rationalizations) for continuing the operation: it diverted large numbers of Communist troops from the front lines; the UN-held islands posed a threat to the Communist flank; and UN gunships could help with the aerial interdiction campaign against Communist supply lines. The harbor islands were useful for gathering intelligence and for supporting guerrilla activities on the mainland. UN aviators in trouble would find Wonsan harbor a refuge indeed. Its occupation gave a psychological lift to UN forces, especially the Navy, and conversely hurt enemy morale. These arguments persuaded such top officers as Admiral Sherman, Chief of Naval Operations, and General Ridgway, Commander in Chief, Far East, to sanction continuation of the siege.

If the primary objective of the operation was to divert enemy resources from the front, it was a success. UN forces were deployed only three thousand yards from the principal Communist supply route to the eastern sector of the entire peninsula. North Korean forces initially tried but failed to throw the UN troops out by counterlandings. The Communists then brought up artillery. Dug into hillsides and artfully concealed in tunnels, the Communist guns (manned almost entirely by North Koreans) num-

The rugged mountains of North Korea dwarf U.S. destroyer *Leonard T. Mason* (DD-852) as she patrols in readiness to open fire on Communist positions spotted ashore. (National Archives)

bered more than one thousand by 1952. In percentage terms, this figure made up 55 percent of all North Korean antiaircraft and coastal defense weapons; 160 of the guns were sizable enough to be a danger to warships in the harbor. Supporting this formidable tube force, sixty thousand troops guarded against another Inchon.

If Wonsan sponged up Communist resources, it soaked up UN strength as well. Soon four or five minesweepers, their tender, and a tug were permanently on station backed by two or three destroyers. Officially designated as the Wonsan Defense and Blockade Unit (Task Unit 95.2.1), it was headed by a commander titled the "Mayor of Wonsan" with his symbol of office a large, gilded wooden key, which he transferred to his relief. Twenty-eight naval officers held the honorific; the key eventually became a prize exhibit in the U.S. Naval Academy Museum.

The unsung minecraft were essential to maintaining the siege. During the spring and summer of 1951, minesweepers cleared and recleared ever-larger areas of the bay, during one short period harvesting 140 mines. The Communists countered by laying mines from small craft (a sampan might carry only two mines) and even floating the lethal devices into the harbor suspended under logs or watertight drums and kegs (shades of 1776 and the Revolutionary War in New York City).

Although the great majority of mines were simple contact mines, some supposedly dating back to the Russian navy of Nicholas II, a few were triggered by magnetic pistols. Early in 1952, the Communists introduced a specialized antiboat mine the size of a beach ball. Floating just below the surface, these weapons could most easily be detected from helicopters.

Constant sweeping was no guarantee of safety as the fate of South Korean PC-704 on 26 December 1951 showed when that vessel struck a mine off Yo-do; the ROKN recovered the bodies of twenty of its Sailors from the craft. Not only was minesweeping inherently dangerous, but also minecraft during sweeps were quite vulnerable to enemy gunfire, "due to their slow speed, lack of freedom of movement, and the necessity for following a definite track." As U.S. destroyer-minesweeper *Thompson* tackled a moored minefield on 19 November 1952, she was taken under heavy fire; but her good luck held; of 174 rounds directed at her, only one hit.

The U.S. Navy went over to night sweeps only. Darkness might cloak the minecraft from enemy artillery but it presented its own hazards, as any mines cut loose from their moorings were very difficult to spot bobbing on the surface. So nerve-wracking was this duty that one section of the bay was nicknamed Ulcer Gulch by the Sailors. Destroyer crews recognized the difficult and hazardous nature of this work by frequently donating their ice cream ration to the sweepers. In fact, the relationship between the sweepers and the gunnery ships was a symbiotic one. Obviously, without clear waters, the larger surface warships could not safely operate inshore. Thus, minesweeper crews could say with justifiable pride, "Where the Fleet goes, we've been!"

For the sweepers to operate—even at night—in the teeth of Communist artillery, they needed cover from the surface warships. Usually the bigger the gun doing the shooting, the better. Early in the siege, LSMRs fired 5-inch rockets by the score. At one point three of the specialized vessels shot off 4,903 rounds in fifteen minutes. But the LSMRs were slow and unarmored. Their vulnerability to counterbattery fire soon confined them to surprise night operations.

Destroyers made up the largest ships permanently under the command of the Mayor of Wonsan and were generally assigned to him for thirty days. One destroyer skipper reported, "Needless to say this is a grueling experience for the ships but also an exhilarating one. It constitutes the ship's most active and interesting assignment while in WESTPAC [Western Pacific] . . . ." Frequently engaging in "stirring gun duels with enemy shore batteries," the destroyers often expended ammunition at an astonishing rate. For example, on 17 July 1951, destroyers *Blue* (DD-387), *Alfred A. Cunningham*, and *O'Brien* (DD-725) shot off 2,336 rounds of 5-inch in less than five hours of counterbattery work. Despite this volume of generally accurate fire, postwar evaluators expressed their disappointment. One commanding officer wrote: "Against well dug in targets such as the Wonsan gun emplacements, it [5-inch] had limited effect in even silencing a battery. At Wonsan, this ship has observed enemy gun flashes appearing through the smoke of our own 5" shells bursting on the target."

Another officer adopted a larger view: "Wonsan Harbor is a good example of the type target that can and cannot profitably be taken under fire by destroyers. Working parties were invariably dispersed by the use of VT [variable time] ammunition, command posts were frequently knocked out and small boats destroyed but very little damage was inflicted on gun positions or bunkers. It remained for the 'heavies' to come in and bury those targets."

In March 1951 light cruiser *Manchester* (CL-83) entered Wonsan, soon followed by heavy cruisers and battleships. When one of these big warships was scheduled to arrive, an intelligence officer living on one of the harbor islands would come aboard to provide the crew with the latest target information. Occasionally VIPs would view the enemy coast from island vantage points or from the bridge of a bombardment vessel. Battleship *Iowa*, commanded by Captain Smedberg and later Capt. Joshua W. Cooper, frequently dropped anchor right inside the harbor, sometime within two thousand yards of the enemy emplacements.

The results of naval bombardment could be impressive. One commanding officer of the heavy cruiser *Helena* remembered, "[We hit a field piece] absolutely square on. You could see wheels and parts flying in the air—we really clobbered it." On 23 September 1952, battleship *Iowa*, with Gen. Mark W. Clark, Vice Adm. Robert R. Briscoe, and Adm. Jocko Clark

Shore batteries emplaced on Hwangto-do, the harbor island closest to the city of Wonsan, engage light cruiser *Manchester* in June 1953. Despite ongoing negotiations for a truce, North Korean coastal artillery continued to harass UN ships. (National Archives)

on board, shot at the Hodo Pando guns and was gratified by a "magnificent secondary explosion . . . the smoke went several thousand feet in the air. These particular guns were permanently silenced." *Iowa* skipper Cooper reminisced, "I don't know where the average one [VIP] went when he left us, but if the Army gave [him] as good a show as we did, he was able to collect enough data to make him a very thoughtful man."

Counterbattery fire was just one of the reasons for the commitment of the gunships. Destroyers, cruisers, and battleships also rendered valuable assistance to UN aircraft by firing flak suppression missions with airbursts over the Communist antiaircraft positions. The warships also devoted much effort to the interdiction campaign, called by the U.S. Air Force Operation Strangle. In just two months, naval gunfire, coupled with air strikes, made daylight movements costly for Communist forces pushing south through Wonsan.

However gratifying this success, the Communists reacted by traveling at night. To halt this traffic, UN aircraft and warships teamed up: the aircraft spotted for naval gunfire, and the ships fired illumination rounds to help the aviators. Evaluators concluded that this effort did hamper rail traffic and forced some trucks inland. Still, it became clear that these joint efforts were only partially successful. Timber bridges with concrete foundations proved surprisingly resistant to shells and bombs. Enemy repair efforts elicited the grudging admiration of UN naval leaders. One Pacific Fleet report concluded in early 1952: "Trains and trucks still pass through Wonsan nearly every night and troops and supplies are still housed in the city." From the harbor islands, observers sometimes counted the headlights of three hundred trucks moving south in a single night, a total made more discouraging by the fact that for every truck with its headlights on, three or four were running blacked out.

The enemy shot back, too, albeit ineffectually at first. Ships frequently anchored to simplify fire control solutions (and for fear of mines), but on 20 May 1951, destroyer *Brinkley Bass* (DD-887) lost one man killed and two wounded. The next day, a nervy North Korean battery on Kalma-gak hit turret one of the battleship *New Jersey*, causing only cosmetic damage, but then an airburst killed one Sailor and wounded three more. These men were the only battle casualties suffered by that vessel in four wars. Given the dangers of firing on the "heavies," the Communist artillery generally fell silent when a battleship or cruiser entered the bay. Captain Smedberg of *Iowa* concluded: "They wouldn't open up on a big ship because they were afraid of giving away their position, and once they gave it away they lost their guns. We'd blow them out."

Still, as the *New Jersey* episode showed, a big ship had no guarantee of immunity. Captain Smedberg recalled: "There's no such prickly feeling as being in a completely landlocked harbor, which Wonsan Harbor is, knowing that there were guns in all the hills and caves all around you." At one point, fog blanketed the harbor: "You could get up on level 8 of the *Iowa* and you were just above the fog. You could just see the tips of our masts sticking up through the fog. That would have been the most marvelous time for them to open up with all their guns because we couldn't see anything to shoot back at. I never could understand why they didn't do it."

Over time, the Communists improved their defenses, both qualitatively and quantitatively. As they added plotting boards and spotting stations, their fire control procedures and accuracy improved. In the last months of the war, the enemy was hitting UN destroyers on a regular basis. Ships responded by reducing to the bare minimum the number of personnel exposed topside. Changing course frequently and staying constantly on the move at speeds of at least fifteen knots (and sometimes much higher), the destroyers performed what came to be called the War Dance.

Despite frequent Communist claims of sinking ships (after three claims for one ship, the enemy said the U.S. had repainted hull numbers to save face), the coastal guns inflicted no fatal wounds. Some U.S. analysts worried that such a loss was simply a matter of time, however. A Pacific Fleet evaluation made shortly after the war concluded: "If hostilities had continued, a destroyer inevitably would have suffered a temporarily disabling hit in the steering system. Steaming at twenty-seven knots, surrounded by islands and minefields, with rudder on and without steering control, it is highly improbable that this unfortunate would ever have left Wonsan."

Given the hazards of the gunnery missions and their seemingly slight return, the siege had to be justified by additional objectives. One that developed rather quickly was the rescue of UN aviators. The Navy's first helicopter carrier, *LST-799*, began operations in Wonsan Bay in March 1951. At first, curious enemy troops waved at the helicopters hovering low over the city. This attitude changed when the aviators dropped grenades on North Korean soldiers using the latrines. The fliers soon found steadier employment spotting mines and plucking airmen from the drink or from behind enemy lines. By November 1952, helicopters from *LST-799* had rescued mostly from Wonsan Bay itself twenty-four UN fliers. One beneficiary of this attention, the commanding officer of Fighter Squadron 54 on carrier *Essex*, was thrice plucked from Wonsan harbor in a period of barely four months, prompting a wardroom sign: "Use caution when ditching damaged airplanes in Wonsan harbor. Don't hit CDR [Paul] Gray."

A solution to this danger was the construction of an emergency strip. Calculations revealed that its costs would be more than offset if it saved a single plane. Navy Seabees finished the work on Yo-do in sixteen days, twenty-nine days fewer than expected, in June 1952. During the next month alone, seven Corsairs low on fuel used the refuge named in honor of Admiral Briscoe.

In early 1953, the siege entered its third year; as a truce became more likely, the level of violence at Wonsan increased. From April through June, the Communists fired two thousand rounds at the siege vessels; U.S. war-

High-ranking Chinese and North Korean military delegates flanked by Chinese military guards leave the conference area at Panmunjom in May 1952. (National Archives)

ships responded in kind. Symptomatic of the bitterness of the war, destroyers *Wiltsie* (DD-716) and *Porter* (DD-800) and cruiser *Bremerton* pumped shells into Wonsan up to one minute prior to the 2200 cease-fire of 27 July 1953. A Pacific Fleet report read: "This city . . . is now a cluttered mass of ruins."

The siege lasted for 861 straight days with the only break caused by Typhoon Karen on 18 August 1952, which drove the blockaders out to deep water. UN postmortems of the siege were skeptical of its "worth-whileness." As one interim Pacific Fleet report observed, "there has been insufficient intelligence to properly evaluate the effectiveness of a large proportion of the firing conducted by the surface forces." Without access to North Korean records, this assessment still holds.

Wonsan represents the Korean War in microcosm. Begun as a tempo-rary expedient, it dragged on far beyond anyone's most pessimistic expec-tations. Although of increasingly dubious merit, it was continued in part

Armistice signing at Panmunjon, 27 July 1953. General Clark signs the document as Vice Admiral Briscoe, Commander Naval Forces, Far East, and Vice Admiral Clark, Commander Seventh Fleet, witness the historic moment that ended the Korean War. (Naval Historical Center)

because its abandonment would have been seen as an admission of defeat. From a much more limited intranaval perspective, the siege, as did the larger war, showed that the surface navy, far from being an antediluvian relic in an air power age, still possessed great value. As one Sailor wrote, "To those who served there, Wonsan pointed up the need for balanced forces *within* our Navy."

MALCOLM MUIR JR. *is a military historian who received his degrees from Emory, Florida State, and Ohio State universities. Currently he serves on the faculty of the Virginia Military Institute where he is director of the John A. Adams '71 Center for Military History and Strategic Analysis. He has also held the Secretary of the Navy's Research Chair in Naval History and positions at Austin Peay State Uni-*

SEA POWER ON CALL

versity, the U.S. Military Academy, and the Air War College. Among his publications are Iowa Class Battleships: Iowa, New Jersey, Missouri, and Wisconsin *(Dorset, England: Blandford Press, 1987) and* Black Shoes and Blue Water: Surface Warfare in the U.S. Navy, 1945–1975 *(Washington: Naval Historical Center, 1996). The latter won the John Lyman Award given by the North American Society for Oceanic History for the best book published in 1996 on U.S. naval history. Muir also edited* The Human Tradition in the World War II Era, *published in 2001 by Scholarly Resources.*

Suggested Readings and Sources

PRIMARY SOURCES

THE OPERATIONAL ARCHIVES of the Naval Historical Center, Washington Navy Yard, D.C., hold most of the primary sources for these chapters. The extensive Korean War collection contains the Pacific Fleet Evaluation Reports representing the fleet's best effort to distill the lessons learned from the Korean War; action reports from Seventh Fleet ships and naval commands; the *Bulletin of Ordnance Information*; Rear Adm. James Doyle's lecture, 14 March 1974, Naval War College, Newport, Rhode Island; message files from the Office of the Chief of Naval Operations (microfilm reels TS–53–62); and the personal papers of Adm. Arthur D. Struble, Malcolm W. Cagle, and Frank A. Manson. The papers of Marine Corps officers Col. Robert D. Heinl and Gen. Oliver P. Smith are held in the Marine Corps University Archives in Quantico, Virginia.

Authors also mined the Oral History Collection at the U.S. Naval Institute, Annapolis, Maryland, which contains interviews of veteran leaders from the Korean War era and at the forefront in the struggle for integration in the Navy. These include interviews by Paul Stillwell with Cdr. Wesley A. Brown (1986), Vice Adm. Samuel A. Gravely Jr. (1986), and Cdr. John Wesley Lee Jr., as well as earlier interviews conducted by John T. Mason with Adm. Arleigh Burke (1979) and Adm. John S. Thach (1977). Some impressions came from author interviews with veterans recorded for the filming of The History Channel documentary "Fire and Ice: The Korean War."

Footnoted manuscripts of the original commemorative booklets are held by the series editor should readers wish to identify specific sources.

BOOKS

Alexander, James Edwin. *Inchon to Wonsan: From the Deck of a Destroyer in the Korean War*. Annapolis: Naval Institute Press, 1996.

Altoff, Gerald. *Amongst My Best Men: African Americans and the War of 1812*. Put-in-Bay, Ohio: The Perry Group, 1996.

Astor, Gerald. *The Right to Fight: A History of African Americans in the Military*. Novato, Calif.: Presidio Press, 1998.

Baer, George, W. *One Hundred Years of Sea Power: The U.S. Navy, 1890–1990*. Stanford, Calif.: Stanford University Press, 1994.

Barlow, Jeffrey G. *Revolt of the Admirals: The Fight for Naval Aviation, 1945–1950*. Washington: Naval Historical Center, 1994.

Bartlett, Merrill L. *Assault From the Sea*. Annapolis: Naval Institute Press, 1983.

Blair, Clair. *The Forgotten War: America in Korea 1950–1953*. New York: Times Books, 1987.

Bolster, W. Jeffrey. *Black Jacks: African American Seamen in the Age of Sail*. Cambridge, Mass.: Harvard University Press, 1997.

Cagle, Malcolm W., and Frank A. Manson. *The Sea War in Korea*. Annapolis: Naval Institute Press, 1957.

Cooper, Paul L. *Weekend Warriors*. Manhattan, Kan.: Sunflower University Press, 1996.

Dictionary of American Naval Fighting Ships. 8 vols. Washington: Naval Historical Center, 1959–1991.

Ferrell, Robert H., ed. *Off the Record: The Private Papers of Harry S. Truman*. New York: Harper & Row, 1980.

Field, James A., Jr. *United States Naval Operations, Korea*. Washington: Naval Historical Center, 1962. Also available online at http://www.history. navy.mil/books/field/index.htm and in *The Sea Services in the Korean War, 1950–1953*. Histories and Photographs to Commemorate the Fiftieth Anniversary of the Conflict. CD-ROM produced by the U.S. Naval Institute and Sonalysts, Inc., in conjunction with the historical offices of the U.S. Navy, Marine Corps, and Coast Guard.

Foner, Jack D. *Blacks and the Military in American History: A New Perspective*. New York: Praeger, 1974.

Friedman, Norman. *U.S. Aircraft Carriers: A Design History*. Annapolis: Naval Institute Press, 1983.

Gaddis, John Lewis. *We Now Know: Rethinking Cold War History*. New York: Oxford University Press, 1997.

Gorshkov, Soviet Admiral of the Fleet Sergei, *The Sea Power of the State*. Malabar, Fla.: Krieger, 1979.

Hallion, Richard P. *The Naval Air War in Korea*. Baltimore: Nautical & Aviation Publishing of America, 1986.

Heinl, Robert D. *Victory at High Tide: The Inchon-Seoul Campaign*. Philadelphia: J. B. Lippincott, 1967.

Jackson, Robert. *Air War Korea, 1950–1953*. Osceola, Wis.: Motorbooks International, 1998.

Joy, C. Turner. *How Communists Negotiate*. New York: Macmillian, 1955.

Jurika, Stephen, Jr., ed. *From Pearl Harbor to Vietnam: The Memoirs of Admiral Arthur W. Radford*. Stanford, Calif.: Hoover Institution Press, 1980.

Karig, Walter, Malcolm W. Cagle, and Frank A. Manson. *The War in Korea*. Vol. 6 of *Battle Report*. New York: Rinehart, 1952.

Kaufman, Burton I. *The Korean War: Challenges in Crisis, Credibility, and Command*. New York: Alfred A. Knopf, 1986.

Lansdown, John R.P. *With the Carriers in Korea*. Winslow, England: Crecy Publishing Ltd., 1997.

Love, Robert W. *History of the U.S. Navy*. Harrisburg, Penn.: Stackpole Books, 1992.

MacGregor, Morris J., Jr. *Defense Studies Series: Integration of the Armed Forces, 1940–1965*. Washington: U.S. Army Center of Military History, 1981.

——, and Bernard C. Nalty, eds. *Blacks in the United States Armed Forces: Basic Documents*, 13 volumes. Wilmington, Del.: Scholarly Resources, 1977.

Manchester, William. *American Caesar*. Boston: Little, Brown, 1978.

Matray, James I. *Historical Dictionary of the Korean War*. Westport, Conn.: Greenwood Press, 1991.

McCollum, Kenneth G., ed. *Dahlgren*. Dahlgren, Va.: Naval Surface Weapons Center, 1977.

McCullough, David. *Truman*. New York: Simon & Schuster, 1992.

Melia, Tamara Moser. *"Damn the Torpedoes": A Short History of U.S. Naval Mine Countermeasures, 1777–1991*. Washington: Naval Historical Center, 1991.

Michener, James A. *Selected Writings of James A. Michener*. New York: The Modern Library, 1957.

Montross, Lynn, Nicholas A. Canzona et al.. *U.S. Marine Operations in Korea, 1950–1953*. 5 vols. Washington: Historical Branch, Headquarters, U.S. Marine Corps, 1954–1972.

Muir, Malcolm, Jr. *The Iowa Class Battleships: Iowa, New Jersey, Missouri & Wisconsin*. Poole, Dorset: Blandford Press, 1987.

Nalty, Bernard C. *Strength for the Fight: A History of Black Americans in the Military*. New York: The Free Press, 1986.

Nelson, Dennis D. *The Integration of the Negro into the U.S. Navy*. New York: Octagon Books, 1982.

Neufeld, Jacob, and George W. Watson Jr., eds. *Coalition Warfare in the Korean War, 1950–1953*. Washington: U.S. Air Force History and Museums Program, 2005.

O'Rourke, G. G., with E. T. Wooldridge. *Night Fighters over Korea*. Annapolis: Naval Institute Press, 1998.

Potter, E. B. *Admiral Arleigh Burke*. New York: Random House, 1990.

Ramold, Steven J. *Slaves, Sailors, Citizens: African Americans in the Union Navy*. Dekalb: Northern Illinois University Press, 2002.

Shaw, Henry I., Jr., and Ralph W. Donnelly. *Blacks in the Marine Corps*. Washington: History and Museums Division, Headquarters, U.S. Marine Corps, 1988.

Stillwell, Paul. *Battleship Missouri: An Illustrated History*. Annapolis: Naval Institute Press, 1996.

———. *Battleship New Jersey: An Illustrated History*. Annapolis: Naval Institute Press, 1989.

———. *The Golden Thirteen: Recollections of the First Black Naval Officers*. Annapolis: Naval Institute Press, 1993.

Summers, Harry G., Jr. *Korean War Almanac*. New York: Facts on File, 1990.

Sweetman, Jack. *American Naval History: An Illustrated Chronology of the U.S. Navy and Marine Corps, 1775–Present*. Annapolis: Naval Institute Press, 1991.

Taylor, Theodore. *The Flight of Jesse Leroy Brown*. New York: Avon Books, 1998.

Uhlig, Frank, Jr. *How Navies Fight: The U.S. Navy and Its Allies*. Annapolis: Naval Institute Press, 1994.

Uya, Okun Edet. *From Slavery to Public Service: Robert Smalls, 1839–1915*. New York: Oxford University Press, 1977.

ARTICLES AND ESSAYS

Bernstein, Barton J. "The Truman Administration and the Korean War." In *The Truman Presidency*, edited by Michael J. Lacey. Cambridge: Cambridge University Press, 1989.

Chisholm, Donald. "Negotiated Joint Command Relationships: Korean War Amphibious Operations, 1950." *Naval War College Review* (Spring 2000).

Doyle, James H., and Arthur J. Mayer. "December 1950 at Hungnam." U.S. Naval Institute *Proceedings* 105 (April 1979).

Edwards, Harry W. "A Naval Lesson of the Korean Conflict." U.S. Naval Institute *Proceedings* 80 (December 1954).

Fleming, Thomas. "MacArthur's Pirate," *MHQ* 12 (Summer 2000).

Harrod, Frederick S. "Integration of the Navy (1941–1978)." U.S. Naval Institute *Proceedings* 105 (October 1979).

———. "Jim Crow in the Navy (1798–1941)." U.S. Naval Institute *Proceedings* (September 1979).

Heinl, Robert D., Jr. "The Gun Gap and How to Close It." U.S. Naval Institute *Proceedings* 91 (September 1965).

———. "Inchon, 1950." In *Assault From the Sea*, edited by Merrill L. Bartlett. Annapolis: Naval Institute Press, 1983.

Holly, David C. "The ROK Navy." U.S. Naval Institute *Proceedings* 78 (November 1952).

Marolda, Edward J. "Cold War to Violent Peace, 1945–1991." In *The Navy*, edited by William Holland. Washington: Naval Historical Foundation, 2000. Also available online at http://www.history.navy.mil/wars/coldwar-1.htm.

———. "Hostilities Along the China Coast." In *New Interpretations in Naval History: Selected Papers from the Eleventh Naval History Symposium*, edited by Robert W. Love Jr., Laurie Bogle, Brian Van DeMark, and Maochun Yu. Annapolis: Naval Institute Press, 2001.

———. "Hungnam Evacuation," "Charles Turner Joy," "Mine Warfare," "Naval Battles," "Republic of Korea Navy," "Arthur D. Struble." In *Encyclopedia of the Korean War*, edited by Spencer C. Tucker. Santa Barbara, Calif.: ABC-CLIO, 2000.

———. "Invasion Patrol: The Seventh Fleet in Chinese Waters." In *A New Equation: Chinese Intervention into the Korean War*, Colloquium on Contemporary History, No. 3. Washington: Naval Historical Center, 1990. Also available at http://www.history.navy.mil/colloquia/cch3.htm.

———. "The U.S. Navy and the Far Eastern Crisis, 1945–1953." In Proceedings of *The Korean War and the Changes of Military Relationships in Northeast Asia Conference*, Seoul, Republic of Korea, June 2005. Available in Navy Department Library, Washington Navy Yard, D.C.

———. "The U.S. Navy in the Korean War." In *The Korean War: An Encyclopedia*, edited by Stanley Sandler. New York: Garland Publishing Co., 1995.

———. "Wall of Steel: Sea Power and the Cold War in Asia." In *Maritime Power in the 20th Century: The Australian Experience,* edited by David Stevens. Sydney: Allen & Unwin, 1998.

Millett, Allan R. "Close Air Support in the Korean War, 1950–1953: A Tale of Two Systems." Research paper, 1980, Nimitz Library, Annapolis, Md.

Reynolds, Clark G. "Forrest Percival Sherman." In *The Chiefs of Naval Operations,* edited by Robert William Love Jr. Annapolis: Naval Institute Press, 1980.

Rosenberg, David Alan. "Arleigh Albert Burke." In *The Chiefs of Naval Operations,* edited by Robert William Love Jr. Annapolis: Naval Institute Press, 1980.

Weems, John E. "Black Wings of Gold." U.S. Naval Institute *Proceedings* (July 1983).

OTHER SOURCES

Korean War Naval Operations: A Bibliography, http://www.history.navy.mil/biblio/biblio6.htm.

The Sea Services in the Korean War, 1950–1953. Histories and Photographs to Commemorate the Fiftieth Anniversary of the Conflict. CD-ROM produced by the U.S. Naval Institute and Sonalysts, Inc., in conjunction with the historical offices of the U.S. Navy, Marine Corps, and Coast Guard.

Index

A

Acheson, Dean, 5
Acheson speech, 9–10, 60
Acronyms, listed, xiii–xv
African American Sailors. *See* Racial integration, U.S. Navy
African American Sailors Project, 250
Air operations, 287–344. *See also* Close air support; air power, major aspects of employment, 30; aircraft carriers, factors affecting use of, 34–35; air-to-air combat, 334; Aoji oil refinery, 333–34; Bedcheck Charlies, 341–42; *The Bridges at Toko-ri* (Michener), 317–19; Carlson's Canyon, 317–18, 321; Carrier Air Group (CVG) 5, 291–92; Cherokee strikes, 334; China coast and Taiwan Strait, patrol of, 292; Chosin Reservoir crisis, 310; Communist leaders meeting place, bombing of, 328; early "guided missiles", 333; F-51 Mustangs, delivery of, 37; final action, 343; Haeju airfield, 36, 293; helicopters, 306, 324–25; Hungnam, evacuation at, 310–11; Inchon, 302–04. *See also* Inchon amphibious assault; interdiction, 39–40; interservice disputes over, 30, 33; interservice rivalry, 288; jet aircraft, integrating into carrier force, 288; Kowon rail and supply center, 334; land-based aircraft from Japan, problems with, 298; Marine Corps jet fighters, 329–31; mothball combatants, reactivation of, 296; napalm, 220, 294; North Korean Air Force (NKAF), 289–90; Operation Moonlight Sonata, 332; Operation Package, 332; Operation Strangle, 323–24; patrol aircraft, roles of, 292; Pohang amphibious landing, support of, 39, 294; postwar changes, 343–44; Pusan Perimeter, 294–96, 300,

302. *See also* Pusan Perimeter, defense of; Pyongyang, 35–36, 64, 293, 294, 332–33; railroad facilities, Pyongyang, 36, 64; Rashin, 327–28; Seoul, evacuation of, 289; Seoul, retaking of, 304–05; Seventh Fleet, 290–91; straight-deck versus angled-deck carriers, 37, 293; strategic bombing as Navy mission, 288; Suiho hydroelectric facility, 332–33; supply lines, targeting, 313–16, 319–20, 323–24; Taedong River, 293; *United States*, cancellation of completion, 287; U.S. Navy carriers, listed, 312; Wonsan, 305–07; Wonsan Oil Refining Factory, 39, 294; Yalu River bridges, 307–09
Air superiority: North Korean Air Force (NKAF), inability to maintain, 34; potential offsets to UN command of, 34–35; as superpower deterrent, 53, 107
Alacrity (Great Britain), 15
Alexander, James, 20, 21, 211, 223, 233
Allen, Halle C., 80, 81
Allies, 3, 15, 20–21, 65, 133, 228
Almond, Edward M., 79, 86, 106, 140–41
Amphibious operations. *See also* Inchon amphibious assault: Amphibious Task Force (Task Force 90), 15, 18, 25, 27; Changjon ruse, 361–62; Chongha, evacuation at, 28–30; civilian evacuations, 362; covert, 186–88; Hungnam, evacuation at, 169–72, 223–27; Japanese Coastal Survey Project, 363; Kojo, sham landing at, 364–65; Operation Order 9-50, code named "Bluehearts", 27; Pohang, landing at, 25, 27–28; prisoner transport, 362; surveys, 230; troop transport, Japan to Pusan, 18; vessels, use of World War II, vii; Wonsan, amphibious landing at, 156–60

415

About the Editor

EDWARD J. MAROLDA graduated from Pennsylvania Military College (1967) with a bachelor of arts degree in history. He completed a master's degree at Georgetown University (1971) in European diplomatic history and a Ph.D. in U.S. history from The George Washington University (1990).

He is the author of *From Military Assistance to Combat, 1959–1965*, vol. 2 in the series *The United States Navy and the Vietnam Conflict* (Naval Historical Center, 1986), coauthor Oscar P. Fitzgerald; *Carrier Operations*, vol. 4 in the series *The Illustrated History of the Vietnam War* (Bantam, 1987); *By Sea, Air, and Land: An Illustrated History of the United States Navy and the War in Southeast Asia* (Naval Historical Center, 1994); the award-winning *Shield and Sword: The United States Navy and the Persian Gulf War* (Naval Historical Center, 1998; reprinted by Naval Institute Press in 2001), coauthor Robert J. Schneller; and *The Washington Navy Yard: An Illustrated History* (Naval Historical Center, 1999). Dr. Marolda also edited *Operation End Sweep: A History of Minesweeping Operations in North Vietnam* (Naval Historical Center, 1993), *FDR and the U.S. Navy* (St. Martin's Press, 1998), and *Theodore Roosevelt, the U.S. Navy, and the Spanish-American War* (St. Martin's Press, 2001).

Dr. Marolda currently serves as the senior historian and chief, Histories and Archives Division, Naval Historical Center, located at the Washington Navy Yard, D.C. Between April 1987 and February 1996 he headed the center's Contemporary History Branch, and from December 1971 to April 1987 he worked there as a professional staff historian. He served as a company-grade officer in the U.S. Army in the Republic of Vietnam during 1969 and 1970.